Ripples
of
Wisdom

A Journey Through Mud and Truth

Written and Illustrated by

Nancy Scheibe

Raven Productions, Inc.
Ely, Minnesota

Text, illustrations and photos
© 2010 by Nancy Scheibe

Published November, 2010 by

Raven Productions, Inc.

P.O. Box 188, Ely, MN 55731

218-365-3375

www.ravenwords.com

Printed in Minnesota
United States of America
10 9 8 7 6 5 4 3 2 1

Library of Congress Cataloging-in-Publication Data

Scheibe, Nancy, 1954-
Ripples of wisdom : a journey through mud and truth /
written and illustrated by Nancy Scheibe.
    p. cm.
ISBN 978-0-9819307-5-6 (trade pbk. : alk. paper) --
ISBN 978-0-9819307-6-3 (softcover)
1. Women--Mississippi River Valley--Social conditions.
2. Canoes and canoeing--Mississippi River. I. Title.
HQ1421.S34 2010
305.409776'091734--dc22   2010041897

TABLE OF CONTENTS

Dedicated to the women whose major contributions
helped make this experience possible for all of us.

Kitty Kennedy

Heidi Favet

Alanna Dore

Gwyn McKee

Sherry Leveille

Nancy Hernesmaa

Cis Hager

Becky Stigen

**And my husband,
Doug Scheibe**

In Loving Memory of Keewaydinoquay

Keewaydinoquay (Woman of the Northwest Wind) Pakawakuk Peschel was a Crane clan elder and scholar. She taught about the gifts and potentialities that each of us is given and how everyone's contributions are needed.

Photo printed with permission from Holy Hill Center, Inc.

Acknowledgments

It takes a community to make an expedition such as this happen. Following are the people and the organizations who contributed to the success of this venture. It is with deep gratitude their names are listed and I apologize if I missed anyone.

Sponsors of "A Day Of Paddling"

A Flock of Nancy's Friends, Ann and Mike Slesar, Anne DesLaurieres, Annette McBride, Audrey Muccio, Barbara Cary Hall, Betsy Flaten, Denice & Bruce Muccio Grout, Diana and Dan Stell, Donald MacDonald, Jane Schraudenbach, Jayne & Brian Grout, Nancy Kibens, Patti Steger, Sandy Scheibe, Susan Cherne

Individuals

Alanna Dore, Beckie Prange, Becky Stigen, Bill Flies, Bondell Rae, Carol & Bob Mucha, Carol Orban, Carla Arneson, Cecilia Rolando, Cis & Charlie Hager, Dan Creely, Danielle Blanchfield, Dave Hernesmaa, Dayna & Eric Mase, Deah & Paul Kinion, Deb Pettit, Diane Henry, Donna Arbaugh, Donna & Pat Surface, Doug Scheibe, Euan Reavie, Gail Haney, Gordon Sheddy, Gloria Bowen, Gwyn McKee, Heather and Wade Jeske Pharr, Heidi Breaker, Jeanne Bourquin, Julie Gellerman, Kathleen Waterloo, Kathy Mindel, Karen & Wayne Nielsen Friedrich, Karen Pauls, Keiko Williams, Larry & Dee Heideman, Laura Kenig, Laura Myntti, Laurie Horn, Lisa Allinger, Lou Harter, Lou Ezza Bradley, Lynn Oelker, Marilyn Hausy, Mary Fogerty, Mary Hyde, Mary & Wes Kennedy, Maxine Jacks, Mike Hillman, Momfeather, Nancy Jo Tubbs, Nancy Powers, Norma Smith Olson, Osahmin Judy Mister, Pam Weber, Pam Webster, Pat Gillett, Pat Jordan, Pat Parker, Sue Chernak, Ray Nargis, Rebecca Kali, Robin Bertelson, Sherry Leveille, Stephanie Bish, Todd Hohenstein, Tom Dore, Tom Rollins, White Buffalo Man

Organizations

Special Thanks to NRS (Northwest River Supplies) and Alan Dooley and the U.S. Army Corps of Engineers for their support.

Carolina Vision—Dr. Fern Powell, Hand Done T-Shirts, Elywear & Ely Sportswear, Front Porch Coffee and Tea Co., Jack Pine Bob Cary Enterprises, PracticeRange.com, Norex Photo, Piragis Northwoods Company, Raven Productions, Inc., Spiritwood Music, The Chocolate Moose, Thea Sheldon—Prime of Life Coach, Wenonah Canoe/Current Design, Wintergreen

My Editors

I am grateful to those who dedicated hours to editing this book.
Becky Stigen, Gail Haeny, Alanna Dore, Doug Scheibe, Pam Webster, and Rikka Wommack

RIPPLES OF WISDOM JOURNEY
SEPTEMBER 4 TO OCTOBER 16
2007

INTRODUCTION

The journey began in 2004 when I paddled 585 miles from the headwaters of the Mississippi in Itasca, Minnesota, to Red Wing, Minnesota. What started as a way to celebrate my fiftieth birthday evolved into a mission to gather women's wisdom. While planning the first trip, a yearning grew within me to connect with the extraordinary women who lived along the river's shore and learn about their lives. As a result, I held nine Gatherings and spoke with fifty-eight women, capturing their stories in my book Water Women Wisdom: Voices from the Upper Mississippi.

While traveling the river in 2004, I listened to the women speak, and I observed how easily women recognized each other's pain, joy, and wisdom. Like tributaries of the river, each woman's voice became part of a greater body of knowledge that embodied a powerful force to bring change and healing. A prophecy held by indigenous cultures—"Now is the time for the feminine to come forward,"—echoed in my mind. That prophecy had been brought to my attention by Native American and Taoist friends before the first leg of this journey down the river. On the last day of that trip I floated quietly, looking downriver, and knew my journey had just begun. I realized I needed to paddle the river's entire length in order to experience how she changed and influenced the lives of the women who lived near her shores.

That realization led to the creation of a mission to guide the journey and a logo to represent it. The mission is: While journeying the waters of the Mississippi, the Ripples of Wisdom venture celebrates the value, power, and sacred abilities of women by giving the Grandmothers a voice, gathering their truths, and sowing those seeds far and wide.

This book is the second in the Ripples of Wisdom series and details the 634-mile journey from Red Wing, Minnesota, to St. Louis, Missouri. During this stage of the journey, I spoke with 116 women and had 26 women paddle with me.

This journey has been a spiritual one for me. Many gifts have come my way since I said yes to this adventure. Had I known how my decision would turn out, I am not sure I would have said yes. Life has a way of presenting us with only the information we need to move in the direction we are meant to go. The journey was born out of a childhood dream to see how the headwaters I had visited as a child transformed into the Mississippi River I played near in Minneapolis. While on this journey, I learned I could do more than I ever thought I could and became convinced that everyone could.

Early on, I began referring to the women I would talk with as Grandmothers. It is a Native American term that acknowledges wisdom and compassion born out of time and experience. I expanded the meaning to embrace women over fifty whether or not they had children or grandchildren. At each of the Gatherings, only the Grandmothers were asked to speak; it was a time for younger women to listen. Five conversation starters were given to the Grandmothers at the beginning of each Gathering, and they were encouraged to speak their heartfelt truth. The topics were:

1. Describe how spirituality has influenced your life.
2. Has life followed the path you expected? How have life's circumstances shaped who you are?
3. What wisdom would you like to share with younger women as they travel their own river of life?
4. What does being courageous mean to you?
5. How would you like to be remembered by family and friends?

While preparing for the first leg of the trip, I struggled with how to set the tone that would best serve the mission. Spirit stepped in, and special people came into my life, offering vital pieces. I was invited to a peace conference in Chicago at Northeastern Illinois University, where I connected with Dan Creely. He gave me a sacred, Native American song to sing at sunrise each morning of the trip. The song calls us to stand together to fulfill our obligations to nature, the spirit world, and the Creator and to care for coming generations. Dan taught me to sing the song correctly in Anishinabe. He introduced me to kinnikinnick, a native, evergreen ground cover used by some Native Americans as an offering to the Great Spirit and the Sacred Waters. I was instructed to make an offering of kinnikinnick each morning and say a prayer of gratitude for safe travel. Gratitude and expectancy were already part of my approach to life. As I received the instructions from Dan, my heart connected to the intention behind them, and I knew I would adapt them to the way I traveled.

Dan also gave me coal from the sacred Peace Fire to carry. The coal came from the first Peace Fire, started in 1995 by Bruce Hardwick, a fire keeper, at an international conference at Lake Geneva, Wisconsin. That Peace Fire was attended by more than fifteen hundred people from all over the world, including Jane Goodall and Aru Gandhi, Mahatma Gandhi's grandson. The purpose of the Peace Fire was to awaken our consciousness about peace, love, sisterhood, and brotherhood. At the end of the conference, which became an annual tradition, participants made coal bundles that have been distributed around the world where people are gathered with peace in their hearts. I was instructed to start each fire in the traditional manner, with flint and steel, and then place a Peace Fire coal in the middle. At the end of each Gathering, I collected

Keewaydinoquay

cooled coals from the fire and carried them downriver to the next fire. Participants at our Gatherings were encouraged to take coals home as well.

During the 2004 trip, I developed a deep connection to herons. They were constant companions on the river and guided us many times when we needed to choose between channels. When I returned and shared my story with Dan, he was not surprised and believed it was his treasured native Grandmother, Keewaydinoquay (Kee), who had been dedicated to bringing peace and balance back to all people. He went on to say that Kee was a wise elder who was no longer alive. Many believed her spirit had returned in the form of a great blue heron.

I had thought about what I should use as a "talking stick" on this leg of the journey and decided a fan made of heron feathers would be appropriate. On another trip to the Peace Fires in Chicago, I met a man named White Buffalo Man. He listened to my story and said he felt guided to make a sacred fan for the trip. He constructed the fan with both heron and raven feathers, beaded his culture's symbol for the world onto it, and put the trip logo on the back. On the day the fan arrived, I was awestruck by its beauty and power.

Fan

The package with the fan included thirteen extra heron feathers. White Buffalo Man's note said they were for the thirteen Peace Grandmothers I would meet. The feathers represented thirteen international native Grandmothers who gathered in 2004 to begin their work healing the world, fulfilling a prophecy held by indigenous cultures around the globe. Those thirteen native Grandmothers concluded that they were merely a representation of the many Grandmothers working to heal the world. I was told to trust that I would know the recipients of the feathers when I met them.

We ended each Gathering with a closing ritual in which each woman was given two sticks and two pieces of yarn, one beige and one purple. The women were instructed to wrap the beige yarn around the first stick, called the releasing stick, while they visualized tying their struggles and the pains of life onto it. The first stick was then respectfully placed in the fire, and the women were encouraged to say a prayer of gratitude. While wrapping the second stick, the aspiration stick, with purple yarn, the women visualized their hopes, dreams, and aspirations. With the aspiration stick, the women were given a choice: They could give the sticks to me to place in the river the following day, or they could place them into the fire.

As you begin your journey downriver with us, I offer you this blessing:

> May the gifts you have offered by your presence here circle back around to reward you.
> May your head bless you with clear thinking.
> May your heart bless you with love, compassion, and joy.
> May your feet always walk in honor.
> May your hands always do good work and respect the things the Creator has made.
> May your ears be sharp to hear the Creator's voice.
> May you be safe from inner and outer harm.
> And may you be healthy and strong.

GLOSSARY

Aspiration sticks The sticks from the closing ritual onto which women tied their aspirations. They were either floated down the river or burned in the fire.

Charts The collection of waterway maps we acquired from the Army Corps of Engineers that gave us information such as mileage, main channel location, island locations, bridges, wing dams, and locks.

Chute A narrow passage between islands, or islands and the mainland, which is not part of the main channel. It may not be navigable by larger watercraft and may link two navigable waterways. In general, the word chute is used for narrower waterways that were not indicated as sloughs by our charts.

Daymark A large, flat sign painted either green or red. When one is traveling downriver, the green daymarks are located on the starboard, or right, side of the river. The red ones mark the port, or left, side of the river. The tugs locate and use them in the dark to navigate around bends in the channel.

Fan The fan White Buffalo Man created that was used as our talking stick at the Gatherings.

Gorp "Good ol' raisins and peanuts." Our snack also had a variety of dried fruits and nuts.

Main channel A channel maintained by the Army Corps of Engineers which is more than nine feet deep. The barges and larger boats must travel within the channel, which is marked by buoys. Outside of the main channel, the water level changes dramatically, and there may be stumps or rocks.

Metallic moose A term my daughter Sara Jo dubbed the many trains that were our constant traveling companions.

Releasing sticks The sticks onto which women visualized tying their struggles and pain before burning them.

Riprap Rocks piled along the shore to stop erosion.

Slough A secondary channel of the river. It may be a shallow lake system, typically formed by the backwaters of the river. In general, when the word slough is used in the text it was the term used on our charts.

Wing dam An underwater wall constructed of rock that projects into the river to direct the water and reduce erosion.

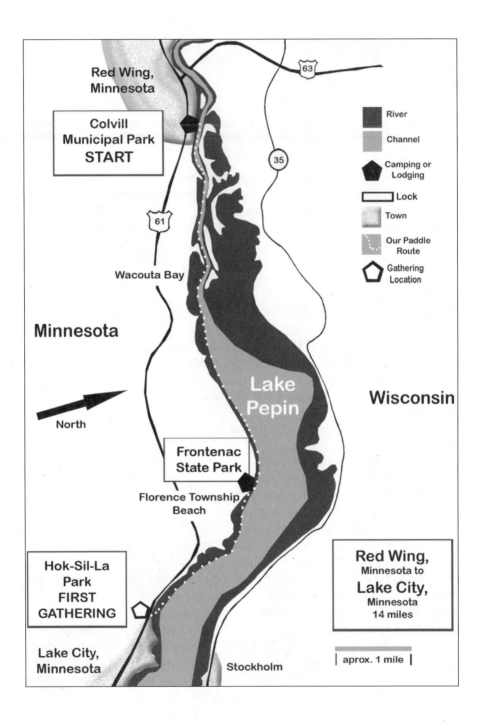

Red Wing to Lake City

September 4, Day One

I slipped away from the motel and headed to the river. As I drove into Colvill Park in Red Wing, Minnesota, two deer stood at the entrance. I felt like old friends were welcoming me back to the Mississippi River and to this leg of my journey to gather women's wisdom. The deer were a reminder to be gentle with myself as I traveled the next six weeks.

I stepped out of the car into the fresh, cool morning air as the sun rose from behind the trees. A sense of calm, expectation, and joy washed over me. High in the sky above me, flocks of geese glided into odd V shapes as they practiced migration formations. I found a large, grey rock poised at the top of the bank of the great river and sat down.

The river had become an old friend, companion, and confidant. Tears filled my eyes; I was at home here with her. Soon the rest of the paddling crew would wake up and we would start our journey, exploring the river and discovering the incredible women who lived near her. I looked downriver and considered my goal of playing a small role in empowering women and creating an environment where they could step forward.

I looked upriver and experienced a vision I'd seen more than once. It was a powerful picture of the women who walked behind me, women who gathered to support me on my journey. I closed my eyes, and the vision grew clearer. The women varied in age and color and represented many generations. They held me up and carried me forward. I looked into their gentle, warm, smiling faces and allowed their love to seep deeply into me. I was overwhelmed and wept.

The vision faded, and I gazed out onto the water, which moved at a quiet and gentle pace. I dug out my journal and a few sacred items I had brought with me. As I did so, the noises of the highway and the waking town behind me faded away. A heron called from above and flew to a tree on the other side of the river. I joyfully said good morning to her and thought of Kee. She came to mind each time I saw a heron. The heron watched me and called again, "I am here. It is time to begin."

Kitty

I made my way to the water with the sacred fan, kinnikinnick, and a small bottle of Sacred Waters from my friend Dan. These Sacred Waters, used to promote peace, had been collected from sacred places all over the world and blessed by many holy women and men.

I sang the sacred song I would sing each morning and felt a profound connection as the tears continued to flow. I was awestruck by the beauty around me and overwhelmed at having been chosen to do this work. Sprinkling kinnikinnick in the water, I prayed for safe travel for the women who would be a part of this journey. Another heron joined the first in the tree.

I wondered how to begin a ritual that would set the tone for the expedition. I relaxed, took a deep breath, and felt directed by Spirit to place the ends of the fan's fringe in the water, letting the great river penetrate the leather and become part of the fan. Pouring a few drops of Sacred Waters into the river, I asked the river's forgiveness for the destructive things we have done to her. As the last drop hit the water, an osprey flew overhead, following the river southward.

Taking the thirteen heron feathers I had received from White Buffalo Man, I dipped the tip of each one in the water, connecting them to the river and thus to all of the water on the planet. As I placed each one in the river, I wondered who would be receiving them. I was filled with a sense of expectancy about meeting those Peace Grandmothers and a sense of responsibility about being able to identify them. I took a deep breath, leaned into the moment, and trusted that I would know them when I met them.

Wispy clouds dusted the deep blue sky. Fish jumped and birds called all around me. The sun, now above the treetops, shone on the trees with an orange hue while the herons continued their vigil. A perfect half moon hung in the sky, and a pair of ducks swam lazily past me.

After a few more moments, I headed back to the motel. The parking lot was bustling with activity as the rest of the team prepared for the day. My husband, Doug, greeted me at our motel-room door with a broad grin on his face. He told me he was proud of me and held me firmly in his arms for a few moments before we headed out into the commotion.

Anticipation was high and the energy electric. With the packing of

Gwyn

the vehicles complete, we headed to the water, and I thought about how it had already been a journey to get to this point.

Kitty, my paddling partner for this trip; Pat P., a volunteer who had helped with details over the past few months; my daughter Sara Jo, who would paddle with us for the first week; and Doug and I had all arrived in Red Wing the previous day. We connected with Gwyn, who had driven in from Gillette, Wyoming, to be our car support for the first week. Alanna, who had been a core person during the past year of planning the trip, also joined us. We spent the afternoon going over last-minute details with Gwyn and then went to a send-off dinner with friends at the St. James Hotel in Red Wing. I recognized everyone sitting at the tables except Sherry. Sherry, who lived in Red Wing, had seen an article about our trip in the local paper that included an invitation to the dinner and decided to join us.

When we arrived at the park the next morning, we were surprised to see Sherry again. She was there with others who had come to see us off. My sister-in-law Sandy S. and her friend Vern were comfortably watching the activity from their lawn chairs. Sherry sat next to a woman whose beautiful harp music filled the air. The harpist, JoAnn, wore a white dress and sat on a rock by the shore. She was a friend of a friend from Ely. The gentle sounds of the harp drifted around us as we prepared the boats.

Sara Jo seemed to feel torn. Having just arrived from California, she cherished every second she could be with her stepdad, Doug, but she was also eager to begin paddling with me.

The paddlers who would begin the expedition with me were Kitty, Sara Jo, Leslie, and Heather—my paddling partner on the first trip. As we gathered near the boats, Sara Jo pointed out several egrets across the bay. They were a brilliant white against the deep green of the trees in which they perched. Kitty beamed and said, "Oh my, and this is just the beginning."

Sara Jo

The women had already launched their boats when I got down to my kayak. I stepped into the calm water and watched the green slime floating on the surface cling to my sandals and thought, "Oh my, and this is just the beginning." I joined the women on the water. Heading out from shore, it was encouraging to see our friends on shore smiling and waving good-bye. We would not see most them until we were back home in Ely.

We paddled out of the canal into the river. Alanna and Doug ran down the walkway to wave good-bye one more time. They caught up with us as we paused to float for a few moments while Kitty performed a ritual of placing an offering bundle into the water for safe travel. The ritual honored the spirit of the river, Mishew Picshew, an underwater panther who lives in the form of a giant catfish. Native tribes believe Mishew Picshew can cause great strife if the spirit is displeased with you. Kitty wanted as many of the spirits in line with us as possible.

After a few paddle strokes, we spotted an eagle high in a tree on the opposite shore. She was the first of many bald eagles we would see that day, all of them lining the river as if leading the way.

We passed Wacouta Bay and saw a flock of white birds in the middle of the river. I paddled out to get pictures. As I neared the pelicans and gulls, they flew away one by one. Determined to get a good photo, I paddled closer but was soon stuck on the sandbar where they had been standing. I was a mile offshore, and the water was less than a foot deep. I attempted to back up, but my rudder dug into the sand. Getting out and walking probably would have been easier, but I kept paddling. After a struggle, I was again floating free and crossed back to join the rest of the group.

We enjoyed a floating lunch of gorp off Presbyterian Point. Floating lunches entailed holding onto each other's boats to keep from drifting apart while passing food from person to person. As we ate, tiny fish jumped around us, thrusting their little, silver bodies up in the air with a twist. Occasionally a bigger fish would splash; one nearly collided with Heather.

After lunch, we saw the first of many tugboats we would see on our trip. The sign on the side of the tugboat indicated that the captain was a woman, Virginia Ingram, which delighted me. We pulled off to the side to prepare for the big wake, but it didn't come. Tugboats and the barges they push pose a danger to paddlers on the river. Due to the boats' massive size and the amount of water they displace, they can easily swamp small boats like ours. We knew to approach each one with great respect.

We had now officially entered Lake Pepin, where the river widened dramatically. Pepin is twenty-two miles long and over two miles wide at points. The Lakota Indians called the lake Pen-vee-sham-day, or Lake of the Mountains. We stayed on the Minnesota side, paddling next to a steep bluff. The lake was so big I found it hard to feel connected to the river the way I had in northern Minnesota, where the closer shorelines created a feeling of intimacy with nature. Here the wideness of the river and the expansive cliffs made me feel insignificant.

Leslie

I noticed a sprinkling around my kayak while paddling next to Leslie. I thought for a moment it was raining but was confused because there were only wisps of clouds in the sky. I noticed white spots on my kayak and then felt warm drops falling directly on me. I realized I had been initiated by a bird. I looked up but not quickly enough to see the culprit who dumped the guano. I looked over at Leslie, who was laughing. The humor was briefly lost on me, but soon I laughed too. I quickly used lake water to clean the droppings from my splattered face and arms.

The day provided us with many sightings of pelicans, gulls, herons, and eagles. The heat rose, and the nine miles of paddling proved exhausting. I thought about the native people who had traveled these waters many years before us. The Dakota and Fox had used these waters for transportation, though their experience was probably more challenging without the modern equipment we enjoy.

We paddled into Florence Township Beach where turkey vultures lined the shore. Some of us joked about why the vultures were waiting for us. Gwyn was waiting for us at our landing down the beach. We were to camp at Frontenac State Park that evening. We had made arrangements to store our boats on the property of a local man named Bill F. After we finished stowing them in the woods, Gwyn shuttled us to camp.

Kitty, Sara Jo, and I set up our tents while Gwyn returned to the river to shuttle gear. The three of us took advantage of the opportunity to nap. Heather and Leslie went to get their car. They stopped at Dairy Queen before they returned and brought a treat for each of us. Sara Jo was particularly delighted because she couldn't get Dilly Bars in California. It took Gwyn longer than anticipated to pick up the gear, so Sara Jo ate Gwyn's Dilly Bar to save it from melting. When Gwyn returned, her response to Sara Jo's sacrifice was, "Thank you for your heroic action, but I am going to eat one at tomorrow's landing and tease you with it."

At camp, we dug through the over-supplied food bins, contemplating our options for dinner. We resolved the dinner question when Gwyn said she was going into town and invited us to join her.

Although miles from home, Gwyn would continue to work at her job, via the internet, while she assisted us. She had spent part of her day using her computer at the Whistle Stop Café in Frontenac. The café staff had been very helpful. She wanted to support them in return by eating there.

We had a great time at the Whistle Stop Café sharing the details of our day with Gwyn. She was particularly amused by my guano initiation. After dinner, we drove to Point No Point overlook. Sara Jo, who has a passion for plants, pointed out a milkweed plant to Leslie and Heather. We picked green apples from a tree nearby, and we enjoyed the bitter

Heather

taste while we walked along the ridge. Sara Jo and Heather celebrated feelings of childish joy with cartwheels and headstands. Kitty was awestruck to see how wide the river was. "It doesn't look that wide when we're on the water," she said.

Before leaving, we stood on a picnic table and gazed downriver at Lake City, our next day's goal, five miles away. It was breathtaking.

Back at camp, we quickly headed for bed. I was more exhausted from nine miles of paddling than I had expected. Even though it was understood that everyone was on the trip at their own risk, the energy I expended being vigilant about everyone's safety added to my fatigue. Sara Jo and I climbed into our tent, and I quickly fell asleep.

September 5, Day Two

Our first Gathering would be held later that evening, and it was important that I sing the sacred song by sunrise. I climbed out of the tent before dawn and drove to the water. I walked along the calm lakeshore, through a group of seven turkey vultures, to a point that stretched far into the water. The vultures watched me closely but stood their ground as I moved past them. Native tribes ascribe certain meaning and medicinal powers to particular animals. Because the turkey vulture has no real voice, it is believed that their message directs us to take action rather than talk. Given the action I was taking with the trip's mission, it was fitting that they were present on the morning of the first Gathering.

I walked the shore of an old bible camp that Bill F. was renovating. At the tip of the point, I stood under a white cross that loomed tall above me. The sun rose like a bright orange ball in a tarnished blue sky. A bass jumped so high that she was easy to identify; it was as if she were momentarily suspended in the air. I sang and prayed again for safe travel. Then I said a prayer of gratitude and stood mesmerized by the soft pastel colors the sun created on the surface of the calm water. The peace I felt was refreshing after the hustle and bustle of the past months of planning. I scanned the water, absorbing its subtle colors and gentle movement. After a while, I made an offering of kinnikinnick and headed back to the car. The vultures were still there, and I saw the fish carcass that had captured their attention.

When I got back to camp, everything was stowed and ready to go. Sara Jo was doing yoga in a nearby field that glowed with blooming goldenrod. We were eating breakfast as Deah joined us to paddle for the day. She was a friend from Ely who had recently moved to the Rochester area. Deah wore a straw hat that Sara Jo immediately liked and jokingly tried to talk her out of, with no success.

We headed to the water and were soon afloat on Lake Pepin. Gwyn headed back to camp to pack the van for her day of traveling the road. Deah's kayak was shorter than any of ours, which meant she would be working harder than the rest of us.

We paddled past an area on the beach that was marked off. Signs stated that it was a native mussel propagation project. Sara Jo was very excited to see the area, since another of her passions is preserving our natural environment. Before we took off that morning, I found a bottle on the shore covered with invasive zebra mussels, which threaten the lake and river. I tossed the bottle in the trash.

As we paddled away from shore, the view was lit with power and calm. Small sailboats, silhouetted against the immense water, created an awesome backdrop as each paddler moved past them.

Lost in discussions, our group did not stay together, and the distance between us became unsafe. I paddled quickly toward the straying group while blowing my whistle. Although there was only a light breeze, they did not hear the whistle until I was close. For safety reasons, we decided we would not paddle any farther apart than the distance at which we could hear the whistle.

We stayed on the Minnesota side of the river as we paddled. Above us, train tracks ran along the shore on a rock levee. Higher above the levee was a busy two-lane highway that skirted the towering bluffs.

Minnows began skipping along the water as we approached a rest stop. They broke the surface of the water and wiggled along it a moment or two as if performing a synchronized swimming routine. The entire school of bright, silver fish jumped in unison each time my paddle dipped into the water.

We were amazed by the swallows that darted around us in the middle of Lake Pepin. I had pictured them as shore birds, so it seemed like a long way for them to come for food. There were sandbars in the lake

where other birds gathered. We paddled close to a small flock of pelicans, but they took flight before we reached them. Sara Jo also took advantage of the shallow water and got out of her kayak to stretch. The next thing we knew, she was doing yoga in the middle of Lake Pepin. She balanced on the sandy bottom on one foot in the King Dancer pose.

As the day progressed, a headwind picked up, and Deah's small boat got the better of her. She and Kitty had dropped back and were traveling slowly, so we waited for them. When they came closer, we saw that Kitty was towing Deah, whose shoulders hurt. We still had two miles to go and decided to take turns towing Deah.

A boat in the distance caught my eye as it pulled up the anchor. I paddled as fast as I could toward the boat. Just before it pulled away, I asked the people on board if they would do us a favor and tow one of our team to shore. They worked for the Department of Natural Resources (DNR) and were just completing studies of the lake.

Moments later, Deah was gratefully on her way to shore at a much quicker pace. When we met her on shore, she said being towed behind the boat had been a rush.

It was only mid-afternoon, so there was plenty of time to set up camp. We stowed our boats behind some trees for the evening. Gwyn appeared, pushing a cart to haul our gear. She apologized for not being there when we arrived but explained that she had been on an unsuccessful mission to get ice cream. She remained determined that we would have some later.

Gwyn had set up the tents and arranged them so Kitty and I had views of the river. Black walnut trees dropped mature fruit around us, making the ground lumpy. The fruit was large and hard and hurt when it hit us. When Deah saw the black walnuts, she said excitedly, "I think

Deah

I'm going to come back here in a couple of days and collect them!"

My tent looked a little odd. Gwyn commented that it had been particularly challenging to set up, and she wasn't sure she had put it together right. She hadn't. My tent was not a typical design. It was rounded instead of rectangular. The poles crossed over each other several places and converged at one point, which was the origin of the confusion. The unusual design proved to be a puzzle to everyone for the remainder of the trip.

We spent a lazy afternoon relaxing. Some of our group went to the beach or for a walk. I chose to nap. My tent was set up in the sun and was too hot, so I lay out on the lawn. I stayed at the edge of the shade to avoid being pelted with walnuts, but the bugs annoyed me. I tried to get comfortable in several positions and draped a towel over my face for protection from the bugs. Sara Jo and Heather walked past and laughed at my contortions. "That doesn't look very restful," said Sara Jo. I abandoned the nap.

Our next van driver, Rosy, had left a voice mail that she would not be coming to be our car support. We had expected her to join us in three days, when Gwyn had to go home. This short notice and her abrupt tone angered me. She made no effort to help us find another driver, and I sensed Rosy had known days ago that she would not be coming.

To deal with the issue, I immediately started calling people back home and hoped for the best. Kitty and I discussed our options, but the only workable one we came up with required Kitty to become the driver. It was not fair, but we could not go forward without a driver, and I was better at navigating the river. With that plan in place I went for a walk down by the river to regain peace of mind before the Gathering. The sound of the gentle waves on the shore, the sun on my face, and the breeze in my hair reminded me that somehow everything would work out.

I began preparations for the Gathering. Kitty was busy checking the list of things to do and setting up what she could. I saw a great sense of responsibility and determination on her face. I walked the perimeter of the Gathering site, sprinkling tobacco and saying a prayer of protection. With great effort I started the Sacred Peace Fire. Using flint to start a fire takes finesse, and I didn't have it that evening.

Our site had a grand view of Lake Pepin and the bluffs on the opposite shore. Soon everything was in place, and the women began to arrive. They came in small groups, and the conversations quickly started buzzing. To our delight, Sherry, from Red Wing, joined us again. She felt like an old friend even though we had only met a couple of days earlier.

LAKE CITY GATHERING

It was a hot, muggy evening, with few bugs to distract us; however, throughout the Gathering, nature provided us with other distractions. Cows mooed in the distance, a squirrel in a tree directly above Sara Jo chattered at us, and an occasional cicada chimed in.

There were twenty-one women in the circle ranging in age from thirty to eighty-four. Kitty and I had collected gifts to give to participants. The first was a bandanna for the youngest woman in attendance. The second, also a bandanna, honored the woman who had traveled the farthest to join us, and the last was a mug for the oldest woman in attendance. The mug went to Katie, who was eighty-four years old.

Just as I spoke to begin the Gathering, two bald eagles came from opposite ends of the river and crossed in the sky over the water just a few yards behind me. Everyone facing the water watched with amazement. Someone said it was a sign of the power of the work we were about to do. My heart knew that was true.

Katie

As the honored elder of the evening, Katie was the first to speak. She took the fan and stood tall to share her story.

"I am a grandmother; I have two great-grandchildren that are four and five and who love the water. We were out on the Misslssippi the other day, and the older one dove off the boat right into the river. He did have a life jacket on, and I was just amazed. I think he thinks he's part fish. I have three grandchildren; one is Jenny, who has Jenny's Greenhouse between Lake City and Rochester. She has a younger sister, Laura, and I have a twenty-six-year-old grandson.

"I grew up in the Lake City area as a youngster on a Grade A dairy farm. We attended school in Lake City from the time I was five until I was fourteen. At that time there was no consolidation of schools, so we stayed with my grandparents in Lake City. I was one of the fortunate people who had two sets of parents, since my grandparents acted as a second set of parents to us. It was frustrating at times, but it was wonderful at times.

"Oftentimes in the winter we would travel the seven and a half miles from Lake City to our home in the country with a horse and sleigh, which was really fun. It was so wonderful to see all of God's wonderful creations and hear all the songs of the outdoors. It was just fabulous. The sound of the horse hooves clapping on the road and the harnesses clinking are sounds I will remember all the days of my life. It was a wonderful song.

"I stayed with Grandmother until I was fourteen, when she broke her hip. There were three of us there, my older sister, brother, and me. One time there were five of us that stayed with my grandmother in Lake City. Two cousins were there, too. We really had quite a time.

"It was not really a problem about how my grandmother would feed these people, because during the summer, my mother had a large garden, and we canned about a thousand quarts of fruits, vegetables, and meats. My parents did all the butchering on the farm. My mother and father made all of their own sausages and wieners. They had a beautiful red-brick smokehouse in the backyard, and they smoked all of the meats to preserve them. I can still smell them; every time I come out to a campfire it brings back these fond memories. I can remember my father getting up in the middle of the night—I would hear him occasionally when I was very, very small—keeping the smoke just right. They used corncobs for smoking.

"I attended the School of Agriculture at the University of Minnesota and lived in the dorm at the St. Paul campus. After that I attended St. Olaf College for several years."

JoAnn spoke next. "When I was three years old, I have no memory of this, but they told me that my phrase was 'I do it my own.' [Laughter.] I don't say it quite that way anymore, but I am that kind of person. It is sometimes hard to accept yourself and sometimes hard to get acceptance when you are that way because we are a community of people and women. None of us walks a path by ourselves. What I like in myself is strength. I like to think of myself as being a strong woman and a woman of courage.

"A few years ago, after I raised my children, I left my home and moved to Red Wing, where I knew no one. I had a job because I am a nurse and I can work anywhere. I got an apartment, and I was careful with my money. When I wasn't working in Red Wing, I was working on call in another town. I made a big change in my life. It had never occurred to me that I would divorce, that I would do that to my children, but I did. I told my husband that I would always respect him and that I would not fight for one item. He could have it all, because to fight would have caused my children further pain. That was the hard part, what I did and what it did to my children. My mother didn't speak to me for about six months, but she got over it. I didn't plan on doing any of that. I didn't plan on being a stepmother. Now I have two of my own children, four grandchildren, and six stepchildren. My God, they're all boys—even the dog. [Laughter.]

"Sometimes I feel like I know exactly where I am going. A lot of times I don't, but the day comes and the day goes, and you wait for what happens, and you decide things as you go along with a certain set of principles and values. I have no great wisdom; I came here thinking that I might find some in all of you.

"I know that being a stepparent is not at all like the Brady Bunch. Being a second wife isn't perfect either, but you love as you go and you see each day new. Sometimes you have to make the decision to be happy because it is better for you. You have to make the decision not to worry because it does not change anything. It does not change any outcome. It only changes you.

"I do have one piece of wisdom I would like to share with you: On a hot night when you are going to be outside and not in air-conditioning, wear a sports bra and put it on wet." [Laughter.]

As Sherry took the fan and began to speak, we heard crows in the background. She said, "I love the idea that the feathers in this fan mean you're speaking your truth. At home, crows wake me every morning. I feel like it means to feel your wisdom, be your wisdom, and live your wisdom." While she spoke, crows continued to call in the distance.

"I think that my divorce was sort of a dividing place in my life. I think we go through different periods, and that was a huge thing for me. It's like a fire, a cleansing, beginning a new life cycle. First of all, there was a death of the marriage and then a rebirth of me. It has been amazing to me what has opened up in my life. I always met with women but not nearly like I do now. I am reaching out, going to drumming groups and spirituality groups. My spirituality had been leading up to that.

"I was a junior-choir director at the Presbyterian Church in Red Wing for twenty-four years. Towards the end, I could no longer choose songs for my kids that fit in with a theology of the church, because I didn't believe in those ideas anymore. The church's dogma was too confining. Spirit is bigger than this, I thought. I changed churches. Now I go to a very liberal church right across the river from here in Stockholm, Wisconsin. It's that beach over there." She pointed across Lake Pepin.

"I've learned about quantum physics. Part of that change was because of a book written by Deepak Chopra called How to Know God. I learned that Spirit is bigger than what they wanted me to believe. It is the connection of every part of my body with every part of the Universe. Where is the mind? It is not up here," she said, pointing to her head. "I believe it is in every cell of my body, which is connected to every cell in everybody else's body at a quantum level. It is connected to the trees and the rocks and the water and the clouds. Just think how far you can go with that theory!

"The idea of being afraid of someone is like being afraid of myself.

I still struggle with this, but the theory makes more sense to me now. Everyone is a part of me, and I am part of them. To see and to be able to find the wisdom in everybody else is so exciting. To understand that most people have similar fears and to respect their struggles with those fears is exciting. To acknowledge the connection that we all have with each other at deep levels is part of the idea of loving ourselves and each other. I practice energy medicine. It is just phenomenal getting into that quantum level of work. I honor all of you so much for your wisdom."

Deah stood confidently and came to get the fan. "I was a city girl up until about six years ago, when I lived in Ely for four years. That's how I know Kitty and Nancy. I moved to an area between Lake City and Rochester two years ago. I highly encourage people to get out of the city. You will experience a whole different lifestyle living closer to nature. It is totally a slower pace.

"One of the mottos I live by is: It can always be worse. It goes along with the gratitude that people are speaking of. I feel a lot of gratitude. I was on the river with the group today and met some wonderful women. Oh, yes, I am going to feel it in a couple of days too," she said, shrugging her shoulders. "I feel a sting like I've been sunburned, too, but I had sunscreen on.

"I am an Aries, and I have this personality of 'I'm just gonna do it.' I am going to travel and then I am going to California and then Chicago. I will study this and that. I don't have anything stopping me. I recommend that you follow your heart. Don't let anything stop you. I guess being the youngest of five kids maybe had something to do with it too. I had lots of mothering at a young age, but I didn't have boundaries set on me. I didn't have anyone say 'No, you can't do that.' It took me eleven years to get a college degree, but I did a lot of things in between.

"I encourage younger people today not to worry about what you are going to be when you grow up. I am an acupuncturist and have been for twenty years. I still wonder what I am going to be when I grow up, but I am moving more into the practice of mindfulness, meditation, and sharing that with my patients because of the power of the breath.

"I have been meditating for ten years, and it has helped me get through crisis. I am a cancer survivor. We all know that change is going to happen. We are going to get older, and we are going to be on our deathbed some day. What is your heart going to be like at that time? The process is preparing us for the inevitable with everybody we know. Kitty is one of my best friends, and I have to prepare for losing Kitty. We lose all of our friends and all of our family, so I encourage you … if you don't have a spiritual practice of some sort, find one. It really is an opening to a greater wisdom, not so much to answer all these questions,

but to provide some peace. I wish peace in all of your hearts to be with you moment to moment in whatever you may be going through in the present moment and in the future."

Leslie chimed in next. "I'd like to share a defining moment for my life. It speaks to the spirituality question a bit, but more to navigating the waters of life as opposed to going with the flow. I've learned the benefits of going with the flow through this experience.

"Almost ten years ago, a very tight-knit group of students and parents from my daughter's school traveled to the Twin Cities at Christmas time to see the Holidazzle Parade and the Dayton's holiday display. We had enjoyed a wonderful day together. Some of us were sitting around a small table at a local coffee shop, warming up, and enjoying each other's company. I got up to use the restroom before we left and was gone only a few moments. We then walked down Nicollet Mall on our way to dinner. I was having a discussion with my friend Kathy about materialism and how we get too attached to our stuff. I ordered my meal and went to pay for it, only to realize that my purse was missing. It had been stolen from the table at the coffee shop while I was in the restroom. The Universe was going to put me to the test about the materialism mantra I had just shared with my friend.

"I spent the next six months being swallowed up by charges on my credit cards, forged checks, the inability to write legitimate checks because my name was now flagged, and trying to identify the person who had 'victimized' me. I was becoming tired, bitter, and angry. The last of the thirty forged checks was the one that led me to the person who had brought so much chaos to my life. I had her name, address, and phone number. I pondered what to do about it. I could drive by her house and throw eggs at it, making me feel better, or I could write a long, rambling letter explaining how her actions had affected me and challenging her to be a better person. Or I could call and chew her out. I am not sure what I thought that would result in. It was a lot to consider.

"My answer came from a book I was reading by His Holiness the Dalai Lama. He teaches that if someone is in the grip of cruel necessity and steals from us, we should dedicate or give them those possessions so they will have obtained them legitimately and not have to endure the consequences of their act.

"Compassion ... for a person who had wronged me? I'd never really had such a new concept so in-my-face until that moment. The woman had, after all, used my checks to buy shoes and coats and toys for Christmas and, finally, to turn the water back on in her home. The compassion came easily for me. I was able to release all the negativity that had built up inside, and this powerful lesson has changed me forever for the better."

Kathy M. began with conviction. "There is a lot of credence in hearing from the elders. I can say that because I am one of those. I must say the older I get, the smarter I feel. Some days I feel pretty smart. When I look back at what things I have learned in the last year, the last five years, or last ten years, I see I am so not the same person I was then. Life experience has taught me much. I have learned I am wiser. When I think about it, most of those real nuggets have come from other women or being in circle with other women, benefiting from their encouragement and their challenging questions. The things I have learned that are making me smarter are coming out of the context of women. I feel like I need to live for a long time, because I am really on a roll. [Laughter.] Even as smart as I am, there is a lot more out there and a lot of work to do yet.

Kathy M.

"I really believe in the concept of honoring our elders and paying attention to their wisdom. One of the things I am really paying attention to is looking at life through new lenses. One of the most important things I have learned is that wisdom isn't out there some place; it's just not. As much as I have learned from and with other women, they didn't have the secret. I did! Now one of my big goals is paying attention to my intuition, the things I knew all along that I didn't listen to, didn't give credence to, didn't name, and didn't recognize. I think most of the really great, deep wisdom comes from inside us. We had it all along! There is more inside us than we really recognize. There is a lot of value in our elders.

"I think it's not just the elders in a hierarchical sense of getting up to the top of the pile. It's a circular thing that cycles through the generations, and we have to learn from both directions. A few weeks ago, my granddaughter, who is four, was at my place and we were reading the children's book The Little Red Hen. I thought, 'Okay, here are some good values; we are going to learn the value of hard work here.' We read through the book; you probably all know it. The Red Hen asks, 'Who will help me plant the wheat and harvest it, grind it, and bake the bread?' You know that she had to do it herself because nobody would help. This was really troublesome to my granddaughter. At the end she said, 'Grandma, you know why nobody helped her? She didn't say please.' And it gave a whole new meaning to the story. Then she insisted that we read this book several more times, but we must do it the 'right way.' So when the Red Hen said, 'Who would help me, please, plant the wheat?' Everyone said, 'I will, I will.' 'Who would help me grind the wheat, please?' Everyone said, 'I will, I will, I will.' And on the last page when she said 'Who will help me, please, help me eat the bread?' they all did, and we had to literally draw all the other characters at the table. Everyone was around the table.

"It was a really good jolt for me, a reminder about all the things we take for granted. That we think we know how it goes. That we have it all figured out that this is the lesson, but you know, there is a whole different lesson there. It is about how we relate to each other and how we treat each other and how we are. We can choose to live in communities and collaborate and support each other, and then everybody is at the table. Everybody, including the Red Hen, is happier in the end. I think there is value in elders, and I think there is a generational cycle that we need to pay attention to and consider while building our wisdom too."

Betsy F. spoke next. "My response gets longer as I listen to everyone speak. My maiden name was Betsy Ross, so I did take my married name.

"What I was thinking about is how important these stories are to share with our children. I mean our general children. I look back and it was the women, but not always the women; it was my dad who told me stories too. I would say 'Tell me about when you were little.' I had a great-aunt who would tell part of a story, and then I would tell part of a story, and then she would tell part of a story. That's something I remember as one of my very favorite things. I remember all these wonderful stories. Some were funny, but some were about struggles. I don't know if that is happening with the next generation of kids as much. Storytelling was more a part of our growing up. Now television and other things, and just running to this and that, means they have no time to just be.

"I have been involved with diversity, mostly through my own daughter. One of my children was born in Korea, and I have a brother who is gay. He has been with his partner for over thirty years. I have a wonderful family, and I had an African-American host daughter that we were mentoring from an inner-city school. I have worked in human rights for many years, and that has always been really important to me. I guess if I am thinking of legacy, human rights is one place I want to make a difference. The differences are so much fun, and we are all a part of it."

Lydia jumped up to get the fan next. "I want to say something about diversity. You can be a middle-class, white liberal, and it is really easy to talk it, but it is different to walk it. I think people are so different from me, and that is the enriching part of diversity. It is living with and getting to know people who are different from us. People used to go in the Peace Corps to do that. That was the 'white' thing to do. We don't know what it is like to be gay, we don't know what it is like to be black, unless we know people who are living differently, living with different bodies than ours. I don't mean to say different lives, but I don't know how else to put it. It is really good. Who wants to be with people exactly the same as them? How boring. Diversity is so much more enriching."

Sherry responded to Lydia, "The thought that comes to me is that it doesn't matter what anybody looks like or thinks or believes in, other than yourself. All we can really know is ourselves and trust that we can learn and expand our experience a bit. We can't actually know anybody else. I don't think we can experience anybody else's life. There is so much to learn from everybody and everything. This life is a wonderful experience on that road, on that journey."

Moved by what she had heard, Deah stepped forward to share an exercise in breathing with us. Then she added another thought. "We can get so lost in our minds thinking of the past and the future and all the possibilities. We can't count on tomorrow at all or even tonight. That is a piece of spirituality that I am happy to share."

Kitty, who had been in charge of the tape recorder, passed her duty on to Sara Jo so she could speak. She stood for a moment grinning from ear to ear before she began.

"Thank all of you for being here tonight. All of you coming together has given me the courage to do just this.

"When we were sitting at the landing yesterday morning getting ready to go, Alanna, who has been helping us plan, came up to give me a hug. She looked at me and said, 'You really don't have a clue what you are getting into, do you?' I looked at her and I was speechless. I thought, I don't know what to say to that one. As the days have gone on, it's like settling into a different routine for me. I haven't been in this kind of space before.

"Before we left, I had visualizations about finding myself in the corner a lot. I am in a corner because my vision has become so narrow that I have to step back to find out what the bigger picture is. I am working with a life coach who told me to walk through the corner. That just wasn't an option to me at that time.

"The morning we left, I had this visualization that I was standing in the corner, and I did walk through that corner, and I walked into this huge, open space. That is all that it was, a huge, open space. And that felt like my heart opening up to what was coming to me through this journey.

"When I think of what Alanna said, I realize I really didn't have a clue. There had been so much preparation and so much work to get ready for this. I did about a tenth of it, and Nancy did the rest. I have never been on a journey like this before, nothing that required this much time off of work. I have never devoted myself to something like this before, and it's been quite an awakening on many levels. I was honored and humbled when Nancy asked me to take part in this journey with her.

"I could not have dreamed or imagined this for myself. One of the things I am learning is when I dream, or if I imagine something, I am actually defining something for myself. I need to dream even bigger than that. I need to open myself up in a much bigger way. Anything else is just a limitation.

"I have two jobs, and the screen saver at one of my jobs says 'It could be worse.' I am working for the government, [Laughter.] so it could be. Every time I look at it I smile because that is my saving grace."

As I began the closing ritual, our elder, Katie, indicated she had one more thing to share.

"It was wonderful listening to all of you younger women. You have really inspired me, and I think, hmm, I have gone through many of those same experiences myself. What I want to leave you with this evening is that the greatest gift of the spirit is love. It is in each and every one of you. Each and every one of you has talked about it. It goes beyond our love for our fellow man. It goes to the love of everything around you, everything that you are seeing as you are looking out today. I feel that one of the most wonderful things you need to do, each and every one of you, is to keep reaching out.

"I have been reading, sorry I can't remember the author, but the story said that with everything you touch you want to be sure that you do it with love, compassion, and understanding. If you are turning on the water faucet to get a glass of water, if your heart is full of love, compassion, and understanding, you can be surprised. That glass of water that you drink, when you turn that faucet on, when your body and mind is full of love, the result is going to be entirely different. It will renew your body in an entirely different way than if you reach for it when you are angry. If you turn the faucet on with love and compassion it will renew your body. This is a proven fact. I just really came upon that in the last five years, and it has opened up a whole new world to me. It is something I want you all to experience.

"The main thing is to keep reaching out. Don't ever really be satisfied. Yes, you can be content, you can be happy with yourself, but just keep reaching out beyond to see what needs to be done. See what you could do to better the lives of each and every one of your friends and your fellow man."

We closed the Gathering with our ritual; then the aspiration sticks were carefully tucked away to be placed in the river the next day. Everyone took coals from the fire after it had been doused with water. This ritual would be repeated for each Gathering.

Katie invited us to come to her home for coffee the next day. She described where she lived and assured us that we would have no trouble finding her. We told her that it sounded like a wonderful idea and we would likely come.

Just then Gwyn appeared out of the darkness grinning like the Cheshire Cat; she had been successful in her ice-cream quest. She handed each of us a Dove Bar.

Constance, who had left the Gathering early, emerged from the darkness. She'd come back to thank us for the experience and the opportunity to be with her mother, Katie, at such an important event. She told me she was touched by what she had heard, and she supported what we were doing. The darkness engulfed her once more as she headed back to the parking lot.

In a later conversation with Sherry, she told us that she went for a walk in the campground after the Gathering and ran into a man by the shore, named White Buffalo, and his son Anthony. She connected with them and told them about our trip. White Buffalo, who lived in Lake City, said he would be praying for us in his native language for the duration of our trip. I was touched by his kindness.

After everything was packed, our heads still buzzed with the evening's events, yet sleep was easy.

September 6th through 11th

Hok-Sil-La Park

Stockholm

Lake City

61

Pepin

Camp Lucpulous

Reads Landing

35

25

Wabasha

North

60

Zumbro River

Lock & Dam 4

Weaver Bottoms

Minneiska

Lock & Dam 5

Bass Camp Resort

Prairie Island Park & Campground

Lock & Dam 5A

Wisconsin

Winona

Trempealeau

Play Mor Campground

Lock & Dam 6

90

35

53

Minnesota

Onalaska

Lock & Dam 7

90

Approx. 5 miles

Pettibone Resort

La Crosse

26

Goose Island Campground

Legend

River

Channel

Camping or Lodging

Lock

Town

Paddle Route

Gathering Location

Lake City, Minnesota to La Crosse, Wisconsin 83 miles

Lake City to LaCrosse

September 6, Day Three

During breakfast, we talked about the trains that woke us in the night. They ran down both sides of the river. Sara Jo called the trains "metallic moose," and the name stuck. Our discussion was interrupted when Sara Jo saw two bald eagles on a log off the shore sharing a fish. We were delighted to have breakfast companions but didn't find their meal remotely appetizing.

Once we finished eating, Gwyn insisted that we leave and that she would haul everything to the van. We argued that the trip was a team effort and that she was not expected to do so much. With an elfish grin, she sternly ordered us to leave. We conceded and headed to shore. Gwyn followed us, strutting like she had won a great battle.

It was a clear, sunny morning. I climbed into my kayak and saw a large, chubby woodchuck on the retaining wall off the shore. Its brown, furry coat blended in well with the background. Undisturbed by our presence, she moved along the rocks and disappeared into a hole.

The lake was expansive. I paused for a moment to enjoy the feel of the waves gently rocking my kayak and watched the other women paddle. The aspiration sticks I had been entrusted with the night before were safe in a bandanna on top of my kayak. I waited until we were out into the lake before I sang, made an offering of kinnikinnick, and released the sticks. I wanted to be sure that the sticks would not float right back to shore. The aspiration sticks were lovely as they bobbed and gently danced together on the water. The shades of purple yarn stood out against the deep green of the water and seemed to radiate hope and peace.

We paddled three miles to Lake City, the birthplace of waterskiing. In 1922, at age eighteen, Ralph Samuelson fashioned skis out of pine planks and invented the sport. We followed Katie's directions from the previous night, which took us around the point and past the marina wall. Just as she promised, we could see her quaint yellow house from the water. We pulled our boats up on the shore and climbed to the road. As we crossed the street, Sara Jo searched unsuccessfully for a Dairy Queen. We knocked on Katie's door, greatly anticipating talking with her again, but she was not home. While Sara Jo played fetch with the neighbor's dog, we went around back and knocked again but still no answer.

We relaxed in Katie's beautiful backyard with its brightly colored flowers. Her home had Victorian style porches in front and back. She told us that the house was built in the 1860s. It had been brought over the ice from Stockholm, Wisconsin, and was a historic landmark in Lake City.

A strong headwind had developed by the time we returned to the water. On the previous trip, while on Lake Winnibigoshish in northern Minnesota, the wind had quickly caused the waves to grow to an unsafe level, and we had to get off the water fast. That experience nagged at me; I could not ignore the intuitive message I was getting. Staying near the shore was important for our safety.

We were soon far from the shore and too far away from each other. I took the lead and headed closer to the shore, assuming the others would stay close as we had previously agreed. However, the distance between me and the rest of the team widened. I paddled on until it became clear they were not following my lead. I blew my whistle, and they at last turned in my direction and rejoined me.

The metallic moose rolled past along the shoreline. Our charts indicated that the tracks belonged to the Canadian Pacific Railroad. Some engineers waved at us. It reminded me of being a child and trying to get them to blast their whistles by pretending to pull the cord.

Past Maple Springs Landing we stopped along the rocky shore. After a snack, Sara Jo stretched out for a nap. Kitty saw a hummingbird and said she had been seeing them all day. She was astonished that she could spot the tiny creatures as they flew along the shore.

We had planned to meet Gwyn for a check-in at Camp Lucupolis, Minnesota, a mile and a half downstream. Kitty looked back at Lake City and remarked how it appeared closer than the seven miles we had already traveled. Just before the boat landing Kitty saw a fake palm tree in a yard. "It just doesn't belong there," she said and went back to take a picture of it.

While we waited for Gwyn, Sara Jo decided to do laundry. She took off her shorts and rinsed them out, using her kayak spray skirt as a cover-up. When she realized her outfit made Kitty and me laugh, she began lifting the spray skirt and dancing around.

Sara Jo and I headed to the road to flag down Gwyn. Sara Jo was still wearing the kayak spray skirt, since she had laid her shorts on the dock to dry. Her attire elicited startled responses from passengers in the passing cars.

We checked in with Gwyn briefly and headed back to the water. As we pulled away from the boat launch, a man in a small, red canoe packed to the brim paddled up to us. He asked if we knew where to get beer. He was from Florida and paddling the Mississippi by himself. He told us that he had trouble getting across Lake Pepin because the wind suddenly picked up in the middle. I didn't see any charts in his canoe and asked if he had any. He replied, "No, I'm just following the waterway and camping on the islands." I wondered how he would navigate when he got further downriver, where the backwaters became much more confusing. We paddled on while he turned toward the shore.

Past Camp Lucupolis, Lake Pepin ended, and we entered the river once again. It was an intimate change from the largeness of the lake. We passed the confluence of the Chippewa River, which had created Lake Pepin by depositing sand into the river over a thousand years ago.

We paddled into the first of the backwaters we would come across on the trip. The shallow water and downed trees reminded me of northern Minnesota. Even though it was beginning to get dark, we drifted for a few moments in the calm water.

We rounded a bend and saw the highway bridge that crossed the river at Wabasha, Minnesota, looming in the distance. We paddled into the channel leading to Malone Park, where Gwyn had set up camp. We passed manicured camping areas for RVs and paddled under the Hiawatha Drive bridge into goopy, green water. The water was a stagnant combination of duckweed, weeds rising from the bottom, and green slime, which clung to our paddles. We groaned as our feet slid into the green goop.

Gwyn was not at camp. Pulling our kayaks onto the shore, we were immediately attacked by mosquitoes. We dove into the tents. Calling through the tent fabric, we discussed how we were going to make dinner and not be eaten alive.

It had quickly grown dark, and there was thunder in the distance. Gwyn returned and announced that she had scouted a good place for dinner. We bounded to the car joyfully, anticipating a peaceful, swat-free meal. We drove to Wabasha's main street, where flags picturing Chief Wabasha hung along the road. The old-fashioned storefronts made it feel like we had stepped into the past. Down the road was the Anderson House. Built in 1856, it was the oldest operating hotel in Minnesota. We ate on the Flour Mill Pizzeria deck overlooking the river. Not eager to return to the bugs at camp, we took pleasure in a leisurely dinner.

Back at camp, the rain had begun to fall. We opened the car doors, made a dash to our tents, and spoke goodnights to each other through the tent walls.

We had paddled fourteen and a half miles in nine hours. I lay in my sleeping bag and realized how the administrative details, such as coordinating things each evening for the following day, continued to cut into my enjoyment of the trip. I was constantly thinking about something that needed to be handled. The lack of car support for the following week had weighed heavily on me all day. Kitty would have to get off the water and replace Rosy as the driver, and that did not sit well with me. Sara Jo suggested asking Sherry from Red Wing to be our driver. As she said that, I got a call from Alanna, who suggested the same thing. We didn't know Sherry well, but it felt like the right thing to do.

I drifted off to sleep with details still churning in my head. Mixed among the details was gratitude that Sara Jo was able to be with me, that Gwyn was a stellar car-support person, and that Kitty was so delightful and easy to travel with.

September 7, Day Four

We dubbed Gwyn the rock star of car support and a Sherpa to boot. She repeatedly anticipated our needs. I would begin solving a problem, and she would already have it handled. I told her that it felt uncomfortable and nurturing at the same time. With an elfish grin she responded, "Get used to it."

Gwyn woke early and worked on her computer in the dim light with mosquitoes as her companions. When we climbed out of the tents, we headed directly for the parking lot, where the bugs were more tolerable. Over breakfast, Gwyn filled us in on her previous night's tent adventures.

"It rained hard, and due to the wind, it was actually raining inside my 'new' tent. At first it was irritating, but I realized it was funny to have bad weather inside, as well as outside, the tent." We laughed. "By the end of the night, I had all my gear 'floating' with me on my air mattress to stay dry. I think I had a couple of inches of water in my tent!"

Rain was threatening again, and the park was dark and gloomy. We coordinated our day with Gwyn and then ran to pull up the tents as quickly as possible, hoping to escape the bugs while we still had blood left in our veins. Slugs were crawling everywhere. We pulled them off our tents and kayaks. Kitty had stored her life jacket under her kayak, and the jacket was covered inside and out with slimy slugs.

Groaning, we slid our kayaks back into the slimy, green shallows, anticipating the clean water of the river ahead of us. Three pelicans flew low over us headed downriver. Three herons followed them. Sara Jo was convinced it was a positive omen.

We paddled past Wabasha and diverted from the main channel to the west side of Hershey Island, where we saw lots of turtles. The tall grass and cattails were again similar to the northern part of the river. On the riverbank I saw a tree stump that I first mistook for a llama. The dead vines lying across the stump gave it the appearance of a hairy llama butt. The others agreed.

We went through a narrow area where the water became shallow. Kitty scraped bottom, came to a stop, and had to walk. Paddling past Kitty, Sara Jo was sure her paddle had hit a fish. She screamed with excitement as the paddle hit another one, which she saw swim away.

In the distance, a large flock of pelicans sat on a huge log that had drifted onto a sandbar. I stopped paddling and allowed the water to carry me downstream so I would not disturb the birds. I was surprised at how close they let me come before they began to fly away. We were awestruck watching them take off. They rose in the air and immediately gathered into a group and spiraled upward. Lost in watching them, we all got stuck on the sandbar.

From a distance, the water where the pelicans had been looked slimy and lime green. The green was duckweed, which we had seen everywhere in the backwaters. I reached into the water to pull some out and examined the three tiny, flat leaves. The leaves floated on the surface and dangled roots in the water below. Kitty said they looked like edible sprouts. Individually, they were so delicate and beautiful. Together, they were a big pile of green goop that hung on everything.

Freed from the duckweed and the sandbar, we headed back across an opening toward the main channel just as my kayak began to vibrate. Confused, it took me a few moments to realize it was my cell phone, which was pressed against the hull. I hesitated to dig it out, but Sara Jo said, "You'd better answer that one. Anything that makes a kayak vibrate must be important." We drifted while I dug for the phone, but I missed the call. I checked voice mail and heard Gwyn's elated voice telling us that she had reached Sherry, who was rescheduling everything in her life for two weeks to drive for us. We cheered, and Sara Jo said, "Hey, maybe that was what the positive omen was for."

To add to our delight, when we paddled into the main channel the wind had picked up and was at our backs. It was strong and created two-foot high swells. Kitty giggled every time a swell picked her up and thrust her forward. It was great fun but a challenge to keep the kayaks in line with the waves.

We stopped for a quick break on an island past Teepeeota Point. Lock No. 4 was in the distance. We saw a large deer track in the sand. I was surprised a deer would swim that far from the mainland. I hoped that the cricket, which had been riding on my kayak and chirping at me all morning, had jumped to dry land, but she resumed chirping once we were back out on the water. It was a pleasant sound, and I enjoyed it all day.

The sky cleared as we headed toward the lock. The Army Corps of Engineers chose to number the locks rather than name them. People who live in the towns near the locks refer to them with the name of the town, so Lock No. 4 was the Alma Lock.

As we approached it, I could see that Sara Jo and Kitty were worried. On the previous trip, I had passed through several locks and felt confident about the process. As we neared the lock, Sara Jo and Kitty were surprised by its size. In a small boat, the 110-foot-wide opening, with its high walls, was intimidating. The bright yellow ends of the walls and the large gates leading into the chamber looked ominous and increased Sara Jo and Kitty's concern.

The light was red as we approached, indicating that we needed to wait. We floated for a few moments while I called the Lockmaster to inform him we were approaching. Soon the light turned green and the gates opened. I led the way into the chamber. The attendant directed us to a spot halfway down the chamber wall and tossed ropes over the side for us to hold on to. The ropes assisted boaters maintain control of their boats while the water level adjusted in the chamber. Within moments, the gate had closed behind us and the water level dropped. The change in water level was difficult to discern. I watched for the water line on the side of the wall to change and pointed it out to Sara Jo and Kitty, who relaxed and watched with great interest.

We dropped six and a half feet, and the downriver gate began to open. Most of the locks we would go through would drop between six and nine feet. I waited in anticipation for the all-clear horn to blast, though it still startled me when it did. As Sara Jo and Kitty paddled out of the chamber and into the open river, they commented that going through the lock was fun and nothing to be afraid of.

We pulled off the water for a break at the Alma landing. We sat for a few moments, enjoying a snack of cheese, crackers, and chocolate. We gazed back at the lock and dam, marveling at its construction and how neatly the town of Alma was wedged between the bluff and the river.

We headed back to our kayaks, feeling overly confident that we had ridden the big waves and moved effortlessly through our first lock. We slid our kayaks into the water and nearly tipped over getting in them. We laughed at how we had become so sure of ourselves and how the river had subtly let us know who was really in charge.

We crossed the channel, ducked into West Newton chute, and headed to our next stop, where we would meet Diana from Wabasha. She would paddle the rest of the day with us. We paddled peaceful, narrow backwaters, finding our way one bend at a time. In confusing areas, our treasured friends, the herons, took flight from trees and guided us.

We came out of the chute and stopped near a massive tree that had fallen over the water. Diana had not arrived yet. Sara Jo and I climbed on the enormous tree for a much-needed rest. We fell asleep while Kitty paddled around investigating the area. We awoke as a tugboat with barges passed us heading downstream. We quietly watched and noted the way it churned up the water.

It took Diana a long time to join us, and we wondered if we were in the wrong location. Kitty decided to paddle up the channel to look for her. As Kitty disappeared around the bend, we saw Diana's kayak approaching from the same direction we had come. We yelled for Kitty to come back. There had been confusion about landmarks, and we were further downriver than she had expected.

Diana was excited to join us and was bubbly and full of smiles. She asked many questions about our trip. She said she preferred backwaters to the main channel, which was our choice as well. We paddled into the waterways behind Fisher Island. Diana told us that her friends didn't like to paddle in Weaver Bottoms, downriver from us, because it was dirty and weedy. Since we usually chose the most adventurous route, that was all we needed to motivate us. At the first opportunity, we headed into Weaver Bottoms.

Nancy, Diana, Sara Jo, Kitty

Weaver Bottoms was part of the Upper Mississippi River National Wildlife and Fish Refuge. Many small islands lined the main channel. Numerous turtles of all sizes stuck their heads up through the duckweed and disappeared under the surface as we approached. Along the shore, tiny turtles on branches soaked up the sun's warm rays. The bluffs in the distance outlined the river. It felt like we were traveling in a large, green bowl.

The waves picked up again in the open water. I regretted taking off my spray skirt as we paddled parallel to the waves to get around one of the islands. I took a big, cold wave into my kayak and squealed as the water soaked through my clothes. Sara Jo and Kitty also squealed as their kayaks took on water. Diana's boat was wider, and she stayed dry.

We passed plants with large, round leaves blowing in the wind. Diana told us they were lotuses, and that she had been told this was the only place they grew in the country. We saw more of them as we continued across Weaver Bottoms.

Sara Jo, who had been talking a lot about Dairy Queen the last few days, mentioned it again. Diana lit up and said her favorite was a chocolate mint Dilly Bar. Sara Jo was thrilled, since that was her favorite as well. As they spoke, they realized their obsessions were the result of living in states that did not have Dairy Queens.

We paddled past Mallard Island. It was strangely shaped on the map, and we realized it had to be man-made. I could not comprehend why an island would be constructed in that shape. Paddling a little further, we passed Swan Island, which was also oddly shaped. I presumed it had to do with wildlife. Cormorants dotted the shoreline on both islands.

Approaching Lock and Dam No. 5, Diana became animated and said she had never been through a lock before. She was nervous, although she said she wanted to experience it. Like old pros, Sara Jo and Kitty told her how it worked while I called the Lockmaster. By the time we got to the lock, the gate was open and the light was green. We paddled in. Diana's eyes

Mallard Island

Swan Island

were wide as she watched the water drop and the downriver gate open. We paddled out, and Diana said it was fun and not at all what she had expected.

Photo by Kitty Kennedy

Bass Camp Resort, where we would camp for the evening, was less than a mile from the lock. We saw our tents and pulled our kayaks on shore. The mosquitoes immediately found us, though they were not as bad as the previous night. Gwyn arrived from town a few minutes after we landed. Diana called for her ride, which arrived a short time later, and headed out. We wished she could have stayed.

The temperature dropped and the bugs remained thick, so we put on warm, dry clothes. We ate dinner quickly. I could not sit still while I ate and kept moving around to keep the bugs from biting too badly. Gwyn supplied us with a dessert called Mississippi mud pie. "How could I pass up something with chocolate in it named after the river?" she asked. While we ate, four-wheelers randomly came out of the woods, and fireworks went off in one of the campsites. We noticed one RV was decked out with lights shaped like tractors and flags. A golf cart playing music drove past repeatedly throughout the evening, playing a different style of music each time. The first time around it played Caribbean music, and the second time it was '70s hits.

It was evident that the campground catered to RVs, as many do. The RVs were parked along the shore of the river, and it appeared that many of them had been there for years. Access to the river was difficult because we had to walk through someone else's space to get to the water. It was the end of the campground's busy season, and the impact of the heavy summer use was clearly evident in the outhouse. The stench created an endurance test that measured how long we could hold our breaths.

I was tired after paddling twenty-two and a half miles in a day, but what drove me to bed early was the bugs. We tried to stay up to enjoy Gwyn's company before she had to leave the next morning. However, the buzz in our ears and the knowledge that Gwyn would be back again in two weeks created a greater motivation to dive into our tents.

September 8, Day Five

In the morning, the moisture from the previous night's thunderstorms caused a mist to rise off the surface of the water in a slow rotating motion. "I like watching the mist rise from the water," Sara Jo said. "It's a dance that connects the earth to the sky. If I were a bird I would make this my summer residence—it's so lush here."

After breakfast, we swiftly packed our gear and loaded Kitty's kayak onto the van so she and Gwyn could get an early start. They were driving back to Red Wing to pick up Gwyn's truck, and Gwyn would then drive back to Gillette, Wyoming. She had a project trapping small mammals for relocation, and it could not wait any longer. We were intrigued by her job and looked forward to learning more about it when she returned.

Sara Jo and I waved good-bye and lazily headed to the water. I relished the special time with Sara Jo. She lived in Riverside, California, with her husband, Doug, and was working on her doctorate in plant and soil ecology. I saw her infrequently, so the opportunity to paddle with her alone was precious. As we started paddling, a pair of herons flew overhead, guiding us downriver, and we shared our delight over them.

We enjoyed a leisurely morning with a cool breeze and warm sun. After a mile on the main channel, we turned into Haddock Slough and traveled the backwaters. We saw many herons and turtles along the water's edge, though we were puzzled by the lack of mammals, particularly deer.

Catching up on family, friends, and life in general was fun. Sara Jo talked about the toll that graduate school and living in California had taken on her marriage. My heart ached for her as we discussed sensitive issues. Courageously honest, Sara Jo took a serious look at her part in the struggles she and her husband faced and defined what she had control over and could change. The subject continued to pop up as we paddled, and we created a plan for how she could take care of herself when she got home. I marveled at her problem-solving skills and her ability to see everybody's side of an issue. When we began talking, her tone was laced with despair, but by the end of the day, she was speaking with optimism and confidence.

We enjoyed the herons that led us down the backwaters. The water was like glass, and paddling was effortless. At one point the slough ran parallel to busy Highway 61. We jokingly decided that the passing cars were our adoring fans. We waved to them and bowed, as best we could in kayaks, as if we were in a parade. A fish jumped right over my paddle shaft and startled me. Sara Jo laughed at me, then squealed as it happened to her.

We talked about my struggle with my sense of responsibility. Sara Jo said, "That's nothing new; you've always struggled with that." She was right, but the issue was magnified on the trip. Knowing that people turned to me for direction triggered my need to fulfill other people's expectations. I told Sara Jo my plan to limit the first three days of the next leg of the journey to the primary paddlers. That would allow time to unwind from the stress of planning and get connected to the water and nature. She thought it was a marvelous idea. Our conversation helped me get my mind off the details I'd been so focused on while preparing for the trip. The joy of being on the water without troubling thoughts of responsibility was coming more easily now.

High on top of the bluffs was a fallen pine tree that looked like a whale diving off the bluff. It was darker green than the rest of the trees around it. Even from our distance, we saw that the tree had fallen a while ago, since its branches grew upward from its horizontal trunk.

We rounded a bend that led into Burleigh Slough and saw an old wooden boat near a broken-down dock. The boat was half sunk and had arrowhead and other plants growing out of it. Near it was a patch of lotus with blooming flowers. We paddled closer, thrilled to see the unusual flower. The plants had enormous leaves that folded up around us, surrounding our kayaks. Sara Jo was intrigued by the seed pods, which resemble shower heads and are often harvested for flower arrangements. I was fascinated by the large petals and how the stem held the flower so high off the water. Water  droplets on the floating leaves resembled flat glass beads reflecting the sun.

Sara Jo paddled to the side to retrieve something from the water. Grinning mischievously, she said, "I found a special prize for Gwyn when she returns." It was a dog toy in the shape of a tiny shoe and a ball with a rope. Sara Jo was reinstating a ritual that had begun in 2004 on the first leg of the trip. "Special prizes" were found on the river for the car-support person. It was our way of making her feel included. The treasures were usually trash that would hopefully elicit a smile from the recipient. That dog toy was worth saving.

We turned down Crooked Slough. The shore was lined with arrowhead plants and reeds that stood three feet out of the water. A boat passed us, and the plants swayed in its wake. Our vision warped as the arrowheads that towered above us swayed one way and their reflection appeared to move in the opposite direction. The picture was surreal. We were mesmerized and turned to each other to ask, "Did you see what I saw?"

Paddling into Polander Lake, we wondered aloud what differentiated one large body of water along the river from the river itself, as there were no land masses defining its edges. On the chart, one large body of water may be indicated as two different lakes. I noticed another strangely shaped island on my charts. It resembled a broken wheel, which increased my curiosity about how it had been formed.

A white bird fished near us. She hovered over the water and dove straight down with a splash. As quickly as she went into the water she popped back out. She was streamlined and had a black head, a sharp beak, and black on top of its wings. Its white feathers were stark against the blue sky.

While we watched the bird, a man in a big fishing boat approached us. As he passed, he slowed down to prevent creating waves. He stopped and asked us if we knew that we were headed for the spillway. A spillway is a structure that controls the release of water into a downstream area so that floodwater would not damage or destroy the dam. Normally water does not flow over a spillway except during floods. The spillways on the Mississippi were a continuation of a dam that stretched to the opposite shore of the river. We told him we were headed for the McNally Landing before the spillway. He nodded approvingly and headed toward the landing. When we reached the boat landing he was tying down his boat. I went over to introduce myself and said, "I want to thank you. Most boats don't bother to slow down for us. I guess they don't realize how challenging big waves can be for small boats like ours. I wanted you to know that what you did was considerate."

He looked at me with a bashful grin and said, "Well, that's what we're supposed to do. It was nothing." I wished him well and joined Sara Jo at a nearby picnic table for a snack.

I read an information kiosk while we waited for Kitty to return and learned that the strange islands we had seen were indeed man-made, designed to restore wildlife habitat. Polander Lake used to be a primary stop for migrating waterfowl because it had a smorgasbord of aquatic plants for them to dine on. When Dam No. 5A was built directly across the river, the high water eroded the riverbed and washed away the foliage. The man-made islands restored the balance.

In addition to fostering aquatic-plant restoration, the islands had become homes to trees, shrubs, and wildflowers, which all supported songbirds. The dredging done to create the islands had renewed the river bottom. Because the water was deep and rich in oxy-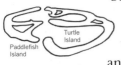gen, it was a year-round home to paddlefish, bluegill, and bass. The island that looked like a broken wheel was actually two islands—Paddlefish and Turtle.

We explored the area around the boat launch and wandered down the short path back to the river. It was lush, quiet, and very buggy. Both Paddlefish Island and the spillway were visible from the path. The spillway didn't appear dangerous, since there was no turbulence around it. I was still glad we didn't have to get too close.

Kitty picked us up, and we headed for Prairie Island Campground.

We planned to get back on the water the next morning at the campground and avoid Lock No. 5A completely. Driving to the campground, Kitty talked about how strange it felt to drive after being on the water. She said that things moved too fast and that the river looked very different from the bluffs above it. "This was a great opportunity to gain another perspective and really appreciate the river," she commented.

Kitty already had our tents set up for us. Well, almost. My tent was distorted and unusable. She told me that, after a valiant effort by her and a man that worked at the campground, they had managed to get it up enough to air it out. I showed her how it went together. We each crawled into our tents to escape the bugs and napped for nearly two hours.

After our naps, we headed to the shower building. A sign on the building read flood relief shower station. A flood had devastated areas along the river a month earlier. Another indication of the flood was the large mosquito population. Inside the building was a sign that said free toiletries were available for flood victims if needed. It was heartwarming to see the campground doing what it could to reach out to people.

We drove south to Winona. Winona in Lakota meant "Chief's first-born daughter." It was the site of many of the Wabasha tribe's ceremonial activities. The town was quiet. I went to the Blue Heron Coffee House while Kitty and Sara Jo went to develop film and buy groceries.

I enjoyed a cup of chai and checked my e-mail. Thankfully there wasn't a lot to respond to, but there was a message from Rosy. I read it and realized I was still angry. I could not grasp how she could make a commitment to drive for us and then not follow through, knowing we depended on her. I understood that emergencies could come up, but that wasn't the case. Her e-mail said she thought she would be a hindrance to us and that she was small and weak. Not true. Thank goodness we had already found a replacement.

Sherry

Back at camp, Sherry arrived to be our new driver. She was bubbling over with enthusiasm about joining us. After stowing her gear, we focused on dinner. Gwyn had made a salad for us the night before, and we had promised her we would eat it. It wasn't until the salad hit our plates that we discovered we didn't have salad dressing. After a few moments of disbelief, I reached for the dill pickles and poured the juice on my salad. At first the others looked at me like I was crazy, but they joined in. Kitty said, "It's not bad in a pinch."

Sara Jo's deep love for dogs emerged when she spotted one across the campground. She ran to meet the dog and the tall African-American man walking him. The three came back to our camp. The dog was named Sparrow after a story in the Bible. Sparrow had a calm spirit, long legs,

Randall and Sparrow

and ears that gave him a lovable cartoon appearance. He loved women, which his owner, Randall, said worked in his favor.

Randall told us that his Minnesota driver's license had been revoked some time ago and he had returned to Minnesota to clear his record. He was hitchhiking and working along the way to pay for his travels. He wanted a fresh start, but to do that, he needed to clean up his past mistakes. He began an intriguing conversation about respect and how to treat women. At one point, he looked at the four of us and said, "You Northern girls don't know how to be treated like ladies." Then he asked each of us if we were married. Kitty acknowledged that she was not, and he zeroed in on her. He told us he was looking for a woman and smiled brightly at Kitty. He made a valiant, but failed, effort to convince Kitty that they would be a good match. The banter became more humorous as he talked about how Northern women needed to be "pollinated." With each comment, he raised his eyebrows, smiled broadly, tilted his head to the side, and looked in Kitty's direction as if to say, "what do you think of me now, Sweetie?" Kitty responded by smiling, tilting her head down, and raising her eyebrows. Her message was, "I don't think so." It was entertaining to watch.

We told Randall about our trip. The more we told him, the more excited he became. However, the bugs soon forced us to end our conversation and seek refuge in our tents.

September 9, Day Six

It rained hard during the night. I lay in the tent listening to the wind and envisioned a rough day on the water. The morning brought a light breeze with a few drizzles. We headed to our kayaks, expecting Randall to appear for another attempt at a date with Kitty, but there was no sign of him or Sparrow. We didn't eat breakfast before we left, which threw off my morning routine. I forgot to sing or make an offering of kinnikinnick. By the time I remembered, it was too late since I had left my deck bag with the kinnikinnick in the car with Sherry. We would meet her for breakfast a couple miles downriver at the Blue Heron Coffee House.

Paddling under a bridge, we approached Winona's beautiful downtown riverfront. A paddle-wheel steamboat, the Willkie, had been made into a museum and was perched on the levee above us. The steep levee bank was constructed of concrete and boulders and was inhospitable to small boats like ours. We each picked a safe place to land and carefully climbed out of our kayaks. Sherry waited on the shore. We pulled the kayaks onto the rocks and walked to the Blue Heron.

While we enjoyed our quiche and muffins, Kitty asked, "Sherry, what is your degree in?"

"Teaching," answered Sherry. "I just started taking classes because I wanted to learn. I never finished any master's program."

Sara Jo stared at Sherry intently and said emphatically, "I just feel like I know you, and it's driving me nuts! It's like we have met before."

"Me too," I added. "When I saw you sitting at the table in Red Wing, I was not surprised you were there. I was just surprised that I didn't know your name."

"Maybe we met in another lifetime," said Sherry. "Just the way this whole thing has come together for me is surprising. I was the only one from Red Wing who came to that dinner. Since then, people have said, 'Oh yeah, I saw that in the paper,' but nobody else came. I know I am supposed to be here."

"Have you spent any time in Superior, Wisconsin?" asked Sara Jo. "I think we have met. I am not ready to accept that it was another lifetime."

"My son lives in Duluth," responded Sherry. "That's where my daughter-in-law, grandson, and dog live. I have the neatest grandson, but doesn't every grandmother say that? He's eight months old."

"That age is always adorable," said Sara Jo.

"Kitty, are you from the Ely area?" asked Sherry.

"No, I grew up in Voss, North Dakota," responded Kitty. "North of Grand Forks. There were probably only seventy-five or a hundred people there when I grew up. It's about forty miles to the Canadian border and about fifty miles from the Minnesota border."

"I used to date a guy that was from there," said Sherry.

"Oh really?" responded Kitty. "What was his name?"

"Olson," responded Sherry. We laughed. "He was very Norwegian, a real loner. When he dies, he wants his friends to make this fancy Norwegian boat, put his body in it, set it on fire, and run it out on Lake Pepin. His friends are all motorcycle nuts, so they just might do it."

"His body will sink and come up later all charred," I added.

"Someone will think he was murdered," Sara Jo jumped in.

"Wouldn't that be fun," Sherry said with a mischievous grin. "He would get a kick out of that."

Breakfast concluded, and we headed back to the bank of the river. A young police officer was blocking off the area where we had landed and was hesitant to let us into the restricted area. He said they were expecting a large paddle-wheel boat to arrive. We looked at each other with great anticipation. It would have to pass us, and we'd get a chance to see it.

While getting into my kayak, I nearly tipped into the water several times. There are a number of ways to get into a kayak; they all required balance, coordination, and a sense of humor. I preferred floating the kayak parallel to the shoreline in shallow water. I stood next to the cockpit facing downriver and then extended one paddle blade to a flat surface on the shore. With one hand, I grabbed both the cockpit rim and the shaft of the paddle. I leaned away from the kayak onto the paddle to steady the boat, placed one leg into the kayak, and shifted my weight so I was sitting on the back rim of the cockpit. Still leaning slightly toward shore, which put the bulk of my weight onto the paddle, I brought my other leg up and into the kayak and then slid down into the seat. A sense of humor was essential because the terrain of the shoreline rarely presented a perfect entry point. Shoreline variables included fast-moving water, waves, rocks, logs, vegetation, slippery mud, or deep water. Any of those could quickly disrupt a smooth entry. Sherry watched intently and commented that she wasn't confident in my abilities. I told her not to worry; the river was just telling me to get focused.

We saw a beaver, though she disappeared under the water after only a quick glimpse. Kingfishers flitted from tree to tree and squawked at us as we passed.

We crossed many wing dams. Wing dams were built in the early 1900s, along with the lock-and-dam system, to improve navigation. They were made of piles of rock and brush that extended from shore, sometimes hundreds of feet out. The rocks had been hauled down from nearby quarries. Heavy equipment was not an option when the wing dams were built, so most of the rocks were thrown by hand onto the pile to construct the dams. The dams were submerged after the lock-and-dam system was flooded for operation. We noted the presence of a wing dam by the ripples in the water as we passed over them.

Katie's words from the Gathering echoed in my head: "Be happy with yourself, but keep reaching," and "The greatest gift from the Spirit is love." She was sure of herself, and I admired that. Her comments made me see that self-love was indeed important. Many of the women that night had spoken of the value of honoring yourself and your "knowing." By making this journey, I was honoring my knowing. I liked that validation. I sensed that my struggle with responsibility was connected to her comment about always reaching. I had always had an internal need to reach and do more. However, being happy with myself required compassion for my humanity and shortcomings, especially when I stretched myself.

It remained sunny, and a strong tail wind developed. Puffy clouds drifted across the sky all afternoon. Paddling near islands past Homer, Minnesota, we came across dozens of cormorants perched in the tops of the trees. Some had spread their wings to dry in the sun. Their shape and the way they took off from the water reminded me of loons. Unlike loons, the cormorants were solid black. They let us get close before they flew away.

Numbness developed in my fingertips. It had been happening off and on during the past few days. My hands, in general, were more tired and sore than they were on the trip two years before, which concerned me.

Sherry waited for us on the dock at Pla-Mor Campground and Marina. Kitty and I paddled to shore while Sara Jo headed to the dock. The day before, she had tried to exit her kayak at a dock and failed because it was too high. This time she was determined. She pulled her kayak parallel to the chest-high dock. Placing both hands firmly on the dock, she pushed down and lifted her body out of the kayak. The boat wobbled. She did not pull her body high enough and sank back into her boat, tilting the kayak over so far that the lip of the cockpit grazed the water. Quickly balancing herself, she tried twice more with the same result. Her eyebrows pinched tight as her determination increased. With a sudden burst of energy and the grace of a gymnast, she rose out of the kayak high enough to twist her body around and sit on the dock. She stood in a victory pose, and Sherry clapped. Her kayak drifted safely to shore.

Pla-Mor Campground was nice, but it felt like an RV park ghost town since there was no one else there. Our campsite had a clear view of Trem-

pealeau Mountain. Trempealeau meant "mountain whose foot is bathed in water." It was the only mountain along the Mississippi and was the site of sacred burial grounds for Winnebago Native Americans.

Photo by Kitty Kennedy

While the others set up camp, I uploaded the day's photos to the laptop. The bright sunlight made it impossible to see the images on the computer screen, so I formed a canopy by draping my pullover and rain gear over my head and the computer. It worked well, but the others giggled at my appearance. They headed into Winona while I stayed behind to finish my project.

While wandering through the campground, I found an old playground with equipment I hadn't seen since I was young. I got the merry-go-round going fast enough to ride two full rotations before it stopped. There was a tall swing that allowed me to get high enough to momentarily hang upside down as the swing changed direction.

When the others returned, I spread out the charts to show them how the train we'd seen across the channel was actually running down the middle of the river. The tracks ran in a straight line for six miles along a man-made levee with water on both sides. When paddling next to it, we felt the train's vibrations through the water. It seemed like a feat of engineering to us, along with the locks and wing dams.

During dinner, Sherry spoke of her family. "My children puzzle over what my grandchildren are going to call me. Recently I have been going with Nana."

"Why Nana?" I asked.

"It's easy to say, and I discovered it has roots in many cultures, including Slovenian culture." answered Sherry. "I'm Czechoslovakian, and my dad was Bohemian. My grandmother never spoke English. She spoke Bohemian. I think she came right over from Bohemia."

"Do you speak Bohemian?" asked Sara Jo.

"No," said Sherry, "I don't understand it either. I was hardly around my grandma because my mom didn't like my dad's family."

"That's too bad," I said. "That must mean that part of your culture was lost."

"It happens in a lot of families," said Sherry. "My kids don't know my family very well, but they know their dad's family."

"I don't know my dad's family very well," said Sara Jo. "I actually don't know either side of my family very well anymore. I don't keep in contact with them. I feel like I should keep in contact with Uncle Mark."

"Why Uncle Mark in particular?" I asked.

"Well, because Uncle Mark was always sort of a rescuer," she responded. "He was sane. I know it's kind of funny to think of him that way, but he remained friends with Dad even through the divorce. So there was still that link. We always knew we would see Uncle Mark. He came and checked on us. That was cool. We knew we could go somewhere if Uncle Mark was there. Dad would be okay with it. Oh, gross, I am eating with a mosquito sucking on my palm."

"Well, there is no meat in this meal, so you might consider him," kidded Sherry.

Our laughter was interrupted by a flock of noisy geese overhead. They were flying in a formation that looked more like a W than a V. Then it changed again to a shape that was nowhere near a V. Struggling to get it together before they migrated south for the winter, they passed over a couple more times before disappearing behind the trees. They had yet to form the V-shaped flight pattern.

We enjoyed a panoramic view as the sun set and the breeze dissipated. The sky turned several shades of orange and pink. Soft colors blended into each other and reflected off the glassy river. The bluffs and islands, reflected on the water, created striking silhouettes. I soaked in the colors of the sky and water and thought about my traveling companions.

Sara Jo exhibited wisdom beyond her age. She always had, but now it had been tempered with experience, giving it depth. Her outgoing, spunky nature drew people in. I was always learning from her and was honored to call her my daughter.

Sherry was good natured, fun, and just plain delightful. She was knowledgeable on many topics, including science and spirituality. I looked forward to learning from her.

Kitty's soft, gentle nature had a calming effect on things. It was like I traveled with a child who had a wonderful way of seeing and perceiving things. For her, the world was always new and tinged with amazement and awe.

As we readied for bed, two barges passed by. We stood on the shoreline, watching as a large searchlight on the tugboat scanned for daymarks on the distant shoreline to get its load of barges safely around the bend. The searchlight was extremely bright, and we could clearly see the trees on the far shore when the light scanned across them. One light off the side of the tugboat shone directly on us. I stepped forward, took a bow, and jokingly said, "Thank you, thank you very much." We laughed, and Sherry suggested that we shine a light back at them. We turned on our headlamps and moved around, sending a playful message to the people on the tugboat, never assuming that our little lights could be seen by them. Sara Jo put her headlamp on strobe and said she was sending them Morse code. Sherry put hers on the red light setting to mimic the red lights on the tugboat. I mimicked their searchlight and attempted to scan the far shore with my tiny light. We continued to play with our lights when a new light appeared from the tugboat. It shone directly at us and blinked and moved in an odd pattern. It was clear they were returning our silly communication. We burst into laughter and jumped up and down.

We watched the barge for a while longer and gazed up at the beautiful starry sky. The prediction of rain the next day concerned us. It could make for a long day.

September 10, Day Seven

It rained most of the night. I snuggled deep into my sleeping bag and listened as the rain gently tapped on the tent. The rain sounded pleasant, but the thought of paddling in it was not. The peaceful sound was broken several times throughout the night by the stark sound of a metallic moose approaching and blasting its whistle.

My thoughts drifted to Sara Jo's struggle with her relationship with her husband. Her compromise to keep the peace was exactly what I had always done in relationships. It was an automatic behavior many women engaged in to keep or bring peace. Culture trained us to some degree to do so, but I believe it was part of our makeup. We couldn't help ourselves if we sensed that compromise would heal a dispute. Some cultures taught women to use that same compromise and compassion toward themselves, but that had not been what I had learned. Sara Jo had learned to compromise herself from me, and it frustrated me. I wished I had learned faster or earlier not to give in so quickly so I could have been a more positive role model. I knew that everybody had to learn their own life lessons, but our teachers made a difference.

Sara Jo loved Doug dearly, and the potential for a great relationship was there. I had listened and struggled for the right words to help her. I encouraged her to be honest and did my best to get out of the way. It did not seem like enough.

I also had not been taking care of myself before we left Ely. I had had an idea that on the water all that would change because I would be relaxed and have more time. That was not the case. I occupied myself more than I should with taking care of everyone and everything. Vigilance rose within me, and I felt like a mother hen watching over her brood with a fox present. I didn't need to take care of everyone, but the thought crept in that the trip was my big idea, so I needed to make sure that everyone got what they needed. Sara Jo stirred in her sleeping bag. I realized I was still modeling behaviors I did not want her to learn.

The first order of business in the morning was to call Cathy R., who had planned to paddle with us that day. We anticipated that she would bow out, since we would have if we were in her position. The weather report predicted that it would pour all day. Cathy R. said paddling in the cold and rain did not sound like fun but that she would wave as we passed by her home overlooking the river in Trempealeau. She had made a smart decision.

We helped Sherry get everything into the van before we left. The rain came down hard, and the drops made sizable splashes on the surface of the water. Mist rose from the water and obscured Trempealeau Mountain and the bluffs. We struggled to get our rain gear adjusted so the ice cold water would not seep in and get our clothes wet.

Paddling past houses at Trempealeau, we watched for Cathy R. We saw a woman on a deck waving to us, and we waved back. From there it was a short distance to Lock No. 6. I called the Lockmaster, who said a boat was locking through and it would be a half-hour wait.

Sara Jo had planned to use the outhouse at the boat launch on the other side of the lock, but could not wait a half hour. Floating on water makes waiting to use the bathroom extremely difficult. I headed to shore with her, and we paddled into an area behind the lock wall that was thick with duckweed and other smelly debris. Sara Jo had a difficult time finding a spot along the shore to get out, so I paddled in next to her to stabilize her kayak. The bugs were fierce. I watched the rain fall on the duckweed. It looked like rain was spouting up from the duckweed in three inch fountains before dropping back down and disappearing.

When Sara Jo got back in her kayak she was covered in duckweed, but waited until we rejoined Kitty to clean it off because of the stench and bugs near shore. Duckweed had even gotten in her underwear. I called her the duckweed queen. We watched a small boat speed out of the lock, and Sara Jo moaned, "That wasn't a half hour. I could have waited!"

Paddling into the lock, we saw a woman in the observation tower with a large camera taking pictures of us. The next thing we knew she was down at the railing, waving at us and taking more pictures. As the

water level in the lock dropped, we realized it was Cathy R. She yelled that she would meet us at the boat landing below the lock.

At the boat landing, Cathy R. offered us warm, homemade tomato bread. We each ate a piece right away and tucked the rest away in a dry place. We chatted with her for a few minutes, but the cold rain spurred us on.

We continued to hug the islands and mainland along the Wisconsin side, trying to get relief from the weather. The islands also offered opportunities to see osprey, eagles, turtles, beavers, and monkey flower. In addition to the wildlife, we found special river "prizes." Sara Jo picked up a ball for her sister, Naomi, who had been car support for us on the first trip.

Paddling between islands, we saw herons standing in the water some distance from the shore. It puzzled us how they could be standing in the water until we realized they were on a sandbar. We decided they had landed there to assist us by marking the shallow spots in the water. They stood like sentries on both ends of the islands we passed.

I acquired a red and black bug as a passenger, who rode on my map most of the day. I wondered if she believed it was safer from the weather there, even though raindrops still pelted her. The bug wandered around on the map as if using it to locate something. She followed the lines that indicated the roads and walked up and down an island. She did not leave my map until we landed on shore at the day's end.

Sara Jo's raingear failed her. Water leaked down her neck and wicked up her sleeves. She was wet and cold, and hypothermia became a serious concern. She said she was doing alright and kept eating to help ward it off. We agreed that if she started acting or sounding odd we would get

her off the water. Stopping for breaks and being inactive made it worse. For a humorous diversion from the cold, Sara Jo made a hat for herself from a lotus leaf floating in the water and claimed it was as nice as Deah's.

We crossed the main channel to the Minnesota side of Dresbach Island. As we crossed, an enormous black bird we could not identify flew eerily overhead. She was the size of an eagle but was jet black, and its wings moved as if in slow motion. We stopped to watch it pass and then looked at each other worriedly, as if we had received an ominous warning. We distracted ourselves from the scary bird by looking at the lovely homes along the shore.

The rain let up as we neared Lock and Dam No. 7. I called the Lockmaster and received an unusual response when I told the woman that there were three kayaks approaching from the north.

"You can't call me here. You have to call us on your marine radio," she responded.

I told her we did not have one, but she told me again that I had to call on our marine radio. I told her that I was instructed to call that number by the main office of the Army Corps of Engineers. She insisted I could not call her by cell phone, even though I was already talking to her by cell phone. Exasperated, I said, "Forget it, I'll paddle up and pull the cord."

I paddled up to the cord, which hung higher than I could reach. I was grateful that the wind was not thrashing the lock wall with waves, or I would have had no chance of getting to the cord. I tucked my kayak up against the wall and pulled myself onto a rung of the metal ladder that was built into the wall below the cord. With a lunge, I grabbed the rope and pulled. I heard the whistle and felt relieved as I carefully lowered myself back into my kayak. The gate opened immediately. As we paddled into the lock, we concluded that the woman on the phone must have been new and trying to stick to the rules as she understood them. We had probably presented her with a scenario that hadn't been covered in training.

Sherry was standing on the lock wall with her camera waiting for us. She was excited and took lots of pictures. She yelled over the side that we would be having spaghetti and a salad for dinner, and the lock attendant joked that he would come join us.

After Lock No. 7, we passed under the Interstate 90 bridge near La Crosse, Wisconsin. It reminded me of the Interstate 35W bridge collapse in Minneapolis a couple of months before. Many had lost their lives while going about their daily routines. I had paddled under that bridge during the first leg of the journey, and it never occurred to me that it could fall on us. I thought about how often we cross over bridges and never give them a second thought, yet many of the bridges in our country are in desperate need of repair. I felt less trusting of bridges and scanned them for potential problems, even though I knew I wouldn't recognize a problem if I saw one.

Clearing the bridge, we crossed the main channel and headed down East Channel near Minnesota Island. The trees were peppered with hundreds of cormorants and a few herons as accents. Most of the birds stayed perched as we paddled past, but others took flight and swirled in the air above us.

"Follow the turtles," Kitty remarked. Dozens of turtle heads breaking the surface of the water lined the channel. Kitty accidently hit one with her paddle. At camp later, Sara Jo looked up the meaning of turtles in Medicine Cards, a book we had with us, and learned that they represent goddess energy. We agreed that the goddesses had been guiding us that day.

We passed under a railroad bridge and approached Taylor Island, where several eagles were perched. Most were immature. Eagles did not receive their white heads or tails until they were a few years old. Scattered among them were seagulls and herons standing guard along the channel.

We saw downtown La Crosse. Its name originated in the 1700s when fur traders came to the area and saw young Winnebago men playing a ball game with sticks. The French called the game lacrosse, and the area was named after it. Hotels close to the riverbank looked inviting to us. We were tired, cold, and wet, so a hot shower and a soft, warm bed sounded divine, but we knew Sherry already had camp set up. I looked right down main street, and the stoplights along it looked odd to me. So much time on the water and in nature had made civilized life seem disjointed.

We paddled toward Pettibone Resort and cut into the slough that led to our campsite. The slough was thick with duckweed. Kitty laughed and pointed at boats in the marina with fake palm trees on them.

Sherry's cheerful face greeted us at the end of our twenty-one-mile day. My tent had again presented a challenge and lay in a heap waiting for me. We went to take showers and do laundry since everything we had on was wet and smelly.

Hot chocolate waited for us when we returned. Sherry was making dinner. Barbara C.H. arrived with her husband of 35 years, Steve. Steve traveled a lot as a train conductor, which gave Barbara the opportunity to pursue her music. She was a professional singer and did music therapy for nursing home residents and Alzheimer's patients. She had moved to Ely a year and a half before, in part to be closer to her parents.

Barbara C.H. would paddle with us the next day. She and Steve were staying at a motel in La Crosse. She was excited about paddling yet a little more reserved than the woman I was used to. They didn't stay long but took coffee and chai orders for a morning delivery.

Sherry shared more of her life story as we ate dinner. "Starting in 1995, I went down to Guatemala with Witness for Peace," she said. "I was a regional coordinator for them. The purpose of Witness for Peace is to take Americans down to Guatemala to learn the political situation from the people who live there. I helped take delegations down for five years, and I learned what our government is doing to the people of these countries.

"The Guatemalans we spoke with asked us to go home and try to change the policies of our government that affected them. They viewed our government as very oppressive. Sometimes we had twenty people in our delegation, and the locals would say to each of us, 'Go back and work to change your government's polices to be more fair and supportive of the people of the world. Change them to be not just about government or money but about people.'

"Then I became involved in the School of the Americas protest in Fort Benning, Georgia. It started in 1990 and happens every year. It was started by Father Roy Bushwa, a priest and a good friend, who is very involved in the Resource Center of the Americas in Minneapolis. The first time I went down to the protest, there were about a thousand people there. Now the number is more like six thousand.

"In 1995, you could walk right onto the base since there was just a white line drawn to mark its perimeter. First I went with Veterans for Peace. Over six hundred of us were arrested because we crossed that white line painted in the road. We carried black caskets painted with the names of people that we knew of who had been killed in Guatemala. We marched across the line, and the soldiers came and told us to lie down. We had all been trained in non-violent protesting, so we lay down. They brought buses along and loaded us up. When got to the base we waited in line and sang songs. It was a pretty jolly group that got arrested. We had to get fingerprinted and get our pictures taken—mug shots. They let us go, but we were all restricted from crossing the line for five years."

"And if you went over the line, what would have happened?" asked Kitty.

"I would have gone to prison," she responded nonchalantly. "My son Allen crossed the line that time with me," she continued. "The next year my son Chris and daughter Ellen crossed the line. Allen and I were there but didn't cross. I am going to go this year for the last time. My philosophy is that we are all in this world together, and we all have to take care of each other. If there is something I can do and still stay centered in who I am and what I believe, then I want to continue to do it. I feel like it's pulling our country to be more positive, if it's possible. If it isn't possible, it doesn't matter to me because I'm still working for what I believe in."

"So you're trying to change our country?" asked Sara Jo.

"Yes," replied Sherry.

We fell silent and turned in for the night.

September 11, Day Eight

I woke in the night to the wind in the trees. My pants slid off the tent, where I had laid them to dry. I got up to fetch them and was treated to a fabulous sky of stars. The wind, which had sounded so loud from

inside the tent, was just a breeze rustling through the trees. It was warm compared to the night before. I shed the layers of clothes I had worn to bed and crawled back into my sleeping bag.

In the morning, Barbara C.H. arrived with coffee and chai and immediately brought her kayak and gear down to the water. She was still a bit reserved, and I assumed she was nervous about paddling. Sherry took pictures of everything. She said she was trying to figure out how the camera worked, but we knew better—she was excited and wanted to document everything.

Barbara C.H.

Mary Ruth and Cheryl joined us. They had camped a few campsites down. Everyone was so eager and efficient that I felt like I was holding things up. They were all already on the water by the time I got down to the shore. Paddling through the channel, Kitty pointed at fake palm trees on the boats in the marina as we passed them. The wind picked up when we got to the main channel. We crossed over to the Wisconsin side and paddled into Laplume Slough in search of calmer waters.

Toward the end of the slough was an industrial site. On Laplume Island were two large white tanks. We debated what they held, and noticed an unpleasant odor filling the air.

"What's with the rotten eggs?" commented Mary Ruth with her nose scrunched. We paddled quickly to get past the area. We were unable to determine the smell's source, but it had caused me enough breathing issues that I had to get out my inhaler. The smell disappeared when we hit a patch of clean air, and I could breathe again.

Mary Ruth

Cheryl

Kitty, Barbara C.H., Sara Jo, Mary Ruth, Cheryl, and Nancy

I saw whitecaps in the main channel, so we stayed near Green Island, which offered protection from the wind. We talked about the lotus plants we had seen over the past few days. Mary Ruth and Cheryl hoped to see some. We came around the end of an island and met an egret slowly walking the shore. We stopped for a few moments to watch pelicans circling in the sky like a graceful, slow-moving tornado.

We came to an open stretch where we were no longer protected from the wind. Waves crashed against the sides of our boats for a half mile before we ducked into Mormon Slough, which led to Goose Island. Barbara C.H. looked nervous about the big waves and became quiet. She mustered her courage and tried to look brave. I paddled over and asked if she was okay. She said she was and concentrated on paddling. Her kayak was wide, so she had stability on her side. I stayed near her until we got into the slough. Her beautiful smile returned as she said, "It was a little dicey out there when the waves started. Then I realized my boat is wide and was taking the waves just fine."

Not far into the slough, we stopped for a break on a point covered in purple loosestrife, an invasive plant species that was a problem in the local lakes and waterways. The loosestrife stalks were tall, hard, and woody. They did not bend easily, and we had to physically struggle to walk through them. There were no other plants around because the loosestrife had choked them out. It left me with a greater understanding of why it was a problem, and I mentioned it to Sara Jo. She nodded and said, "It's a serious problem, and people just don't understand."

Continuing on, we faced the wonderful challenge of finding Goose Island in the backwaters. The charts were not accurate because the flow of the water had changed the landscape over time. The charts indicated that we should follow the channel straight ahead until we reached open water and then turn east. Since the channel was not straight at all, we decided to explore. Laughter filled the air as we paddled among islands covered in tall grasses. Mary Ruth and Barbara C.H. discovered their common appreciation for an old song, and sang "I'm Gonna Sit Right Down and Write Myself a Letter".

We followed a narrow channel that appeared to wind through the islands in the direction we wanted to go. The water in the channel became shallower, and the reeds on the bottom grew thicker. We came to

a fork in the channel. The path to the right seemed clearer, but the reeds underwater pointed to the left with the current. We went right. The duckweed quickly became thick. Sara Jo paddled ahead and discovered we were in a dead end. I followed everyone back out of the channel and smiled as I passed the reeds under the water, which had tried to warn us.

Mary Ruth and Cheryl paddled over to a patch of lotus with me. The wind blew us into the shore while we studied the dried leaves and pods. The dried stems were stiff and scratched our skin. In their canoe, Mary

Ruth and Cheryl got out of the plants more easily than I did in my kayak. Their paddles effortlessly dipped in and out between the plants. One side of my paddle would go through the water easily, but the other side would get caught on the stems each time. I had to lift one end over the stems while dislodging the other end with each stroke. I laughed at the predicament I was in. I freed myself with effort, and we rejoined the group.

Everyone seemed disappointed when the campground came into view. "We can't be there yet," said Barbara C.H. "Haven't we only gone half a mile?"

"No, we only have half a mile left," I responded.

"I'm not ready to be done," Barbara C.H. lamented.

"I'm not ready to be done either," Sara Jo chimed in emphatically. It had a different meaning for her, as it was her last day with us before she returned to California.

We pulled our boats up on the beach near our campsite. Sherry bounced down to shore to greet us. Barbara C.H. called her husband on her cell phone, and he was there in no time to pick her up. She would return for the Gathering that evening.

We turned our attention to putting up the tents. Sherry hadn't attempted it because she was afraid the wind would blow them away. She had been chasing things clear across the campground while unpacking the gear from the van. We helped each other put the tents up one at a time. We staked them down with extra stakes and weighted them with our gear so they would stay put.

My daughter Naomi and her friend Suzanne arrived for the Gathering. They would give Sara Jo a ride back to Minneapolis the next day to catch her flight home. Naomi was a special-education administrator, and getting away during the school year took effort. It meant a lot to me that both my daughters were able to share this adventure with me.

Naomi

Suzanne had been Naomi's friend since seventh grade, when they went on camping trips together. She felt like family to us.

Our campsite became a tent city, with coolers and five tents surrounding the picnic table. Sherry gave Cheryl a ride back to La Crosse to get her car. Cheryl

Suzanne

brought ice cream when she returned. We huddled behind the van while we ate it to keep the wind from blowing it out of our hands.

I took advantage of having internet in the campground and checked my e-mail. Doug had e-mailed to tell me that the mother of a dear friend, Lou Ezza, had died. Her mother had been sick in the hospital when I left. It was painful to hear the news and not be home to support Lou Ezza. I grew quiet as I uploaded the day's pictures onto the computer.

I could not truly relate to the depth of the loss Lou Ezza felt. My mother died when I was eleven. I had not had the opportunity to build a relationship with her over the years like Lou Ezza had with her mother. I had watched other women with their mothers and observed what an integral part of each others' lives they were. I hadn't experienced that. I knew this would be one of the biggest losses of Lou Ezza's life.

As I opened my journal to make a few notes about my thoughts, I found a brilliant red maple leaf tucked inside the pages. I looked over at Sherry, who smiled at me. She had snuck it in earlier.

The campground had many black-walnut trees, which reminded me of a story about my first husband that I shared with the group. When he and I lived on a forty-acre hobby farm near North Branch, Minnesota, he came up with a retirement scheme. Because the price of black walnut was high at the lumberyard, he purchased eighty black-walnut saplings and planted them on our property. He was convinced that when we retired forty years later we would make a fortune harvesting the mature trees. A year later we had moved off the property and were no longer together. I didn't know if was a feasible idea or not, but it certainly was creative.

While we ate dinner, Barbara C. H. wrote in the paddlers' journal:

> *I am so lucky. I turn 60 next year, and so far life has been a joyous journey. Today I paddled the Mississippi with gifted, strong, and spiritual women. Tonight we gather and share.*
> *Bless each of you.*
> *Safe Journey.*
> *MiiGwitch (Thank You)*

Ice Cream Refuge, Cheryl, Sara Jo, Nancy, Mary Ruth, and Kitty

LaCrosse Gathering

Everyone pitched in to prepare for the Gathering by collecting sticks and arranging chairs. The women arrived and took their places in the circle. There were fourteen of us ranging in age from twenty-eight to seventy. We had sleeping bags ready to help ward off the chilly wind, and as the evening progressed, some of the women bundled in them.

Bonne O. began the evening's sharing. "What wisdom would I like to share with younger women as they travel the river of life? Like you, Nancy, I grew up on the Mississippi River. My father taught me to ice skate on the backwaters and to swim in the river. I like the fact that the first highways in our nation were the rivers. They were the first source we had for communication with the outside world. When you talk about the river of life, life meanders just like the Mississippi River. It meanders from its youth to its maturity, and its mouth becomes a wider resource. I like the analogy of comparing the river to our lives. It's changing as we are. My life has not gone the way I expected, actually very little the way I expected. That's what makes life enjoyable and a journey.

"I have three daughters. They are all married and have their own families now. I think, in the course of my life, I have learned more from my children than they ever will from me. I think it's a blessing to gain knowledge from them."

"I also grew up on the river, in Wabasha," added Linda B., "and I still have family that lives there. I learned to swim and fish on the river. A cute memory was something my dad always did. I always wanted to go fishing with him. 'Well,' he'd say, 'if you get up we will go fishing.' But he would never wake me, and he would always be gone by the time I woke up. It took me a long time to figure that out. If I was going to go with him, I had to get up. I did a few times, but most often, by the time I woke up he was gone.

"What is so neat about the river is that it carries sound. We kids would either be down at the river fishing, or we'd be across the river on a sandbar with the boat. All mom had to do was go out the front porch door and yell 'Linda, Nancy, Diane,' and we could hear her. We could be two miles away, and we could still hear her. Then we would have to head home. That was neat.

"When I first saw the article about this trip, I realized I had always wanted to do that–paddle the Mississippi. I did do a very small portion as a college student. A friend of mine and I paddled from Wabasha down to Winona. We stayed a night on an island.

"All the things we experience teach us something. We learn from it all. I like learning the ways of life on the river. How things flow and how things are ever changing, like the different ways of your life. I look back on myself now, and I think 'Why did I do that?' I wished I had known what I know now. We all say that. We all make our mistakes. We all hopefully learn from them.

Edna was our honored elder for the evening but arrived after we had begun.

"I am definitely a mother: a mother of ten, a grandmother of nineteen, and great-grandmother of four. Spirituality has saved my life. I was kind of going the opposite way when I was having all these children, and I'm a Catholic, as you could have guessed. The church and the priest said, 'Oh no, you can't have anything that would prevent. Oh no.' I went through a terrible depression that would probably be called postpartum now, but this was forty years ago.

Edna

"My spirituality, even though I was bitter toward the church's stand, saved me because I went to church every day and prayed 'Let me get through this day and accept my life. I know this is what I have to do.' Yes, it was a lot of work, but you just do it. It took me years, and finally, just like that, I knew what my life was. Fifteen pregnancies in thirteen years. I lost three babies, and that was enough. I had my tubes tied and I started living my life. My life! I felt that if I couldn't take care of me, then how could I take care of anyone else? I didn't think it was possible. After that, life was wonderful. It was so much better.

"My parents were ailing. So I did a lot with my parents. I lived next door to them. My sister, thank goodness, lived in the same town, and we shared a lot of the responsibilities. My brothers would stop for five minutes and say that they had too much to do and couldn't stay. When our parents passed away, my sister and I had a wonderful feeling that we had done so much for them.

"As the children grew up and became independent, my husband and I decided we needed a change, so we moved. We were originally from the southeastern part of Wisconsin, by Milwaukee, Racine, and Kenosha. After being born and raised there, coming to La Crosse changed our whole life. Wonderful! I got involved in the spirituality center at St. Roses, such a marvelous facility. It has good programs of all different faiths. I think it is very interesting to realize that you don't have to live only in your own faith. I have gotten into some Native American faiths and Buddhism. As far as the philosophy of it, I think it all helps you grow. If you don't keep growing, you aren't whole; you just aren't living life.

"I had a life-altering experience a couple of years ago. I had a disagreement with a couple of my girls. I have four girls and six boys. I was hurt terribly by their words. The thing that hurt the most was that their father, their brothers, and the extended family members said nothing in my defense, so it was okay for them to say and behave toward me the way they did. The indifference hurt so much. Then this year my husband's brother and his wife called. I wasn't going to be down for a shower for their daughter because I had made previous plans for that date. They read me the riot act and told me what an awful and uncaring person I was. Again, not one family member gave me any support. This family had meant so much to me, and it now seemed that I must not mean much to anyone else.

"I am a little bit discouraged right now, but I know that because of my spirituality, because of who I am, and because I know who I am, I will get through this situation. It is hurtful when you feel that somebody has betrayed you. Yet it probably really is only your ego that is causing it, and you have to get past that.

"Now I am on this journey to build myself up again to find out who I really am at seventy years old. My sister, Mary, who was so cute, said I am stubborn, which I am. I am Irish, and we are all stubborn. She also said, 'You are entitled to your choices at seventy years old. You are entitled to live your life. You sacrificed, you gave to all these children, and you did all of it. So now why do we have to do what they want us to? Why do we have to change everything because it suits them?'

"Life is so good. I feel that every day is a blessing! I am so grateful, and I love things like this. I love women's groups because I think you can share more than you can with couples or whomever. To me, women really understand. You have to be a crone to have the knowledge to understand what life is all about."

Sherry took the fan and held it for a few moments, admiring its design. "I have no idea what I will say, but I just trust it will be something important for me to share. I am very grateful and feel very honored to be part of this group, and it was a huge surprise to be asked to drive the van. Right now I don't have a job. I had all kinds of commitments, but it was possible to cancel or postpone everything and make a two-week space in my life to do this. A space that allowed me to be part of this phenomenal group of women who are doing such important work.

"When I worked in Stockholm, Wisconsin, in an antique shop there, the owner was also trying to get groups of women to share their stories and put them into a book, but in a different way. Her vision was to have women just write their story based on the basic facts of their lives. In Nancy's vision, the purpose seems more rich and solid. There is much more spirit in this and an energy of connection that we all share. It's not just my story, but it's also everybody's story; everything that we share is so powerful.

"I honor all of you that came to this Gathering to be part of this. I think that it will be through the women in our country, maybe in our world, where change and healing will originate. There are definitely some men that understand how this works, but I think it is the women that are going to get this going and do the healing that we are very much in need of. I feel energy changing toward that end. I really honor all of you for coming and allowing me to share this healing energy with you."

I took the fan next. "I am going to take the opportunity to speak tonight. I wasn't able to on the last trip because I was under fifty and had to follow my own rules. [Laughter.] I can relate to the big family. I come from a family of eight. My mother passed away when I was eleven. I was the oldest girl, which meant that I was expected to handle mom's duties. I have older twin brothers, but they were boys, and that was not their role. I learned so much from that experience. I resented the heck out of it at the time. My relationship with my grandmother changed dramatically into one that I did not appreciate. As an adult looking back, I understand what she was doing, and that her intentions were to help all of us, but at the time, I thought she was just being mean and unfair to me. I felt that her expectations were too high, and they may have been, but I learned that I could do more than I believed I could do. And I continue to do more than I think I can.

"I find that if I just keep putting one foot in front of the other it is amazing where life takes me. I never dreamed that I would be paddling down the Mississippi River and having wonderful conversations with women like this. It was not even on my radar, and yet here I am. So stay open; if you get an opportunity, go. That's what Sherry did. She saw an opportunity by coming with us and grabbed it."

Barbara C.H. took the fan and spoke thoughtfully. "I had the wonderful opportunity today to paddle here with these ladies from Pettibone. My husband drove me to the starting point, and I was saying to him, 'I don't know what I am getting into here. I'm going to be sixty next year, and I have a feeling that my bones are going to be hurting tonight like crazy.' We start off, and I'm paddling along pretty good. I'm thinking 'not too bad . . . feels pretty good.' And then we got to the windy place, and it was okay. I was feeling proud of myself. I had a lot of courage going out on those waves, and Nancy was right there beside me saying, 'How are you doing? How are you doing?' I got through that and I was thinking 'Hey, this isn't too bad, I could probably take another four or five hours of this.' And then I heard someone up ahead of me say, 'About a half a mile.' I thought 'What? We've only paddled a half a mile?' *[Laughter]* We had gone all the way, and I didn't even realize it. I was having too much fun. What an honor to get to be a part of today.

"I am sure you all know the date today is 9/11. We honor those people who unknowingly went to work that day and went somewhere else between there and home."

Amanda had a tone of concern in her voice as she took the fan. "I was thinking that our mothers passed down a lot of stuff that we don't do anymore. A lot of folks don't do it because they don't have the time. I think those of us who are grandparents should be teaching our grandchildren some of those things, even simple things. Today, young folks go in and grab something out of the dairy counter and chop it up and call it cookies. [Laughter.] Nobody bakes anymore. Nobody teaches them how to roll dough out. Nobody teaches them how to make dough. Nobody teaches them how to bake bread. I could never bake bread like my grandmother. My grandmother took a bag and just shook it in a big bowl, and it turned out bread. I have to at least use a recipe, and I say, 'Use this book when you do this the next time.' Elders did so many things that are going to be lost."

Linda B. continued. "When I go visit my grandchildren, my three-year-old grandson says 'Did you bring brown bananas? Grandma, where is your cooler?' I just finished a four-day stint with them. I went and picked up the three-year-old from day care so we could come home and bake banana bread. That is his thing. Grandma has to either bring banana bread or bring the brown bananas to make banana bread."

"But you know it is not just the making of the items; it is the tradition of sharing and talking while you are doing it that is being lost," added Barbara C.H. "I am so grateful for the times we went fishing or sat around a campfire telling stories. I want to leave you with a little thing that my mother used to say. My mother, Lillian, was a very shy person. She didn't like to talk about her Native American background. She was taught not to; in fact, it was considered something to be ashamed of, so she acted very white. Since my father was a writer, outdoorsman, and fisherman, they went fishing together maybe four or five times a week. They went a lot. Every time she went she would wear a little hat, earrings, and she would put on lipstick and a little scarf. Every time she went fishing. She just always looked cute. One time I asked her, 'Mom, nobody is out there in the woods. Why do you get all dressed up to go fishing?' She said, 'Barbara, even an old barn looks better with a coat of fresh paint.' [Laughter.]

"You mentioned that she was taught not to talk about being Native American," Mary Loraine jumped in. "I am in the process of doing genealogy on my father's side. There is rumor of there being Cherokee blood on my grandmother's side, but when I tried to ask my cousin about it, he quit talking to me. I think it's because he won't lie about it. He quit answering my e-mails about it. He cut off all contact when I asked him what he knew about the rumors and whether it was true or not, because I know Grandma came from West Virginia. They won't talk about it. There are not that many elders left in the family to ask about it. It's such an interesting mindset.

"I think perhaps some didn't talk about it because they had been through such hard times that they were almost ashamed of it. My father's family didn't talk much about family because my grandmother came here from Norway as a stowaway at sixteen with a toddler. Grandma was not considered legal. I think it was not that long ago. It was in the 1800s, but they didn't talk about it. It was the skeleton in the closet. There wasn't much sharing of heritage. I had to find it all out after the fact."

Ruth

Hesitantly, sitting with a cute camping hat on her hairless head, Ruth shared her story. "Bonne O. and I have become friends through kayaking. I did not grow up on the river. Three years ago I was introduced to kayaking and the river. I can't believe I have lived here this many years and have been ignorant of this wonderful river. Now we go kayaking all the time, as much as we can. It is the most beautiful, peaceful, lovely experience. It is instant beauty when you get out there. That is wonderful. When we saw the article about the trip we just immediately had to find out who these women were who were kayaking the Mississippi. This Gathering has been great.

"I have, as of May 1, been diagnosed with breast cancer, so that is why I have my little hat on. It has been an all-consuming experience, I must say. I have been sucked into the world of Western medicine to the max and am spending hours and hours at the hospital and clinic for treatment. It has been a terrifying, life-changing experience, not only for me, but for my family as well. The river has been a terrific source of serenity and peace this summer. We hope to be able to join you on a leg in another day or two."

There was a lull in the conversation. The silence was broken when Ruth said, "I am very happy we came. This has been a very important and meaningful interchange. I wish I could hear from some of the grandchildren here who get off the hook because they are not old enough to speak. That would be interesting as well."

"You're right," I said. "I am going to break with Gathering protocol this evening and open it up to the younger women. A request was made earlier by the young women to do that if there was time. We have the luxury of that time this evening. Do you young women have any questions for these ladies? Things you want to know from your position early in life as you sit looking at them with the wisdom they hold?"

Sara Jo spoke first. "More and more women in our generation choose not to have children and do not marry. Do you have suggestions on how we can pass on tradition? I am not going to have children, and people say that will change, but I don't believe it will. That said, I want to make a difference in children's lives. I am not a teacher, I am a scientist. So what are your suggestions for those of us that would like to be a part of sharing wisdom?"

Mary Loraine responded. "Be a mentor. Join the Big Sister program. There are a lot of wonderful youth groups you could volunteer for: Girls' Club, Girl Scouts, church groups."

"Find someone who needs somebody," said Amanda. "You'll see somebody on the playground or wherever they hang off to the side. You could offer them so much, so much. A lot of times you can make a major difference being with one child. Those who are not in a major clique would dearly love to hear whatever you had to say. You are a scientist, which is awe-inspiring. Just think of all the things you can do! It's the small things, not the big things. These children will remember it for forever.

"Help yourself by learning your heritage. Learn from your grandmother if she is still around. Learn from your mom. Keep those things alive. Share that heritage with someone else. I have a daughter who has been saying not only is she not planning on having children, but she is never marrying. So I am looking at that from the viewpoint of not having grandchildren. We are probably not going to have a son-in-law in our circle, but I have seen her changing the world in small ways. What is meant to be will be. That is kind of the Native American way of looking at it too. Don't set yourself up. Don't say, 'I am never having children!' You might be surprised. Sometimes life is like that. As soon as you say 'I am never . . .' you just never know."

"I have so many girlfriends who have grandchildren, and they are so willing to share them with me. So through them I have grandchildren and children. We share," said Barbara C.H.

"I think it is so important to always be influencing children," Sherry said. "They all have a free spirit, and they are always going to run into people that might not influence them in a healthy way. It's important that you know how to be with them and you, Sara Jo, do. Family or elders or anybody. You are healing them through the healing of your own sprit. You don't have to have a child. You are good with people in the way that you respect them, listen, and respond to them with wisdom and love. They feel that. That is just who you are. You are making a difference to children and all of the people you encounter by just being yourself. You make a difference by sharing your truth and enjoyment of life with them."

Naomi, who had been quiet, mustered the courage to speak. "You guys have so much wisdom and knowledge here. For younger people, I think it's easy to give up when a challenge comes and to not think that you have the energy or power to get through it. So how is it that you made it through all of your challenges?"

"Friends!" everyone responded enthusiastically.

"Friends, not necessarily family," Amanda added. "Friends will be there to listen if you need somebody. They will give you suggestions if you ask for suggestions. They are not going to be hurt if you don't take their advice and actually act on it. They are only suggestions."

"They will give you a different perspective on a problem or situation. Like Amanda said, you might not take their advice right away, but after you are away from it, you may start thinking about it," said Linda B.

"Your friends will tell you what it looks like from the outside when all you can see is what it looks like from the inside," said Amanda.

"Be nice to yourself." Barbara C.H. said, looking directly into Naomi's eyes. "Be kind to yourself. It's not so bad. If you wake up in the morning and you have the ability to see the world, to hear the world, to move your arms and legs, you are totally blessed. Sometimes knowing that is all you need. Sometimes that important thing that is driving you nuts can seem so small to someone who has no arms, has no legs, and has no eyes. Be kind to yourself. Love yourself. You are special. You are going to be okay. I can sense your spirit, and you are strong."

Amanda continued. "One of the things my grandmother always told me is that 'you are not going to die, you are not going to starve to death, and you will be here tomorrow. There is no more you really need. So, Naomi, you are not going to die, you are not going to starve to death, and they are not going to kick you out of your house. So what else do you need? You are down to your basic needs. People live with less than that."

"I think you also have to set some goals to live by," said Edna. "But not super high. Take it a little bit at a time, and just get through it. Live one day at a time. If you do have any spirituality—anything, no matter what denomination—it can really make a difference. Get some good reading. Buddhism and Tai Chi are amazing. I just think that is what you need sometimes, quiet time and other people who will listen to you."

"The other thing I found with sharing struggles with friends is that you hear it outside your body," added Bonne O. "You know what it is inside, but when you hear it through your ears, you look at it differently."

"You need to let people in," said Mary Loraine.

"Sometimes it is all you can do," Sherry responded. "Sometimes you are just there at rock bottom, and you can't even think of anything to do when you're so low. That is where you are, and you don't even know where else there is to be. That is why you have to let the healing happen from the inside out because we truly have that innate wisdom. Somewhere inside, you know how to get out, but it doesn't hurt to get some help if you think it might help you. On the other hand, there are people who will more or less always be in a state of melancholy, possibly doing their soul's work there."

Staring into the fire, Mary Loraine added, "We have become a society of instant gratification, quick fixes, and sometimes we just have to realize that there are things we have to experience. We have to feel it. In order to get over it, we have to go through the feelings. I think we are fixers by nature."

"You have to learn to let go of the things that you can't change. You have to just let it go," said Edna emphatically.

Barbara C.H. chimed in. "It can mean letting go of other people. There are people who can harm you and will keep your spirit down. Those people are poison to your spirit. You will recognize them. Those people are the ones you have to let go of. You have to keep them out, but do it in a kind way. Just keep them out of your life. You have to stay away from those people. Respect your spirit and trust your inner voice."

Nodding in agreement, Mary Loraine said, "If you can't get them out of your life, at least distance yourself from them for a while."

We ended the evening by honoring Edna as our elder and giving her a mug. She responded, "I told some friends what I had gone through, and they said this about being stubborn: 'That, Edna, is what we love about you. You are who you are. You are not wishy-washy. We know where we stand with you and that you stand on your principles and your beliefs. You can bend when you have to bend. You can't be so straight because there are always shades of grey in everything, but you still have to be true to yourself. You are who you are, and we honor that in you.' After they said that to me, it really made me feel good. For my seventieth birthday I got a tattoo. [Laughter.] It says love. I gave it to myself."

Barbara C.H. played the guitar and sang for us. She started with "Watching the River Run" by Loggins and Messina. "Listening and learning and turning, run river run…"

We held hands and ended the evening by singing "Peace is Flowing Like a River."

Peace is flowing like a river.
Flowing out of you and me.
Flowing out into the desert, setting all the spirits free.

Love is flowing like a river.
Flowing out of you and me.
Flowing out into the desert, setting all the spirits free.

Truth is flowing like a river.
Flowing out of you and me.
Flowing out into the desert, setting all the spirits free.

Peace is flowing like a river.
Flowing out of you and me.
Flowing out into the desert, setting all the spirits free.

Anonymous

September 12th through 16th

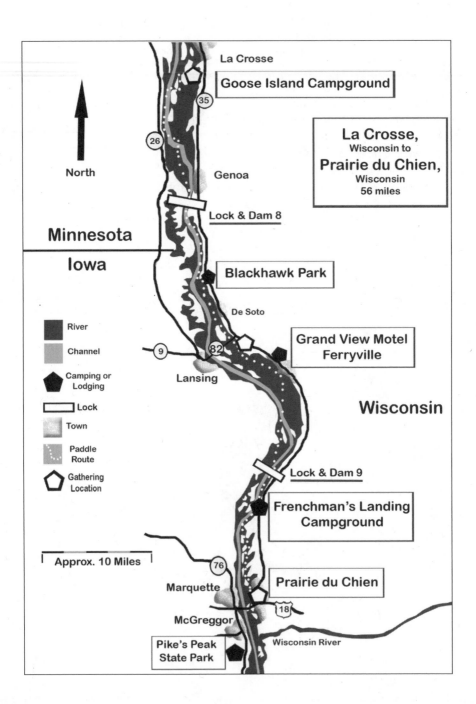

LaCrosse to Prairie du Chien

September 12, Day Nine

A sandhill crane's call woke me. I bolted from the tent to catch a glimpse of her through the mist. The grass was blanketed with hints of the previous night's frost. Cheryl was on the shore with her camera, also in search of the crane. Her call weakened as she flew deeper into the mist.

The air was filled with Sherry's uplifting voice singing "I've Got Peace Like a River" while she prepared breakfast. Sara Jo had been quiet all morning. She didn't want to leave, and I would be sad to see her go. Naomi and Suzanne were squirrelly, which helped Sara Jo with her transition. They kidded around and caught up on each others' lives.

Sara Jo wrote in the paddlers' journal:

> *Today our journeys part. Yesterday I started to paddle thinking my trip was over, but as the words of the grandmothers and the lessons of the river flowed through my thoughts, I realized that the trip never ends—the journey just takes a new turn.*
>
> *I take away a slower pace and a broader mind. It is so easy to become lost in the details of daily life, but it isn't necessary.*

As long as the important plans are set, the rest will follow. Planning a schedule too tightly closes out so many unplanned gifts and opportunities.

Being far from home for so long has made me take a new look at the role of the people in my life and how they came to be there. Even when I am feeling slightly detached from intuition, the universe is working for me and bringing the people I need into my life. The number of powerful souls that come forth when we are in tune with our intuition is even more amazing. I am so grateful to have been given time on the water with so many grandmothers, young women, and nature's spirits.

I return to California strengthened and open to what is meant to come, but I am also bringing back the power to change and direct my future while adapting to the elements, which are not mine to change.

I wish for all the women that they are joined by the same uplifting and mind-opening experience. For you, Mom and Kitty, I wish calm, joy, and safe adventure. I know the river will take care of you; the herons will guide you when the channel is not clear, and your intuitions will take you where you need to be.

I love you both, and you too, Sherry and Gwyn.

Peace, health, and joy.

Naomi wrote:

Last night was just what I needed to revive my energy. So often, life can suck you in so you feel like you are going down the rapids without a paddle. Being around others gives you the guiding force to steer through the rapids.

Thanks for the honor to sit with and hear such powerful women, their stories, and their advice. It means so much to hear their wisdom while I'm at an age where I have so much left to do in life. Last night reminded me that no matter the challenge, I will achieve what I am meant to achieve. I am also blessed to have such a strong and encouraging mother and sister to help me remain strong and let my inner spirit out!

Love you.

Keep paddling.

Suzanne wrote:

Thank you for being such an inspiration, not only for me, but to all these women. We need more, more, more, more examples of women in leadership, defining their own way to fulfillment and success!

I told Naomi that it's a good exercise for me to shut up and listen. Although I would say that in many scenarios I'm quite good at speaking, in a group of dynamic women I have a very hard time. Dialogue and commonality is so natural and organic. You are so creative, and, may I say, daring, to have the ideas to do what you're doing and then put one foot in front of the other and actually make it happen! Edna's at a point in life where she said it is one day at a time to get through, undoubtedly after 10—gasp—children. It occasionally strikes all of us in the overwhelming era of 2007 . . . cell phones, laptops, too much communication, but very little quality interaction.

Anyway, so much good stuff. I could write a book. Oh, wait, I probably should . . . Maybe when I'm 50.

Happy Trails.

Terry

Terry joined us to paddle for the day. She has four children and four grandchildren, with another grandchild on the way. She volunteers as a nurse and quilts. Her family lives south of La Crosse, having moved there from Muscoda, Wisconsin.

We all gathered at the shore. I hugged and said goodbye to the girls and Sherry. Sara Jo quietly paced the shoreline while we paddled off. Sherry yelled to reassure us that she would see us at the lock.

We traveled through the backwaters to the Minnesota side to see the effects of the flooding that had occurred in Brownsville a month earlier. We quickly discovered that some channels were overgrown, and at times, we didn't know where we were.

We found ourselves in a narrow channel and watched muskrats playing in the water. I noticed very few birds and joked that they must have had it with the cold and migrated overnight.

The bluffs on the Minnesota side were clearly visible, but find-

Terry, Mary Ruth, Cheryl, Kitty, and Nancy

ing our way through the backwaters became comical. Cheryl relied on a compass, which she used while canoeing in the Boundary Waters Canoe Area Wilderness in northern Minnesota. I determined direction by studying the shapes, sizes, and location of the land masses compared to the bluffs. Cheryl and I had been using an island that looked like a face on our map as a base point to explain to each other where we thought we should go next.

"I think we should go to the left of the island that looks like a face," I said.

"Wait, which face?" Cheryl responded. "I see a couple of faces."

The others laughed at us while we pulled our boats together to ensure we were talking about the same island. We weren't. While we consulted our maps, Mary Ruth, who is rather short, kept standing up in the front of the canoe and saying "This ain't helping."

"Could it be your height that's not helping?" Kitty teased. After running into a few more dead ends, I wondered if Terry was asking herself what she had gotten into by joining us.

Finally, we stumbled upon a channel that led to the Minnesota bluff. I said, "We did it. I don't know how, but here we are." We paddled victoriously into the main channel of the river.

Brownsville was a short distance away. Below a section of the bluff that had been washed away in a mudslide there was billowing smoke with trucks and cranes nearby. The remains of a house were being burned. Homes nearby had also been damaged in the mudslide. It was hard to comprehend how the earth could suddenly just give way and destroy a home.

Terry shared stories about the flood. She told

Photo by Cheryl Mast

us about a couple who were living in their dream home at the base of the bluff overlooking the river. At two o'clock in the morning, the husband went to help a neighbor who had mud in his basement. Standing at the neighbor's, he watched as the mud sent his house with his wife and their eight-year-old grandson inside tumbling down the hill toward the river. They were both rescued, but the house was destroyed. We wondered if the burning house we saw was the house she described.

Terry said that most of the people killed in the floods had been in their cars. One couple was coming home from a family event when their car plummeted twenty-five feet as a section of the road washed away. People's lives had changed overnight due to the storm, and yet the town looked like it was doing business as usual. I couldn't imagine the great sense of loss they must have been experiencing.

We moved through a shallow spot thick with weeds. The water was crystal clear and every detail of the plants below the surface could be seen. I watched for fish among the various shades of green but saw none.

Paddling toward Turtle Island, we spotted birds floating on the water but couldn't identify them. They didn't seem to be moving, and one was holding its neck at a strange angle. We burst into laughter when we realized they were decoys.

We stopped on Turtle Island and disturbed five immature eagles perched in a tree. Bits of turtle shells speckled the beach. A large, green buoy grounded in the shallow water offshore listed to one side. We joked that since it was retired it chose to spend the rest of its days on an island with a fabulous view.

Mary Ruth stepped onto the sand and saw a baby turtle roll down the embankment. She looked dehydrated and lay motionless. Cheryl moved her back and forth in the water for a few moments until she perked up. Cheryl let the turtle go, and she immediately took shelter under the canoe.

Out past the island and across the main channel, we paddled through several shallow weed beds teeming with fish. Occasionally we hit a fish with our paddle, or one would jump unexpectedly out of the way with a splash. We felt startling bumps on the bottoms of our boats. The bumping began to feel like a game of tag, which the fish were winning. Watching the water to see what type of fish was playing with us, I

spotted the most enormous carp I had ever seen.

Paddling past the quiet town of Genoa, Wisconsin, a quaint church steeple rising high above the trees captured our attention. Genoa was the site of Lock and Dam No. 8. Mary Ruth, Cheryl, and Terry looked anxious as we paddled in. Kitty and I reassured them. Sherry was already there and had shared our story with the lock attendant. She had become such good friends with him by the time we got there that he let her come down from the observation area and stand next to the railing overlooking the lock.

The attendant told us that the water level in that lock dropped nine and a half feet at a rate of one foot per minute. The distance of the drop was determined by the levels of water above and below the lock. The Army Corps of Engineers called these bodies of water "pools."

Several barges laden with coal were parked along shore to the left of the lock. A crane unloaded them and dumped the coal onto a conveyor belt that deposited it in a large pile at the Dairyland Power Cooperative. We were amazed by the enormous amount of coal in a single scoop.

We paddled into the backwaters opposite Twin Island and appreciated being among the trees. The channel narrowed dramatically and became extremely shallow. Mary Ruth and Cheryl paddled on in their

canoe while the rest of us had to get out and walk. Hundreds of minnows darted around and away from us with each step. After thirty yards, we were afloat again and rejoined Mary Ruth and Cheryl.

We passed the confluence of the Bad Axe River and headed

Photo by Cheryl Mast

toward the bluffs. Bad Axe River acquired its name in 1827, when Winnebago Native Americans got into an argument with a boat crew. One of the Winnebago men was killed. Later, another boat ran aground in that area and Chief Winneshiek avenged the brave's death. Seven Native Americans and four crew members died in the encounter.

The bluffs lining the river at the end of the channel loomed high above our heads. In the main channel, a tugboat approached, pushing nine barges upriver. We were excited and positioned our boats to ride out the large waves we expected the barges would create. Our excitement died when the waves did not materialize.

Approaching the Blackhawk Park landing, Mary Ruth said, "I think there's a man on the dock."

"I don't see a man," I said.

"The thing that looks like a post," she responded, and we broke into laughter. Then the post started moving.

The man walked to the end of the dock and yelled, "Apparently you guys need to know where you are going?"

"I didn't think so," I replied.

"Well, that's what I'm here for. I am your welcoming committee. Sherry said you were coming." Sherry had asked the park ranger, Dan, to wait for us and direct us to the lower camping area. Before arriving at the park, we had been talking about how divine sinking into a hot tub would be. Mary Ruth asked the park ranger, "Do you have a hot tub ready for us?"

"Nope," he responded, then stuck his hand in the river and said, "Not too bad here though." We laughed.

We moved through a narrows between the shore and an island as the sun set. Out of the darkness on the island a great horned owl called. The darkness made the call sound eerie, yet somehow welcoming.

Terry had been quiet for most of the day and at times paddled a distance from the rest of us. Because of her distance, I wondered if the paddling was too much for her. She said that she and her husband paddled quite often, but never twenty-one miles in a day and rarely more than two hours at a time. They usually went at a leisurely pace so her husband, an amateur photographer, could take pictures. But that day she had kept our pace for the entire six hours.

Cheryl, Terry, Nancy, Kitty, Mary Ruth, and Sherry

When we landed, Terry climbed out of her kayak, looking a bit stiff. I told her she'd done a great job. "I'm proud of myself," she responded. "I have never done anything like this before, and I wasn't sure I could do it." Her husband greeted her, his face beaming with pride. She became animated while talking to him, and she took a moment to write in the paddlers' journal before departing.

This is a day I will always remember. The beautiful serenity of the river and great companions. Thanks for the great memories.

Mary Ruth and Cheryl went to pick up their other vehicle from Goose Island Campground. We took a break at the picnic table before we made dinner.

"Terry sure has a lot of courage, like the other women that join us," Kitty said.

"They must feel inexperienced around you guys," said Sherry.

"I think there is a synergy with groups, and it's hard when you are the new person," I responded. "Especially if it's a close-knit group. If our places had been switched, I think I would have kept on driving when I saw all of us this morning."

During dinner, Sherry confessed that she'd had trouble with the stove earlier and set the picnic table on fire. In the process she burned our tarp, which had been sitting on the table next to the stove. There were several holes melted through it. She felt bad about the tarp and was now leery of the stove. "I don't know what I did to make that happen," she said. We tossed the tarp, which now looked like a giant doily, in the trash.

Attempting to divert the conversation, Sherry said, "I'm sad to see Sara Jo leave. She was a delight and added so much to the experience. It sure looked like she didn't want to go."

"Yes," I replied. "She struggles any time she leaves water and nature. She worked really hard on some big issues while she was with us and gained a fresh perspective. She felt validated by everyone for the direction she plans to go. You all helped her more than you realize."

Dan came by to make sure we were settled into our campsite. He was talkative and very interested in our trip. He said his wife would love our adventure, but these days her great adventure was getting to the post office with their two young children. He spoke lovingly and admiringly of his wife. We learned that he was from Cook, Minnesota, which is not far from Ely. He was pleased to be talking to "folks from home." He admired what we were doing and was particularly impressed with the three-ring binder full of information sitting on the table. "You have more paperwork than I do, and I work for the government," he smirked and then disappeared into the night.

Mary Ruth and Cheryl returned. Mary Ruth wandered over to our table, and we offered her our leftover macaroni and cheese. She hesitated. We told her she didn't have to "take it for the team," a phrase that generally meant eating all the leftovers so nothing was wasted. It could mean eating more when we were already full, or eating something we didn't like.

Fatigue nudged me toward my tent even though I wanted to linger under the stars and soak up the remaining time with Mary Ruth and Cheryl. The tent felt cavernous without Sara Jo next to me. I slipped my feet into the fuzzy, purple socks that Naomi had given me and felt closer to my girls.

September 13, Day Ten

During the night, I crawled out of the tent into the crisp air and gazed at the fabulous sky full of stars. In the morning, Mary Ruth debated paddling with us one more day, but commitments called her home. She wrote in the paddlers' journal:

> *I left Ely Monday mid-day to join this journey, and on my way I wrote a poem. Interesting to come back to it after these two days on the Mississippi with beautiful, wise women on the water and on land. Here it is . . .*

> *Driving South*
> *Towards La Crosse, WI.*
> *A paddle on the*
> *Mississippi*
> *Ahead*

> *Alongside Hwy 53*
> *A great blue heron*
> *Flies into my view*

> *Always a good sign*
> *Beckoning me to go forward*
> *Beckoning me to go deeper*

> *I've hit the farm country*
> *South of St. Paul fields of corn along I-90*
> *Full like the land*
> *In Holmes County, Ohio*

> *My phone rings*
> *You say your alternator's bad*
> *Waiting for the tow truck now*
> *You remind me*
> *That you've got the tent, the canoe*
> *A new twist to this adventure*

> *And I say, "It's alright."*
> *The beckoning don't mean*
> *Perfection*

And anyway
This morning
The great blue heron
Passed by
Thank you so much for creating the space and the opportu-
nity for us to travel too!

Cheryl wrote in the paddlers; journal:

Departed from Sturgis, Michigan, Monday morning excited
about joining up with Nancy and Kitty in La Crosse. That
energy carries me into the afternoon even though I'm weary
from long days at work these past few weeks.

I ponder what happened to that slower pace and renewed
spirit that I left Ely with just a few weeks ago after having
spent six weeks leading canoe trips in the BWCA. I glanced
down at the gauges on my dashboard and sensed something
was wrong. The rain began to fall on the windshield and I
attempted to turn on my windshield wipers, but they were in
slow motion. Off with the headlights, ah, improved action of
the wipers, but with each passing mile they slowed and my
anxiety grew.

In the end, Lord, you've orchestrated it all. Peter B. was there
to give me a tow and he was willing to replace the alternator.
Within two and a half hours I was back on the road. That lit-
tle glitch was just the beginning of the adventure. The
experience beckons me to once again reevaluate and TRUST. I
am again reminded that I just need to remain open to the
opportunities each day brings and flex as needed.

Now here I am two days later having experienced many
firsts, some more challenging than others, but all have been
blessings! As I leave here tomorrow and part ways with you
folks, I leave very RICH. Paddling from Pettibone Resort to
Blackhawk Park on the great Mississippi has been a wonder-
ful experience. Being a part of the Gathering was amazing. It
was hard to remain silent, yet good for me. I was blessed by
just listening. Images of herons, egrets, eagles, and pelicans
will linger. Sounds of kingfishers, sandhill cranes, and the
great horned owl will reawaken the memories. Sore muscles in
the morning will remind me that I am fully alive and that I've
been with you for part of the journey.

Thank you for the privilege of spending two days paddling
with you.

God's blessing to you all.

Mary Ruth and Cheryl drove off in separate directions. We got a late start at ten o'clock. Strong headwinds forced us to cross the main channel and hug the opposite shoreline in a futile search for protection.

The Wisconsin bluffs continued to frame our journey. They exhibited a variety of shapes as we moved downriver. Colors changed as the sun moved across the sky and sent shadows in new directions. Some bluffs were bare of trees, and it looked as though there had been major mudslides that had swept the trees away.

Crows dotted the trees and flew above us. A flock of vultures dined on a carcass on shore. The day grew more blustery. We crossed back over at De Soto, Wisconsin, and went into Winneshiek Slough, where we finally had protection from the wind.

Fishermen chose the backwaters too. Kitty asked one of them what they were fishing for and he said sheephead. He described them as almost white and similar to bass but without many teeth. Always curious, Kitty stuck her head in the large wooden crates that were sunk along the shore to get a closer look at their catch.

We pulled into Winneshiek Landing for a break from the growing heat and a lunch of dried fruit, gorp, and apples. Two fishermen walked past, and Kitty asked them about snakes. "There are hog snakes and garter snakes along here," one of them responded enthusiastically. "Hog snakes are in the brush along the shore. They look ferocious, but they're not. They get big, but they're harmless."

The fishermen wandered away, and a pontoon boat with two older couples on board landed. The women, Maxine and Janet, started talking with us right away. One of the men meandered slowly toward the parking lot. His bib overalls seemed out of place on a pontoon boat; I visualized him on a tractor out in a field with a piece of straw sticking out of his mouth. I asked Janet if they had been farmers. She said they had, but they had also worked for Oscar Mayer for thirty years.

While the men futzed with getting the pontoon on the trailer, we talked with Maxine and Janet. They were fascinated by our boats and could not imagine how we managed to stay upright in them. "I would never fit in that," said Maxine. When Kitty said that she had just started kayaking in June and was now paddling the Mississippi, they were speechless.

We said good-bye to the women and ventured on. After reemerging from a dead-end channel, we paddled wherever we found shade for relief from the heat. The wind was nonexistent in the backwaters. Monarch butterflies flitted around us. The trees along the shore were primarily cottonwood, maple, and elm, with a smattering of others.

We had a tailwind as we entered the open water of Lake Winneshiek. Exhausted from the heat, we welcomed the gentle push for the last three miles of our thirteen-mile day. The river was four miles wide here yet was only three to six feet deep, with the exception of the main channel. We rounded a point and saw Ferryville in the distance but discovered a barrier of reeds and dead lotus between us and the shore. We paddled on, taking any opening that headed toward the shore through the weeds. We moved through dead plants and patches of celery grass growing up from the bottom. In some places, the grass lay across the surface of the water, making it difficult to paddle.

Kitty and I experienced the celery grass differently. I saw the brown fuzz that grew on each blade of grass and noticed that when the blades reached the surface they were fuzz-free and bright green. Occasionally, a thin, round stem rose from the bottom in a spiral, as if it had grown around a pipe. The stem had a thin, three-inch pod on the end. The shapes and colors intrigued me. Kitty focused on the clarity of the water and noted how each time we paddled into the celery grass the water became crystal clear. Away from the grass the water became murky again. She said the water was clean because the celery grass was doing its job. The situation was a perfect example of how diverse backgrounds generate different conclusions. Kitty was a scientist and had worked on the Great Lakes National Program, where she studied diatoms in water samples from the Mississippi River and the Great Lakes. As an artist, I noticed shapes, patterns, colors, and how things worked together visually. The discovery delighted me. It was an opportunity for us to learn from each other.

Waiting for Sherry at a boat landing, we watched a man pushing his boat with a pole. We assumed he used the pole because of the thick weeds. His cussing grew louder as he approached us. He cussed about his kids, money, his poor health, and his broken boat motor. Attempts to assist him were greeted with a gruff no. His wife stood quietly on the shore. Her body was stiff and her lips tight. When we passed her on the dock, she quietly said, "Thank you."

Ferryville, Wisconsin, in the background

Sherry was late to pick us up because she went shopping for dinner. We arrived at the Grand View Motel and enjoyed the luxury of a kitchenette. Sherry prepared a feast of baked salmon and spaghetti squash. I updated my journal. It had been hard to find time to write, and my notes had been brief because I was usually physically spent at the end of the day. Kitty watched hummingbirds buzz around colorful flowers that hung outside our window. Even though the motel was on a tiny strip of land at the base of the bluff, Donna L., the owner, had flowers everywhere. She and her husband, Todd, had owned the motel for a year and a half. When they bought it, there were few flowers. She was proud of the lush environment she had created.

Rain began to fall as we sat down to eat. Being warm and dry and not swatting at bugs in the motel made it feel like a palace to us. The metallic moose were still our companions here. There were train tracks just below the motel, but thankfully the train whistles didn't blow close to us.

"There's a couple two doors down from us who are from Menomonie, Wisconsin," said Sherry. "We got into a discussion about where they were going to eat. Since they're both former smokers, they won't eat where smoking is allowed. She's disabled and uses oxygen. We talked about states passing no-smoking laws. I agreed with them that lawmakers shouldn't pass such a law because it controls people too much."

"I bet you didn't like the seatbelt law either, did you?" joked Kitty.

"Oh yes I did," answered Sherry.

"How is that different from the smoking law or the helmet law?" asked Kitty.

"The helmet law I agree with," said Sherry. "I don't know—I just feel the smoking thing is too infringing."

"For me, the lack of smoking is great. My asthma means I can't go into some places." I said. "It's about health. People work in smoky places because they need the job. Smoking, helmets, and seatbelts are all health related. I find it curious you separated smoking out as too controlling."

"I have a passion against government control," Sherry said. "Government control is scary to me."

"I was a smoker for thirty years, and I never thought that I would become antismoking," added Kitty. "There are very few places I go these days where I am around cigarette smoke, and I really notice it in my clothes and hair afterwards. I quit almost eight years ago, and when somebody goes by lighting up a cigarette, I say a silent thank you. I am grateful that I am not smoking these days. I quit drinking twenty years ago, but it was harder to quit smoking."

"Doug quit smoking as a wedding gift to me twenty-five years ago," I said.

"Nice, wow," commented Sherry.

"After he had not been smoking for a while, he became so sensitive to smoke that he couldn't be around it either," I added.

"That is what these people said," Sherry said. "They just can't be around it. In college, I smoked a little bit. I was really never a smoker, just a social thing really."

"I was a gifted smoker," Kitty joked sarcastically. "Two packs a day at times. By the time I quit, I was down to one pack a day. It took three years to finally stop. I did it with my buddy Carl in Ely. He was retired from the hospital and wanted to quit smoking too. We agreed we would quit smoking on January 1 of 2000. Before either one of us was going to have a cigarette, we had to call the other one and let them know. For about three months we were on the phone to each other daily. We yelled and screamed. We walked over to each other's homes to say 'I really want a cigarette.'"

"Your own Smokers Anonymous, huh?" responded Sherry.

"Yes," said Kitty. "I don't think I could have done it without him. He still doesn't smoke to this day either."

"I don't understand how people afford it," I added.

"After I quit, I couldn't figure out how I afforded it either," said Kitty. "It was like drinking. After I quit drinking, I would look at the money I had spent on alcohol and wonder how I afforded it."

"And you did both at the same time for a while, right?" asked Sherry.

"Yes, that was before my daughter, Erin, was born," answered Kitty. "I did a lot to protect my bad habits then. I worked to support those habits so I could afford to smoke and drink. Work, work, work! That's interesting–I never thought of it like that before." Kitty stopped speaking, and a broad grin crossed her face. "There is that hummingbird again. Look at those wings go. It is just a blur. Today we also saw dragonflies, eagles, turtles, herons, pelicans, seagulls, and an osprey."

A large, black spider walked across the floor. Kitty began to whimper. Sherry jokingly called it a tarantula, and Kitty retreated to a corner. From across the room, Kitty gave Sherry directions on how to get it out of the room using a pitcher and piece of paper. Later, Kitty headed outside to make a phone call and jumped as another spider crossed her path. She joked that she would find the next one in her shoes.

Without bugs buzzing around us, the urgency to get to bed early was gone. The evening lingered on. It felt decadent to stretch out on a double bed by myself after the confines of my sleeping bag.

September 14, Day Eleven

Sherry started our day singing "My Paddle's Keen and Bright." We packed the car as I quietly struggled with my asthma. It had grown worse the past couple of days, and an air freshener in the motel room had put me over the edge. My inhaler did nothing to stop the coughing. I began treating myself with a stronger asthma medication I had brought just in case. I was not going to let asthma slow me down.

From the motel, our view of Pool 9 was stunning. Todd told us the pool was one of the major staging areas for migrating birds. He explained that a staging area is a place where birds rest and recharge for a few days during migration. The celery grass in Pool 9 drew them in because it was a nutritious food source.

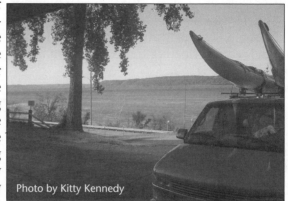

Photo by Kitty Kennedy

The river was four miles wide at Ferryville, Wisc.

Swallows swarmed the Ferryville boat launch as we unloaded the kayaks from the van. The swallows were primarily brown with a white underbelly. We thought they might be bank swallows, but they moved too fast to determine any other markings. The birds feasted on the bugs overhead.

We paddled through a section of lily pads. Beads of water danced on the surface of the leaves as they bobbed on the waves. They captured tiny rays of sunlight, which glistened and bounced around inside the water beads as they rolled on the leaf.

The weather prediction that the day would be unseasonably cold was correct. The high was fifty-four degrees. A high tail wind carried us quickly across the first three miles of our fifteen-mile day. The angle of the wind required extra effort from us to keep going in the right direction. The waves caused bitterly cold water to splash us. Our paddling gloves left our fingertips exposed and stinging from the cold. We had not anticipated this problem. Water soaked the cuffs of my shirt and seeped up the sleeve. My arms became as cold as my fingertips.

Ahead of us, a long black line extended a half mile across the surface of the water. Hundreds of cormorants were perched on a wing dam constructed to protect Pool 9 Island. Our presence spooked the cormorants, and they took flight. The solid black line moved as a unit and then shattered into black dots, filling the sky. They swirled in the air around us. The sky was alive with black wings, soaring and playing in the wind. After a few moments, they dissipated.

Kitty's joy about being on the river caused her to giggle a lot as she paddled. She also had a bad case of hiccups. We had changed the brand of electrolyte-replacement drink we used. Each time Kitty drank some, she got another round of hiccups. She decided she was done drinking that stuff.

We paddled toward the wing dam and watched a small flock of pelicans a few yards away. We stopped with a thud when we hit rocks. Kitty got herself loose quickly. I also freed myself, only to have another rock claim me. The pelicans watched me closely while Kitty paddled on ahead. Finally floating free, I said good-bye to my audience and caught up with Kitty.

Photo by Kitty Kennedy

We passed a tiny island. The only visible inhabitant was an eagle perched on its nest high in a tree. The wind continued to assist us, and at one point, we stopped paddling and held our paddles up like sails to catch the wind.

A barge crossed from the Minnesota to the Wisconsin side, following the main channel to the lock. We considered racing ahead of it so we wouldn't have to wait for it to lock through, but it would have been too dangerous. We would have to wait.

Kitty suggested that we surprise Sherry, who was waiting at the lock to watch us pass through. We paddled into the small bay behind the lock wall and pulled our kayaks up on the rocks. We walked up the road to the parking lot and burst into laughter when we saw our van. Its contents were spilling out the back door onto the ground, but

Sherry was nowhere in sight. "There has got to be a good story here," said Kitty.

Sherry was on the observation deck talking with people about our trip. She had pulled the van apart to get to a book and other merchandise we carried with us and sold to support the trip. One of the women she was talking to was wearing our sweatshirt and looking at the book. Sherry cheerfully introduced us to Lannie and Dorothy, who had stopped at the lock while on a road trip from Chicago.

Lannie was sixty-seven and had been diagnosed with lung and brain cancer sixteen years ago. She had been told she only had months to live.

Smiling enthusiastically, she told us about the surgeries, treatments, and her determination to prove the doctors wrong. She was a special-education teacher for both kids and adults. She loved the river and told us she had once traveled through a lock in a cabin cruiser with her father. Lannie was excited about our trip and attempted to talk Dorothy into coming to the next Gathering.

Dorothy was sixty-nine and more reserved than Lannie. She was an accountant for small businesses. She had worked in corporate America for many years and ultimately left because of the way women were treated. Dorothy seemed to be protective of Lannie.

The American Beauty locking through and exiting the lock

Jay, the lock attendant, told us the lock dropped seven and a half feet and answered my questions about how the tugboats and barges locked through. Often, a tugboat's load was too long to fit in the lock. Only six barges, or two barges with a tugboat, could pass through at a time. The front barges were disconnected and sent through first. If they were traveling downstream, they generally floated through the lock, carried by the current. If headed upstream, the barges were pulled through by a winch along the top of the lock wall. Once through the lock, they were tied off while the tugboat and remaining barges locked through. Then they were cabled together again and were on their way. Jay told us the clearance between the lock wall and the barges was tight—only five feet—which meant only two and a half feet on either side of the barge.

Once the American Beauty was through the gates, we ran back to our boats. We paddled out around the lock wall, turned in toward the lock, and entered challenging waffle waves. When waves bounce off a solid object, like a wall, they move back out with the same force they hit the object with and cross the incoming waves. It creates what looks like a waffle on the surface of the water as waves cross each other. Paddling waffle waves was challenging because a wave would lift the kayak so high in the air that the paddle wouldn't reach water. A surge of adrenaline rushed through me each time my paddle hit air and threw my balance off for a moment.

The waves were two to three feet high and required focused concentration to get through. I was concerned about Kitty and how she would handle them because she had never experienced anything like those waves before. I knew that I might capsize if I turned to look. I spotted Jay walking out onto the wall to watch us. I occasionally looked up, watching the expression on his face. I decided that if Kitty got in trouble, his casual demeanor would change.

Once we were inside the lock the waves disappeared. My adrenaline surged, and I felt like cheering. Kitty gushed, "That was quite a ride. Wow! What fun!" I greeted the guys on a fishing boat in the lock with us a little too loudly, and they looked at us like we were nuts.

The calm water below the lock left me with a sense of peace and tranquility. I had been waiting for that feeling. I was enjoying the river that day rather than constantly worrying about the details of the trip. I had disconnected from the constant sense of responsibility.

Vines along the shore crawled over the tops of other vegetation. The vines were dead and stringy. We were curious about what had killed them. They carpeted large areas and formed eerie shapes. I pictured creepy bugs and snakes living underneath them.

In the backwaters, lines of mud and watermarks were unusually high on the tree trunks. Clumps of green celery grass hung in tree branches above our heads, indicating that not long ago the water had been much higher. We passed houses along the shore that were in poor shape but showed signs that people still lived in them.

We paddled in silence. I recalled a recent conversation I had with a friend about the trip and its purpose. At the time, I had been struggling to understand the full scope of it. I had heard myself say, "I am just doing what I am supposed to do." That was true, but it was more complicated than that. When I discussed the trip with other people, I saw amazement on their faces, followed by concern for my safety. My friend made an obvious point: "Not many people take on the biggest river on the continent." I had overlooked that. It had not occurred to me that the Mississippi was a danger. Instead, my perception of her was as a childhood friend, and that played an enormous role in my choices.

While planning for the trip, I had come across many people who needed me to hear their fears. One woman was adamant that I would encounter snakes and told me that "some of them swam." A friend sent me a video of the invasive, jumping Asian carp, which were moving their way up the Mississippi. On a few occasions, the carp have collided with people in boats while leaping out of the water, knocking people into the water or breaking their noses. Faces grew somber when I said we would go through the locks. People's concern for our safety was justified. Many things could go wrong on the water. I had heard stories of people who ventured out ill-prepared and met with disaster. I listened to each concern, not dismissing them, because they held useful information. However, if I took on everyone's fears I would be paralyzed. The knowledge that I was meant to do the trip overrode the fears I had. I took precautions, studied the areas I traveled through, and continued to be vigilant. I would not let fear deter this journey.

I had been told I was courageous, but the trip didn't feel courageous to me. I felt that most people could achieve the same thing if they tried to. I believed that each person was doing what they were meant to do and was doing it the best they could.

Then again, perhaps the trip was a bigger deal than I wanted to admit to myself. My reluctance to acknowledge that was because being courageous sets people apart, which can be lonely and painful. I didn't want to be set apart or disappoint people because I did not meet their expectations. I decided, for the time being, to continue my dance with denial and move forward, paddling one section of the river at a time.

Cold and tired, we spotted Sherry on shore. She led us to the dock at Frenchman's Landing campground. The ground at our campsite was soggy and squished with each step. Weeping willows covered the campsite. Sherry had again made a valiant attempt to get my tent up, but it still puzzled her. Her efforts created a different shape each night.

A hot spaghetti dinner was just what we needed. Sherry, like Gwyn, made sure we ate very well. We resumed a discussion we'd started earlier about relationships.

"I am sort of changing my definition of abuse," said Sherry. "I realized I went along with it, partly because it was all I knew."

"Does that make it okay?" I asked.

"No, that does not make it okay," responded Sherry, "but I am more able to say that I made choices that created it. My ex-husband, Jack, is in a better relationship now than when he was with me. I am much more accepting of the fact that it wasn't good but see that the purpose of our marriage was to have our neat kids."

"For me there are abusive relationships," added Kitty, "but it's more about dysfunctional families. People use their dysfunctional family as an excuse to explain their negative behavior. It isn't an excuse, because all families are dysfunctional on some level."

"But mine was more dysfunctional than yours," I teased.

"I want to let go of all of that negative stuff to help my kids," Sherry continued. "Holding on to all that negative energy affects them and encourages them hold on to it as well."

"Holding on to negative energy affects everybody around you," added Kitty.

"Do you know the Sedona Method for healing?" said Sherry. "It's so simple and is designed for letting go. Basically it is three questions you ask yourself about a given situation. Could I? Would I? When?"

"That has to be a simplified version," said Kitty.

"No," responded Sherry. "It isn't simplified. It's just that basic."

"Wow," said Kitty.

"Kitty," said Sherry, "I want to know more about the lab you work in."

"The waters of the upper Mississippi River, the Missouri River, and the Ohio River are what we are testing in the NRRI lab right now," Kitty said. "The waters in the river are very different from other rivers. The upper Mississippi has a lot more diatoms and life in it than the Ohio River does."

"What's a diatom?" I asked.

"A diatom is siliceous yellow-brown algae," answered Kitty.

"Oh, that clarifies it," I responded, and we laughed.

"It is an algae that incorporates silica, which is sand, into its form." continued Kitty. "They don't decompose, which means that they are found in the sediments. The type of diatom found in the sediment specimens we are working with can be an indicator of the water quality for that particular part of the river. There are almost no diatoms in the Ohio River compared to the Mississippi and Missouri rivers. So the question is, what kind of pollution is killing them, and what is the overall water quality in the Ohio River?"

"Basically, a diatom is at the bottom of the food chain, is that right?" I asked.

"Yes," Kitty replied.

"So if the diatoms die off, eventually everything else in the river will die as well," I concluded.

"That is the concern, and that's why we are doing the testing," said Kitty.

The sun was setting, and a stunning moonrise over the river captured our attention. A thin orange curve hung above the western horizon. The temperature dropped as fast as the sun. My asthmatic coughing had grown worse in the cold. I put on an extra layer of clothes to sleep in while a barred owl serenaded us.

The metallic moose tooted their whistles as they chugged past our tents. As we snuggled into our sleeping bags, Sherry joked, "It's nice that those engineers want to say hi to us every time they pass."

September 15, Day Twelve

My coughing woke me in the morning after a poor night's sleep. Four trains had passed during the night, timed so that the next one would rumble by and blast its whistle just as I was falling asleep again. A hard frost covered the ground and crunched under my feet. The frost formed delicate crystals on the edges of the grass and plants. It was strikingly beautiful, unlike my frosty internal attitude.

It felt good to warm my fingers around my bowl of hot oatmeal. In an attempt to distract myself from my cranky mood, I asked, "Sherry, last night you said you needed time to pull back from things. I think that is a very real reaction that many people have after a life tragedy."

"It is," she responded. "As we learn new things, we have to process them. If we are in a new situation or if we are with new people some of us need that. But when we have to, we all can deal with difficult situations."

"Have you ever questioned being with us?" I asked. "You didn't know us at all before this trip."

"I guess it never really went that deep, because I trust you and Kitty," answered Sherry. "This whole project seems so honest and straightforward and really doing good stuff, so I don't feel threatened at all here. Well, sometimes I do, because I compare myself to other people and think I am not a strong person. I let myself go there when I am feeling sort of low. I think my ex-husband knocked a lot of strength out of me, which happens to a lot of abused women and men. Although I really fought it at the time, I think our divorce freed both of us. Now we are both better; at least I am healthier as a result of it."

"I don't think strength is really beat out of a person," I said. "I like to think that it goes underground as a way of self-protection, a survival skill of sorts. That way there is still hope of bringing your strength out again."

"Either way, our true essence gets held back, and that is sad," said Sherry.

After breakfast, we packed quickly to stay warm. Sherry teased us about the heat she would enjoy in the van. The air was crisp and clear when we got out on the river. We had a light tail wind, and Kitty said she needed to have a talk with the wind gods. She felt our tail wind should be stronger and warmer.

High in the sky were two spirals of pelicans. We drifted and watched their graceful performance. One group was so far away that the birds looked like black pepper flakes spiraling in the wind. The second group was closer, and we could see the individual birds as they rode the updraft. The column switched from black to white and back again as the birds rotated peacefully.

We approached the beginning of Ambrough Slough. Compared to other sloughs, it was narrow and felt more like a large stream. It wound around, bend after bend, and the water was shallow and murky green.

We maneuvered around downed trees that stretched into the slough. Birdsong filled the air. We sighted a bright yellow bird slightly bigger than a finch, a flicker, and a few sandpipers bobbing and chirping along shore. A large turtle sunbathed. Startled by our appearance, she dove into the water. Rather than disappearing under the surface, she crawled at an amazing speed along the bottom and created a large wake. She looked like a torpedo trailing through the water, and the image made me laugh.

The sun began to warm the air around us. Crickets chirped. A kingfisher called as she flitted from one tree to the next. More dead vegetation hung in the trees, making them look like forts children might have built with chairs and blankets. More trash dotted the shoreline than we had seen before–white Styrofoam cups that anglers kept their worms in, plastic in all shapes and sizes, big black garbage bags, and a plastic thermos.

Rounding a bend, we discovered a fallen tree that extended the width of the slough. We were too far in to consider turning around, so we chose to go over the top. One at a time, we carefully stepped out of the kayaks onto layers of logs, branches, mud, and green goop. Debris floated next to the tree trunk. We searched below the surface for a stable foothold so we would not slip deeper into the muck. Slowly, we pulled the kayaks over the log. The bank on the downriver side was slick mud, which made getting back in the boats a challenge.

Around the next bend, we startled two fishermen enjoying the calm of the slough. They knew about the downed tree and could not figure out how we got past it. They were equally surprised to learn that we had paddled from Red Wing and confused about why we had wandered into the backwaters. One of the men told us that during the flood, water in the slough had been seven feet higher. I looked seven feet up into the trees, attempting to fathom that much water in such a small channel.

As I paddled, I thought about Edna, from the Gathering. Her commitment to her beliefs was inspirational. She had paid a heavy price for following church doctrine, but her spirituality allowed her to have an intimate relationship with her God that ultimately allowed her to take charge of her life. Her faith gave her strength. Edna's lovely sense of humor and gentle nature helped her through significant challenges and kept her from becoming bitter.

The women at the Gathering had reached out to my daughters when they asked questions. It warmed my heart each time I saw women reach out to each other. Everything the girls heard from the women I had told them before, though sometimes it's easier to hear truth from strangers than from family.

Gunshots interrupted my thoughts as we passed Big Missouri Lake. While planning the trip, I had apparently overlooked hunting season along the river. The gunshots grew louder. We became concerned for our safety and were greatly relieved when they stopped.

We enjoyed a lazy, peaceful paddle past houses along the shore, each with its own dock and boat. On top of one of the boathouses stood a plastic flamingo, which had been painted white to look like an egret. The boat traffic picked up. Small fishing boats passed us first, then larger and faster ones. I found it interesting that the smaller fishing boats slowed down as they neared us so they would not create waves, while the larger ones sped past leaving huge wakes.

We pulled into Ambrough Slough boat access for lunch. We were serenaded by crickets, and a heron kept vigil near us as we ate. Suddenly, ten vehicles lined up to put their boats into the water. We entertained ourselves during the commotion by rating how well the men launched their boats and observing their boat-launch etiquette.

A large boat towing a smaller boat with two people in it came around an island. The two people in the smaller boat held canoe paddles and pretended to be paddling. Three men, four boys, and one girl, all dressed in camouflage, came ashore with gun cases. My fear of guns resurfaced. The thought that these young hunters probably didn't consider kayakers while hunting left Kitty and me both unnerved.

The girl had long, red, curly hair. Her boots came to her knees. She fidgeted as she quickly removed the camouflage jacket and revealed a bright orange baseball jersey.

"How did you do?" I asked one of the boys.

"Oh, we did fine," he responded with a lot of bravado.

"Enough for dinner tonight?" I asked.

The young man didn't answer me. One of the adults laughed, shook his head, and said, "Only if you're not hungry." The young man reached down and held up one little duck.

All the activity at the boat launch drove us away. Boats sped past a little too close for comfort. A large flock of pelicans floated along the shore, watching the commotion. We stirred them up as we paddled by. Approaching Prairie du Chien, Wisconsin, we passed a salvage area where old trains were stored. Rusty cabooses parked next to the water intrigued me; they reminded me of the trains I saw as a child. I wanted to stop and check them out; however, the high boat traffic was a growing concern, so we focused on getting to our destination.

After eight miles, we met Sherry at the North Water Street Landing. A houseboat passed us heading downriver. We broke into laughter when we spotted another fake palm tree standing on the deck of the boat. We had been counting them since Kitty spotted one in Lake Pepin. This was the twelfth palm tree.

We drove to Lawler Park and located the shelter we would use for the Gathering the following night. The buildings in Lawler Park were rich with history, most dating back to the 1800s. We then drove across the river to Iowa and Pikes Peak State Park.

Pikes Peak is a 1,000-foot limestone bluff, named by Lieutenant Zebulon Pike when he explored the area in 1805. He also named Pikes Peak in Colorado. Atop the bluff was a breathtaking panoramic view of the Mississippi river in both directions and its confluence with the Wisconsin River. While admiring the view, we met Bonnie, a retired math teacher who worked for the park. She pointed out the highlights from our vantage point.

We set up camp in the group campsite next to a troop of boy scouts. We wondered how rowdy the boys would be and expected they would interfere with our sleep. However, as the evening progressed, we hardly knew the boys were there.

Kitty took a phone call from her boyfriend and then announced, "Greg is coming down tonight."

"He is?" I asked, confused.

"Neat, I'll get to meet him!" Sherry responded.

I asked Kitty what his plans were, but she didn't know and couldn't say how long he planned to stay. Kitty's demeanor changed as soon as she found out Greg was coming. He immediately became her focus. He had not even arrived yet, but he had already changed the dynamics of the group. It bothered me that she had not discussed his joining us with me. Later I talked to her about my struggle and made it clear that he could not be present at the Gathering.

It continued to amaze me how men affected women and how we unconsciously changed our behavior for them. I had no control over his arrival; he had already been driving for a few hours before he called, so I did my best to let it go.

We headed into McGregor, Iowa, for dinner and ate at a Mexican restaurant that vibrated with music. By the time our food arrived, we were deep into a conversation.

"It seems hard for men to connect," I said. "Is that something we teach them?"

"Connecting seems to be a female thing for sure," said Sherry.

"I wonder if it's part of that macho thing that is pervasive in our culture," I said. "You know, the attitude they project that they don't need anyone because they can handle it by themselves."

"I know some men have learned it from their dads," said Kitty. "I can see it when they talk about how they interacted with their dads. I know a man who works sixteen hours a day, and he thinks that is something to be proud of, rather than saying, 'Oh my God, is this what I want my whole life to be?' Women seem to bring other women together for conversations with each other. Is there any forum where guys do that? If we were a couple of guys floating down the river, inviting other men to Gatherings, would it work? Would men come?"

"I know of one organization called the Warriors," said Sherry. "The problem is that after a weekend retreat like that is over, they go home where there are no support groups and they have to make it on their own."

"There is a lot of richness brought to a relationship when both parties have connections outside of the relationship," I added. "Both people bring new ideas and concepts into the conversation."

"I had been dating a guy that had a lot of interests," said Kitty. "He pursued them by himself rather than with me or other people. I realized that communication worked best when we went off during the day, lived our lives separately, then brought what we experienced back in the evening and shared with each other. I need that connection. I feel very fortunate to have the community of women I have. I only became friends with women after I moved to Ely, which was when I became more comfortable with myself and was finally able to have meaningful relationships with women."

We drove back to camp to set up the tents. After searching out the right spot on the sloping ground and laughing as we watched Sherry wrestle with her tent, our conversation continued amidst the background noises of outboard motors, cars, train whistles, and birds.

"I was listening to what you were saying earlier and realized that when I was married, all my friends were happily married. I had no friends that weren't married," Sherry said.

"In my first marriage, my husband didn't like it when I had friends that weren't married," I said. "I guess it was too threatening."

"When you come out of a relationship like that, you have none of those friends to talk with anymore," said Sherry. "My husband and I had been active in the church and kind of holding the church up in some cases. It was us and a few other people. Then when the divorce came, I didn't trust anybody and had no women friends for five or six years. I had only my kids, and that was too much responsibility for them. It's tough for a kid. It's a lot of pressure, and it's not fair."

"My daughter, Erin, said that too," added Kitty. "When her dad and I broke up, it was the same thing. The whole situation is unfair no matter which way you look at it."

"To me, it's the worst when your kids are your only support," said Sherry. "In my case they absolutely were. I curled up in a ball and just about died. They took care of me and made sure I was eating. It was that bad. I don't know what would have happened without them. I'm coming to a place in my life where confidentiality is no longer as important. I am who I am, and I have got to come out. I have to stop being afraid of hurting people's feelings. I am going to try not to say things that are hurtful but still say it the way it is."

"I feel like the more of us that can be real out there, the better off the world will be," I added.

After another phone call to Greg, Kitty learned he would not arrive until two o'clock in the morning. With darkness falling, we decided to turn in.

September 16, Day Thirteen

I woke during the night to the howl of coyotes in the distance. After living in Ely and hearing wolves howl, the coyotes sounded like wolf pups with high-pitched voices.

The morning light woke me, and I heard cows bellowing in the field near us. The group campsite was a grassy area on the edge of the park between the lush trees and farm fields. One of the fields had corn that grew taller than me. A semi was parked in the group campsite a distance away. I assumed it must be Greg, though I hadn't heard him pull in.

Before everyone else got up, I walked down to the overlook to sing and make the offering for the Gathering. I stood looking over the river and across into Wisconsin as the sun rose. I began to sing and was over-whelmed with a feeling of gratitude that the song was being heard by the entire river valley. I felt extraordinarily connected to everything around me. The breeze felt like a gentle hand caressing my face. I was engulfed in nurturing energy.

Pulling myself away from the overlook, I headed to the bathhouse. Sherry was talking with a woman named Sue H., who was retired and worked for AmeriCorps doing park restoration in Iowa. Sherry was try-ing to convince her to come to the Gathering.

Sue H. was a petite woman with a dynamic and powerful spirit focused on helping to heal the earth. She told Sherry she worked in the park because she hoped to change how they did things. The parks burned downed trees and brush. Sue saw the trees as a valuable resource that was being wasted. She wanted to make wood chips to fill the gul-lies, which would be more effective at absorbing water and preventing washouts than rock.

After breakfast, we split into two groups and headed to town. Kitty and Greg went off to enjoy time together and to find a sporting-goods store to purchase neoprene gloves. Sherry and I went to do laundry and find internet access.

After she started the laundry, Sherry joined me back at the Mexican restaurant while I attempted to upload pictures onto the website and put in a weekly update. We shared Mexican sodas and chips while Sherry came and went, managing the laundry. After three hours of frustration with the computer and only one photo added to the website, I quit.

I went on the internet to find information on wind gods for Kitty. I found more information than I expected. The Hopi had Yaponcha, while the Greeks had a god for each cardinal direction: Boreas for the North; Notus for the South, who also covered the storms of autumn; Eurus for the East; and Zephyrus for the West. Kitty would have to decide which one to talk to.

Sherry and I explored McGregor. We went into a quaint shop called Paper Moon, which had a wide variety of books and unusual gift items. The shop was run by a mother-daughter team. The daughter, Jennifer, was dressed in retro '50s clothes. She had the style down pat, with a big, pulled-back hairdo, shoes with fat heels, and bright red lipstick. The mother, Louise, dressed conservatively. Several cats meandered around the store. Jennifer sat for a moment holding a kitten with a cast on its foot. She told us they had a soft spot for cats, especially ones in need of a home or medical attention.

After a bit more exploring, Sherry and I headed back to camp to pre-pare for the Gathering. "I think partly what is happening to me on this trip is that I am opening up to all kinds of possibilities that I never thought of before," said Sherry. "I have wanted to get rid of most of my stuff and live at a basic level. Because we've been camping, I now have a glimmer about how to accomplish that. There are people who are doing it, but I have not been around those people.

"I had a friend die a month and a half ago. He was fifty-two years old, but he was so ready. He lived very simply. He didn't have a car or a TV or any of that stuff, but he had people. He and his sister ran a coffee house, so they employed a lot of kids. He mentored many of those kids, particularly with music. He played the guitar and had his own band. When he was young, he traveled all over the West. He worked whatever job he could find, like logging, picking apples, or playing in coffee houses. That was just who he was. The cancer started in his esophagus about a year ago, and the people started to come to visit him. He knew so many people. They were always there with him, even at the end of his life.

"Usually when you go to visit someone who is dying, you worry about what you are going to say and you feel sad. People would leave uplifted after visiting Bill. It was amazing. For his funeral they had to find a big place. Bill didn't exactly have a funeral because he donated his body to the University of Minnesota for research. That was a new concept for me. Now I am committed to doing that as well. His funeral at the Camp Pepin chapel was more of a celebration of his life. The chapel is no longer used. It's an old Methodist camp right down there on the lake."

"Is there a big, white cross down on the end of the peninsula?" I asked.

"Yes," answered Sherry. "How did you know?"

"It's in Old Frontenac and owned by Bill F.," I answered. "I sang my song that morning right there under the cross. The energy in that area was incredible."

"Bill would have been there with you," Sherry said. "He was a major biker too. For his funeral there was a bunch of people that biked out from Lake City, even though it was raining and cold. On the way to the funeral, a spoke broke on his biking partner's bike. People commented that Bill was playing with people that day."

"We lost a friend last April," I said. "He went for a hike with his dog and didn't come home. They found him on one of his favorite hiking trails, sitting at the base of a tree with his head down, like he was resting. His dog was next to him. He had been missing for thirty-six hours. He also had a huge heart. Everybody had a Mike story. They had to have Mike's funeral in the Catholic church because it had the biggest seating capacity. Even then, it was standing room only. I felt his presence there too. Sara Jo was very good friends with Mike. It really bothered her that she could not come home for his funeral. When I told her about his death, she said, 'People like him are not supposed to die–they're just too big and full of life.' She was right. It really shakes you up when you lose someone that young."

We climbed into the van to leave for the park just as Kitty and Greg pulled up. We left Greg at camp and headed to Prairie du Chien to set up the Gathering. We passed through Marquette and had to stop to take a photo of Pinky the Elephant and her three palm trees. Pinky stood in front of the Isle of Capri Casino. She was a brilliant pink. Her palm trees brought our count up to fifteen.

PRAIRIE DU CHIEN GATHERING

While we got things in place for the Gathering, Sherry connected with every woman she saw, inviting them to join us. She spent extra time with a blond woman. I couldn't hear what they talked about, but it was evident that the woman was troubled.

Sherry returned and brought the blond woman, whose name was Irene. She was on the fence about staying and asked questions about what we were doing. While we continued to set up, Irene wandered back to the railing and stared out at the river. Sue H. and a few other women arrived. A woman named Shelly said she knew she was not old enough to speak but still wanted to soak every-thing in. Irene rejoined our group. By the end of the night, we had eleven women, ranging in age from thirty-nine to sixty-one.

Sue H.

As the honored elder of the evening, Sue H. began speaking. "Has life taken me where I thought I was going to be? No, thank God. I have definitely tried not to fall into the nor-mal paths and traps that I know a lot of women of all ages get into, and I have suc-ceeded. I was searching for honesty, openness, and adventure in a mate, but I found I needed to develop those in myself first. I try to be honest around people. I am open and have as much fun as possible. It has been a lot more fun this way."

"Today I was in McGregor, doing laundry for the three of us," Sherry chimed in. "In the laundromat were Oprah magazines and one Family Circle. It is interesting what you can learn from Oprah. One of the articles that really struck me said, 'Once you are aware that you are searching for God, you have found God.' I thought, 'Wow, that is really neat wisdom.'"

Lynne continued. "I'm sitting here feeling that, for women in gen-eral, it's courageous to come to a circle and speak your truth and speak your heart and share your experiences. I am seeing more and more women not talking about soap operas or their neighbors or their clothes. They are talking about their truth, and they are talking about their spirituality. They are talking about things that are or used to be very hard to talk about. Up until recently, for my little section of the world, it was difficult to even say, 'I don't know if I am Christian, but I believe in Christ and Christ's walk.' Oh, how scary that is to say. It took me some time to stop having my heart pound if I said that, because 'Oh God, I am going to get it.' All that fear and I am finally free of it.

"Then it took courage to be with other women who are sharing those truths. For me that is raising the vibrations of the earth. We are all teachers of light, just like Gandhi, Mother Theresa, Jesus, Mary, and all of those people. We become connected to the light that they had because we are speaking their truth. We are trying to share that with each other and bring more light to the Earth to make the dark stuff a bit grayer. I think it is important because we are all dark and we are all light. We have to take the darkness and shade it out a little bit and get that lightness to shine brighter. It takes courage to sit and share those things and not feel like you are going to be struck by lightning."

Kitty added, "This has been quite an adventure, to say the least. I only met Nancy about two years ago. How it happened was one of those crossings of paths that normally I don't pay attention to in life. Something drew me back to the coffee shop to say 'Well, I am going to the Cities. You can ride with me,' to a woman that I did not know at all. We spent four hours in the car together. I don't know if that trip began the transformation that has been taking place in my life, but it definitely has had a lot to do with it.

"I am a recovering alcoholic, and I have been in a twelve-step program for a number of years. In that group, they talk about God a lot, but I didn't subscribe to any kind of religion. I was raised Catholic and came to describe myself as a recovering Catholic because there seemed to be so many things to undo that I learned from that religion. For me it was about having confines put on my beliefs. I didn't even know I had other beliefs when I was being taught to be a good Catholic. That came much later in my life. I had a hard time with the concept of God. It just seemed like there were so many other spirits out there that are guides in my life. It was through the twelve-step program that I learned the difference between religion and spirituality. That is one of the great things I have learned.

"I am a snowball that started at the top of the mountain, and I am going downhill. It kind of leveled off for a while, but then I decided to go on this trip. When Nancy asked me to go on the trip, the snowball started downhill again. I think it hit base camp and went over the other end. It just keeps moving, sometimes faster than I am able to keep up with. Yet if I can keep myself open, I will be okay. That is what I am learning.

"Being in tune with the river is my pace. I am slowing my thought process and my movements. Being on the river is serving me right now. I am not moving so fast that I can't catch up with what is going on around me. I have learned so much.

"There are many teachers tonight. I am learning to discern what works for me and what doesn't work for me. I don't have to accept everybody else's truth. I can develop my own truth and move forward with that. That has been a gift."

Irene, who had been listening intently, spoke up. "I am tired of all the priests getting away with molesting children."

"I am glad it's starting to be talked about instead of just shoving it under the rug," responded Sue H.

"They ought to be in prison," replied Irene. "They should not be sent to another congregation. Where is the wisdom in that?"

"I know a lot of people—women—who have been affected by molestation at a young age, and I know how it has affected their entire lives," said Sue H. "I get angry. I mean really bad angry. So I usually try to stay away from that subject. I am so glad those preachers are getting caught."

"But they are not being held accountable," continued Irene. "They are just sending them off to another parish. They send them from parish to parish to parish where they can just do it again. They are not in jail."

Sue H. continued. "If people don't see this, if they don't connect with this, they are really, really afraid. Fear is how they control people. It is the fear of death that they control with. Not the fear of life. Life is eternal—that is one thing. It is always eternal."

"Brenda G. and I have been talking for the last twenty-four hours straight," said Lynne. "One of the things we were talking about is being frustrated with the abuse in churches, which happens anywhere. It is about the experiences of power over people. We came up with some ideas and conclusions together. One idea is that we have to start seeing everyone as an equal. When you start putting people above you, or the power of anything above you, you start looking up to all that and saying, 'Oh I want to be that,' or 'They are so great.' Stop it! That is a sure sign that you are going to get hurt. You are going to be abused one way or another, either by yourself or by someone else. The idea is to keep everyone, including yourself, on an equal plane. You don't need to be above anyone, and also know that nobody has the right to place themselves in a position above you. That is where you are safe. The safety net is right there and fluctuating either way is a real red flag. The way to protect ourselves from these kinds of abuses of power is to wake up to our own power rather than getting angry about the abuse. We need to teach our children, daughters, and grand-daughters to respectfully be in their own power. Teach them to never be subject to abuse because they gave their power away, thinking it was the right thing to do. How do you do that? What is the key? The key is to never put anyone above yourself. I think that is an important concept."

"The tough thing is when we send our children to school, where authority runs everything," responded Sherry. "I am not really sure how to handle that, except to respect our children so that they know they are respected. Listen to them as we want to be listened to. Maybe that is the best way to do that sort of thing. It is also good not to put out a lot of rules for kids to follow. They need freedoms so they feel that their ideas are important and the things they do are okay and accepted by their parents and friends. There have to be some parameters for safety and respect, of course, but maybe that is as far as it should go."

Sherry noticed the look on Brenda G.'s face, who was under fifty and struggling not to chime in, and said, "Brenda G. wants to talk and she can't." Brenda G. covered her mouth and everyone laughed. Then we noticed that Shelly was also trying hard to stay quiet, and we broke into laughter again.

Sherry continued. "How do we do that? It is a tough one. We have to teach our parents how to parent in the right ways. Irene was talking with me about parenting issues earlier. Would you like to talk about it or just share your story of your own children?"

After a few moments of silence, Irene began to speak and quickly choked up. "I just got a granddaughter about a month ago. My son and daughter-in-law are following a book on how to do it. So according to the book, you are not allowed to touch her, and you can't pick her up. You have to be clean and can't smoke. They live in Decorah. They won't let me around her; my mother, her own great-grandmother, has not even seen her. The longest time I picked her up was for fifteen minutes and they told me to put her back down. They are unbelievable. My daughter-in-law is following the book, and my own son is doing everything she tells him."

"My daughter-in-law said to me, 'I know more than you do,'" responded Sue H. "Babies need to be held and loved. Irene, you need strength to get through that."

Irene continued, "I told them that they need counseling. Nobody is allowed to see the baby. Yesterday was my second trip over there, and I could only be there fifteen minutes before I had to leave. I think they will have a lot of regrets if they don't go to some parenting classes. What do you do? My son is twenty-seven, and he wasn't raised that way. He was doing everything on the farm. Even the parents in the hospital pick the babies up. It's just so hard." Tears ran down her face.

We sat quietly for a few minutes, taking in her words, until three more women joined us. They had been lost and driving around for the past hour, though they had been very determined to find us. One of the newcomers, Julie, began speaking.

"My friends Paula and Kristin and I got started on a bit of a journey of our own. We go to the Boundary Waters together in the summers on canoe trips and have bonded in a very special way. Last spring when we were in Ely, Minnesota, we were at the Front Porch coffee shop and they had information on this trip, so we decided it might be kind of a fun thing to extend our friendship and go to a Gathering together. We didn't know what to expect, and we got a little lost, but we are here.

"I am a teacher, Paula is the secretary at my school, and Kristin is her sister-in-law. The fourth one of our group is also a teacher, but she couldn't make it today. We have created quite a friendship, and it is a good thing in my life.

"I have raised three children; well, one is not quite raised yet. I devoted my whole life to my husband and my children, and now I am devoting some time to myself and nurturing my friendships. That has been a great gift in my life."

Lynne

"I want to speak to one of the things I am seeing, which is a change in our children," added Lynne. "The good thing I see, though they might be a little bit more in the technical world or riding the grid of life a little bit differently, is that they are connected to light-working women, women who are healers or bring healing to the world. And that is good. You, Irene, are a bright light, and that is going to make a difference in your son. I don't even know how to start the conversation, but I do see a difference in this twenty-something group of parents. Brenda and I have talked about this. I have noticed that our children are beautiful. They are incredibly intelligent—look at what they can do with those computers! The studies they have in school, what they have to do to get by in life is phenomenal.

"My son's wife just had a baby. She is three months old now. I remember hearing them say, 'I don't know if we should have anybody come over to see her for the first little while. And if someone is smoking they can't hold her because, oh my goodness, she is going to smell that, and that is as bad as having someone smoking next to her.' Some of the same things you were talking about. What I am saying is that our children are being fed different information, and it is not all bad, and it is going to work its way out. Maybe we need to go through this new moment of 'Oh my goodness,' because many parents haven't necessarily tended to their babies with such intense interest for a while. This unconditional love for a child is beautiful and will turn out for the good of all. Not that we don't all love our babies—I just feel there is a new devotion that is different. I wanted to say that because there is a bright lining that will eventually shine from all of this. There is something called an "indigo child," and I think we have all probably had one. And that is something to be proud of."

"Will you say more about the indigo child?" I asked.

"I still don't know much about it," Lynne relied. "The indigo children are children that were born into this world with special powers or abilities to communicate on a higher level. There is a movie out, which is where my information comes from, called Indigo. These children have access to a higher plane of consciousness where they can communicate through clairvoyance at a very young age. I think the special gifts of these children become more evident as they grow older and have more input in the world. They may be the greatest gift to this planet in a long time. It appears to be a different way of using the brain, a different intelligence, a different connecting.

"But look as us. We would not be sitting here if we didn't have a different way of connecting with each other. Listen to what we are talking about, for heaven's sake. This is different than if this were ten years ago or twenty years ago. Well, twenty years ago we would not be sitting here. We would not have these conversations. We would not be that free to speak, well, maybe underground, but not as free and as open as we can be today. I compare these indigo children to what we are doing now and how we reach each other and communicate on higher levels. They are open to other dimensional forms of thought processes and are freer to use them. New progressive parents of today are less likely to force their children into the box that we have all been raised in. This opens all sorts of possibilities for a child's mind to grow in ways we have not seen in the past."

"I wish my daughter, Christine, were here tonight." Sue H. said. "Unfortunately she is going through some pain of her own. She lost a friend, her last roommate. This girl died last week and Christine is feeling a lot of guilt because she left to come up here after the girl had begged her to stay in Texas with her. Now, because of the pain and guilt, Christine is beating herself up, and she can't feel this person's spirit. If she would stop beating herself up and let this girl come through to her, she would find out how happy she is now that she is with her dead husband. This girl had a car accident years ago and was crippled to the point of not being able to get around. She would fall down constantly because the doctor had her on so much medication that she couldn't stand. Her family disowned her. She was totally alone. I know this woman is trying to get through to Christine, but she has got to let go of the pain first. If she lets this woman get through to her, she will see that her life is so beautiful now. I wish Christine would stop crying long enough to feel the message this woman is trying to tell her from where she is. I wish Christine were here tonight."

The sun was setting and the air grew cooler as the Gathering came to a close. "I limit the women who are able to speak to fifty and older for a specific reason," I said. "In this generation, we have given a great deal of permission to women to speak, and younger women are doing just that. It is the women who are fifty and older who come from a generation where we were told not to speak. We were told to be quiet. Our wisdom is lost because we are keeping quiet. I am trying to create an environment where the younger women have to be quiet and the older women say what is on their mind and in their hearts before some of that is completely lost."

"I still have a problem speaking, even with as much as I talk," Sue H. responded. "I can't do it around men. My brother, to this day, refuses to allow women to talk to him. He is two years younger than me. To him a woman is supposed to sit like this," she posed with her legs daintily crossed, hands folded in her lap, "and she is not supposed to carry on a conversation. God forbid if she interrupts a man. If he has to take his own plate to the sink, oh my God. There are still men like that, and it is hard. They were raised like that. I find it very difficult to speak openly and freely around men."

"I have noticed that a group of women can be having a great time talking, but then one man walks in and it changes," I added. "He doesn't even have to say anything. He doesn't even have to come into the circle. For example, the gentleman with the cell phone that walked by a moment ago captured everybody's attention for a while. I felt our energy go out there checking to see, 'Is he coming? Is this okay?' I watched us do it, and when he was a distance away, we all came back. When other women walked by we did not have the same response. We barely noticed them. There are not too many men who are sensitive to how their presence impacts women. I am delighted to say that is changing too, but it may be a while before that completely gets transformed. That said, we have a few more moments this evening, and I would like to open the conversation up to the younger women."

"I have been just sitting here soaking it all in," Shelly said, seizing the opportunity to speak. "You, Sue H., are one of the most beautiful women I have ever met. Listening to your wisdom and the things that you have said today, you've touched me. Your courage . . . obviously you have huge amounts of courage. I hope in another ten or twenty years I am right where you are. I am extremely glad that I came tonight. I had some friends that were going to come with me and couldn't, but I came anyway."

With a broad grin Brenda G. jumped in next. "I have been so good. I am so proud of myself. You have no idea. I am really grateful to be here listening to the women's wisdom. I am so glad that you gave me the opportunity to be quiet and to listen so that I could learn, because it is something that I need to do. I am very truly grateful. Blessings to you on your journey. Everybody's stories were great. Thank you, thank you, thank you."

"I feel very grateful to be here too," said Paula. "I am reading Nancy's first book about the first journey. I am halfway through, so I thought I had an idea about what this was about, but it has really been more than I expected. It makes me want to go home, shut up, and listen to my mother." Everyone broke into laughter and applause.

With some encouragement, Kristin spoke. "I have enjoyed listening to everyone also. Being the youngest one here, I am truly inspired by your beauty—both inside and out. I have a blue, Water * Women * Wisdom mug that I use every day at work. It will now remind me of you and how thankful I am to have been invited to come here. Hopefully this will be one of many Gatherings for me. As I get older, I realize that the destination is not the most important; it's the journey. Paula, Julie, and I really did have a journey tonight! Have a safe and beautiful journey."

Lynne and Brenda G. treated us to Native American flute music and drumming to end the Gathering. They gave me a drum to join them, which delighted me. They taught us how to sing a Lakota thank-you song. The music echoed under the shelter and drifted off into the dark night air. The air was filled with the extraordinary connections between each woman, the river, and the earth.

Brenda G. turned to everyone and said, "Pilamaya. It's Lakota for thank you. Tunkashila, Pilamaya is Lakota for Grandfather, thank you"

"Megwich is thank you in Ojibwa," I responded.

Lynne continued, "Gitchi Manidu is Creator, or Great Spirit, in Ojibwa, and Megwich Manidu is Thank you Creator in Ojibwa."

After the Gathering I gave Lynne one of the thirteen heron feathers. She became quite emotional and said, "I feel honored and do not take this lightly. I will wear it proudly and promise to keep doing my healing work." She had not heard of the thirteen grandmothers but was going to get the book Grandmothers Counsel the World to learn about them. Lynne invited us to a sweat lodge on our way home from the trip.

Back at camp, Sherry was not ready to be done with the day. She sat at the picnic table and described the moon in stunning detail to the rest of us as we snuggled in for the night. A barred owl hooted, and a grey tree frog chirped in the woods behind her.

September 17th through 22nd

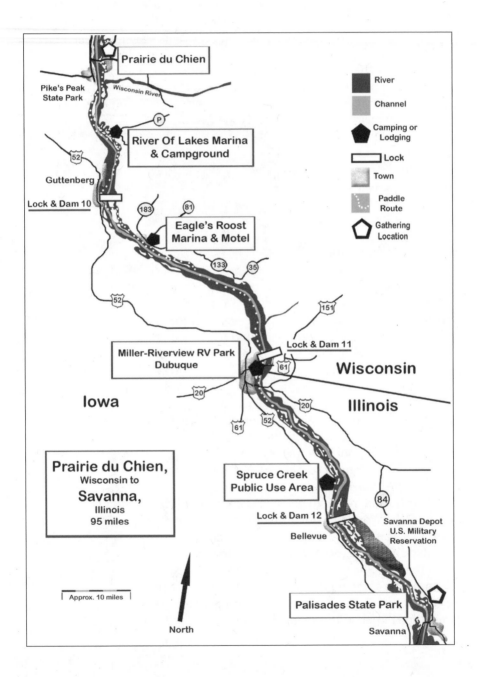

Prairie du Chien

Pike's Peak State Park

Wisconsin River

River

Channel

Camping or Lodging

Lock

Town

Paddle Route

Gathering Location

River Of Lakes Marina & Campground

52

Guttenberg

Lock & Dam 10

183

81

Eagle's Roost Marina & Motel

133

35

52

151

Miller-Riverview RV Park Dubuque

Lock & Dam 11

61

Wisconsin

20

Iowa

20

Illinois

61

52

Prairie du Chien, Wisconsin to Savanna, Illinois 95 miles

Spruce Creek Public Use Area

84

Lock & Dam 12

Savanna Depot U.S. Military Reservation

Bellevue

Approx. 10 miles

North

Palisades State Park

Savanna

Prairie du Chien to Savanna

September 17, Day Fourteen

It was my husband Doug's birthday, so we sang 'Happy Birthday' to him into the tape recorder; I'd play it for him later. Kitty said good-bye to Greg, who headed home. Our motivation to pack up camp was low, so we talked as we packed.

"I wonder sometimes why we can't see what is right in front of us," I said. "There were signs before I got engaged to my first husband that there was trouble, but I just made it okay. One example happened in my first apartment. He was my boyfriend at the time and was always in my apartment. Once while I was at work, he decided to heat up a can of tamales for dinner. That was fine, but he didn't open the can. He put it in a pan, brought the water to boil, and the can exploded. There was tamale goo and fragments of tin can all over the apartment. It hung from the curtains, the ceiling, the walls, the cupboards, the couch . . . Everything in my tiny apartment was covered with red, greasy slime.

"The fact that he didn't know to open the can was one clue, but that wasn't the worst part. My neighbor heard the explosion and ran over to see what had happened just as he bolted out the door. He made no effort to clean any of it up, left no apology note, nothing! It wasn't his apartment, so it wasn't his mess. He timed his return the next day to be well after I was done cleaning. Still no apology. He made a quick joke about it and changed the subject. I overlooked many clues and married him anyway. Do you think it's a mom thing, cleaning up after everybody and thinking nothing of it?"

"I told Greg to be safe when he left," added Kitty. "Then I looked at him and said, 'My God, I feel like your mother.' We have had that conversation before. I don't want to be anyone's mother anymore."

"I think my first husband was very controlled," said Sherry. "I think I was afraid of him."

"Controlled or controlling?" asked Kitty.

"Both," Sherry answered. "I think he was first attracted to me because I was fun and light and he wasn't. And then he knocked that out of me because he felt threatened by it. He was threatened by my ability to talk with people and do all the other things that he couldn't do. He had to be the center of attention and the one in control of our relationship. He saw me as part of him, and I when I acted out he gave me looks. I still have a bruise on my leg from where he slammed into me. Well, that should have been a clue, but it wasn't."

"He slammed into you with what, a fist?" asked Kitty.

"Yes," answered Sherry. "He was angry but not at me. He was angry at something, and I was there."

"Did you ever think about fighting back?" I asked. "I know I did at first, but later I felt too intimidated."

"I always withdrew," answered Sherry. "My husband left because he said I was not intelligent enough for him. He wasn't so smart either, but he didn't understand that."

"I think he left because you challenged him," I said. "You started resisting, and he probably had to get out while he was still the top dog."

"You know, I think you might be right," Sherry said.

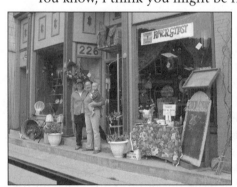

After leaving camp, we stopped in McGregor and saw Shelly from the Gathering. She owned a store on Main Street called River Gypsy. She and her grandson were waiting for us and gave us a tour. Her shop was an eclectic mix of candles, antiques, jewelry, and more. She told us she also ran a crisis help line for the area. We commented that it sounded like a lot for one woman to do. She smiled and said, "It needs to be done."

We put in at the Prairie du Chien Marina landing. While Kitty and I prepared to paddle, Sherry skipped rocks across the surface of the calm water. We saw the little girl inside her bubble up to the surface.

It would be another cold day, so we put on warm gear. As we paddled away, it didn't look like Sherry would leave the shoreline anytime soon. Kitty and I followed the channel that hugged town, passing fishermen and enjoying a peaceful paddle.

We saw a bird on shore that we couldn't identify. After a debate, we decided she must be a green heron because of its

Photo by Cheryl Mast

shape and the green hue to its legs. It was the first time either of us had seen one.

Every time the side channel opened to the main channel we were blasted with a bitter headwind. We followed the river to Garnet Lake. I told Kitty there would be pelicans around the next bend. She looked surprised and asked how I knew. "I'm starting to recognize their smell. I am sure we are downwind of a flock." As we came around the bend, we saw hundreds of pelicans floating and standing on sandbars. It was stunning. Staying on the outside of the channel, we moved quietly toward them. They spooked and took flight, surrounding us. They were like a white wave lifting off, moving in unison. We heard their wings splashing on the water and flapping in the air as if amplified. They flew toward the main channel in perfect formation, like a silk scarf blowing in the breeze, and eventually disappeared behind the trees. We floated motionlessly. "It's like being in a National Geographic special," Kitty whispered in awe.

Out in the main channel the wind pounded us. We crossed to the Iowa side at the base of Pikes Peak and hugged the bluff, hoping for relief. I realized the numbness in my hands was no longer an issue and my asthma was better, even in the cold wind. Fish jumped around us as we approached a tiny peninsula. It sounded like the water was bubbling. The fish were shiny, gray, and three inches long, and they moved in unison.

We watched how the wind played with the water and the current. To the south of the point, large waves crashed on the shore, while to the north, it was much calmer. Paddling around the peninsula, the current drew me directly into the big waves. I angled my kayak straight at them to ride through. I passed through the worst of them, and the current eased.

We entered Johnson's Slough, where the sound of cicadas filled the air. A train parked on the track deep in the trees had its engine running. No one was around, but its hissing sound echoed eerily down the channel. Its cargo, giant tubes made of metal, stretched out before us. Kitty decided that they were secret missile silos and the train was laying low so it wouldn't be spotted.

It grew warmer, and by two o'clock it was hot. We shed our layers, while along shore, sandpipers darted ahead to keep away from us as if playing leapfrog.

Toward the end of the slough the land above the bank was mowed. The groomed area continued on for quite a distance. Signs were posted facing the mowed area. Curiosity got the better of me, and I climbed the four-foot mud embankment to read the signs. When I reached the top, I knew immediately where we were. Kitty joined me. Before us were the rolling green hills of Effigy Mounds National Monument. The monument has more than one hundred Native American burial mounds that date back several hundred years. From the air, the mounds resemble marching bears and large birds. The sacred ground had a refreshing and calming energy.

Astounding oak trees stood like giant guardians above the mounds. Before long, the true guardians of the land, mosquitoes, descended. Our peaceful moment ended, and we raced back to our kayaks.

Past Wyalusing Slough, we headed into the main channel, hugging the islands along the way. We faced relentless wind and waves for a mile of open water. Exhausted and hot, we paddled into Ferry Lake then followed channels that wound through the backwaters until we arrived at our campsite outside of Bagley, Wisconsin.

We arrived later than we had expected, and Sherry said that she had been worried. Cis and Karen P., who would paddle with us for the next three days, were with her. Fatigue and hunger got the better of Kitty and me. We were better hostesses after we had eaten and enjoyed a warm shower, but it didn't take long before the mosquitoes drove us into our tents.

Cis

Karen P.

I positioned my tent to watch the sunset through the screen door. It was stunning. I read mail and called Doug again to wish him a happy birthday before falling asleep.

September 18, Day Fifteen

Our new paddling partners were eager to get on the water the next morning. The narrow channel had remnants of the not-so-rare-after-all lotus plants. Pelicans skimmed the surface in a long, white, fluttering line. I thanked them for a splendid start to our day.

We hugged the Wisconsin shoreline, traveling the backwaters for four miles before crossing to the Iowa side toward Lock and Dam No. 10. Through the narrows, we spotted an island-like barge near the main channel. It was two stories high, with boats and all types of equipment aboard. We dubbed it Mystery Island. When we got closer, I spotted the Army Corps logo on top. We assumed it was a dredging station. We saw a similar barge structure tucked into McMillan Island further downriver.

A strong headwind caused us to hug the shoreline of islands in the middle of the river. When we ran out of islands, we aimed our boats into the waves and paddled hard to the other shore. Kitty and I discovered that slowing our pace in the big waves to stay with the others was more physically exhausting, but we needed to stay together for safety. A single small boat crossing the main channel was more difficult to see than several boats together, and if one of us capsized, the others could get to them faster.

We paddled along the shore of a large peninsula and into a calm bay. My mind drifted to the last Gathering and Lynne's words about speaking your truth. It was such a difficult thing to do. I had spent so much of my life not knowing what my truth was and, therefore, being unable to speak it. In my mind, Lynne's idea about needing to see others as equals wrapped around the idea of speaking your truth. It became a simple theory that, if implemented with compassion, could end power struggles. Ego, insecurity, and other personal issues made that hard to do.

I had been astonished that a powerful woman like Sue H. said she struggled to speak around men. She spoke confidently when she talked about asking for equipment from the park managers and shared her ideas about the changes she wanted to implement. I sensed that she found the appropriate words in most situations, whether she knew it or not.

A mile before the lock, we stopped on an island across from Guttenberg, Iowa. I noticed milkweed plants whose pods had burst open. The silky seeds were blowing in the breeze, beginning their journey into the world. Each white, thread-like strand attached to the seeds glistened. I wished Sara Jo were with us. She was particularly fond of these plants because they were one of the few plants monarch butterflies eat. I had noticed that there were fewer monarchs than when I chased them as a child, perhaps because milkweed was becoming scarce.

My attention was drawn from milkweed to cell phones. Cis was discussing lunch plans with someone. We carried a phone for safety, to communicate with our car support, and to let the Lockmasters know we were coming. Hearing a personal call struck me as odd. Civilization was right across the bay from us, but we were in the wilderness where phones seemed out of place.

We entered the lock with a cabin cruiser. The lock attendant threw down ropes for us to hold onto as we dropped. Cis and Karen P. were wide eyed. They had been through a lock before but not in a kayak, and our small size dramatically altered the experience.

Once out of the lock, we crossed the main channel and headed for an opening between the islands that led to Cassville Slough. Kitty and I shared our concerns about Cis and Karen P.'s ability to stay together. Karen P. was often out front, while Cis lagged behind. The next day we'd be on big water, and staying together would be a priority. We struggled with how to handle the issue. Cis and Karen P. both had a great deal of kayaking experience and knew about safety, so we didn't want to insult them. When someone joined the trip with a lot of experience, it was easy to assume that they worked with the same guidelines we did. That assumption and my "Minnesota nice" personality were sometimes a problem. I wouldn't say anything, attempting to be respectful of someone's expertise, but then I'd see them do something that did not fit my guidelines and feel forced to say something that felt even less respectful. I was learning that I had to work on my communication skills and clarify my expectations for paddlers up front.

We stopped for lunch on small, sandy outcropping with a picturesque view of Guttenberg. Karen P. pulled out a bright blue tarp and spread it out on the ground. Kitty and I had already plopped down on the sand and were eating. Karen P. turned the sandy beach into a fine picnic spot, complete with plates and napkins. She and Cis dined like royalty on tuna, fresh fruit, and homemade bread. I watched them with envy as I brushed the sand off my fingers and reached for another bite of my squished cheese sandwich, which had turned oily in the heat.

There was a tree at the edge of the beach with most of the soil washed away from its roots. The tap root extended four feet up from the sand to the base of the trunk. There were few other roots left on the tree, yet it was lush and healthy.

During lunch, we debated our next route. The charts often did not match the actual shape of the river because it was constantly changing, so we made some choices by instinct alone. Kitty had learned to trust my instincts and ability to read the charts, so we decided to go the way I suggested.

Back on the water, we rounded a bend and encountered what Cis called "squirrelly water." Wing dams spanned the width of the waterway, which was lined by revetments. A revetment was a concrete retaining wall built along the edge of the channel. The wing dams and the revetments created whirlpools. At times our rudders were no help, and dipping our paddles into the water felt like paddling pockets of air because there was no resistance to our strokes. The water gently pushed and spun the kayaks around until we broke free and moved into the next slough.

Cassville Slough was wide and offered little protection from the wind, but it was beautiful. The bluffs in the distance reached up like mountains. We passed a group of turkey vultures, who were undisturbed by us. Rounding a bend, we saw a fisherman using a round net that was about five feet in diameter. We watched as he set the net in the water and then pulled it back in again. He wasn't catching much. He looked rough and unkempt. His long straggly hair and ratty beard hung down to his chest, and his wide-brimmed hat shadowed his eyes. We startled him when we approached, and he was not happy to see us. He quickly packed up and headed downriver. After he disappeared around a bend, we burst into laughter.

Fatigue began to get the best of us. Cis and Karen P. asked how much further we had to go. I told them only a couple of miles, knowing that it was actually four. I was really trying to fool myself–four miles sounded too disheartening to admit. We came out of Cassville Slough and saw the town of Cassville, Wisconsin, in the distance. We paddled close to barges parked at the Dairyland Power Cooperative and the Wisconsin Power and Light Company plants, where Cis and Karen P. got their first taste of waffle waves as they bounced off the barges.

I called Sherry to let her know we were finally getting close. She said a pontoon boat was on its way out to find us. Moments later, a pontoon sped out of a channel ahead of us and turned in our direction. As the pontoon got closer, the elderly man driving shouted, "That lady back there on shore said you guys were late so she was going home without you!" Grinning broadly, he circled around again and added, "Keep going, you only have twenty miles left!" He stopped his motor and pointed at Cis, who was a distance behind us, and asked, "What's the matter with that one?"

His name was Len. He hadn't slowed down as he circled us, and we understood why when he tried to start the engine again. It ran, sput-tered, and died several times. With some effort he got it going again. He sped away at full throt-tle, with an occasional bang and puff of smoke from the engine.

The sun was setting when we turned into Jack Oak Slough. Cis caught up with us, but Karen P. was so far ahead that she couldn't hear us calling to her or blowing our whistles. The van was parked next to the motel we would stay in, a welcome sight after seventeen long and windy miles.

We dragged our kayaks onto the grass. Cis and Karen P. were cheer-ful but looked particularly done in. Food was a priority for all of us. We enjoyed burgers, sodas, and a cucumber-onion salad at Vogt's Town Pump. Kitty and I were fascinated by Cis and Karen P.'s fresh perspective of things on the river that had become commonplace for us.

Back at the motel, Len pulled up in his pickup truck to check on us. He was as feisty as he had been out on the river. He told us he made trips to Haiti to build schools for impoverished kids. He was a widower with time on his hands, and the people in Haiti needed help, so it made sense to him. He wished us luck and drove off.

Cis and Karen P. headed into their motel room while Sherry, Kitty, and I sat up to talk.

"I was thinking earlier about a spirituality group that I am a part of," Sherry said. "There have been so many times when I felt like I was on the outside of it. Now, I know I don't have to feel like that. I know I belong. You guys helped me to feel totally accepted right away. I haven't really felt that in very many groups."

"I can be sitting in a room full of a hundred people and feel alone," added Kitty, "though I know it isn't about anybody else. It makes me pause and say, 'Okay what is going on in me that makes me feel this way?' Usually, I am feeling inadequate as a result of comparing myself to the people around me. It has to do with my self-esteem and where I am in my life. I have made great strides in the last three years, but I still feel that way at times."

"I am so in tune with what you are saying," responded Sherry. "It's also about asking yourself 'Where do I want to be? Do I even have a concept of where I want to be?'"

"I don't think our generation was given much permission to really think about what we wanted," I added. "We had roles and we moved out into those roles. Society has changed, and we have more choices, but here we stand, saying 'I don't know what I want because nobody ever asked.' It's very confusing. While I was in therapy after my first marriage, I was asked, 'What are your hopes and dreams?'" We all burst into laughter with recognition. "I was so confused by the question that I could only respond with 'What?'"

Sherry, still laughing, said, "Hopes, dreams, what is that?"

"I have come to realize that I couldn't create dreams for a very long time because I believed I was never going to have them," I continued. "So, why set myself up for a huge disappointment?"

"Exactly," Kitty said emphatically.

"I didn't even go that far," said Sherry. "I just never thought of it. People would ask me, and I would just say that I didn't know."

"I was the same way," said Kitty. "I found that if I dream about something specific I am putting limitations on where I am going. The trip is a perfect example. I could not have dreamed this trip up."

"At the same time, if you don't allow yourself to dream, life doesn't move forward," I responded. "We need to allow ourselves to dream because it gives us direction."

"That's an advanced way of thinking and feeling," said Sherry.

"Let's consider me going to China," added Kitty. "I don't dream about going to China, I know I am going to go, even though it isn't a reality right now."

"For me, considering something as a possibility puts it into that dream world where I test it out—'Oh, that feels good, yeah, I am doing that.'" I replied. "It becomes a possibility. How I am going to get there is a completely different story, and that's where I often get stuck in the details. At least if it's a dream it's on my radar."

"That's a lot to sleep on," Sherry concluded.

September 19, Day Sixteen

We had twenty-five miles to paddle. I was concerned. It had taken us nine hours to travel seventeen miles the day before. If we moved at the same pace, it would take more than thirteen hours, and that didn't even factor in our fatigue.

Down at the boats, Kitty was talking with Cis and Karen P. about safety concerns, staying together, and how we had to pick up the pace if we were going to make it to our destination. When we got on the water, the previous day's roles were reversed. Cis was out in front and Karen P.

was behind, but we were in a tighter formation. Cis wore headphones and listened to music, which may have contributed to her change in speed.

I watched the rhythm of the waves as they moved with us and became mesmerized by their pattern. The more I watched, the deeper I went within myself. I was brought back to reality abruptly by a large fish that jumped over my paddle and came down with a big splash. Startled by the surprise and the cold water splashing my face, I screamed and burst into laughter.

Cis and Karen P. shared their knowledge of the river with us. They said Valmeyer, Illinois, was relocated after it was severely flooded in 1993. It had stood at the base of the bluff for years, but after the flood, they built a completely new infrastructure, including utilities, schools, and the fire house on top of the bluff. Since I didn't live in a flood zone, I couldn't understand why people repeatedly built in an area that continued to flood. I understood a love for the land and history, but the turmoil, expense, and pain that floods cause would probably have overridden that love for me.

The bluffs had hints of yellow, and an occasional red maple created a blazing contrast to the solid mass of green. Fall was my favorite time of year, but it would be over by the time I got home.

We paddled past a tugboat pushing two small barges upriver. A man walked the length of the barge and climbed into a tractor parked on the end of the barge. For fun, we made the signal for tooting the horn. A big puff of smoke came out of the stack when he fired up the engine, followed by a long blast of the horn. Karen P. dug out her foghorn and tooted back at him while we waved. The contrast in loudness seemed hilarious to us.

The tail wind saved us that day. We made much better time than the day before with little effort. We praised the wind gods. Kitty and I got into a discussion about how the wind gods affect the weather. I jokingly asked, "We always see pictures of a wind god blowing out, but what if the wind god breathes in—does the wind change direction?" Kitty pondered it for a while, then said mischievously, "Wind gods only blow out."

North of Lock and Dam No. 11, on the Wisconsin shore, was a picturesque farm at the base of the bluff. The bright silver silo next to the huge barn glowed against the vivid green trees. I couldn't see any fields, and there seemed to be very little space between the farm buildings and the base of the bluff. I wondered what they farmed that made that location worth working.

Once we cleared the lock, it was a mile and a half to the Miller Riverview RV Park and Campground. Pelicans at the end of an island across the river huddled down for the evening. Along shore, a fire truck drove north and tooted its horn at us. The firefighters waved out the truck windows.

Sherry directed us to a beach near our campsite. The campground was different from the others we'd stayed in. There were other people camped near us, we could hear noise from the Highway 61 Bridge adjacent to us, and there was a casino and dog racing track right behind us. The dog kennels bordered the campground. It didn't take much for the dogs to start barking.

Sherry said that she'd met a woman named Gail M., who had come to the campground to find us. She'd heard about our trip from a newspaper article and made arrangements with Sherry to join us the next day with her daughter, Lisa. Gail M. had helped Sherry find the best spot for us to take our kayaks off the water. She was looking forward to joining us and had ideas about the best route to take the next day.

I bristled when I heard the last part. There had been too many people that had been more than willing to tell me the "best" route and the "best" way to do things. Many were adamant that I should do something their way. It took time for me to figure out how to handle those situations. I realized I was projecting my previous experiences onto Gail M. and assuming she wanted to control things, which was unfair. I took a deep breath and tried to let it go.

Kitty and I had packed several kinds of dehydrated foods that would be quick to fix at camp, but Sherry, as Gwyn had done before her, ignored our food bins and bought fresh vegetables, fruit, and meat. I always ended up eating more than I needed because the food was so tasty. Until that night, we had still been putting pickle juice on our salads, but Sherry had bought salad dressing, which tasted heavenly in comparison.

One of the lock attendants who had locked us through earlier stopped by our campsite to make sure we had found it okay and said he had called the local newspaper about us.

I lay on a picnic table away from camp to check voice mail; I had one message from Doug about payroll tax questions. I struggled periodically with feeling like I had abandoned Doug to go on the trip. I had been managing our coffee shop since we opened it. Doug had been working full time as a chemical-dependency counselor and working at the coffee shop in the evenings. Just before I left on the trip, he quit his job and only had two weeks to learn the bookkeeping and day-to-day management of the shop.

Doug sounded good on the phone and reported that he was figuring everything out okay. He said both he and our pets missed me and that the pets had needed much more attention since I left.

After hanging up, I lay on the table admiring the large cottonwoods throughout the campground. An enormous one stood near our campsite. Sherry, Kitty, and I decided to see if we could reach all the way around it, but none of us could.

Karen P. took an opportunity to write in the paddlers' journal.

It was the second day of paddling for me and Cis. We're both from St. Louis and paddle the Mississippi around the Alton pool, north to Louisiana, Missouri, and down to Clarksville.

This 25 mile trip is the longest I've ever done. Hillsides around the part of the river are high on both sides with train tracks running along the river. The occasional town, some memorable houses high on the hilltop, and barges were the only interruptions.

The kayak I am paddling is a loaner from a friend. It carries more volume than mine, it feels heavier (because it is) and acceleration is slow. I do like the rudder, which my boat doesn't have. I was trying to paddle in long cadences and find the most efficient stroke that wouldn't need the rudder for adjustment.

The Mississippi is an urban river with all the great river towns and the small farming towns that sprang up along its waterway. Fishermen and transportation companies use it; pleasure and escape are part of its job. It holds up the middle country with its life.

Rivers have a wildness about them. They are unpredictable because they flood. The floods can be mellow sometimes, but also quite angry, like the people who frequent them.

I thought of my neighbor Bill G. today. He's a retired riverboat captain who likes to share books with me about the river from a tugboat's point of view. So today when the tug gave us a friendly toot on the horn I knew it was someone who liked seeing four small boaters making their way down a pretty stretch of river. They love the river too. How could they not, being on it day after day?

Thank you, Nancy, for letting us come with you.

The night cooled off, and the bugs came out to play. In my tent, I pondered better ways to handle communicating with the women who joined us to paddle. My preconceived notions of how things should work, of safety procedures I had been taught, and of how I had always done things were part of the problem. It was a constant balance of letting go of things not done how I thought they should be and watching for things that were truly unsafe. It drained me. I was used to traveling with well-seasoned paddlers or people who had led canoe trips in the Boundary Waters Canoe Area Wilderness, so my standards were high. The skill levels of the women who joined us were unclear until we got on the water. Terminology was challenging. If they said they had paddled for the past three years, that might mean only twice a year on calm water. Paddling the Mississippi required more skill than that. Kitty and I had already concluded that on the next leg of the trip women would need to document their completion of a kayaking course before joining us. There was just too much at stake.

It was also difficult to explain to someone who had only paddled a few hours at a time what a full day of paddling was like. It was always more taxing than expected. A gentle breeze in your face could leave you completely exhausted at the end of the day. I had to trust that Gail M. and Lisa were experienced.

September 20, Day Seventeen

The campground "alarm" went off at six o'clock in the morning–feeding time at the dog track. It was a toss-up which was more annoying: the dogs barking or the people who kept yelling at them.

The pelicans were ghostlike as they floated in the thick mist rising off the water. An osprey flew in the clear sky above us while we enjoyed breakfast. Gail M. and Lisa arrived, as did a newspaper reporter who had heard about us from the lock attendant the day before and who wanted a photo of us departing. Gail M. introduced herself and handed me her business card, on which she called herself "Cracklen Rosie." The canoe Gail M. and Lisa paddled had "Cracklen Rosie" painted on the side. Lisa raised her eyebrows and said her mother had nine boats, all named after Neil Diamond songs. She was not as big a fan of Neil Diamond as her mother.

Gail M. had been a medical technician for thirty years and participated in the Mississippi Great River Rumble every year. The Great River Rumble was an annual week-long paddling trip that travels a different section of the Mississippi River each time. She proudly described herself as a river rat. River rat was an affectionate term for locals whose lives were completely enmeshed with the river and who spent a lot of time on the water. I asked her what her favorite things were about being a river rat, and she replied, "It's the nature and wildlife. It's calm and takes you away from the stress of life."

Lisa was much quieter than her mother. She had worked at the casino for six years making change for people. She beamed when she told us she had gotten married in July.

After some comical coordination, we got together for the reporter's photo and departed. Gail M. shared her knowledge of the area. When we passed under the Highway 61 bridge she said we were at the corner of three states: Wisconsin, Illinois, and Iowa. Passing downtown Dubuque, she pointed out a red brick building. It was the Dubuque Star Brewery, which was one of the oldest standing breweries in the country.

Next to the brewery stood a tall brick structure that looked like a smokestack. Gail M. informed us that it was a shot tower, used to make lead shot for muzzle-loading guns. It was built in the 1850s. She described how hot lead was poured through the screens built into the  top of the tower. The lead fell in spherical droplets into the water below, where it cooled and solidified into bullets. Most of the lead shot for the Civil War came out of that tower.

Gail M. talked about how button factories that used to be along the river had almost wiped out the clam population (which is still low). We passed a grand building on top of the bluff, which Gail M. said was a convent. On the bluff downriver from the convent stood a round, white stone tower that resembled the corner of a castle. It was a stone monument to Julien Dubuque, who established mining in Dubuque. He had been so accepted by the Meskwakis, a local Native American tribe, that he married the chief's daughter.

At Nine Mile Island, Kitty found a great horned owl feather lying on the beach. I found small pieces of river-worn clam shells with appealing spiral shapes. I gathered a few for future art projects. Ahead of us, Karen

P. drifted right under a tree limb stretched out over the water that had a bald eagle perched on it. The eagle watched her float past.

In Molo Slough I spotted what looked like two bright orange balls caught in some downed trees. I mentioned that they would make great gifts for our car support, and Cis fished them out of the debris. They were buoys with wire attached to them, so Cis and I tied the wires to our kayaks.

Gail M. and Lisa were strong paddlers and had no trouble keeping up with us in their canoe. Gail M. reached into her bag and pulled out a small bottle, faced us, and said, "This is how I determine the direction of the wind." She began blowing bubbles. They drifted and filled the air around us. It was ingenious and playful. Gail M. brought out the bubbles a couple more times before the day was done.

We began searching for a place to stop for lunch. A strange object ahead of us caught our attention. It looked like a jumble of blue and white pipes just off shore. When we got closer, we discovered the jumble

Kitty, Lisa, Gail M., and Nancy

was a table and chairs arranged on a small peninsula. We were astounded by our find. Karen P. pulled a fancy umbrella out of her kayak, stating that we needed an umbrella to complete the effect. We pulled up chairs and enjoyed lunch. Afterwards, we tied one of our orange buoys to a chunk of cement near the table for decoration and anchored a thank-you note in a Ziploc bag with a rock on the table.

Still buzzing with conversation, we noticed a man paddling upriver toward us. He introduced himself as Brian. He said every year he paddled 30 miles a day for three days from Clinton upriver to Dubuque. When we asked him why, he said, "It all started because of a woman. It's a long story." Unwilling to go further with the story, he said his wife would be waiting for him when he arrived in Dubuque, and he continued upstream.

At the mouth of Bates Creek, a squawking flock of crows swarmed out of the trees. The Twilight paddleboat headed in our direction. It was painted a stunning white with bright baby-blue trim and accents. Gail M. said it and other paddleboats traveled the river regularly, taking people on sightseeing tours.

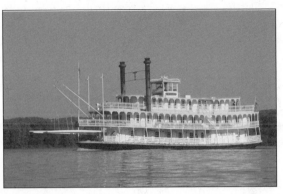

Fatigue was setting in, so I focused on simple things to distract myself. A barge passed, heading upriver. The waves gently lifted my kayak, and as I reached the peak of the wave, my boat twisted slightly. I hadn't noticed the subtle exchange between the water and my kayak before. I listened to what the waves sounded like as they hit the shoreline. Along shore, delicate, white asters dangled from the sandstone cliffs.

After turning into Bellevue Slough, I was relieved that it was only two more miles to Spruce Creek Public Use Area, where we would spend the night. Along the slough were homes of various sizes and colors. Kitty was astounded by another palm tree on a deck. This one was real, but dead.

Sherry had been busy again. Several people waited on the beach with her to greet us. Sherry directed us to a narrow slough that ran through the campground to our campsite. Cis, Karen P., Kitty, and I headed up the slough while Gail M. and Lisa headed to the boat launch, where they would meet Gail M.'s father. People ran to a footbridge over the slough to take our picture as we paddled into camp. I joked that the paparazzi were camping with us.

Photo by Karen Pauls

Sherry was quite proud that she had all the tents up, and even mine needed only minor adjustments this time. Cis and Karen P. set up their camp while Kitty, Sherry, and I went to the boat launch to say good-bye to Gail M. and Lisa. Gail M. said, "It was just great to meet two women who love the river as much as I do. I wish I could paddle a few more days with you, but I could only take one day off work." Her father arrived. He was a pleasant man and obviously proud of his daughter and granddaughter.

Gail M. wrote in the paddlers' journal:

> *Awesome day! Weather was perfect. It is always such a pleasure to enjoy the Mississippi River with other women. I have lived in Dubuque and on the water for 54 years. I really enjoyed sharing the local history with other paddlers. It was really special to have lunch at the table and chairs next to the water. Great group of women, just wished I could have done the whole trip. Good luck the rest of the way. May the river gods be with you.*

Lisa wrote in the paddlers' journal:

> *The day went so well. I feel that as I've gotten older I don't get out on the river as often, so it was very enjoyable to get out with my mom and meet other women who enjoy the river just like us. It was nice to hear the other people's experiences on the river. Everybody seamed to be having a great time, and it's too bad we can't continue. Wish you the best! Keep on paddling.*

Kitty, Sherry, Sue, Joe I., and Karen P.

Back at camp, Cis and Karen P.'s dinner was ready. While we prepared dinner, the strong and unpleasant smell of a pig farm wafted through the campground. We sat down to eat, and our neighbors, Sue and Joe I. from Enfield, Connecticut, brought us a lemon cake they had made for us in their RV. Sue said, "Just bring the empty pan back in the morning." Our eyes grew big; we knew there was no way we would eat the entire cake in one evening.

Trying to keep a straight face, Joe accused us of smelling up the place. Sue told him to knock it off, but he had us laughing. Later in my tent, I called Doug, feeling depleted. He offered me a lifeline by listening, and I went to bed feeling reassured.

September 21, Day Eighteen

Bellowing cows behind us and geese on the other shore woke us. The distant noise of traffic and civilization mingled with the sounds of nature. Trains were quieter than we were used to because the track was farther away and there were no whistles. Bellevue, Iowa, was one of the few towns in the country that had a law forbidding train whistles.

It was a rough night of sleep. I knew I needed a break to escape the feeling of being in a race. I raced in the morning to get on the water early, raced to get the details handled in a timely fashion, and raced to capture my experiences in my journal. The constant rush was dampening the fun, and I was beginning to question my abilities as a leader. We had a layover day scheduled in Savanna, so I focused on that.

The past few days I had begun to process my issue with people I viewed as controlling and who needed to tell me the "best" way to do something. I realized I was especially sensitive about the trip details, and I didn't like how I had responded to people who were just trying to be helpful and sharing opinions. What I heard instead was "You're doing it wrong." My fear of being wrong dated back to childhood, when I tried to follow in my mother's footsteps after she died. I felt like I could never do anything right. I realized I was taking things too personally on this trip. I wasn't that eleven-year-old kid anymore. That was a powerful realization. For me, understanding the reasons behind my reactions and behavior was half the battle.

I shared my realization with Kitty, who said that she thought I was having trouble with people on the trip partly because I had drawn such powerful women to participate in the adventure. She thought I had better get used to it. It felt like Kitty was justifying or defending the other women. Feeling unheard and resentful, I defended my position. I felt like she was analyzing me, and like my personal realization had been brushed aside while I listened to her tell me what was "really" going on. Sharing is a necessary part of how I process and learn. It helps me solidify issues so I can see what needs to change. When I shared my thoughts with Kitty, I was sensitive about being told how I should be doing something. I realized I needed to start conversations by stating that I just needed to be heard and didn't want an opinion. I wanted to say something to Kitty but didn't have the words just then, so I grew quiet. I talked to her again the next day and felt that we communicated better and that she heard me.

Traveling with Sherry gave us a sense of what it must feel like to be famous. Other people in the campground continually showed interest in us. On my way to the bathroom, two different people stopped me to ask questions about the trip. Both were amazed that women "our age" had traveled so far on the river.

Returning to camp brought my focus back to the day's travel. I went to Sue and Joe's RV to return the cake pan. Sue was surprised that the pan was still half full and insisted we take it in our kayaks for lunch. I appreciated the offer, but an unrefrigerated frosted cake on a day that was predicted to reach ninety degrees was not a good idea. As I said goodbye, she excitedly told me that we were on the cover of the Dubuque paper.

Back at camp Kitty and Karen P. were already floating in their boats in the slough. Cis was attempting to find a way to get in without stepping in the mud. A look of surrender crossed her face as her foot disappeared into the muck. Paddling past the campers who had lined up to bid us farewell, my earlier frustrations were washed away by a sense of accomplishment and pride. We were touching people.

Karen P. shared a story about a woman in camp who had asked why I was doing the trip. The woman assumed it was because I was recovering from a divorce or other major life trauma. We wondered why it was so hard for people to understand that women like adventure too. If a man were traveling the river, she probably wouldn't have asked the same question.

Asters in full bloom lined the shoreline leading to Lock and Dam No. 12 in Bellevue, Iowa. Cis pulled the cord to signal our arrival. As we paddled into the lock chamber, we heard Sherry overhead. She stood with a small group of people from the campground, and they all waved enthusiastically.

After fighting an exhausting headwind, we landed at Pleasant Creek Public Use Area and looked back four miles to the lock, feeling defeated. The lock looked too close to be worth the energy we had expended.

We looked at the charts during lunch, and I read aloud: Navigators are cautioned not to land or trespass on the Savanna Depot Activity, a U.W. Military Reservation, which extends from the main channel easterly to the Burlington, Northern, Santa Fe Railroad tracks between miles 542.2 and 558.5. For the next sixteen miles, we were not allowed to land on the eastern shoreline of the main channel. We wondered how strict they were about the heightened security after 9/11. The shoreline didn't appear to be any different than the one that we were sitting on.

A hot, blustery wind swirled at us from every direction. We searched for shade, but the channel offered none. To our delight, turtles visited us and fish jumped around us. I caught a glimpse of their tails as they disappeared into the dark green water. Leaves drifted down from the trees and blew onto the boat launches and shoreline. It felt like summer but looked like fall.

Trees on the eastern shoreline had been cleared and signs had been posted. The first signs for the military reservation tempted Cis to see what would happen if she landed on the shore. She wanted to know if there were cameras hidden along the shore to catch people. We waved toward the distant shore as if we were being watched.

We talked about the purpose of war and concluded that it had none. Life in all its forms was destroyed on both sides. We thought there must be a better way to handle disagreements and issues between countries. Kitty thought it must be a male thing. "Only men would do that. A woman wouldn't start a war. Maybe it is that warrior thing for them."

Pelicans graced our day. Small flocks floated near the shore or sat on sandbars. We passed a dock with car seats bolted to it. The seats still had the seat belts attached. Kitty joked, "That must be so they don't get pulled in when they catch a really big one."

Cis continued to move fast. We knew when her music changed because she paused while waiting to connect with the new rhythm. The type of music determined her pace. When we teased her, she said the music made paddling easier.

Looking for a shortcut, we turned into the narrows to get off the main channel. It was peaceful and shady. The water was clear with a sandy bottom. We didn't get far before we got stuck in the sand and had to walk. We got back into our boats near a dead tree that had

been chewed by a beaver. The wood showed no signs of weathering, which meant that the chew was relatively fresh. The beaver must have chewed the tree during a flood, because the chew was seven feet up the trunk of the tree.

We took another shortcut into a channel that would dump us into Savanna Bay, where our boat landing was. The waves and current at the mouth of the channel were strong and made it tricky to enter. Just beyond the mouth, tall grasses and lotus plants lined the channel. I paddled ahead, and suddenly the water became very shallow and vegetation closed off our path. Savanna Bay was just over the reeds, but we would have to turn around. The others were disappointed when they saw me paddling back in their direction.

Fatigue made the turbulent ride back out into the main channel more challenging. I paddled ahead to be sure the next route was not going to be another dead end. I rounded the end of the last island leading to Savanna Bay and saw wide open water. While I waited for everyone to catch up, I was surprised by the number of kayakers along the far shore. I counted fourteen boats in various sizes and colors, with some tandems in the mix.

A white kayak headed our way at full speed. When the kayaker reached us, he introduced himself as John and asked if we were the Minnesota ladies. When I said yes, he replied, "I thought so because of your graceful paddling." He went on to say that he had been sent by Sherry to escort us to the landing.

John and the rest of the kayakers were with a group out of Chicago called Moving Mountains. Moving Mountains provides opportunities for people with spinal-cord injuries to experience outdoor adventures. The group was at Mississippi Palisades State Park to enjoy rock climbing, biking, and kayaking. When we joined them, it was evident that they were

new at kayaking. All the activity of them maneuvering their kayaks looked like a game of bumper boats. Paddling to the landing among them was inspiring.

Sherry was focused on how she would get home the next day. Kitty and I looked at her with disbelief; it couldn't really be time for her to go. Getting Sherry home proved to be a challenge. I had misunderstood when she needed to be home. Gwyn, who would be rejoining us, was to drive her on Sunday, but Sherry needed to be home on Saturday. First thing in the morning, Kitty would drive Sherry back to La Crosse, where a friend of hers would pick her up.

Pat G., a friend of Cis and Gwyn's from St. Louis, arrived. Pat G.'s arrival was a planned surprise for Gwyn. I was surprised when Donna G., a friend of mine from Appleton, Wisconsin, strolled into camp. Then Karen P. was joined by her sister, Kay W. The women had all come for the Gathering. We sat around a picnic table talking.

Pat G.

"I grew up on the farm and I stayed there until I left at nineteen years old," said Kitty. "That was the only place I had ever lived. I moved Erin, my daughter, around quite a bit. We lived in the same town but in thirteen different houses or apartments before we settled in Ely. I never thought much about it until I was visiting with a lady who said her daughter had a hard time building long-term friendships because of all the moving they had done. I thought about what it had done to Erin, but it was too late to do anything about it."

"I married the exact opposite of what I grew up with," said Cis. "I grew up with my mom, dad, and two brothers. We were transferred coast to coast to coast all the time. My dad was in the Air Force, and my family was transferred sixty times in thirty years of service. I was lucky since I was the youngest. We would take a quick sweep through Texas where we had family and say hi to anyone who was around and keep on going. I couldn't even understand my relatives. I needed an interpreter because they had such a strong Texas twang. I said, 'Mom, who are these people?' 'These are your cousins.' 'Are you sure? I can't understand a word they say.'" We laughed.

"In hindsight, I realize it really did take me until my mid-forties to come out of my introverted shell. I think moving all the time became like shutting a door. I never kept in touch with anyone. I would have a best friend, but I would leave them and never think of them again. I did that all the time. Wow, what was that all about? My reaction time on that was like twenty years. I think I was just in shock the whole time."

"For an introvert to go through that all the time would be pretty tough." responded Donna G.

"I was so shy that I don't know if I would have even made friends in that situation," I added.

"I didn't have many friends," said Cis. "But if I had anyone, you'd think I would want to keep in touch with them. But no."

"Even with my stable base, I lived like that too," added Kitty. "Once I moved away from home, I didn't keep in touch with people for many years."

"I think keeping in touch with people is actually pretty rare," I said. "I see it in workshops where people connect in an intense way. They are convinced they will know that person for the rest of their life. Six months later, if you ask them if they have talked to that person, the answer is usually no. Maybe it is really about being here now. Maybe we can only concentrate on the people who are in front of us."

Fatigue set in, and one-by-one everyone drifted off to bed. Before I went to sleep I read what Cis had written in the paddlers' journal:

> In my 20s I once misheard the lyrics to a song. I thought they were "Being alone together." And being a loner in a world of people . . . it made perfect sense to me.
>
> We come into the world alone. We go out alone as well. It's what we do in between . . . I chose to be alone for more than 40 years even though I worked, married, and raised two children.
>
> In my 40s I learned the actual lyrics were "We belong together."
>
> Ahh . . . How true . . .
> We are all one.
> One river.
> One journey.
> Thank you.

September 22, Day Nineteen

Gunfire echoed across the river valley at sunrise. I headed to the river to sing. The gate to the campground was closed, so I stepped out of the van to open the gate. I put my foot on the ground and both felt and heard my knee pop out of place and snap back in again. A sharp pain shot through my leg. I stood next to the van, anticipating the intense pain to last, but it was short-lived. The consequences of what an injury would mean for the trip briefly passed through my mind, but I couldn't think about it. I proceeded to the water, stepping carefully on that leg.

Trucks with boats on trailers lined the parking lot, waiting their turn at the landing. Several more boats floated near the landing. I asked one of the men what was going on, and he said they were waiting for a fishing contest to start. I wandered down the shore for privacy and sang while the men in the boats watched with curiosity.

Back at camp, the pain in my knee returned, and I walked with a slight limp. The others noticed. Cis did healing energy work on it, and Karen P. gave me a homeopathic ointment to rub on it. The combina-

Kitty, Sherry, and Nancy

tion eased my discomfort, and Cis produced an ACE bandage to wrap my knee in.

We pulled everything out of the van we needed for the Gathering in case Kitty did not get back in time, and Sherry wrote in the paddlers' journal.

> *This has been quite a journey with Nancy and Kitty. Hearing about and seeing things on the river and experiencing the land and people and the towns was memorable. The trip has been rich for me. Plus it was the universe's answer to my desire for a long overdue vacation.*
>
> *Thank you for asking me to drive your car on the portion of your journey. Thank you for sharing your Spirit with me. The people that were pulled together to share themselves and their wisdom were the rich gifts you gave me.*
>
> *Much Love,*
>   *Sherry*

Donna G.

This was our layover day with no paddling, so after breakfast, Donna G. and I headed into Savanna, Illinois, to find internet access. On the steps of the closed library, our third attempt at finding internet access, a passerby said we would find it in Clinton, Iowa, 20 miles away. We headed across the Highway 52 bridge. The expansiveness of the farm country felt like a strange new land after so much time on the water. We arrived in Clinton, where the nation's first sawmill was built and which was once the world's largest lumber producer. The town used to be known as "Sawdust Town."

We located a coffee shop in an older downtown area. I made myself at home in a booth, got my laptop going, and discovered that they no longer had internet service. I was discouraged, but Donna G. remained determined. We ate lunch while I wrote the update for the past week. At the Clinton library I was finally able to load the update onto the website.

Our driving time ate up the day, but I enjoyed the time with Donna G. Approaching Savanna, we saw Council Bluffs. The bluffs had been a favorite place for Native American chiefs from a variety of tribes to meet and trade.

Back at camp, I headed to the shelter to set up for the Gathering. The other women jumped right in, hauling things and putting everything in place. Pat G. collected enough dead grass and pine cones for starting fires to last the remainder of the trip. Kitty pulled into the parking lot just as we finished setting up.

We were joined by Joyce and Marsha, who had seen an article about us in the local paper. They came to make arrangements to paddle with us. They didn't understand what the Gathering was about, but after some encouragement, they stayed. We had ten women in attendance ranging, in age from fifty to seventy.

SAVANNA GATHERING

Following protocol, we gave Joyce a mug as the elder, and I asked her to speak first. She began hesitantly. "Thank you all for being here. This is a new experience for me. I look forward to seeing what it is all about. I must say that turning seventy last month was not without trauma. But I get something free for being seventy," she said, holding up the mug, "so this is a first good step. Thank you."

Joyce

"I would like to talk a little bit about how spirituality has influenced my life," Cis chimed in. "I was raised without any spiritual life or religious life. I am only now finding out many, many years later why that was. What I learned was that my father was raised going to Presbyterian church services each week. He lost all faith when he was a prisoner of war in Germany. After seeing the ovens at the concentration camps, he said, 'God would NEVER have let that happen.' He never spoke about faith again.

"In many ways, it was a blessing not to be biased or influenced one way or the other. I have gotten to experience many paths, and I have learned that at the heart of them all is the one single truth, which is that we are all one."

"What struck me about this Gathering is that we're called grand-mothers whether we have children or not," Donna G. added. "I do not have children. So often when people ask me if I have kids and I say no there is a dead silence. Yet I have never felt like I haven't had children. I have wondered why that is. I think it goes back to my high school days. I went through a lot of parochial school, which was after the changes had happened in the church. We got a lot of 'love, love, love' classes. Each student took it their own way. One of the books given to us was called the Radical Bible. It talked about the population explosion and all sorts of stuff. One of the things it talked about was that we are all really responsible for children. We all have a part to play in raising them and helping people move forward. I just remember thinking to myself 'That is where I am at. That is for me.' So I worked a lot with youth groups in the past, I have done a lot with my nieces and nephews, and I have done a lot with friends' kids. I watched them grow up, and now they have kids. I feel like I am a grandma even though I am not. For some reason, it taught me to be a parent, and now grandparent, to a larger family. I appreciate being able to say I am a grandma."

"I just had to say something because Donna G. inspired me," said Pat G. "I am not one for saying how I feel, because I have a hard time doing that. What Donna just said is pretty much how I feel. Everything she said about being a grandmother is exactly how my life has been. I do not have children, but I have lots of nieces and nephews. I feel very blessed that I get along with all of my siblings, even though there are rough spots here and there. Basically, I have seventeen children, plus other children not even blood relatives. I feel very fortunate that I have that in my life. Even though I didn't bear children I feel like I have."

The talking stopped because Donna G. had a large number of caterpillars crawling on her. We helped her pull them off. She was the only one that happened to, but it happened twice more that evening. "What do you suppose they mean?" she asked.

"With that many climbing on you, I think you should look it up and find out, but I speculate they mean good luck and transformation," replied Cis.

"Oh, I like the sound of that," said Donna G.

"When we were paddling," Karen P. said, "sometimes people asked, 'What do you think about when you are paddling?' Part of the reason I like to paddle is that it gets me outside and it gets me outside myself. I tend to struggle too much within myself. So the ability to go out and have time to be responsible for myself on the water, paddling and having fun, is great. It is really like meditation for me, but when we're sitting around here and we're talking about what we would like to share in terms of wisdom, she is a whole lot smarter than me." She pointed to her sister Kay.

"I guess one of the things that keeps running around in my head, and I'm not sure if I just put it there as an excuse or a reason, is that I have been working at a religious publishing house for twenty years. I am not necessarily a denominational Christian. I am not necessarily a Christian, but I definitely believe in Christ and his good work. I am not concerned with the fine details of what happened and what didn't happen. Sometimes I think the reason I continue to work at the publishing house is that I am still trying to grasp some truth. I guess it's my own truth. I haven't found it yet. I am not waiting for an epiphany. I am not waiting for something to completely change. I keep kind of wondering and hoping that there will be something that will really click for me, but I am kind of slow, so the clicking takes awhile. I am sure I have changed significantly from when I first started working there. In terms of what my faith is, I guess I'm just not quite there yet."

"I want to talk about what I wrote in the paddler journal the other day," said Cis. "Like Karen P., when I am out paddling I am just in the moment. I don't think about anything. I am just part of the water, nature, and birds—just the beingness of heaven, earth, and the human realm.

"Back in my twenties I misunderstood a lyric in a song, but it made perfect sense to me. 'Being alone together.' That was pretty much how my life was. I am a loner, I am an introvert, and I am not a joiner. Even though I am together with a husband, raising a family, and working with people, I always felt like I was alone in the world. Then in my forties I had the epiphany, and the correct verbiage of the lyric came to me, which was 'We belong together.' [Laughter.] At that time in my life, I also had an awakening that this is a team effort in the world. It is okay to accept help and accept compliments, which I could never do. If somebody complimented me, I just, well, I didn't believe them. We belong together. Not being alone together." She shook her head, grinning.

"I have been married and I have two wonderful children," began Marsha, already tearful. "I lost my husband at fifty-five. He passed away of cancer. I have always been comfortable by myself and I understand what you say about being alone. I have a quite a bit of property, and I get out there on my tractor in the woods and think about everything. I just got a kayak last year. I enjoy the river. I enjoy nature, the birds, the fish, and the beautiful water. We go out on the Mississippi and I really have enjoyed it. I go out by myself a lot but also with friends. Life always takes a turn that you don't expect."

"I don't often speak at the Gatherings because I am busy writing notes," I interjected. "But there have been a couple of things I heard tonight that speak to me. I don't often tell my story anymore because it means something different to me than the way people often interpret it. I come from a family of eight kids. I was the oldest girl, with twin brothers one year older. My mother died when I was eleven, and I became the mother of my seven siblings. Cooking, washing, cleaning, all of that. When people hear about it they think it is a tragedy, 'Oh my God, you had a horrible childhood.' And yeah, some of it really stunk, but I look at it now as a huge gift, because I learned a lot of things as a result. I learned to make something out of nothing and to be independent. I learned many skills that people who didn't have to struggle at that age don't have.

"I've had things happen in my life that are often deemed to be tragedies, but I learned from them. I have been divorced. My ex-husband was an abusive alcoholic. As a result, I learned how to speak up and how to get out of there. My daughters were sexually abused by a family friend. I learned a great deal from them about how to heal a devastating wound by watching and assisting their healing process. As soon as the older one got into counseling, she started speaking about her experience in her junior high. She helped other abused kids get help.

"All of these perceived tragedies were opportunities for me to learn. I have learned so much from everybody involved in them—my sister, my grandmother, my father, my daughters, and my ex-husband. It all helped shape who I am. I learned persistence and endurance, sometimes to a fault. I did not have a role model for how to take care of myself, but I am getting better at that. For me, taking care of myself and relaxing is hard. When I do relax it doesn't always work out." Kitty started laughing.

"Kitty is laughing because she knows an experience I recently had while attempting to relax. Three weeks before this trip, my husband was mowing the lawn. Out of character, I decided to take a break. The weather was perfect, so I crawled into the hammock. I was lying there noticing the brilliant blue sky with the wispy clouds drifting by, watching Doug mow the lawn, and feeling slightly guilty. The rope holding the hammock was about five years old. I was three feet up in the air when the rope broke. My lower back slammed onto the rock-hard ground. Walking was very difficult. The next day we went to Duluth and I couldn't even carry the shoes I'd bought because they were too heavy. I was really concerned because it could have ended the trip. Luckily, with chiropractic care and exercises I was completely healed. It was one of those things where, damn it, I finally relax, and see what happens." [Laughter.]

"I obviously still have lessons in self-care to work through. When Cis talked about taking compliments, I related to that. Taking compliments has always been a challenge for me. As a child the adults in my life did not give compliments. They criticized. As an adult looking back on what they said to me, I see their perspective and I understand why they said things the way they did. As a child, I didn't hear them the way they meant them. I heard that I was bad, I was wrong, and I couldn't do anything right. Grandma, in particular, was just trying to teach me how to keep the house clean, how to do the laundry right, how to cook, and how to know when the floor was not quite clean enough. It was all well-intentioned, but that eleven-year-old girl who struggled to grow up fast got hurt. We were all in survival mode after my mom died."

Kay W. spoke. "I am an alcoholic. This Gathering is similar to AA meetings in that each person is given an opportunity to speak without being interrupted. I really enjoy AA, but it took me a long time to get there.

"I have three boys. I have been divorced for about five years and it has taken me that long to get to this point. I think age has something to do with it. I now feel more comfortable with who I am and comfortable with the authenticity of my life.

Kay W.

"From early on, I have always had a lot of mentors. I am the youngest of five. I would say that my siblings were a great influence on me but so were a lot of other people in my life that were spiritually directed. I think for a long time alcohol was a way for me to try and get in touch with that. It's really been in the last couple of years of not drinking, and it took me a long time to deal with the not drinking thing, that I began to deal with life on life's terms. In the last couple of years, I have gained a lot of acceptance as to what that means for my life. For a long time it was 'I have to accept that I am an alcoholic. I have to accept; acceptance is the key.' You hear that all of the time, but it was just in the last six months that it sunk in for me. I have read a fair amount of books on meditation and spirituality, and I am at the point now where I can accept it. I can accept the joy in my life. I am worthy. There is love and oneness in life, and now I can say, 'Hey, I am a part of it too.' And that is just so simple, yet it took me a long time to get to that point."

"Life is taking turns and I am wondering where it is going," Kitty said. "I think I must have started on the top of Mount Everest, and I am on the switchbacks coming down. Life has taken more turns than I could have imagined. I didn't realize it until tonight. The name of the poem I read at the start is 'Imagine a Woman.' I have been reading it at the beginning of every Gathering. Before we came on the trip, people would ask me about how I decided to go on the adventure of a lifetime. When I talk about it myself, frequently I can't imagine that this is my life I am talking about. And so the 'imagine' came in even before I started reading that poem. Today I sit here and I can't imagine this is my life. I could not have dreamed this up a year ago. Something like this wasn't even on the horizon. I am very grateful that I am in a space to be open enough to accept this kind of challenge, this kind of adventure.

"Life's circumstances have not taken me where I thought they would. Not at all. I also am a recovering alcoholic. I have been recovering for a number of years. This is only the second place where I am able to sit with people who listen to what is being shared at this level.

"When I started the trip, I thought I was on this mission to just shut up and listen, and that hasn't quite been the case. I have so much to learn, and I hope I never get to a place where I think I have learned all there is to learn. I think back on life and what I thought were miracles going on in my life. Here I sit, and I am whole and healthier, well, I don't know about physically, but I am healthier spiritually than I ever have been in my life. That has truly been a gift for me."

"I was thinking about the importance of joy in everyone's life even when you know that you are going through a bad time or that things are not quite right," Karen P. said. "I think Kay was saying things have changed in the last six months and that sometimes when something does click with you, you almost don't believe it at first. We think 'That was too easy.' I may not be having a good day, but suddenly in my head and in my heart I can say, 'Well, you closed down a little bit; you have got to open up.' Mentally I think about unfolding and opening up and softening and not being so hard on other people, or so hard on myself. Suddenly things start being joyful. Suddenly I am able to see something new; it might just be a vine growing up on a red building, which is exquisitely beautiful because the sun is shining on it. I might not have seen that if I had been closed down inside. That is part of the thing about opening up: we can feel more and see more. It is an everyday process for me. It isn't easy. When I am one hundred I hope to still be seeing more and feeling more and still reminding myself that I have to keep opening up."

During a lull in conversation, my thoughts turned to something I had been pondering while paddling. "I would like to pose a question that I have been thinking about on the river. What does it mean to be a powerful woman?"

"I think what it means to be a powerful woman is to trust yourself and to know when to trust others and to be authentic," responded Cis. "I see it in the vastly contrasting life I have had. I would spend a day scraping bird shit and cutting up rats, mice, and road kill for the hawks I was working with. Then that night, I would dress up and go out to some cocktail party with my husband. [Laughter.] The contrast has often left me in doubt, maybe until my fifties."

"I found that losing my husband at such an early age helped me realize that there is not much I can't do for myself," said Marsha. "I found I could change the oil in the tractor. I have a chainsaw, and I go back in the woods and cut up trees. I don't like asking people for anything unless I can pay them. I don't want to be obligated. I can do almost anything I decide to do. There hasn't been anything I have tried to do that I haven't done. Powerful woman!"

"There have been a few comments made by different people about being present in the here and now, whether it is kayaking or something else that brought you to that point," added Donna G. "I know when I get to that point I feel my own power. I think that is part of it, not being in the past or the future, but being present gives power. As I listen to people talk about power, one thought I have is that getting in touch with your power and honoring that power puts you on a solo path, and you feel like an outsider. I think having that power gives you a different perspective than what other people have around you, but you recognize them when you find someone who has also been on that path."

"I don't think of myself as a powerful woman," Kitty said. "Yet, to have even gotten this far in life there has to be power for survival and existence. What I am trying to do with my life from here forward is enjoy it more. To get out of the survival and existence mode and to find what it is that I like to do in life."

The air had grown cold as the sun set, and Donna G. stood up and said, "I am not going to sit down, because I have discovered, with my utmost wisdom, that I will be purchasing a sweatshirt, right now." We all laughed. She and Kitty headed to get a sweatshirt for her while we continued.

"I know that sometimes when we say something, we think it isn't wisdom; it's just common sense," I continued. "But it can be the simple things we share that are absolutely profound to other people who have not had the same experiences or thought about it in the same way. Maybe you thought that what you shared was just a cute story, but it has the power to deeply touch someone. People found things profound that I did not necessarily find that way. Our paths set us up to see and experience things differently."

After the closing ritual, the conversation continued. Marsha asked me, "We thought we might like to join you if you'll accept a couple of vagabonds."

"Absolutely. These two vagabonds joined us for the past few days," I said, indicating Karen P. and Cis. "We can go over our itinerary tonight before you leave. Some days we do long paddle days, but you don't have to do the whole thing."

"Well, we weren't going to," Joyce interjected. "We're just here for the dessert." We laughed. "I'm not out there when it's hot. I don't need any more hot flashes."

"Oh, please tell me you are over hot flashes," said Kitty with concern.

"Oh, my estrogen levels just keep playing around," Joyce replied.

"I don't think I even want to hear that," responded Cis.

Marsha and Joyce headed home while we congregated around the table at camp to enjoy an eclectic feast. We shared wine, juice, cheese curds, salami, veggies, and more.

"Donna, what do you do?" asked Kitty.

"I'm an instructor at a technical college, teaching web design and development courses," Donna G. answered. "I am a long-term sub for someone on sabbatical. I'm hoping it's one foot in the door, but right now it feels like one foot out the door."

"See it like you want to see it and make it happen," Cis said.

"That's what I'm trying to so," Donna G. replied. "Last week one of the other teachers asked me how things were going. She said 'I remember how it was. I was underwater for a whole year, just reading, studying, and trying to keep up.' She went on to say that she thinks the people who have been there for a long time forget what it was like when they started."

"The first year I taught a wetland class at the two-year college in Ely, I struggled with all the prep," said Kitty. "I was working four jobs. I felt like I didn't do the class justice. The second year was a bit better. It is very time-consuming to figure out how you want to present it."

"I'm teaching overtime," said Donna G. "I have six courses and five subjects."

"Oh, my God," said Kitty, Cis, and I in unison.

"I have only taught one of the subjects before," said Donna G. "I am constantly learning the material to stay ahead of the class."

"Are you teaching HTML or other programming?" asked Kay W.

"I'm not doing HTML, I'm doing scripting," answered Donna G. "I'm doing Java Script, PHP, and XML."

"Anyone else hearing a foreign language here?" I teased, acknowledging the confused looks on everyone's faces.

"Java–that's coffee, right?" Cis joked. We laughed. Donna G. and Kay W. continued to talk computers while the rest of us moved on.

"Did you see the paper? We are in the paper," Cis exclaimed. "It wasn't the front page, but we are all in the picture, and it is a very esoteric shot. If you look carefully you can tell who we are. The reporter didn't need to take names, but it was sweet. The caption is hysterical, 'Oars Away'." We giggled. Cis retrieved the paper and said, "I'm sorry, it's even better than I remembered. The caption is 'Oar Else.'"

"You're kidding," I responded, and read the caption to the photo out loud. "'A group of women head out on the Mississippi River after camping in Dubuque. The group of paddlers is part of the Water Women Wisdom group that is making a 620-mile journey from Red Wing, Minnesota, to St. Louis, Missouri.' It's not a bad photo."

"Where is the rest of the story?" asked Kitty.

"No, that's it. That's all she wrote," answered Cis.

"At least they got the information right," I said. "A reporter interviewed me for an hour and a half by phone and I gave her the website for more information. When the article came out, I was astounded: she got the river, the year, my name, and the state wrong."

"Yes, but was it positive?" teased Karen P.

I wanted to talk all night, but I knew I would be sorry in the morning if I didn't sleep. I snuggled into my sleeping bag, delighted by the warmth it provided on a chilly night, and drifted off to sleep feeling grateful.

September 23rd through 27th

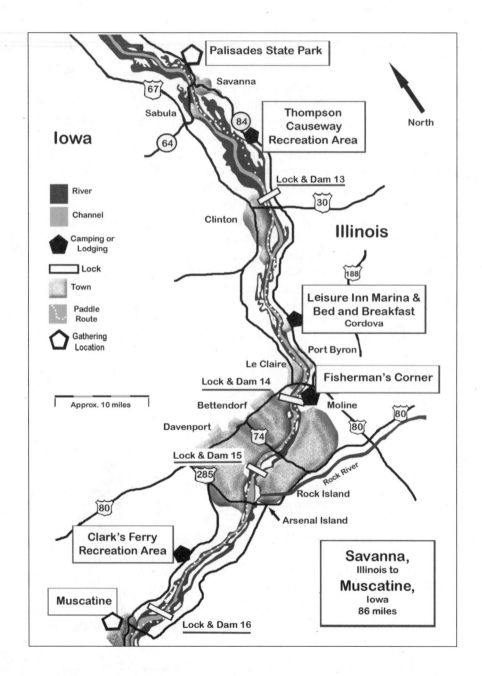

Palisades State Park

Savanna

67

Sabula

64

84

Iowa

Thompson Causeway Recreation Area

North

Lock & Dam 13

30

River

Channel

Clinton

Illinois

Camping or Lodging

Lock

188

Town

Leisure Inn Marina & Bed and Breakfast
Cordova

Paddle Route

Gathering Location

Port Byron

Le Claire

Fisherman's Corner

Lock & Dam 14

Approx. 10 miles

Bettendorf

Moline

80

Davenport

74

80

Lock & Dam 15

285

Rock River

80

Rock Island

Arsenal Island

Clark's Ferry Recreation Area

Savanna,
Illinois to
Muscatine,
Iowa
86 miles

Muscatine

Lock & Dam 16

Savanna to Muscatine

September 23, Day Twenty

My knee was still tender and slightly swollen, but the ointment and wrapping had helped. The campsite buzzed with activity. Cis handed me a clamshell pendant. The shell had been polished until the mother-of-pearl glistened. She said, "This shell represents your journey down the river healing broken spirits. As I travel the river, I often see little clamshells that have been opened like butterfly wings. That is well and natural, but when I look at this and consider the journey you're on, I know you are making many spirits whole again." I was touched.

A few moments later, Gwyn arrived with another woman. Gwyn walked up to the table and joined our conversation. When she finally noticed Pat G., her surprised reaction was hilarious. Gwyn and Pat G. had not seen each other for several years. Gwyn introduced her companion, Kay M., an innkeeper in Savanna at the bed-and-breakfast where Gwyn had stayed.

"Are you coming to the Gathering in Muscatine?" Kitty asked Kay M.

"Yes, she is," announced Gwyn with a firm tone we recognized.

"I just met Gwyn and she's already telling me how to run my life," Kay M. laughed. "You guys opened a door that I didn't know was there, and now I am seeing all this wonderful stuff."

Kay M. had recently separated from her husband after fifty years of marriage. At sixty-nine she started over and was confident about her decision. She said if she had stayed with him, she wouldn't have met us because he never let her go anywhere.

While we broke down camp, Kay M. and Donna G. sat at a table near us talking.

"I didn't even know about this group," Kay M. said. "There is so much out here I don't know about. Everyday life is like a circus with everybody busy running their lives. When my kids were young, I was

PTA president, which was the usual routine. In my generation that's what we did. Even if you became a nurse or a teacher, your first responsibility was as a wife and a mother.

"Isn't it marvelous here! I wish I could capture this all in paintings, but I have it in my mind. It's the same way with writing—I just don't have the patience to sit down and put my thoughts in a journal."

"Ever think of tape-recording your ideas?" asked Donna G

"You know, I kind of wondered about that," responded Kay M. "I'm always encouraging other people to tape their parents' stories. I recorded my mother's stories several times. I learned how to ask the right questions. You know, not just when and where you were born, more like what you and your friends did when you were teenagers. I found out she was quite a rascal. Things have changed a lot for people at my age. My kids don't know what an outhouse is or what it means to pump water. Kids don't understand what it was like before computers or cable TV. When I was first married, we were thrilled to have a TV; we all had to decide what station to watch when the children were little. It's a whole different life-style now from the way it was ten or fifteen years ago, let alone fifty. When I was a young married woman, our attitudes were different. Oh, there is another mosquito. They must like me; I must be getting juicy or raunchy."

"They say that if you go a month without a bath, the mosquitoes will leave you alone," I said.

"Them and everybody else," joked Kay M. "My husband was never one to worry about what people thought, or else he was too busy working all those extra hours to notice. I was the one who was involved in the small-town activities. Once in a while I wonder what Ol' So and So thinks now that I've left town and I'm on my own. I just love being different now and, God willing, I'm healthy. I want to be the older lady in town that folks talk about and say, 'Oh God, now what is she up to?' I would like that. I got a tattoo a few years ago. It's just a little shamrock with a harp on it. If I end up in a nursing home, I want them to say, 'I think the lady with the shamrock tattoo needs her vitamins today.'

"There is so much in the world that people miss, because they are distracted by everyday living. You got to feed the kids and do this and that, when what we need to do is just sit still and look at the world. How can anybody deny that there is a higher power?"

"Exactly," agreed Kitty.

While the women were talking, I called WELY—the radio station back home—because radio host Ray Nargis had wanted to interview me about the trip. I told the women, "Let's get on the water and I'll call the station again. Ray said he just got a long list of personal and emergency messages to read."

"Is that a reporter?" asked Kay M. "What personal messages?"

"It's our home-town radio station," I answered. "They regularly do personal and emergency messages because there are people in Ely without phones."

At the boat launch, a peregrine falcon soared overhead. Kitty and I floated offshore while I was briefly interviewed by Ray. Swallows swirled

above the water. They flew so fast and so close to the surface that we imagined they would do a somersault if their beaks touched the water. In Savanna Bay, the morning sun turned the trees along the rolling bluffs vivid green. Boat traffic was already buzzing.

People fished along shore. We saw four women doing jumping jacks on the beach. We laughed when we realized it was Gwyn, Pat G., Karen P., and Cis trying to get our attention. They had gone to Kay M.'s bed-and-breakfast to prepare lunch for us. We landed our boats and walked across the railroad tracks to Kay M.'s. We saw small, round pellets lying on the railroad bed. They looked familiar, but I couldn't recall where I had seen them before.

Kay M. gave us a tour of the Blue Bed-and-Breakfast and showed us one of her paintings. Back in the kitchen, a variety of cheeses and lunch meats were laid out. We ate our sandwiches on the deck overlooking the river.

Crossing the tracks after lunch, Kitty picked up one of the round pellets and asked if it was taconite.

"That's why I recognized it," I replied. Taconite pellets are produced on the Iron Range of Minnesota, and we are used to seeing them back home. We wondered where the pellets were being shipped that had brought them through Savanna.

Back in our boats, we ducked into narrow Savanna Slough. We heard something that sounded like an airplane approaching. Around a bend came a DNR airboat, which quickly passed us. I felt like I had been transported to the Florida Everglades. The large fan on the back, which propelled the boat, fascinated me. I wondered how the DNR could catch poachers if their boat could be heard a mile away.

A muskrat swam along the shore next to us, undisturbed by our presence. The river was calm and peaceful. We noted the stark difference in water quality between the sloughs and the big water. The slough water was green and muddy, while the channel water was clear.

The weekend boat traffic became a challenge to navigate. Teenagers on Jet Skis and knee boards raced past. A speedboat headed straight at us as we passed between two islands. It didn't veer away until the last moment and made no attempt to slow down. It was especially disturbing because the driver had been looking right at us the entire time.

There were more duck blinds in a large bay. Some were built from scrap lumber, and some had been out there so long that they had deteriorated and weren't safe to use. One duck blind had a garage for the boat. The blinds were covered with vegetation, which was called brushing. We began to refer to duck blinds as "big boys' forts."

We passed through dense weedy areas, which made paddling difficult. The pelicans and herons ahead of us were easy to identify from their silhouettes, but a taller bird was among them. Standing in shallow water near an island were sandhill cranes. We paddled slowly to enjoy the rare sighting. The cranes emitted their prehistoric-sounding call and flew a few yards ahead, landing in a larger group of pelicans. Shallow water prevented us from getting any closer.

Randomly throughout the day, a single monarch butterfly would flit over the water and provide us with a distraction from the growing heat. We put on long-sleeved shirts to protect our skin from the sun and dipped our arms in the water to cool ourselves down.

The last three miles of our fourteen-mile day were on big water. The river here spanned four miles, which made us feel like we weren't making any progress.

Gwyn and Pat G. greeted us at Thomson Causeway Recreation Area. The shoreline was rocky and was thick with duckweed and an unpleasant smell. Frogs of all sizes croaked in unison and jumped across the top of the duckweed before submerging along the shore.

We were surprised to find Kay M. sitting at camp, awaiting our arrival. She chatted for a bit but headed home before long to avoid driving after dark. Pat G. had decided to stay with us for the weekend and

intended to do a lot of cooking. Using an electric skillet, she made a dinner with fresh vegetables from her garden. The meal was incredible.

A woman pulled up with a kayak on her car. She eagerly introduced herself as Bonita. She bubbled with enthusiasm as she told us that she wanted to paddle with us in a couple of days. She had become an avid paddler when she retired. She participated in the Great River Rumble every year and had paddled the length of the Missouri River in 2004. After visiting for a while, we exchanged contact information and she headed home.

As the sun set, a large, squawking flock of terns flew overhead. The hazy sky turned several soft shades of orange as darkness settled in, and a great horned owl called long into the night.

September 24, Day Twenty-One

A distant industrial plant droned throughout the night. There were gunshots at sunrise again, but it was a nearby sandhill crane's call that motivated me to get up. I dressed quickly and crawled out of the tent. The muck and stinky duckweed were worse than the night before. Dozens of frogs leaped in every direction. Pat G. was making bacon and eggs when Gwyn crawled out of her tent and introduced us to her sleeping companion. She had discovered a tiny, lime-green tree frog that had crawled into her sleeping bag with her. We sat at the breakfast table noticing how the cornfields across the river looked like sand dunes. The gold of the dried cornstalks contrasted vividly with the green around them.

Over the past few days, Kitty had begun to join me in singing the sacred song in the mornings. As we finished, a flock of geese rose off the water. Then a flock of ducks took off, headed toward the Iowa shore. Kitty and I warned them, "Turn back! Iowa is not safe for you right now!" They didn't listen.

Under a clear sky, we crossed four miles of big water to Lock & Dam No. 13. Because of the width of the river, I had assumed that the water would be deep, but even in the middle we passed weed beds and tree stumps. I had forgotten that much of what we paddled used to be dry land with trees. I couldn't picture what it looked like before it had flooded.

We passed through Lock No. 13 uneventfully and missed Sherry waving to us from up top. We paddled between Fulton, Illinois, and Clinton, Iowa, beneath a railroad bridge that was under construction. One of the workers yelled down that they wanted to join us.

Immediately after the bridge the waves became intense. The breeze that had cooled us earlier became a warm headwind. For relief from the wind, we ducked into Beaver Slough and paddled next to the Clinton industrial area with Beaver Island on our left. The island, lush with trees

Photo by Kitty Kennedy

and foliage, stood in dramatic contrast to the industrial area. We stopped for a break on Beaver Slough Ramp. A fisherman pulled in and was surprised that we had chosen to stop there. As he loaded his boat on his trailer, he told us that the area was known as Stinky Clinton.

I grew concerned that we would not arrive in Cordova, Illinois, on time. I was scheduled to make a presentation about the trip at the public library that evening. The headwind had slowed us, and we were pushing harder than I wanted to. I would need to rest, eat, and cool down before I could deliver a good presentation.

We hugged Beaver Island while observing the construction and industrial buildings on the opposite shore. A heron sat on a log, also apparently watching the industrial activity. Across from the heron a large pipe dumped something into the water. We speculated that it might be toxic and paddled so our hands didn't touch the water.

The headwind had churned up three- and four-foot swells in the main channel. We paddled hard and aimed at a slight angle across the waves, headed for Meredosia Island. For the rest of the day, there was no escaping the wind. It whipped down every possible opening and only grew hotter. A desire to quit rose in me. It took a great effort to push forward.

A tiny island three miles from our destination provided a brief respite from the heat and waves. We floated for a few moments and enjoyed a drink of warm water. As we neared the end of the island, the Cordova water tower came into view. I dug for my camera. Kitty asked what I was doing as I took a picture of the water tower. I replied, "I am taking a picture of hope." She laughed.

Cordova supposedly got its name because one of the original residents, a Scandinavian immigrant, had only learned to count to ten in English. He sold cord wood to the paddleboats. When he told the captains how much wood he loaded onto their boats he told them how many "cords ova" ten it was. The captains started calling the landing "cord ova." However, that story was disputed. It's also believed that the town was named after a city in Spain.

Even with the end in sight, the desire to quit was relentless. The water tower didn't seem to get any closer. Discouragement multiplied with each paddle stroke. I told Kitty that if we saw someone with a pontoon I'd ask for a ride, but we were alone on the water. We knew we could pull up on shore at any time and Gwyn would pick us up. I found myself scoping out the docks and the embankment for a possible landing spot, but each time I picked one out, I told myself, "Just keep going; the end is right there."

At last our hotel, the Leisure Harbor Inn Bed & Breakfast and Marina, came into sight. We were greeted by Gwyn, Pat G., and Del, who eagerly helped us get our boats out of the water. My discouragement melted when I saw their smiling faces. Del, dressed in coveralls, was a Cordova resident I had met while he was vacationing in Ely. He was excited to learn that we would travel through his town, and he had connected me with his daughter Cheryl, the town librarian, who scheduled the presentation. Del came to check on us because he was worried about the heat and wind.

Nature taunted us. Shortly after we arrived, the wind stopped. We had paddled for nine hours with only one break. I went up to my room, showered, and lay down for a few moments. On the porch, Pat G. was making stir-fry for dinner. Walking through the lobby, I met Linda, the owner of the inn. She served us heavenly ice-cold lemonade.

The Leisure Harbor Inn was lovely. Linda had a fascinating collection of antiques and knickknacks displayed in the rooms. It had been Linda's dream to run a bed and breakfast and Bob's dream to own a marina. They seemed very happy. One of the striking things about Bob was the way he treated his wife. He adored and respected her. Seeing the way he spoke with and watched over her warmed my heart.

The screened-in porch had a view of the calm water and was a perfect place to unwind before the presentation. As I walked to the library, I saw my name in lights on the Cordova library marquee. We walked into a modern library, which was larger than I expected for a town of only six hundred people. The local power company had been generous during the library's construction. Inside, the library had murals on the walls painted by a local artist. Del greeted us and made sure we had everything we needed.

During the presentation and slide show, I talked about and shared women's stories from the previous trip. I told the audience that, contrary to what many people believed, the trip was not about man-bashing. Many of the women I had spoken with focused on how men and women could communicate better. The presentation concluded with questions from the delightful audience about the details of the current trip.

We walked back to the bed-and-breakfast under a beautiful, starry sky. There were lights in the distance across the calm water. We received a message from Barb H. saying that she would meet us in the morning for breakfast. She had been traveling and was headed home to Ely.

The gentle sound of wind chimes ended our day. We decided it was angels letting us know that they traveled with us. I easily drifted off to sleep.

September 25, Day Twenty-Two

The bed was so comfortable that I had to pry myself out of it. Tantalizing aromas drifted in from the kitchen where Linda was preparing breakfast. I called Doug to wish him a happy twenty-fifth anniversary. I thought he would be up getting ready to go to the shop, but he was enjoying a lazy morning in bed.

Linda, Pat G., Barb H., Gwyn, Nancy, Kitty

The table was set elegantly, and the food had been prepared from scratch. There was egg bake, coffee cake, muffins, fresh fruit, and juice. The conversation about our trip with Barb H., Linda, and Bob was lively.

Bob said he was glad I had pointed out at the presentation that the Gatherings were not about man-bashing. He had been nervous about that before the presentation, and he thought it was important that I keep sharing that information. He felt the project was extremely important. His wife, Linda, had struggled with cancer. It helped to him to hear what other female cancer survivors had said about enjoying life after cancer.

It was drizzling and looked like it would rain all day. We paddled across the river to Princeton, Iowa, to meet Marsha, sixty-nine, and Joyce, seventy, the oldest paddlers who would join us on the trip. We met them in front of the Go Fish restaurant, and despite the rain, they eagerly climbed into their kayaks.

Paddling with them was delightful. At one point, Joyce called out to a man on the shore about a pickup truck parked near his home. She seemed to be very familiar with that model. She said she had a '57 pickup that had been her father's. She stated proudly that everyone in the family had learned to drive in that truck.

Joyce was divorced. Her husband had been a political reporter and hadn't been home much. Her daughter used to think that Joyce went to the airport to pick up her husband when she wanted to visit with him, and when she was tired of him she drove him back to the airport. Joyce pointed out her house and farm as we paddled past it. She owned the last farm in the area, and it had a large orchard. She was proud of her home and its heritage.

Marsha told us she had been a stewardess for United Airlines. Kitty and I found it interesting that she used the term stewardess rather than flight attendant, since stewardess has not been used for over a decade. Her husband was a pilot for United Airlines. When they got married, the United Airlines policy was that the wives of pilots had to quit their jobs. When

Marsha

United changed the discriminatory rule, her husband mentioned that she should get retroactive pay like some of the other wives. She decided not to because she didn't think it was fair to United.

Nearing Le Claire, we spotted a swan among a small group of decoys. A barge had its front end pushed into the shore. Joyce and Marsha told us that the barges pushed up against the shore like that when they needed supplies. Once they were stable against the shore, the crew members got off and went into town. It hadn't occurred to me how they got supplies on the barges, but it made sense that you couldn't just pull a barge up next to a dock and tie it down for a few minutes. Paddling around the back of the running tug that was holding the barge in place, Joyce tooted a little "ooga ooga" horn at the barge.

Joyce and Marsha told us about the annual tug-of-war contest between Le Claire, Iowa, and Port Byron, Illinois, located directly across the river from each other. The tug-of-war was the only time river travel was shut down. The Tug Fest had been going on for twenty years. Ten twenty-member teams pulled on a 2,400-foot, 680-pound rope that spanned the river—over a quarter mile. The prize was an alabaster statue of a bald eagle in flight.

Nearing Le Claire, Joyce pointed out a tiny, white house where Buffalo Bill Cody had grown up. It began to rain harder. For lunch, we all headed into a restaurant called Sneaky Pete's.

Kitty, Joyce, Marsha, and Nancy

All along one wall were thousands of business cards, many yellowed from age. Hanging from the rafters were thousands of ties that had been cut off of men who wore them into the restaurant. The staff didn't used to ask before cutting them off.

"Has there been anything on the river that has scared you?" asked Marsha. "When Joyce and I talk about kayaking we always hear, 'Isn't that dangerous?'"

"Oh sure, and it usually had to do with fast-moving water." I responded. "I just bought my kayak in June," Kitty added. "I am not real experienced. Kayaking at this kind of level is not something I thought I would be doing. We took a class before we left. We learned to flip it over and get back in, which is the hardest part. Learning how to do all of that took ninety percent of the fear out of kayaking for me."

"We go out in the big water sometimes," Joyce added, "but not if the weather is bad."

"For the most part we are out there, bad days and good days," I said.

"If there were lightning you would get off the river, wouldn't you?"

Marsha asked, concerned.

"Absolutely, if there were lightning," I said. "If we see a storm coming, we prepare for it."

"We found it is just as hard to paddle downriver as it is up," Marsha joked.

"We noticed that too," replied Kitty, smiling.

Our time with Joyce and Marsha ended, and we launched our kayaks. At Le Clair, the Mississippi makes a ninety-degree turn and heads west for forty-three miles until it reaches Muscatine, where it flows south again.

Paddling up to Fisherman's Corner North Recreation Area, we discovered a wall of dense, green lotus and reeds standing tall out of the water between us and the shore. We could see the campground but no boat launch. We made our way through the lotus, using any openings we found. A man named Dale guided us to a spot to take out our boats. He had met Gwyn and Pat G., who had asked him to watch out for us, and said they were not back from town yet.

Dale was talkative. He told us he was an old Harley rider who used to go to Sturgis for the big bike rally, though he didn't go anymore because he said there was "a new breed of idiots" that he didn't want to be a part of. Dale was knowledgeable about hunting season and filled us in on what we could expect for the rest of the trip.

Kitty and I lay down in the tents for a short nap. Gwyn and Pat G. returned from an afternoon spent touring Le Claire with Barb H., who went back to her campsite to tend to her dog, Ginger.

A large RV was parked next to us with a huge picture window facing us. A gentleman sat at a table inside, and I felt him watching us. I teased that the window was his "big screen TV" and that we were the entertainment. The man in the RV came out and began talking. He was a retired sheriff. He had heard about our trip and wanted to see who was paddling. He wanted to know how old we were. After a long look he said, "I guess you're not old and not young." He headed back to his RV and after a few moments came back with a soda for each of us. He and his wife lived at the park because it was closer to his wife's work than their home. She had worked for the government for thirty years. Living at the park saved her a fifty-mile commute each way. They could stay in a given campground for two weeks, and then they switched with another couple at a different campground. People in the park visited with each other often. RV parks were little communities.

A light rain started as Pat G. and Gwyn began cooking dinner, which included a freshly baked pie. Pat G. pulled an umbrella from her car to cover herself and the frying pan. By the time we ate, it was raining hard. We were huddled under the one umbrella in our rain gear as best we could when the sheriff came out of the RV with two large umbrellas for

Photo by Kitty Kennedy

us. Dale came running up with another one. We had enough to cover the entire table. We laughed through dinner, clustered under the umbrellas.

"This is my wedding anniversary," I announced.

"Happy anniversary!" everyone said.

"We had a conversation with Joyce and Marsha earlier about the magic formula for relationships and how they transition through things that come along in life," I said. "They said it was about acknowledging an issue or challenge in the relationship and then working on it."

"They said it was important that both parties know there is a transition happening and have a willingness to stick with it," added Kitty.

"I know when Doug and I do that we come out ahead of where we started," I added. "Things seem to be stronger and more meaningful."

"Wow, that's cool," commented Barb H.

We took turns holding the umbrellas. The barge we had paddled around passed through Lock No. 14 on the other side of the river. "I was thinking that hot chocolate would be good right now," I said. "But that means a whole different arrangement for us and the umbrellas, so I'll just wait." We laughed. Along the shore, lotus leaves danced in the wind and rain, and I pointed them out.

"I was looking at them when we pulled in," commented Kitty. "The only way they photosynthesize is that one huge leaf on top." We watched the leaves dance for a bit, then did the dishes and headed for bed under the constant rain.

September 26, Day Twenty-Three

Barb H. headed home early. We drove to Fisherman's Corner South Recreation Area with our kayaks loaded onto the van. Pulling away from camp, we saw a newspaper reporter's car and slowed so it could follow us. While we put the kayaks in the water, the reporter asked several questions and the photographer snapped pictures. I always got nervous about what to say during impromptu interviews. When it was over, I hoped I'd been articulate.

The sky was clear and the water calm. We looked forward to the lack of wind but knew the heat would take a toll if it stayed calm.

Paddling past Campbell's Island, we noticed a tall, white pillar constructed near the shore. We pulled over. According to the inscription, the monument was built in 1906 in memory of four Illinois Rangers, one woman, and one child who died in 1814 during a fight with the Fox Native Americans. A copper relief depicted the fight. Adjacent to the pillar, four cannons were aimed out at the water. Kitty could not resist looking down the barrels.

South of the monument was a peace garden. The garden honored the history of the Native Sauk and Mesquakie tribes who lived in the area in the 1800s. Animal figures were carved into the concrete floor, and tile mosaic risers depicted Native beadwork. At the center was a turtle with a flower garden on its back.

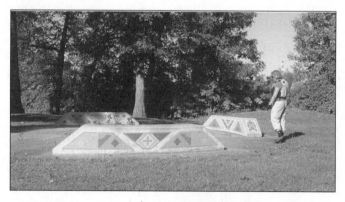

We paddled between the towns of Moline, Illinois, and Davenport, Iowa. They are part of the Quad Cities, which is a source of great pride for the residents and which also includes Rock Island, Illinois, and Bettendorf, Iowa. Above the shoreline in Moline was a strikingly green, manicured, terraced hill. Downtown, paddleboats were parked along the shore, and the shoreline became more industrial with loading docks and warehouses.

Rock Island came in sight. My daughter Naomi had toured Rock Island—a military arsenal—earlier in the year. She had been told that anyone docking on the island would be immediately arrested. There were beautiful brick buildings on the island that made it resemble a private estate.

A barge was parked on the Iowa shore. We assumed it was waiting to go through Lock No. 12. We called the Lockmaster, who said a tug was locking through and it would be a forty-five-minute wait. We paddled around the lock wall, got out, and went inside an interpretive center that was part of the lock complex.

Davenport homestead on Rock Island

Rock Island was used as a prisoner-of-war camp during the Civil War. Some buildings were part of the George Davenport homestead, built in the early 1800s by the Confederate prisoners held there. Before the dam was built, there was a dangerous set of rapids in the area called the Rock Island Rapids, and the island was named after them. Standing on the observation deck, we watched the tug lock through. The barges were already waiting on the upriver side. The lock was unique because a bridge crossed directly over it. When a tall boat locked through, such as a tug, the section of bridge over the lock rotated open in a circle. Traffic stopped on the bridge until the boat cleared.

Once the tug was through the lock, we scrambled back to our kayaks, knowing the Lockmaster would be expecting us to get into the lock quickly. We floated behind the lock wall, waiting for the tug to pass. I called Naomi to inform her we had passed Rock Island safely. I got her voice mail and whispered into the phone, "Hello Naomi. I wanted you to know we put on our invisibility cloaks as we passed Rock Island and were not detected. We have safely passed the danger zone. Over and out, Mom."

The tug and its barges cleared the end of the wall, and the horn blasted to signal us to enter. We began to paddle around the end of the wall with the tug twenty feet away from us. We had not seen water churn that fast before, and it made me nervous. The tug slowed its engines and the churning water behind it died down a bit. I paddled into the whirlpools and turbulence and felt my kayak toss and spin. Steering was difficult, and adrenaline surged through my system. Kitty had cut too close to the end of the wall. Her kayak got caught in the current boiling around the end of the wall and was thrown toward it. I watched her paddle hard to stay upright, and I heard her paddle hit the wall. She recovered, and we rode the turbulent water into the lock. When we were safely in the lock, the tug began to run at full speed again. We realized that he had paused for our safety. On the downriver side of the lock another barge approached, so we quickly crossed over the main channel to get out of the way.

The adrenaline rush had made me hungry, so we stopped in Davenport at a park above the high concrete levee. A found-object sculpture depicting four people stood at the base of the stairs built into the levee. Artists had assembled random found objects to create an image of something recognizable. It required unique vision to accomplish. The sculpture was constructed of concrete, driftwood, lumber, and a variety of metal objects.

We sat on a park bench with a view of the river near downtown Davenport and the John O'Donnell Baseball Stadium. A tall man had watched us paddle to shore and came to talk with us. Floyd had a gentle way about him. He was retired and had recently moved to Davenport from Georgia to be closer to his mother. He couldn't believe that we were headed to St. Louis or that we came from Red Wing. He shook his head back and forth and said, "Why would you want to be on the water in those bitty boats? I'm quite fond of solid ground." Floyd headed off, still shaking his head.

As we pulled away from the park, a group of people wearing tattered clothing and pushing empty grocery carts leaned over the bridge railing and called to us, "God Bless. God travels with you." A woman in the group yelled, "Keep doing God's work. He is taking care of you." It was heartwarming; we had only said hello to them.

Past Horse Island, dozens of green and brown balls bobbed in the water. They were black walnuts. Around the end of the island was Walnut Grove, aptly named. The terrain was flat, and farm fields abutted the road along the river.

I saw a small, blue football floating in the water and paddled over to

pick it up. I reminded Kitty about the football we had found on the first trip. We had used a marker to draw a face on it and named it Penelope. I tucked the football into my kayak. We bantered about a name for it and decided on Penny because it was a smaller version of the first one. At camp that night we drew a face on her, and her imaginary, playful personality was born. She rode in my kayak for a few days, but the waves made her seasick, so she became Gwyn's companion in the van.

I found myself thinking about what Donna G. and Pat G. had said at the Gathering. They said they felt like they had children even though they had not given birth and that every child was their child. We needed to share the care of all of the world's children. I'd heard that sentiment before, but not how it had so greatly impacted other women's lives. In a world where families have become so fragmented, it was refreshing and hopeful to hear. Life has become complicated, and I believe that it takes more than just parents to help children navigate our world.

The heat gave Kitty a craving for ice cream. She reminisced about the Dove bars Gwyn had given us, and she wanted one immediately. My mouth watered as she described them in detail. We spotted a mini-mart downriver in Buffalo, Iowa. We pulled up on the rocks and ran to the store. Ice cream in hand, we sat on the sidewalk outside the store. We decided that sitting took too much effort, so we lay down. It took intense, mutual pep talks before we could muster the motivation to stand, though we encouraged ourselves by saying that it was only five miles to camp.

Upriver, the same barge approached that we had been seeing all day. It wasn't moving fast, but it was still gaining on us. We decided to race it to camp. It continued to gain on us even when we picked up our pace. Our destination in sight, we gave one last push and were victorious. We hoped Gwyn and Pat G. would be there to greet us and take our victory picture, but they were nowhere in sight. I asked an older gentleman on the dock if he would take the picture and hurried him along since we wanted the barge in the background of the picture.

We had paddled twenty-seven miles in record time, landing two and a half hours earlier than expected. Gwyn and Pat G. were surprised when we walked into the campsite. Kitty was immediately drawn to our neighbor's RV, where a cat was outside enjoying the sun. Kitty missed her two cats.

Gwyn and Pat G. said they'd had a great day hanging out at the park and catching up with each other. Time together was precious to them, so we were glad to hear that Gwyn had not worked on her computer all day.

During dinner, a train parked on the tracks near us. When the train started moving again, it created a chorus of screeching and banging. It sounded like an off-key orchestra warming up, which changed to rolling thunder as the train gained speed and its cars banged into one another.

We headed onto the dock with hot chocolate as the sun set over calm water. The sun set on one side of us while the moon rose on the other side. Both created hypnotic reflections on the water. I couldn't decide which direction to look. There was enough of a breeze to keep the bugs away, and after the sun set we stared at the full moon and watched sticks float by. It felt restorative to talk, laugh, and enjoy each other's company.

I barely remembered my head hitting the pillow but woke a short while later when my phone rang. My feelings of tranquility were shattered during a discussion with Doug about money. The call ended poorly. I tossed in my sleeping bag for a while and then called him back. The second call went better but sleep was hard in coming. I resented that issues from home were imposing themselves on the trip.

September 27, Day Twenty-Four

Halfway through a restless night, I discovered that my Therm-a-Rest mattress wasn't holding air, which explained why the ground had seemed harder the past couple of nights. I experienced a number of equipment issues on the trip, which included the broken kayak seat, the camera cord, a lanyard for my glasses that continually fell off, gloves that gave me blisters, and the flat Therm-a-Rest. Gwyn had ordered a new seat for my kayak, which we would pick up in Burlington. My current seat was held together with athletic tape, safety pins, extra foam padding, and the ever-reliable duct tape.

At daybreak, I walked to the dock with Gwyn while Pat G. started breakfast. I was honored to have Gwyn witness the song and blessing for that night's Gathering. When we returned, Gwyn again ordered Kitty and me to sit and relax. Being waited on made me feel both special and uncomfortable. I grappled with releasing my need to do an equal share of the work. Kitty fidgeted watching Gwyn and Pat G. and stated it well: "It's difficult to accept someone doing something for me that I am capable of doing myself." Gwyn responded in a firm tone, "Get used to it."

We laughed at Gwyn and Pat G.'s breakfast bowls. Gwyn's was tiny, while Pat G's was huge. In her preparations, Pat G. had forgotten to pack a bowl to eat out of, so she used the mixing bowl. Over breakfast, we told Gwyn we wanted to treat her by having her paddle for a day. She lit up like a Christmas tree. Her job was to decide which day. Grinning widely, she thanked us several times, saying, "I never even dreamed that might be a possibility. I secretly wanted to be out there."

Gwyn and Pat G. left camp to shuffle cars. Knowing we'd hear about it later, we ignored their orders and broke down camp. They would be back to pick up our gear.

I spotted a dragonfly resting in the mowed weeds next to the boat launch. She was covered in dew. The morning sun glistened off the tiny beads of water. I thought the dragonfly was dead, but she moved slightly when my hand came close to her. Choosing not to disturb her further, I headed to the kayaks.

Along the main channel past Fairport, Iowa, we saw hundreds of small chirping birds in the trees. They were too high in the trees to identify, but they filled the air with a cheerful song. The aroma of a bakery traveled several miles downriver with us. We had hoped we would discover its origin when we passed through Fairport, but it remained a mystery. Though it was a pleasant smell at first, it became a nauseating odor with time.

The previous night's conversation with Doug gnawed at me. He had said his intention was to keep me informed, but I recognized a subtle tone which implied that he wanted my help. There was nothing I could do from the river to help him. I resented the situation. He seemed to be handling it and promised to call again to let me know how his plan worked.

In Wyoming Slough, butterflies fluttered past, crossing from the mainland to the islands. No two butterflies were the same size or color. We joked that they must be headed to a party on one of the islands. The shady, peaceful, narrow chute that cut through Geneva Island would be the perfect place for a butterfly party. It was heavily wooded, and rays of light broke through the green canopy. The water reflected a mirror image of the surrounding beauty. We drifted, enjoying the crickets and birds. A heron squawked from a treetop. Lush, green vines climbed the trees. Fish brushed the top of the water. I wondered if they were scratching themselves on the air like a cow would on a tree. A squirrel chattered angrily at us from high in a tree. Further along, dried lotuses had been stripped of their seed pods.

We cut around Hog Island to get to Lock & Dam No. 16. The lock marked mile thirteen of our fifteen-mile day. In the lock, we were directed to ropes at the far end, closest to the gates. The gates were especially impressive from that vantage point. They were designed to create a slight upriver V where they came together. The design utilized water pressure from the current to help hold the gate tight. I found the entire lock system to be an engineering wonder.

Large waffle waves greeted us when the gate opened. Pelicans floated near the wall and in front of the dam. They seemed unaffected by the bobbing as the waves tossed us around. We had come to realize that we could not predict what to expect on the other side of the lock. It could easily be calm on the upriver side and choppy and windy on the downriver side.

We arrived at the boat landing at Muscatine, Iowa, where a large heron walked the shoreline. While we ate our sandwiches, we wandered over to admire a statue of a man harvesting clams. Clamshells harvested from the river near Muscatine were used to make buttons. Muscatine was also known for the sawmills that had once been there. Muscatine was a

Kayak parking

Native American term meaning "people of the prairie."

While loading the boats onto the van, we noticed the heron was floating on the water. It was unusual behavior for a heron. We watched her bob on the waves for a while until she took flight.

When we arrived at the motel, we took showers and a quick nap and headed to Riverside City Park for the Gathering. We weren't there long before Kay M. joined us from Savanna. She would be staying in the same motel that evening. Other women began to arrive. I had forgotten that Heidi, a friend from Ely, was going to come. She and her mother, Gail H., had driven two hours from Gail H.'s home in Illinois. Heidi made a point to check in with me. She said Doug had told her I was struggling and unable to relax. I told her I had reframed the trip for myself and that things were better. She was relieved.

MUSCATINE GATHERING

Marion

The Gathering began with twenty-five women, ranging in age from thirty-six to eighty-one. As the elder of the evening, Marion hesitantly started sharing.

"My husband and I had Bamford Photography Studio for twenty-five years. George worked for Helen Bamford twenty-one years before he bought the studio, so he was in the business for fifty years. We retired in 2005, and my children had a real nice retirement party for us right up here in that building over there. Was it ever nice.

"George and I used to go waterskiing on Saturday mornings because that was some of our free time. Then we would come home, get cleaned up, and take a wedding that afternoon. By the end of the day we wondered why our knuckles were dragging on the ground.

"I lost George this summer on May 30." Tears flowed down her cheeks. "Anyway, I think that is about as far as I will go now. My overflow is pretty low."

"I'm not shy," Gail H. jumped in. "You have to be careful when you give a teacher the privilege to speak. I've been married for forty years this last August. My husband and I experienced a big change this year. Don't ever think nothing good is ever going to happen to you or that your life is too routine, because that is what we thought. We thought our lives were too routine. Then, all of a sudden, my husband's boss walked in last March and said, 'I've decided I'm not going to move the business to the other side of town. I have sold the building and I'm just going to liquidate.' Mike had worked for this man for thirty-two years and—boom!—no job, no insurance, no severance, no pension, no retirement. That was it.

"We are going to move up to Ely, Minnesota, where my daughter and grandson are. Mike's going to start looking for a job. I have already pulled my teacher's retirement because that's the only way I can get insurance. I have MS, and no one wants to insure me. That was a big problem, but things are working out. We were beginning to panic, but we sold the house, and we are ready to move on and try a whole new life. So, don't think your life is in a rut, or maybe you'll find it was not such a bad life after all."

"I just want to speak to your courage," Betty responded to Gail H. "Don't you think that it's one of those things that you look back on and say you didn't choose this, but it turned out to be a blessing in disguise?"

"Yes, I know. Thank you." replied Gail H. "Before the layoff, one of the things we did was to buy this house on a lake. I appreciate the idea that water is relaxing, because I think just being by the lake helped keep us sane during all this craziness. We are going to miss it, but I am excited about being near my grandson and Heidi. I have known my son-in-law, Matt, for a long time. They have been married for . . . what . . . nine years?" She turned to her daughter, Heidi, next to her, who nodded. "But I really don't know him because they live so far away. I know he has been a good husband, a wonderful father, and a good man. I am looking forward to getting to know him as a person. I know life is going to be better.

"The other thing I haven't said is that there are a lot worse things in life than losing a job. The worst was when our daughter Lori died. It has been fourteen years and we are doing pretty well. Sometimes we just need to talk about it more, because I don't think there is anything worse than losing a child. Ever!"

Krystyna spoke next and captured everyone's attention with her accent. "I am seventy-three. I came to the United States when I was seventeen. Because I came from Poland, and even though I went to German schools, this lady in Kansas had formed an opinion that I wouldn't amount to much. She believed that because I didn't have a high school education and I had just turned eighteen. Well, that one person propelled me to make something out of myself. I was cleaning house for her, and I didn't know how to wax the floor properly. In my country and in Germany we had wooden floors, and they were beautiful. I had never waxed the floors. She thought I was kind of dumb. So I decided then, and it is a kind of wisdom that you have to believe in yourself. At eighteen I made that promise that I would believe in myself.

"I have three daughters and I went ahead and I believed in them. I became an RN later on, got an education. There were many different things I was doing. I believed in my three daughters, that they could accomplish things. And they did, because they believed they could do everything because their mother did."

Brenda R. spoke next. "What Krystyna said started my thoughts. I married the baby of a family and he is a wonderful man, though I think my mother-in-law was often very jealous that I took her baby away from her. Over the thirty-five years of marriage I have learned some things about being a mother-in-law and a grandmother. I think I am a good mother-in-law and a good grandmother. Miraculously, my mother-in-law thinks I am too. I am glad it didn't take me thirty-five years to realize that my daughter-in-law is a wonderful woman. People say things happen for a reason and sometimes you don't think that it's true. From my own experience I really do think it is true."

Pat I. took the fan and sat for a moment with a contemplative look on her face. "The question that touched me is about whether your life turned out the way you thought it would or whether it followed the right path." She choked up. "I never dreamed of this day. My life is so much bigger than I ever thought was possible. I am a kid from the wrong side of the tracks, with a drunk for a father and just a real terrible background and childhood, but I had a mother who believed in education. As sexist as this sounds, her thought was, 'You educate a woman, you educate a family. You educate a man, you educate a man.' Sorry, but that was her philosophy. All of us kids were educated, but particularly my sister and I got really good educations. Even with that education, I chose to stay at home with my children. My daughters' and my sons' friends will ask 'Your mother has a degree in philosophy, well, what does she do with that?' You raise four kids! That is what I did. Anyway, it's just a bigger, better life than I ever imagined. Like I said, I never dreamed this big. I feel very fortunate and extremely blessed."

"Melanie is the only one that I know in this group," Lorrain began. "I am her realtor and now I am a broker and owner of a new real estate business. I am also a three year widow, twenty-seven years married. I have a son that just got out of the Corps after four years and he goes to the International Affairs department at the University of Miami. I have a pill of a daughter named Jillian. She might end up being a two-year senior at the rate she's starting the school year. I guess people say that God does not give you more than you can handle. I have always believed that, and I wished He didn't have so much confidence in me. [Laughter.] I about lost my sanity three and a half years ago. We didn't have a perfect marriage, but, I tell you, since my husband has been gone, almost every day he comes closer to being a saint." We laughed again. "Funny how your memory plays them up. My husband is almost like a god to me now. Anyway, it has been rough being a single mom, working, and trying to get through life. I had a lot of trouble at the beginning. It was three hospitals and forty days after the car accident that he died up in Chicago. After the funeral, which we had to put off because it was so close to my birthday, we got his body back here. Two weeks later, I was robbed in daylight while I was with my pastor. That fall, the house burned down and I lost everything we owned. In the meantime, my son was in a war zone. I was really about fed up! I want you to know that, as far as learning to tie a knot and hang on, I always think it is worth it. I had to do that in my marriage too.

"I am dating a guy who used to be an executive chef, but he is in sales now for wholesale food. I don't think my kids will ever like anybody I like because of the memory of their father.

"My daughter has had a hell of a time. The morning my husband had the car accident he was taking her school books to her. She has had therapy three or four times, but I can't get her to go in anymore. She is a handful for me, and I hope she can get through this and get her education and think a bit bigger. I don't know what to think about counseling nowadays. They say it is all in your frontal lobe and it's not developed enough when they are teenagers. I don't know. My son is struggling in school in English. It's been five years since he went into the service at age seventeen. Jill struggles in school too. Every day is a struggle, but you just keep plugging through it. Don't quit. I have moments when I think it would be easier to quit, but we all have to keep bearing our cross and keep carrying it on.

"By the way, Melanie and I are river rats. I have my husband's johnboat. He used to duck hunt and all that kind of stuff. We enjoy the river. I know the river from here to the Quad Cities and from here to Burlington, Iowa, on my own. The johnboat is a sixteen-foot, extra-wide, extra-deep boat with a four stroke Suzuki motor that will go about thirty-five miles per hour. I can get down to Oquawka on one five gallon tank of gas."

We were interrupted as two trains passed. The women studied the trains and began to discuss which trains they were and where they were headed. Then Melanie began to speak loudly over the trains. "This kind of reminds me of my own backyard because this is what we have to do too. I am fortunate enough to live on the river, but that means trains. I have been married for twenty-seven years to my husband, Doug. We raised a couple of boys. We moved to the river in 1990 and decided to build and do everything the old fashioned way, basically with the old pioneer spirit. Some people told us we were kind of crazy, but you don't listen to those kinds of people. You just do what you think is right. We had friends and family involved with the project that was supposed to take a couple of years. After we had dealt with the flood in '93, in '94 the house burned down. It was a unique experience because we learned so much about all of our friends—so many rallied to help us. We don't own our land. It's government land. It has made us very aware of how we treat our land and the things we put on or don't put on our lawns. My boys have always liked being on the river. They are river rats too. We used to always take them out in an old pontoon boat. We looked like the Beverly Hillbillies whether we were heading upstream or downstream.

"I always question why women are so scared to go out on the water by themselves. It's such a tranquil, beautiful place. We always feel comfortable enough to come down to the riverfront and it makes us happy. If we are sad it gives us relief. When I try to get other women to go out in a johnboat or a canoe, I have always found it very hard. It's awesome for me to meet other women who like to go out on the water and are not afraid of it. It's a great adventure. More of us should start doing it."

Bonita, whom we had met a few days earlier, took the fan next with a concerned look on her face. "I am a schoolteacher too, so I will try to keep it short. I want to respond to your comment about going out on the water by yourself. That is something I don't do even though I have paddled from St. Cloud, Minnesota, to St. Louis, Missouri, on the Mississippi. I had an experience where I went over and I was caught by my life jacket. It was going to kill me. If I hadn't had other people with me, I might not have made it. I don't recommend going out by yourself because things happen."

"I agree it is a scary thing," Melanie replied, "but we just have to have the courage and confidence in ourselves to go out and do it. Like Lorrain, sometimes she goes out on the johnboat by herself."

Waltroud began to speak; she had an intriguing accent too. "I think we always have a number of life-changing experiences during our life, but my most recent one was that I lost my hearing on the left side—overnight. I went to the doctor. Because of my grey hair, I was treated for old age. They were bound and determined to prescribe a hearing aid for me. I said that I wanted to know the reason for the sudden hearing loss and whether I could maybe see a specialist. Very reluctantly they sent me to a specialist. They gave me the hearing test and said, 'You are deaf.' I remarked,

Waltroud

'That is why I came here.' [Laughter.] They stated, 'You know, if we just put you on steroids it probably will come back.' So they administered steroids to me and I asked, 'I still would like to know why the hearing goes away overnight. May I have an MRI?' They questioned, 'Do you know how costly an MRI is?' This is because I have grey hair. I said, 'Well, I never used my insurance, and I would like to use that. If they don't pay it I'll pay it out of my own pocket. It is for my own curiosity.' Anyway, they gave me this MRI, and then a little office girl called me and she stated, 'The results are in. You have a brain tumor.' 'Oh, okay, well thank you,' I said. Then she stated, 'We just have to make arrangements.' We made arrangements at the local hospital. They called me from the hospital and the first question was, 'Who is your insurance carrier?' So I told them, and they said, 'Oh, we don't work with them.' I asked, 'Why not?' 'Because they don't pay enough.'

"So I was left without any doctors and had to find my own doctor. Luckily, there was a support group. A nurse there recommended a wonderful doctor in Iowa City. I trusted him wholly, and since it was a rapid-growth tumor, they had to treat it right away with radiation treatments. I am doing really well. Since my husband was very sick, I didn't have really any time to think about my own fate. I had to take care of him. Six months later he died. I think it made me stronger. I think we all need to be our own advocate. We have to talk for ourselves. I think sometimes we tend to be very timid. Particularly when one is a grandmother, an over-the-hill person, one is treated as not valuable enough to invest a lot of money in.

"I really think that whenever we have something going on we need to be courageous for ourselves. I think maybe I learned a lot. A lot of things have happened to me too. I was burglarized and I lost my identity after my husband passed away. The house was such a mess. It had been ransacked. I think adversities make us more resilient and we keep going. I am grateful for my curiosity. I think it was so amazing that this little office girl called me from the doctor's office with the verdict and I thought to myself, 'See, there was something more to it.'"

"I am Mary and I am fifty-five," stated Mary R. "I saw the article in this afternoon's paper after work, and I live in Davenport, but it's mating season, so I can't stay until dark because I just had a new transmission put in my truck, and I do not need another big bill from hitting a deer. I was intrigued by the article because I am in my fifties. I think if you grew up in the 'sixties, being age fifty is different. I see women that are more than ten years older than me and it is more of this timid kind of thing. Not all of them, it is unwise to generalize. Hey, I grew up in the 'sixties. That was a rebellion for women, let me tell you. I didn't do drugs, drinking, or any of that stuff. Just refusing to take my mom's side against my dad was rebellious enough. They did not have a good marriage.

"I have been a letter carrier for twenty-seven years. I have a live-in male companion. He is a fourteen-year-old half-Siamese cat. He is a sweetie. I think it is providential that I am in this occupation. I like it a lot. I kind of stumbled into it. Even with all the negative male influences I had as a child, I really like the guys I work with. I have really great male friends, and now I met a bunch of guys at church. They are strong and considerate gentleman. That is a good counterbalance to my childhood. Of course I have women friends too, but I think sometimes guys get a bad rap. I am fortunate to be in the situation I'm in where I have experienced a lot of good men."

"I was afraid this fan was eventually going to get here," Carolyn started. "I should have run when I had the chance. [Laughter.] I am not a public speaker. I have to echo what I heard Pat I. say, that life is just

more fantastic than I ever dreamed it could be. I think what has influenced me most consistently through my life is the fact that I was taught at an early age about the Lord Jesus Christ who has come to be my savior. It was a decision that my parents told me at age five I needed to make. I did, but it was not until I was about age forty-five that I realized my parents had nothing to do with that choice. It was something I had to do on my own because I wanted him to be my guide and my leader.

"I have been so thankful for that relationship throughout the forty-four years of my marriage. I was the kind of girl that was timid, couldn't talk, and my tongue stuck to the roof of my mouth every time I got near a boy. I just knew that I was never going to have a husband. God blessed me at twenty-one with a husband—a Christian man—and eventually four kids and seven grandkids.

"I guess I thought early on to put my husband on that pedestal and let him be what God himself wanted him to be for me. I have been through a lot of hard places when my husband disappointed me and my children disappointed me. I had a daughter that was very rebellious. Well, with four kids, life was not simple, but those hard places have been doable because I knew that crying was an okay thing, as long as you didn't do it for the rest of your life. You know, you cry and get done and then wash the dishes and do the laundry or something else. I am very thankful for my relationship with the Lord Jesus throughout my life. I know I can trust him to lead and guide me.

"Recently my husband and I purchased an old house, built in 1890, that sits on a bluff high above the Mississippi. It has a gorgeous view, both upstream to the lock and dam as well as downstream to where the river stops flowing west and heads south. We see both the sunrise and the famous Muscatine sunsets!"

Kay M. took the fan with a smile and began, "My husband and kids think I talk too much, but I only talk when I find someone who will listen to me. So you guys are in trouble. [Laughter.]

"I was raised in the 'fifties. I graduated in the 'fifties and I was the good girl of the two sisters. I didn't become a teacher, a nurse, or a nun, but like most of us in those days, I didn't go to college. I couldn't afford to go to college. I ended up getting married at nineteen, and by the time I was twenty-six, I had been married for six years and had six children, one at a time.

"I had three or four big events in my life." She began to cry. "I am a weeper too, besides a talker. It was a big decision, after being pregnant for six years to go against my faith and my upbringing, to not have more children. I was busy raising these kids, and they turned out to be pretty good kids. The decision not to have any more children and go against my upbringing was difficult.

"When I was forty-two, my fifteen-year-old son killed himself," she said, crying. "Oh, I thought nothing worse could happen, and it hasn't, but I have grown by it. Then this May was my fiftieth wedding anniversary, and I wasn't there because I left him in February. I had always said that I would never put up with physical abuse. It wasn't bad, it was always verbal and power, his power. This time, he pulled my hair and accused me of some things, so I left and I haven't been back. I did stop in and pick up my stuff. Everybody thinks 'Fifty years, boy, you've got it made. You can put up with that.'

"I always wished there were groups of women, especially older women, going through the counseling I am doing as part of preparing for the divorce. The counselor and I have looked and looked and there is nothing, nothing on the internet or in books. Even this young woman who is my counselor doesn't know what to do with those older women. Who gets divorced when you are sixty-nine? We should be quiet and live with it and hope you outlive them. [Laughter.] I'm sorry. I don't mean evil for the man. He is a good man and everything, but . . . well . . . you know. . . ."

"There is a wonderful book called Men Are Just for Dessert. You should get that one," responded Waltroud.

"I love books. I'll have to get that one. I have nothing against him, and I have no plans. I am just taking one day at a time," Kay M. replied.

"These are your days," said Gail H. encouragingly.

"I told a friend today," Kay M. responded, "that if my husband knew this is what I was doing he would say, 'Oh, for cripes sakes. What do you think you are doing? You are wasting all that gas driving somewhere. You don't even know these people. You don't know if they are a bunch of ax murderers or whatever.' [Laughter.] The more I thought about it, the more I thought, by God, I am going to go just to see who else is in some situations."

"Years ago, when I got a divorce, I found a book called I Feel Guilty When I Say No," Jan F. added. "That was the best book I ever read! You deserve to be treated with dignity and respect. You are worth it. You go girl. You grab all the gusto you can get, because you are worth it."

"That is what I am learning," replied Kay M. "Well, I am not any younger or skinny, but I am a new me, that's for sure."

Krystyna enthusiastically jumped in. "This young lady over there, who is only fifty-five, said because we are a little older we are a little more timid. Well, let me tell you, yesterday I called Mr. Grassley and Mr. Harkin in the White House because I was so upset. I didn't feel like we, as taxpayers, should pay for Colombia's security. Colombia should pay for the secret service and all of this. So I am not very timid even though I am seventy-three. I speak up with whatever has to be said." She finished speaking and her face shone with pride.

During the Gathering, a man on a bicycle circled us a couple of times and left. I noticed him but didn't think too much of it. Twenty minutes later he returned, parked his bike, brought a bag and handed it to one of the women, then turned and left without a word. The bag held a couple of copies of a newspaper with an article about us in it. Nancy L. scurried off after the Gathering to the newspaper's office to get additional copies for the rest of our group.

A full harvest moon rose over the Highway 92 Bridge as everyone headed home. Its bright orange, smiling face hung serenely over the calm, reflective water.

On the drive back to the motel, I thought about the eleven feathers still in my possession. I had given one to Sherry after the Lake City Gathering and another to Lynne, and I wondered if I had been so focused on details that I had missed someone. It had not occurred to me that I might bring feathers home. I had faith that I would meet all thirteen grandmothers, but perhaps they would not be along this stretch of the river.

Gwyn and Pat G. were delayed getting back to the motel due to a Dove bar excursion. Gwyn handed Dove Bars to everyone and realized she had bought too many. She headed down the hall and gave them to anyone who answered their door. No one was ready to call it a day. Kay M. pointed out how women at the Gatherings said "my husband and I" instead of just "I". She commented that it was typical of that age group to not see themselves as separate from their husbands.

After everyone left, I briefly spoke with Doug. He had a solution to the financial issue, and we were both relieved. He listened while I told him about the Gathering, and he said he was proud of me.

SEPTEMBER 28TH THROUGH OCTOBER 1ST

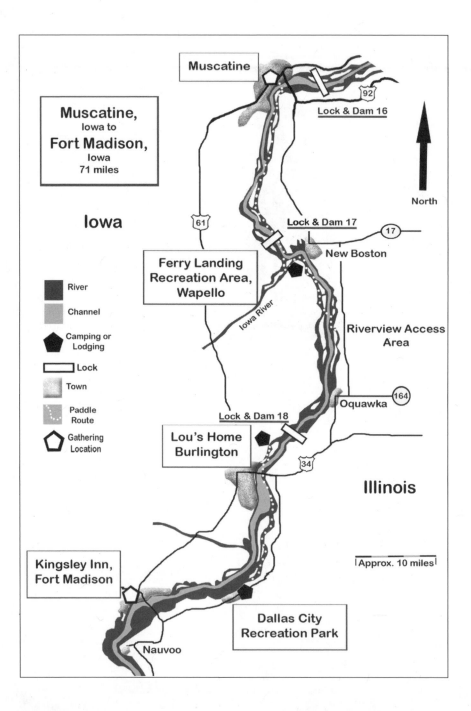

Muscatine to Fort Madison

September 28, Day Twenty-Five

Penny the football sat in the middle of our breakfast table. While we chatted, Kay M. revealed a secret of Gwyn's by thanking us for the flowers. "What flowers?" we asked. All eyes turned to Gwyn, who was trying to look innocent. She had become a self-appointed flower fairy and was sending flowers on our behalf to everyone who had helped us along the way.

At the river, Kay M. wrote in the paddlers' journal:

> As long as I can remember I've always loved any form of water: Lake Michigan as a child in Milwaukee, later a creek or small fishing lake at the cottage, or the power and beauty of the waters in Ireland. Recently I was drawn to the river. Now I know why I am here at this special time of my life.
>
> The stream of my life has led me to those who also love the waters—the wise women of the north. How fortunate that we met just when I needed their friendship so much! Thank you, Creator, for these times of friendship. Who knows where my journey will lead me. Thank you, friends, especially for stroking my needs right now. Till we meet again!
>
> May the spirits guide you each day, whether here on the water or back in our daily journeys.
>
> Peace and God Bless.
>
> Kay

In the center of the channel I sang, made an offering, and one by one blessed and released the aspiration sticks from the Gathering. I felt hopeful and peaceful as I watched the sticks gently bob in the water. The colors of their yarn seemed brighter that morning.

As we paddled on, two men in a fishing boat drove straight at us. We reached for our warning horns, but they slowed down and pulled in close. They asked if we were the women paddling the river that they had read about in the paper. They had come to the park during the Gathering the night before to meet us but quietly left so they wouldn't disturb us. They wanted us to know that they thought what we were doing was important. They drove off, leaving us amazed that anyone would go that far out of their way to talk with us.

My aching knee was healing well, but sitting in the kayak required my knee to be slightly bent and turned out, which irritated it. I continued to keep it wrapped for extra support and got out to stretch occasionally. That morning when it started to ache, we stopped at a public use area. We climbed to the top of the levee and saw miles of flat farmland with crops ready for harvest. Storage buildings and barns were scattered among the fields. The flat terrain and bright gold colors seemed surreal after the blue water and green bluffs. A bad smell we had noticed the day before reappeared and was even more pungent and nauseating. It was probably a grain processing plant we could not see, and we hoped to leave it behind soon.

We turned down a chute where fish jumped in front of us and landed in splashes of light. The banks along the shore were high and muddy, with exposed tree roots growing back toward shore. Trying to avoid the bugs on land, we ate lunch floating on the water. There were several herons standing in the water and perched in trees. Some quietly watched us pass while others squawked and flew downriver. One fished along the shore, thrusting its head into the water and coming up with small fish. Long, snake-like fish brushed the surface of the water. The water in the chute moved nearly as fast as the main channel, so we continued to make good time even though we weren't paddling.

Comments from the night before about how nice it was that Doug was "letting" me go on the trip implied that I had needed his permission and spoke to our culture's view of a woman's place. Doug and I shared an equal partnership. If one of us wanted or needed to do something, we didn't need to get permission from the other. We made choices for ourselves while being respectful of the other person. A relationship that required getting permission would have been too confining for me.

Before Pat I. had spoken the night before, I had sensed a level of joy in her that warmed my heart. I was deeply touched by the depth of her gratitude for how her life had turned out. Living in that place of thankfulness altered everything for her. I envied her attitude, and hoped I could adopt something similar in my life.

We drifted on glassy water while waiting for a barge to pass through Lock No. 17. The reflection on the water seemed to magically brighten the colors. A flock of pelicans called from a nearby island, and from another distant island, we heard a busy woodpecker. The time spent waiting for our turn was a gift.

We floated in the middle of the lock as the water level dropped. The heat had taken its toll. I felt baked and was grateful we only had three and a half miles left of our twenty-two-mile day. In Keg Slough we took advantage of the shade the trees provided. A downed tree lying in the river some distance away had several cormorants perched on it. Each bird looked like it was a branch of the tree, which made the tree appear to fall apart as the birds dropped from their perches and ran across the water before taking flight. Cormorants are similar to loons in the way they take flight. They can't lift off like other birds because they're too heavy, so they run across the water to gain momentum first. By the time we reached the tree, the limbs were bare.

When we reached our campsite, Gwyn and Pat G. were nowhere in sight. The campground had flooded not long before, and a thick layer of dried mud extended across most of the area. The flow of the river was evident in the way the mud had moved around the tree trunks. The water created a swirling pattern that wrapped around the trees and left a depression on the downriver side.

Gerry, a scruffy-looking man with a long, gray beard and long hair, introduced himself. He was camped a couple of sites down. He asked if we were part of the singles' paddling club and enthusiastically told us that he was a member. We explained what we were doing while he acted moderately interested but still clearly disappointed. He headed back to his campsite mumbling that he liked the singles' club. Kitty and I grinned at each other as he left. We each took a nap, which felt heavenly after a hot day.

After Gwyn and Pat G. had returned, a woman came over and introduced herself as Patricia. She said she had been tracking us on the website and had wanted to be at the Muscatine Gathering, but had, unfortunately, had a conflict. As Patricia sat down with us for dinner, I observed how Gwyn, Pat G., and Kitty all reached out to her. I had watched them do it each time someone new came into our circle or stood on the edge wanting to be a part of it. They made everyone immediately feel like part of the group. That was a skill that Sherry had too, and it had been an unexpected gift on the trip.

Patricia had two teenagers and was in school to complete her master's degree. She was a teacher and a writer who particularly enjoyed writing poetry. I asked for a poem for my book. She looked surprised and then smiled. She was working on one that was inspired by the drive into the

Patricia

campground and would give me a copy when she finished it.

The sun set during dinner, and we walked down to the sandy beach. The sky above was a deep, clear blue, while the horizon was shaded with orange and had wispy clouds above the tree line. It looked like an artist had quickly and lightly stroked her brush across the sky. Pelicans on the distant shore shuffled around, searching for the best place to bed down for the night. Gwyn discovered a fat toad hopping along the sand and picked her up to pet her. Across the river were the lights of New Boston, Illinois. Our constant companions, the bugs, hastened the end of our leisurely stroll.

It would be Pat G.'s last night with us. She wrote in the paddlers' journal:

> *What a wonderful reunion to spend a week with one of my all time favorite friends, Gwyn. She has been such a wonderful friend to me over the years, and to get to spend a whole week with her was a wonderful treat! I thank you both, Nancy and Kitty, for drawing her to the Midwest! You really made an impression on her! I am so grateful to you both for that.*
>
> *I truly admire you both for your courage, enthusiasm, love of the river and water, and your willingness to share all that you have with new people. You both are an inspiration for all women.*
>
> *I have enjoyed my time with you both so much. I cannot tell you how much this week has meant to me. To find strength in other women and to share that strength with others is such a valuable gift. You both do it so well!*
>
> *Thanks for the birds, white pelicans, and sandhill cranes to wake up to at Thomson Causeway. What a way to wake up! I will treasure this experience and your friendships!*
>
> *Ferry's Landing was the end of my journey and the first day that I saw the contents of the breakfast box! Wow!*
> *Much love*
> *Your new friend,*
> *Pat*

From my tent, I watched the last of the sunset and listened to the pelicans continue their shuffle. Their wings splashed as they moved from one place to another. A canine chorus echoed across the water from New Boston, and late in the night, a pack of coyotes howled at a passing barge.

September 29, Day Twenty-Six

We enjoyed a cool, sunny morning with a slight breeze that kept the bugs away. With two weeks left of the trip, I felt a mixture of homesickness and an ache to keep paddling. The responsibilities at home felt heavy. I had a nightmare that Doug had died, followed by another nightmare about rescuing a gray tabby cat from a green buoy in the middle of the river. Both dreams seemed so real that they left me feeling restless that morning.

The campsite was abuzz. Everyone cheerfully prepared for the day ahead. Patricia joined us for breakfast. We ate oatmeal and reminisced about how much we enjoyed Linda's cooking at the Leisure Harbor Inn. Patricia also shared her completed poem with us.

The Levee

That short steep hill
We just drove over
Was made by those
Who wish to contain
This river that flows
Untrammeled by my feet.

When she seeks to grow
Beyond her bounds
She will beat upon the hill
Year after year after year
Until those who restrain her
Bow to the goddess she is.

As usual, Gwyn ordered us to leave everything and get going. Pat G. smiled and became teary-eyed when we said good-bye to her. She assured us that we would see her in St. Louis. She left the electric skillet and a few other comforts with us. Gwyn had plans for the skillet—we would have steak for supper.

A truck with a kayak in the back pulled up just as we headed to the water. A woman named Nancy G. got out of the truck and beamed as she said she wanted to paddle with us. She had gotten her kayak two years prior and loved to paddle, so joining us on the Mississippi sounded exciting. Her husband, Jim, had convinced her that she should join us and was there to support her.

We welcomed her and discussed how our twenty-five-mile day might prove to be too much if she was not used to paddling all day. We made a plan with her husband that she would paddle as far as she could, and then we'd meet at a boat launch. A lone pelican floated and watched our departure.

Everything thrilled Nancy G., and we enjoyed watching her reactions. She did not paddle at our pace. Kitty and I liked the idea of a leisurely day, but knew we would not reach our destination at the slower pace.

The wind came up early, so we ducked behind Corsepius Island and enjoyed the serenity of the backwaters for two miles. Reaching the end of the island, we saw that the waves had grown in the main channel. We hugged the shoreline and turned into Blackhawk Chute, where the wind was merely a breeze.

Nancy G. told us she was a nurse. Every November her husband traveled to Texas for five months for hunting season while she stayed home to help her elderly mother. Her adventurous spirit and ability to roll with the punches became clear when we stopped for a break near a railroad bridge. She came out of the woods laughing and covered in prickly burrs. It took the three of us to pull them all off of her. She realized that we were not making very good time paddling and sensed she was slowing us down. She said she would understand if we needed to drop her off so we could go on ahead. We told her we would let her know if our pace became a problem.

We watched pelicans take off from a log. They made a mighty leap, but the weight of

Nancy G., Nancy, and Kitty

their bodies made them drop to the water. After they took a couple of steps on the water they were able to take flight. Near the end of the channel, we came upon large goose decoys. I paddled among them; they were

Photo by Kitty Kennedy

as tall as I was. Our leisurely paddle ended at the main channel, where the wind had created tall whitecaps. We decided to cross to the opposite shore where we would be sheltered from the wind and where we could find a boat landing if we needed to get off the water.

The waves in the channel were big, with some swells nearly three feet high. We told Nancy G. to aim straight into them and that it was important that we crossed together. We let her set the pace, encouraging her to move as quickly as she could and never stop paddling. The slower pace was challenging for us. We could see her fatigue increase during the painfully slow progress.

We pulled off at a small, sandy beach to rest and snack. Nancy G.'s exhilaration about what she had accomplished overrode her fatigue. She had moved slowly, but grinned from ear to ear while we discussed what we should do next. We decided that the waves had become unsafe and that we all needed to pull off for the day, though we still had another opening to cross before we reached the next boat landing.

Moving south, we searched for the small channel that led to the boat landing. Once inside the channel, relief from the wind was immediate. I was exhausted and couldn't imagine how Nancy G. felt. We paddled the tranquil water of the channel and rounded a bend to the landing. We pulled our boats up and took our gear over to a picnic table in the shade. I dug my cell phone out and called Gwyn, but was not sure the message went through since my phone had such poor service there. Nancy G. dug hers out to call her husband and discovered she had the same problem. We looked at each other and laughed.

Munching on snacks with the wind at our backs, we watched a young couple put their Jet Skis in the water. The woman did not want to go out in the big waves, but the man was determined and kept assuring her that it would be fine. He looked in our direction and acted macho. She conceded to going out to make him happy. "That is a clear example of how women do things against their better judgment for the men in their lives," I said.

"And she will probably tell him she liked it," added Kitty. We nodded in agreement.

The couple disappeared around the bend. There was no traffic at the boat launch. Fifteen minutes passed and a car approached. We waved it down. The couple in the car happily let us use their cell phone. I connected with Gwyn, who said it would take a while for her to get to us because she was on the other side of the river. Nancy G. connected with Jim, who also had been driving the other side of the river looking for us because he had been worried about the big waves. We thanked the couple for the use of their phone, and they drove off.

The wind gusts were relentless and kept blowing our gear off the table. It was the worst wind we had experienced on the trip so far. Each gust reassured me that we had made the right decision to get off the water. We were tired and sitting was all we could manage—we didn't even talk. We were relieved when the couple on the Jet Skis returned. Apparently the waves were too much, even for the man.

Nancy G.'s husband arrived first and told us he was glad we had pulled off the water. He thanked us for taking care of his wife while he loaded her kayak into their truck. When we said good-bye, Nancy G. said, "It's really exciting to find people like you, people who do things. I get tired of people who just watch TV. I want to be active and more involved in the world. Thank you for everything."

She wrote in the paddlers' journal:

> *This has truly been a lifetime adventure! Joining you at Wapello was supposed to be an adventure, but I never realized it would turn out so dramatically. The waves were four feet high, cell phones were useless, and we barely knew where we were. (We did know we were in Illinois.)*
>
> *What fun meeting you both. I feel like I learned a lot about the river. You are both excellent teachers and role models. I want to be just like you!*
>
> *I'll always remember Riverview Landing.*
>
> *Nancy II.*

Gwyn pulled in some time later, and after loading our kayaks, we drove south toward Burlington, Iowa. The wind made the van ride a bouncy one. We passed through Oquawka, Illinois, and I remembered that the town's claim to fame was that Norma Jean the elephant was buried there. We found the rock memorial marking her grave. The plaque told the tale of when the circus came to town in 1972 and Norma Jean was struck dead by lightning.

We moved on to Lou's river home north of Burlington. I had met Lou on a trip through Burlington while setting up the trip. I hadn't been able to find a camping spot next to the water and had stopped at the welcome center for information. Lou was a volunteer there, and after a few minutes talking with her, she offered to let me stay at her cabin. She insisted on driving there with me to ensure that it was okay. I looked forward to seeing the feisty eighty-eight-year-old woman again.

We pulled the van—kayaks and all—under the

Lou

cabin. Her home and a few others sat on pylons twenty feet high on the river side of the levee so they were above the flood level. Catwalks ran from some of the homes to the top of the levee.

We took showers and enjoyed a relaxing afternoon after paddling only nine and half miles. We watched the wind whip the trees and thought about how luxurious it felt to be safe and comfortable inside. We enjoyed the magnificent view of the river.  Lou arrived and cooked up a storm, making spaghetti and a fresh fruit salad. Her friends Marian, Jeanne, and Jeanette arrived and asked lots of questions about the trip. We enjoyed our dinner as the sound of crickets streamed through the windows.

Nancy, Gwyn, Kitty, Jeanne, Jeanette, Marian, and Lou

"Is farming the main industry around here?" asked Kitty.

"Yes it is," Jeanette replied. "We used to have more industry here. A lot of plants have closed, like Case Company, which was a big farm machinery plant. We had the Iowa Army Ammunition plant, and they made bombs. The ammunition plant made the town grow to almost 40,000 in 1941 during the war. Of course, things toned down, but there was the Korean War and Vietnam, so they were always producing, just not on as full as schedule as during World War II."

"This used to be a big railroad town," said Jeanne.

"Lumber and railroad," added Jeanette. "The lumber yards are no longer here, but the railroads are. We had what was called the CBQ, the Chicago, Burlington, and Quincy line. Now we are the corn state, but soybeans are kind of taking over.

"We saw a sign today that said 'forty years of corn in this field,'" Gwyn added. "We wondered how much fertilizer it took to grow forty years of corn if you aren't rotating your crops."

"Ladies," I said, changing the flow of the conversation. "We are traveling the river to gather women's stories, and we have some fabulous women before us."

"I can't imagine us having anything too exciting for a book," Lou said.

"That's what most of the women start out saying," I replied.

"Then you can't shut them up." Lou responded, laughing.

"Pretty much," I replied. "We want to hear about your lives."

"Did you tell them anything about us, Lou, or can we just make up anything that we want to?" kidded Jeanne, and we laughed.

"Things have changed in our community just like everyplace else," Jeanette added thoughtfully. "People have left and come back and they say it's different. It's so gradual that when you live here you don't notice it. I know it's different from when I was young."

"What was it like when you were young?" I asked.

"Well, there were lots of new businesses. When I was young, Roosevelt Avenue out there was like a lane," Jeanette continued. "It's now the busiest intersection in town. Our Tri-State fairgrounds were out there. It felt like you drove far out when you went to the fair."

"The fair was a big thing," added Marian, who had been listening quietly all evening.

"I didn't grow up in Burlington. I came to Burlington when I was seventeen years old," interjected Lou. "I went to Business College and stayed at the YWCA while I went to college."

"They rented rooms to young ladies then," Jeanette added.

"I could take the train back to my hometown on weekends," Lou continued. "Then, while I was going to school, I got a job. I grew up on a farm, so I was really very naïve, but I went down to the hotel and got a job waitressing. I knew nothing about waiting tables, and they were really very kind to me and taught me how to do it. I was probably a pretty good waitress, except that one time when I spilled some soup in a person's lap. I was just mortified. I went back to the kitchen, and I was just sure the hostess would come and I would get fired. She came back and said, 'Oh that's okay. We'll send the guy's pants to the cleaners. Don't worry about it.' I never really forgot that. The kindness people have shown me through the years has been really meaningful in my life. Then I met my husband, and we married and had two sons. It was then that I kind of grew up a little."

"Having kids tends to do that to a person," I commented.

"It does," agreed Lou. "I was active in the community. After I got out of school, I was the secretary for the probation officer with the county.

That was an interesting job. I met all these little delinquents. Some of them were wards of the court for various reasons. I think that process has pretty much changed now. There, again, I had a boss I couldn't believe; she was really one of the greatest. Later on I worked for the YMCA. That was interesting. Then we moved to Texas, and I worked for the YMCA down there. It was just really wonderful. I've had a very nice life. When I look back, I have no regrets. It just seemed like everything has just gone along good. I just more or less make the best of any situation I'm in. I guess I'm pretty much satisfied with life. Now, look, you can't shut me up. I admired your spirit when I first met you and what you are doing."

"You must have," I responded. "Last spring, I wasn't in the welcome center more than five minutes and you said, 'I'll put you up.' And you," I indicated Jeanette, "were looking at her like—"

"Is she crazy?" Jeanette said cutting me off. "You don't know this woman."

"I don't know," said Lou. "I guess it's because people have been kind to me all through my lifetime. For the most part, I'm quite a trusting person. Not everybody can be trusted, but I see the three of you sitting there and I think, 'I can trust them.' It's kind of neat.

"So back to my story now. I have two sons and two daughter-in-laws. I am very fortunate because I got two nice daughters-in-law. I have two granddaughters, who are in college now. They are fun; I've enjoyed them through the years. This little grandson, he is a little bit different. He is, what would I say?" She paused, searching for the right word.

"He's a boy?" I said. We all laughed.

"Yes, he's a boy," Lou continued, smiling fondly. "He's a good guy. It's just that he is growing up in this tech age that I have not really quite kept up with, all these games and stuff. When I talk to other seniors and grandparents they are all in the same predicament. Their grandchildren can't sit down for two minutes before they have this Gameboy out, playing games and things like that. That's why I have all these games and puzzles here at the cabin. When they come to the cabin they have to do old-fashioned things where people interact with people rather than people interacting with a machine. That's basically where I am coming from with all of that."

"My oldest grandson was thrilled to death when he found out I finally had a remote control for something," added Jeanne with a grin. "He thought it was a major accomplishment that I could push a button." We laughed.

"My daughter is sixty tomorrow," added Jeanette. "When she went to college she majored in math and computer science. I remember thinking, 'Computer science, what in the world is that?' The computer was huge then. They had to go over to the campus building that housed the computer. It was massive and it poured out reams of paper. I thought,

'What is she ever going to do with that?' I remember when computers first started, my daughter said we would never be able to keep anything private anymore; everything was going to be available to everybody. It's getting to be that way. I don't have a computer and I feel safer without one. I wouldn't know what to do with it if I had one. My husband always used to say we ought to get a computer. I said, 'What would we do with it? We can't figure out this VCR.'"

Jeanette

"How many children do you have, Jeanette?" asked Kitty.

"Four," answered Jeanette. "I have seven grandchildren and three great-grandchildren. They're all spread out from one end of the country to another. Nobody decided to stay in Burlington."

"That must make it hard for you to see everybody," I said.

"I don't see them as often as I would like," Jeanette replied. "I feel lucky if I see each one once a year."

"Have you always lived here?" I asked Jeanne.

"No," she answered. "I moved here. I became a divorce statistic and I went back to college to get my master's in institution management at Iowa State University. That was an exciting adventure to do with a teaching assistant's salary, two kids, and getting a master's."

"That seems unusual in that time to be trying to get through school," I said. "That must have been tough."

"It worked out fine, and I was the director of school food service for Burlington Community School District after I got my master's," Jeanne continued. "It worked out because my kids and I were on the same schedule. I had a ten-month contract, so I was off in the summers when they were."

"I was Jeanne's secretary," said Jeanette. "She kept the place running. We kept it running smooth for quite a lot of years. I retired in 1988 and spent a lot of time traveling with my husband in Canada, Mexico, Europe, and many trips in the United States to visit our children, other family, and just sightseeing. I have had a full and happy life. I was born and raised in Burlington, was married to my high school sweetheart for fifty-nine years until his death in 2006. We raised our four children here. They all graduated from college, married, and raised their own families in various parts of the country. They are my pride and joy."

"Jeanne, did you remarry?" Kitty asked.

"No," Jeanne replied. "I have lived in Burlington some thirty years, I guess. I have fantastic neighbors. I'm one of the golden oldies."

"We are getting that way, aren't we," commented Lou.

"When we first moved to our neighborhood we were the youngest," added Jeanette. "When we left we were the oldest. All the other neighbors had left. We lived in the same house for fifty-five years. Not a lot of people do that anymore."

"Marian, have you lived here all of your life?" I asked.

"Yes, all but a couple of years when Bob first started with the telephone company and we were in Davenport," Marian replied. "Right after we were first married he got transferred for a couple of years and then transferred back again. I have two boys and a girl."

"We were talking the other day with my kids, and they were saying how fast the years go by," said Jeanette. "They are just beginning. Of course their kids are all grown up now, too, and getting married or in college. I said, 'Just wait until you get to be a few years older than that, the years seem to click off just like nothing.' We were talking about how when you're a child the summer vacations are endless. It feels like forever, like you have a year to play. I can still hear my dad when he was in his nineties saying, 'Where have all the years gone?' Now I'm saying the same thing."

"I hear even the young people say it goes fast," added Marian.

"I think it's maybe the pace," Jeanette responded.

"I think it is too," I added. "We run to keep up with technology and all the other demands the world puts on us."

"Nancy and I went into some backwaters yesterday," Kitty said. "We floated along and discovered that there was finally enough current that if we stopped paddling we were still moving, so we just floated while we had lunch. I thought, 'Here we are, living life at one mile per hour.' It's almost incomprehensible how when I go back to Ely, to the rest of my life, how fast it will be. It just doesn't happen at one mile per hour."

After dinner, the other ladies headed home and we went to bed. Later that evening, I wandered out of my room and found Gwyn working on her computer. She worked on her job back home every free moment she had. That night she was motivated to get things done so she could paddle worry-free the next day.

September 30, Day Twenty-Seven

We started with a hearty breakfast of hot oatmeal, raisins, and walnuts. Gwyn was bubbly. It was strange to pull our kayaks off a van parked under a house. It was a way of life for Lou, who had arrived from her home in town to give us a "good send-off." She watched and said she'd never been in a kayak and was uncertain how they worked. I told Lou about my aunt Joyce, who at age ninety still sent Christmas cards with pictures of her in new places doing unexpected things. She sent one with her in a NASA suit and another with her riding a four-wheeler, dressed in blaze orange, and holding a shotgun. I suggested that Lou get in one of the kayaks, and we'd take her picture to use for a Christmas card. Her face filled with a mixture of excitement and fear.

Down at the water, Kitty was giving Gwyn a quick kayak lesson and covering safety tips. Lou was relieved that we had life jackets. We pulled Kitty's kayak onto the boat ramp for Lou. She put on a life jacket and carefully climbed in. Gwyn and I took either end of the kayak and slid her into the water next to the ramp for the picture. Lou was tickled. We got her safely to dry land, and Gwyn and I departed.

Lou wrote in the paddlers' journal:

> *I enjoyed having you. May your trip be safe and your experiences as great as our pleasure in sharing with you. Getting to know ladies' adventurism is awesome.*
>
> *Lou and friends at the cabin.*

Photo by Kitty Kennedy

We paddled a short distance, and I began to sing. Gwyn loved hearing the song because it spoke to her, so being on the water while I sang was a special treat for her. We paddled O'Connell Slough, heading toward Burlington with herons as our companions. Palm tree number twenty-two grew in a pot on a deck of another home. At the end of the slough, we passed an industrial area with a barge scrap yard. Half of a barge was sunk in the water, so we paddled in to get a better idea of how big they were.

Gwyn was surprisingly talkative. She was normally quiet, observant, and didn't open up to people easily. With no other paddlers around, she spoke freely. We were too busy off the water to really connect, so I felt honored to be able to talk with her in a personal way. We talked about how some people came into the world knowing who they were and the boundaries that confine them, while others spent a lifetime trying to figure it out. Gwyn said sometimes she felt guilty because she was so clear about where she was headed that it was hard to watch others struggle to discover something that seemed so basic to her. We discussed how some people can be born knowing their purpose, but their environment strips that purpose away and forces their identity underground. The more valuable the characteristic, the deeper it was hidden. We acknowledged that, for some people, struggle was necessary in order to learn.

Gwyn and I discovered that we had things in common, like our fear of being incompetent. We frequently feared we had let other people down, when in reality we had done a stellar job. Gwyn admitted that was how she felt at the start of the trip, and that Pat G. had helped her get over it. I was stunned she had felt that way. I assured her she had not let us down and we had all experienced her as nothing short of a gift.

Gwyn's keen observational skills didn't miss a thing. Everything fascinated her. She repeated over and over how excited she was to paddle and how much it meant to her. She felt guilty that Kitty was giving up a day paddling, but I reminded her that Kitty wanted a day by herself to process her thoughts.

The Highway 34 bridge stretched over the river at the end of the slough. The numerous cables used to construct it looked spectacular against the blue sky. Gwyn called it a "string art" bridge. Out on big water, a strong wind came from the east, so we crossed the channel and hugged the opposite shore. Passing underneath the bridge the wind suddenly got stronger, and Gwyn said, "It's like a wind tunnel through here."

The big waves were more fun, but required skill and balance. The front of the kayak rose up and slapped back down into the water. Our paddling had to be strong and constant, and the rudder was used to hold the line directly into the waves. Each wave hit us in the face with a cool splash. The waves rolled off our  spray skirts, which kept us dry and kept the kayak upright. Without a spray skirt, a big wave could fill the cockpit and throw us off balance.

We took a break near a boat launch where three men loaded branches onto their johnboat. The branches were piled high, leaving room only for the driver. They were bringing brush to a duck blind to prepare it for hunting season. A load of brush on the flatbed waited for their return.

The waves grew even more intense. People along the shore dropped their jaws and stared at us in disbelief as we battled through the waves. At Two Mile Island, we found shelter from the wind and took a floating break. I asked Gwyn if the wind was too much for, but her let's-go-for-it attitude was still strong. Gwyn's hard paddling was rewarded with a large flock of pelicans on a sandbar. We drifted near them until they took flight.

We found more relief from the wind in Turkey Chute. The tree canopy arched over our heads. Downed trees jutted into the water, and trees floated under the surface. Turtles sunned themselves on the trunks of the downed trees and scrambled into the water from their posts when we paddled by. Turtle heads poked out of the water in front of us.

Gwyn spotted a downy, white feather stuck in a tree and went after it. Being a former falconer, she knew about the Migratory Bird Treaty Act, which provided protection for migratory birds. The law prohibited the collection of any migratory bird feathers, eggs, and nests. Gwyn studied the feather for a few moments before letting it go.

Duck blinds lined both shores. One resembled an old railroad car and looked like it could fit fifteen people. Some duck blinds were directly across the channel from each other, which seemed dangerous. Many had ramps so

dogs could easily get back in after retrieving a bird. Around a bend was a duck blind with decoys floating around it. As we paddled closer, real ducks took flight and surprised us; we hadn't noticed them among the decoys.

Soon the water was too shallow to paddle in, and we walked in the slimy mud, carefully placing each step so as not to sink. For several yards, the narrows presented one muddy challenge after another, until it suddenly turned into completely dry land.

We left the boats and scouted how far we had to portage. It was 200 yards to the water. An old tire sat partially buried in the sand about halfway across. We dragged our kayaks near the tire and used it as a tripod for the camera. We over-dramatized our plight, as if we were lost and confused, and took a photo.

More mud waited for us at the other end of the dry riverbed. I put my kayak in the water and slid my muddy feet into the cockpit, making black smears across the bottom. I paddled ten feet from shore and got stuck on the muddy bottom. Drained from portaging, I leaned back to rest while I waited for Gwyn. Once her kayak was floating, she made several attempts to get in while avoiding the mud. "I don't want to get Kitty's kayak dirty. There has to be a way to do this." She eventually surrendered and stepped in the mud. Seated in the kayak, she hung her feet over the sides into the water while she rubbed and rinsed her shoes. Learning that Mississippi mud does not release its slimy grip easily, she gave up. Her muddy feet went into the kayak.

Paddling hard and lunging forward, I released myself from the mud's grip. Our paddles scraped the muddy bottom in places, while the headwind created high waves. We realized that the combination of big waves and our exhaustion was unsafe and that we needed to pull out. We called Kitty to determine a pick up location. Describing the meeting spot to Kitty on the phone reminded me of the confusion Cheryl and I had experienced in the backwaters south of La Crosse.

"There's a little road that crosses the highway just after a tiny creek that creates a little peninsula on the north end of a bay. Across the tracks from that is a broken line that could be a road. Do you see it?" I asked.

"You mean the road that is just past the road that looks like an upside down U?" she responded.

"What upside down U?" I asked.

Eventually we settled on a spot and hoped our descriptions matched up.

Dark clouds moved in and threatened rain. Coming around a small point, we saw the top of the van over the thick vegetation along the shore. Kitty directed us to a shallow channel through the weeds that was barely wider than our kayaks. I drove my paddle into the bottom of the river to determine how soft the mud was, and it sank ten inches. More mud waited for us on shore. I felt the it ooze between my toes and wrap around my ankles as I stepped out of the kayak. The mud held tightly. Each step required extra effort to release my foot from the mud, and I nearly lost a shoe.

We pulled away from the landing and headed to Dallas City, Illinois, while Kitty filled us in on her day. She had met a woman named Ruby and her husband, Rich, who live in Dallas City. They offered us water and the use of their garage if the weather turned bad. Ruby had given Kitty a tour of Dallas City in her golf cart and had found a place to store our kayaks for the night. She told Kitty how, shortly after they moved to Dallas City, Rich had decided to do something about all the garbage along the waterfront. He began the dirty job of pulling 150 tires out of the water and made arrangements for them to be picked up. Walking past the pile of tires later, he saw a young boy rolling a tire down the road and back into the river. Astonished, he asked the boy what he was doing. The boy said, "I'm putting the tires into the river where they belong." The boy had already put nearly 100 tires back "where they belonged." Ruby and Rich were appalled that no one had taught the boy differently. While some worked tirelessly to care for the river, others were clueless about the damage they did.

Ruby had a sign in front of her house that showed the water level from the flood of 1993. She described how they had sandbagged the house to keep the water out.

At camp, we had the luxury of a shelter with electricity. With the tents up, we opened the well-supplied food bin and began preparing dinner.

"Kitty, I got the full deal today—high waves, relatively calm water, crossing the channel, pelicans, egrets, eagles, crows, seagulls, and lots of turtles. It was everything I could have hoped for," beamed Gwyn.

"I am glad you had such a rich experience," said Kitty.

Darkness came quickly. The cool, swirling air felt refreshing as it swept through the trees and softened the train whistles 100 yards away. A searchlight from an approaching barge moved through the foggy air.

More exhausted than usual after a fifteen-mile day, I snuggled into my sleeping bag, grateful for a cool evening. Rain tapped at my tent, which twisted and bent in the wind. Lightning flashed like a strobe light while thunder rolled across the sky.

October 1, Day Twenty-Eight

I did not sleep well and was frequently awakened by the trains. Each time I woke, I fell back asleep praying that the wind would blow itself out by morning. Morning came, and though the high wind continued under a heavily clouded sky, the rain had moved on.

I walked down a road along the river's edge. After I sang, I stood, with the spray from the waves splashing my feet, and stared at the rolling water and the big trees that bowed to the wind. The waves were bound to grow stronger as the day progressed, and my energy resources were depleted. Eight miles of paddling on wild water was eight too many. We would not paddle that day.

Back at camp, Kitty was concerned about paddling. I told her we were not going out and she replied, "I was not very excited about taking on those waves."

We had begun packing up camp when Nancy Leigh and Lionda arrived to paddle with us. They also looked relieved to hear we weren't paddling, though they had been willing to give it a try. Lionda said she could use the day to get her pottery ready for an upcoming show. We thanked them for coming and encouraged them to join us at the next Gathering.

We headed to Nauvoo, Illinois, best known for the Mormon temple built there. The temple was a sacred place for the Mormon community. The name Nauvoo meant "pleasant land." We walked around the outside of the impressive white-marble temple. A golden angel trumpeted its horn on top of the steeple and the gardens and lawn were spectacular. The temple was built in 1846, later burned down  by radicals, and rebuilt in 2002. Mormons traveled from the world over to visit the temple. We knew little of the Mormon history, so we headed to the information center. Inside, I felt uncomfortable because we were dressed in our paddling attire, while all the other women wore shin-length dresses and the men wore suits and ties. My discomfort grew when I saw we were being discussed, and a woman headed our way. She told us there was a women's garden around the side of the building we should see and said, "It's dedicated to you." From a brochure I picked up on the way out, I learned that the Mormons arrived in Nauvoo with Joseph Smith, their leader. They were run out of Missouri and, in the early 1900s, returned to begin reconstruction of Nauvoo.

The garden was exquisite, with several large bronze statues depicting women's lives. The sculpture faces depicted warmth and beauty. The gardens were lush and green with a rainbow of flowers. I was enthralled by each sculpture. It surprised me that there was one of a woman sculpting clay, which was dedicated to honoring women's talents. A statue of an elderly woman quilting in a rocking chair captured my attention. The detail in her face and hands and the quilt were stunning. We walked from one sculpture to the next, enjoying the peacefulness. However, hunger soon drove us to a nearby restaurant for lunch.

"A few years ago, I had an experience with my mom that changed our relationship," said Kitty as we ate. "I always felt like a little girl when I was with her. While I was sitting at my mom's house decorating cookies at the kitchen table, she started instructing me on how to do it. This time, I spoke up and told her I was not a little girl anymore. She didn't turn around at first. She stood and looked out the window. When she turned around, she acknowledged what I was feeling, which validated it for me. She trusted my knowing. Our whole relationship changed. I remember that was the point where I found my balance with my mother. It's still vivid in my mind how I grew up that day in my eyes and my mother's.

"Gwyn, it is interesting to me that you didn't tell your mom you were doing this. Nancy, your mom isn't here to tell. When I told my mom I was going to be doing this, her first reaction was about safety and then about taking the time off from work. As our departure time got closer, both Mom and Dad had all kinds of questions. I felt supported by them when they sent a contribution to help sponsor the trip. I cried when I got it, because I really wanted their support in doing this. My mom and older sister are going to be at Cis's in St. Louis when we get there. They are going to stay three days and come to the Gathering. It means a lot to me that Mom is going to be at the final destination when I get there. It was important that our relationship changed when I was in my mid-thirties, but I still feel a little piece of me that wants her approval."

"Has it shifted from approval to pride?" I asked.

"Yes, there is a piece of that in there," answered Kitty. "I have this thing about pride, thinking that it is a negative thing. I haven't clarified the difference between being prideful and being proud."

"I meant her pride in you," I said. "For me it's different to want someone I care about to be proud of me. I think a lot of people want their parents to be proud of them. Sometimes I still wish my dad was alive, because I know he would think this was great. I also know he'd think it was a little crazy, but you know." We laughed.

"I actually decided last night that I would tell my mother I was here for the second week, but not for the whole three weeks," said Gwyn. "That might not seem quite as irresponsible as being here for three weeks. She will be happy that I was doing something for myself. The complication is that recently I've backed out every time I was going to go to see my sister or my parents, who only live across the state ."

"And then you traveled this far to do this," I added.

"Exactly," said Gwyn. "My mom has been pushing me to do more things for myself lately, because she knows my work has gotten so stressful, but this would be more about priorities. I'm afraid she would think, 'You don't come to see me, but then you drive halfway across country to do this with strangers?' If I don't come because of work she understands but maybe not for something like this. I'm trying to avoid all that by not telling her how long I'm really here."

"So, you're afraid she is going to think you are choosing something else over her, and she is going to be hurt," I said.

"Yes, and I'm not sure I want to go there," Gwyn said sadly.

"The work ethic with that generation was always very clear to me as I grew up," I said. "'Can't come because of work.' Well, okay. 'Can't come because I am having fun someplace else.' Well, that is not okay."

We drove to our hotel in Fort Madison, Iowa. Crossing the bridge, the aerial view of the river was enthralling. From that vantage point, the water was expansive and the whitecaps were intimidating. Our rooms at the Kingsley Inn were stately. The building had been impeccably restored to its original, graceful style, down to the furniture and wall hangings. Each room had the name of a historical person significant to the area posted on its door. Kitty's and my large room had a king and queen size bed, dresser, desk and chairs, and it offered a view of the river. We took a quick nap before heading to Fort Madison's Riverview Park for the Gathering.

It was a cool, sunny evening. We began the Gathering with twenty women ranging in age from forty-nine to eighty-one. Jane E. walked up to join us, and before she said much more than her name I immediately had a knowing that she was to receive one of the thirteen heron feathers.

Faye was the elder of the evening but was hesitant to speak.

Faye

"I came to listen, but the wisdom I would like to share with the younger ones is to enjoy every day. Take time every day to look around you and not spend a lot of time fretting about the next day. As I have grown older, I have learned that each day is precious and each little incident is wonderful. I look forward to each day when I wake up, and even though I have aches and pains and a lot of problems health-wise, I look forward to and enjoy each day. One of my favorite things to do, as my friends know, is watch the birds. I guess as I have gotten older nature has grown more important to me. I enjoy birds. I am feeding hummingbirds and thoroughly enjoying them."

Sandra spoke next. "I was looking at these questions, and these are the meaningful questions that we approach and all ask ourselves during our lives. The one I feel I could talk about a little tonight is 'What does being courageous mean to you?' I think it takes so much courage just to be our authentic selves. I think it is so difficult for women, and people in general, to be truly authentic. It's something that takes courage. I see these women here, some of who I know personally. I know how courageous they are and how much I admire them. I think a lot of us have been on this path for a long time, trying to be courageous and just being true to ourselves."

"I agree. It's very hard to be your own authentic self," responded Ann L. "I am finally finding, through many trials, that is where my path is leading me. They weren't really trials; they only strengthened me. In my sunroom, I have a duck with tennis shoes on, and it says 'Dare to be different.' That is kind of what I am doing. I don't need to follow the crowd. I am becoming more and more secure with my own beliefs. This is my spiritual path that I'm on."

"When I first started my career, I was a teacher, and I did that for five years," said Juanita. "I taught some of you here tonight. Then I decided that I wasn't a very good disciplinarian. I decided the day I went to one classroom and about threw up that it was time to change. [Laughter.] That was a big change for me because I always believed I was going to be a teacher. Then we had a fabric shop, but the chain stores scrunched us out of that. Then I went to work for the state as a job-placement person. I have met wonderful people, and some of them are here. I really, really loved and love helping them find jobs. My life has had several twists and turns, and I think I ended up where I belong."

"The question that appeals to me the most is how spirituality influenced my life," continued Cindy. "We live in a Western culture where we believe in God in a traditional way, and that has never really touched me very much. I have read about the Native American beliefs, and that appears to me to be the way the world works. I had the opportunity, at Bald Eagle Days in Keokuk, Iowa, to watch and participate in a ceremony they held. It was called an Honorary Dance. The first thing they did was have the elder couple that was honored dance around the circle. Then all the people who were Natives danced around the circle with them. Then they invited everyone that was there to dance around the circle. I'm the kind of person to sit back and watch. I don't like to dance, and I don't like to be in the middle of the circle, but my friend said, 'We have to do this.' I said, 'Okay, all right.' As soon as I entered that circle the tears started streaming down my face. It was very powerful to me for some reason. I thought, 'What a neat way to honor our elders.' I just can't imagine how neat it must have felt to have been those honored people at that ceremony."

"I also like the spirituality question," said Jane E. "I started out as a minister's daughter. I was adopted. It was a wonderful family to grow up in. About twelve or thirteen years ago, I moved back to Iowa from Connecticut. I left my ex-husband. I had already started going to a different church and discovered that there were a lot of things I thought I believed that I really didn't. When I came to Burlington, I got to go out to the reservation three different times. It was very eye-opening. I felt like I was at home. Then I discovered my birth mother and that I am part Native American. Wow, that really opened my eyes. I remember a bumper sticker that I saw at one of the powwows that said "We are not human beings having a spiritual life; we are spiritual beings having a human life." I love the thought that we keep going."

Nancy Leigh took the fan and tape recorder from Jane E. and said, "This feels awkward, doesn't it, talking to a box." Speaking directly into the tape recorder as if it were a walkie-talkie, she said, "Hello box, this is Nancy. Over. [Laughter.] The questions all sort of overlap for me, but I will talk about the wisdom I would like to share with younger women. The thing I have learned, particularly in the past few years from my spirituality group, is to be something every day. Like Sandra said, 'Take time to just enjoy every day.' Don't worry about tomorrow or yesterday, just simply be where you are today. For me it works to be outdoors; it doesn't matter what the weather is. Nature really helps me connect with whatever the 'Source' with a capital 'S' is anytime. So my advice to everyone is just take time to BE."

She handed the box to Esther and said, "Talk to the box," and we laughed again.

Esther smiled and said, "Today is my birthday. I turned fifty-six today. Every year on my birthday I go to the river and sit and contemplate what went on in the last year of my life and where I want to head next year, which leads into the question about following your path. It is really neat when things just happen. Like when things are really going bad, or good, and all of a sudden something happens, things change, and you realize why it went the way it did. You can't see it when it's in front of you, but you look back and see how everything that has happened to you has influenced where you are right now. In the last few years, I have realized that there is a difference between being religious and being spiritual. I was religious for a long time and then I became spiritual. There were so many things which, for me, didn't fall into place. Religion told me what to think. Spirituality let me see things in a different light. I like to think of myself now as a spiritual person, one who is just following the path."

Joni spoke next. "I was a stay-at-home mom for twenty years. After my husband lost his job, I was on the Internet looking for a job for him when I found my calling as a police dispatcher. I looked forward to going to work every time I could. I worked every hour I could. I loved my job. In 2004, my husband passed away. I was a single mom with two kids, one in high school and one in college. I knew I had to go out and find a full-time job. It wasn't until that point that I realized God had been preparing me for this all along, because I found strength at the police department. I had a huge fear of being by myself, so what shift did I get to work? The graveyard shift. All by myself in that police station, but I was a button away from three officers out in the field.

"As of about two weeks ago, I found out that I am losing my job, but I feel God has chosen this path for me because he has bigger and brighter plans for me. Most recently, I have been working as the secretary for public works. It came time to put together a résumé, which is something I never thought I would have to do. The gal that helped me put the résumé together said, 'Honey, you're not going to have trouble finding a job. You have the qualifications that everybody is looking for.'

"No, this isn't the path I would have chosen. I loved being a stay-at-home mom. I loved being a mom period. I probably would have had more kids if I could have afforded it. I loved being pregnant. I know that God is looking out for me and my two kids. My daughter is now in graduate school. She was an art major, and she couldn't get into grad school to blow glass. I told her when she was applying to grad school for the second time, 'Did you ever consider applying in a different field?' Well, she applied in three fields: glass blowing, art history, and women's and gender studies. What program do you think she got accepted into? Women's and gender studies. So she's now at the University of Northern Iowa studying women's and gender studies. She just called me tonight all in tears and said, 'I can't stand all these women.' [Laughter.] She has always been a loner because she didn't want to fall into the bad crowd. In fact, she was a police dispatcher in her first few years of college. She has always kind of kept to herself and done her own thing. This year, she's finally making friends and going out to eat with these kids and I think, 'Oh, finally she has a social life.' Then she calls in tears saying 'I can't stand these women.' Anyway, I know God is looking out for us, and I know we will be all right."

Esther

"Something that I have realized from the topics we are talking about tonight is how difficult it is being your true self," remarked Esther. "When I was younger I looked for somebody I really liked. Then I wanted to grow up to be like them, but that is not the way it went, trust me. There is no one like me, yet we are all alike. I grew up in a very dysfunctional family without a mother. Everything was really crazy in our household, but it made me everything I am today. I went through alcohol and drug treatment. I did learn new ways to cope. I always knew that there were certain things in life that happen and that everything happens for a reason. Those reasons are not always clear to us until we look back on them. It's remarkable when you have that "aha moment" and you can say, 'Wow! That's why this or that happened. It was to get me prepared for what I would be doing next.' I have no idea what I am going to be doing next. Sometimes I get stuck. Friends see me as a courageous person, but I don't see me as a courageous person. I wish we could just look in the mirror and see ourselves the way others see us.

"It takes courage to become wise. Wisdom comes from living life. Life comes from God. Like that poem that was read earlier, we could be a lot happier if we just let things go. I think it's wonderful that you talk about the elders and the older people and how we should respect them. I think that's getting lost in our society. We don't respect our elders the way Native Americans do. Unfortunately, I think the lack of respect is getting worse and worse."

Ann L. responded to Esther by posing a question. "What can we do as women to change that?"

The women broke into laughter and all agreed that was deep—question number six.

"Ann," I responded, "in asking question number six, you get to be the first person to respond to number six." There was more laughter from the group.

Ann L. smiled thoughtfully and said, "When I originally heard about this, I thought there should be a lot of world leaders here to listen to us women. We need to first of all respect ourselves and then somehow share our wisdom with younger people. I am not a grandmother, but I'm an aunt and great-aunt and great-great-aunt, and I hopefully have been a role model of some sort to the younger kids and my family. I wish they would show up more often, but they are teenagers now, so that doesn't happen. I'm not sure what all we can do, but I think it does need to be done. Women need to have a voice and be heard. I would like to hear what everyone thinks about that question."

A train whistle blew loudly and drowned her voice out, so I attempted to get her message across. I was drowned out by yet another train blasting its horn. I waited until I could be heard again. "I wanted to make a comment about what Ann L. said. There are indigenous cultures around the world that have had a prophecy that a time would come when the grandmothers would come together to heal the world. The prophecy specifically stated that there would be thirteen grandmothers who would come together, speak, and begin to heal the world.

"In 2004, thirteen grandmothers from all over the world came together and held council. There is a book called Grandmothers Counsel the World, by Carol Schaefer, about their gathering. One of the things they realized as they met was that they were merely representatives of the multitudes of grandmothers around the globe who do healing work. Grandmothers, like us, who meet, share their wisdom, speak, and ask important questions. It is happening. Taoism prophesies that the feminine will come forward to heal the world. And they say the time is now. You are part of it by being here. That was a great question, Ann."

"I think what we can do is have more respect for women in our culture," said Sandra. "One of the things I have become aware of as I grow older is that I'm becoming invisible to younger people. At family gatherings or maybe just out doing my business, clerks don't make the eye contact that they once did. They're slow to help me. I just think it starts with each one of us. Each of us can honor our elders. They're all around us. We can make eye contact and we can hear them. We can listen. Wouldn't it be just wonderful to dance around them? It touches my heart to hear that story. All I want to say is that we can do that."

"I want to add to what you were saying, Sandra," said Carol T. "The way we can make changes in the world is by setting examples for the younger ones, for our daughters. If we want to be respected, what we do with our elders is a way of setting examples for our children. Are we short-tempered with them? Do we have time for them? Do we go out of our way to do things with our parents and grandparents? Aunts? Uncles? Do we take them to our family gatherings? I do home health care, and I'm also a hospice volunteer, so often, I see families that are very loving with their older people. I see so many more older people who either don't have anybody or the kids stuck them in a home somewhere or in an apartment someplace. The family doesn't want to be bothered with them. Well, what about when it's our turn? If we are treating our elders that way, how are our children going to treat us? We all can make a difference."

"Several people mentioned growing up," Jane E. said, taking the conversation in a new direction. "Because we were girls, we felt like we shouldn't like math. We shouldn't be able to do math, because if we did, then we won't be able to find a nice boyfriend. Boys don't like smart girls. Yes they do, I have discovered. I have a little granddaughter who is two and a half years old, and I'm already planning that when she turns thirteen, or whenever she gets her first period, we are going to have a ceremony welcoming her into womanhood. I just can't wait! It's going to be so exciting! I can hear her say, 'Oh grandma, please.' [Laughter.] But if all of us had something like that when we were children instead of hearing the whispering and 'you can't tell anybody about this,' we would have been proud. What a difference it would have made for us. So, I am planning that for when Sophie turns thirteen."

"This speaks to the boy versus girl thing," said Ielah. "There were three of us girls in the family, and my father would obviously rather have had three boys, because he left us for somebody that had three boys, who then refused to go hunting with him. [Laughter.] I always wanted to build things and do outside things and thought dolls were really stupid. I would rather build a house than play house. For as long as I can remember, starting with a card table and blanket, I wanted to build a house. I always thought, 'I probably never can because I'm a girl, and girls don't do that.' So back in the '80s I moved to Colorado from Kansas and met another gal who had the same dream. She had been married twice to construction workers, and she had never built her own house either and thought she would never get to because the men would do it. We moved to Minnesota, and we built our own house. We lived in a tent for three months while we tried to get the shell of this house up to keep us from freezing to death the first winter. It was wonderful to be able to sit in that house, even though it wasn't finished, and look at the rocks in the fireplace and look at the ceiling that we put in board by board and know that what we had been through was incredible. I had no idea when I started that it would be the thing that would change my life. It was just something I always wanted to do, but after that, the sky was the limit. I haven't done anything fantastic. It's just that I know that whatever I want to do, I can do.

"We built it in Bemidji, Minnesota, and were the entertainment on Sunday afternoons. It was the Minnesota version of tailgating while we built that house. People would come with their coolers and their lawn chairs and sit. The first couple of weeks we thought, 'Oh, how nice if we really need another hand.' Uh-uh. We found out they were there because they believed two women could never build a house and they wanted to be there when we broke to see what broke us. If that doesn't fan your fire, I don't know what else will. [Laughter.] We put that house up, and after that, we were the place to come drink coffee because everybody thought we were just great. We were the 'witchy women' I guess, because we managed to do it. Whatever you want to do, go do it, because you can if you want it bad enough."

"I was listening to Ielah and thinking that so many of us who were raised in our generation were taught limitations," Connie K. added thoughtfully. "I'm sure my parents meant well, but my father did his best to try to steer me into one of the three approved jobs—teacher, nurse, or secretary. And you might possibly stretch that to airline stewardess. I rejected all of those. There is nothing wrong with any of those professions; they are wonderful jobs if you feel called to do them, but I was rebellious, even at that age, and decided, 'I am going to show you.' I went after the men's jobs because they paid well. That's why I was a truck driver for about six years. It was a very hard, physical job. The men did their best to run me off. They sabotaged things. I could curl your hair and you wouldn't need a perm for a year with all of things they did to me to try to run me off of the job. I'm certainly not any saint by any stretch of the imagination. I probably could have done all kinds of nasty things to them in return, and several things occurred to me too, but I chose to do helpful things. When one guy got stuck in the ice, I got my log chain out and pulled him out. When one of them dumped his truck with all the merchandise, I went over and helped him pick it up. Eventually you win them over. They finally just gave up. 'Well, we are not going to run her off, so we might as well just settle and just tolerate her.'

"I noticed as I went through life that I seemed to want to choose things that were hard to do. I set myself some kinds of challenges. I certainly didn't intend to marry three alcoholic husbands, I can tell you that. I divorced all three of them and wish them well. The good side of that was I chose to go into a career as a chemical-dependency counselor. I also have two of my own children and thirteen great step-kids that I helped raise along the way. There are some benefits. I learned I can't walk somebody else's path for them. I just have to walk my own."

Faye spoke next. "I don't know if I can express how I feel. I have just been fascinated by listening to all of you. I grew up in a household where mother tended to the children and listened to the father, and my father went to work and came home. I never had any challenges. I never did. I just envy you and think how wonderful for you, because I never did get brave like you all did. It's just wonderful and I want to say again and again: don't quit, don't stop. As long as you have energy and you can move, just keep going. I think it's just wonderful!"

"Thank you for saying that," Karen R. responded to Faye. "I have a mother who is your age, and she would be on the other side of the fence. I sit now and look at what she taught us then and I see she's still thinking like she lives back then. That's a great thing to hear from one of our grandmothers. I totally agree with doing what you want to do. Sometimes we have to be coerced though. [Cindy giggled.] Cindy laughs because she knows she coerced me into cleaning a fish. I'm married, and my husband is an avid fisherman. He has always baited my hook and cleaned and cooked my fish, but now the cat is out of the bag. He knows I can clean a fish, but he still does it. I have eight grandchildren, and I think it is important to take the time to go and participate in whatever they need. We must show them where we are coming from and what we have done. Encourage them to do what we are all talking about. Teach them they can move on and do anything they want to, whether they are girls or boys."

Cindy quickly chimed in, "I would like to tell the rest of her story. I got to witness Karen cleaning a fish for the first time at an outdoor adventure camp for girls aged fifteen to eighteen. It's kind of funny because she wasn't going to do it. 'No, I'm not going to do it.' I kept egging her on, 'Now, you came here to teach the little girls to do things, so you have to try this.' She said, 'No, I'm not going to do it.' I finally gave up on her and didn't think she was going to do it. The next thing I see, she's over there cleaning that fish. It was really cool! Her daughter and granddaughter were also at the camp. Her granddaughter was really scared to climb up into a tree stand. She got about halfway up, froze, and she came back down. The next day she tried to shoot a gun, and she was kind of scared to do that, but she did it. She took on some challenges that she wouldn't normally have done. The next day she had developed so much confidence that she climbed all the way up in that tree stand, two or three times at least. Then her mother went up in the tree stand, too. They were really inspired by Karen just cleaning the fish. She did something—I don't know if you would describe it as scary exactly, grossed out probably—anyway, she did something she didn't want to do and she inspired her daughter and granddaughter to do something new. I thought it was really neat to see them grow by watching her take on something difficult."

"I look for the magic in what happens all of the time," added Jane E. "A couple of years ago, five of us girls from Cedar Falls High School, class of 1962, got together. We hadn't always been that close when we were young, but we've grown together as we've gotten older. For our gathering, I bought little beads and had them strung on some string for each one of them. I put it in a bag, and you know what happened to those strings? I opened the bag and they had gotten so tangled. I thought, 'Oh no, what a shame,' and my friend Mary said, 'Well, let's just get busy and untangle them.' I think I have a picture of the five of us sitting around in a circle together untangling the strings. While we were doing that one of them looked up and said, 'You know, that's what life is all about, you hang together and untangle the strings.'"

"I was sitting here thinking about how when we first started this evening everyone was sitting around and nobody wanted to say anything," commented Esther. "It was like 'I don't have anything to give; I don't have any wisdom.' Then Cindy brings something up about Karen, and Juanita brings something up about Cindy. We can see it in others. I hope that someday we can all get to a point where we can see the value in ourselves. All of us!"

After the Gathering was over, I approached Jane E. and gave one of the heron feathers. She held it tightly to her chest, cried, and thanked me.

"Thanks for the opportunity to gather with other grandmothers," Connie K. said to me afterwards. "This was the first time I saw my forty-nine-year-old friend silent for such a long time. I was expecting her to explode any moment. She's not used to being silent, but she said it was a wonderful experience listening to the rest of us."

Nancy Leigh, who is a poet and an author, shared a poem about

the river with me.
    Colors of the Mississippi
    By Nancy Leigh Harless

The mud green water turns tawny umber as the sun burns
a path behind the oak-lined shore,
the sky paints herself a rosy shade of wonder.

In the calm surrender of evening
Old Man River begins to sing his blues,
in the most unforgettable shades of indigo,
deeper and darker, until sometime after midnight,
he inks down to a cyanotic slow, dark as the devil's own colon.

And there he swings, between misery and melancholy,
until morning sun spills over the dark water
and the spirit of the river unfurls her silk scarf—
a garnet whisper undulating in the gentle
morning breeze and slow crimson current.

You gasp in awe of the scarlet wonder,
but sooner than your sigh,
that ole river rolls back over,
returns to drab muddy green, and you wonder
if that silk scarf was real.

October 2nd through 6th

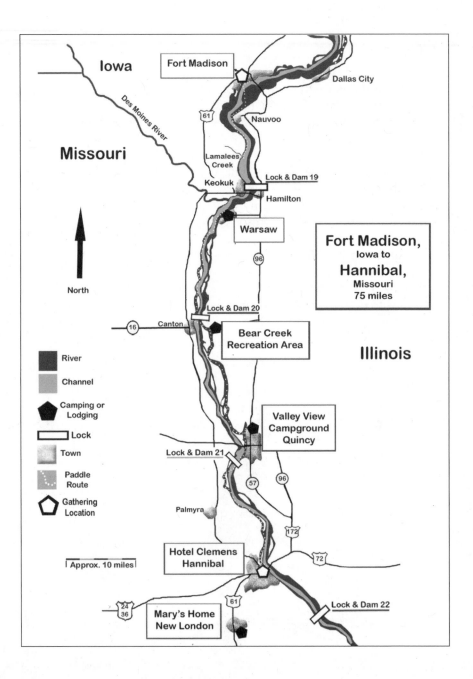

Fort Madison to Hannibal

October 2, Day Twenty-Nine

The weather forecast predicted high winds and thunderstorms. I was not looking forward to paddling twenty-five miles in that. At breakfast, Gwyn and Kitty talked about the Gathering with awe. They were impressed with the openness of the women and how they supported each other without judgment, only with compassion and recognition of their similarities.

We headed to the Fort Madison boat launch, which was bustling with activity. A long line of large boats with big motors were launching as fast as they could. We quietly readied our kayaks and waited for a break in the action. Kitty started to adjust her rudder as we floated in the small marina. I said, "Let's get out of this marina and on the river first. I don't want to start my day off getting yelled at by some man." Kitty looked startled but followed me to the river.

I paddled away from shore, sang, and released the sticks from the Gathering. As I watched them drift away, Kitty paddled close and said she'd had a realization about her life. My comment about getting yelled at first thing in the morning had struck a chord. In her job, she often dealt with people who bumped up against regulations that wouldn't let them do what they wanted. She was the person on the other side of the counter whom people took their frustrations out on. She said her day often started with getting yelled at, and often it was by a man. Getting yelled at had become normal for her, but it was actually an awful way to start the day. She decided she needed to do something about it. She said, "That must be part of the reason I dread going to work in the morning. Who wants to start their day that way?" Lost in thought, we headed across the channel toward Everingham Island.

My thoughts drifted to the Gathering and Cindy's story about Karen R. cleaning the fish for her granddaughter. It was such a simple thing that had had such a great impact. Inspiration was often delivered in simple acts that were easy to dismiss. A moment of courage could speak volumes to everyone around us.

I thought about Ielah's story about building a house and how the neighbors had come to watch, not to help. Women are often perceived as not being able to accomplish something like that on their own. I thought nothing of swinging a hammer or running the chainsaw. I forgot that for many women those things were not a part of their lives. I had learned early on that there were different rules for girls, but necessity often caused me to cross the established gender line. If something needed to be done, I would do it. For me, the gender line had become blurred by constantly competing with my brothers, which made me more comfortable doing less-feminine things.

I scanned both shorelines and saw nothing but green trees with an occasional yellow tinge. I was disappointed. "It's October, and it's just too green," I sighed. For a Minnesota girl, October was alive with reds, oranges, yellows, and golds. Back home, the landscape would be filled with bright red sugar maples and golden aspens and birches. The road leading to our home would be a brilliant orange corridor of tamaracks. I had assumed that I would see more color along the river, but it was still too early.

I began to feel discouraged, thinking about home, which added to my fatigue. We followed the shoreline and stopped at a boat ramp for a quick break. Thousands of water bugs skated on the surface of the river. Their quiet dance created a pleasant distraction for me.

From the water, we saw the Catholic church and the Mormon temple, which stood near each other in downtown Nauvoo. The steeples rose into the sky as if racing to see which one would get to heaven first. Down the shore, a man stood in the water and read from a Bible while people on the shore watched. We paddled quietly past them.

We crossed to the Iowa side of the river for Lock and Dam No. 19. The high waves in the middle of the river added to my discouragement. The strong winds day after day were breaking my spirit. We still had two more weeks of this, and our longest paddling day was yet to come. I wanted to go home, but my fear of letting people down kept me going.

I wondered how long that motivation would last. When would I stop taking care of everyone else and trying to keep them happy? I was a reluctant leader but had a mission and a passion to paddle the river and gather women's wisdom. My attitude had to change.

Kitty had been contemplating male suppression of women since the day before, but our morning discussion brought it to the forefront of her mind. She said she had felt it in the air lately and had become anxious to get out of town. She spoke about the government jobs she'd had and the suppression she had felt there. She asked, "Why is it a competition with men—between them and everyone else?" Neither of us had an answer. We guessed that cultural influences, training, and genetics all contributed to their competitive nature. Women, by nature, didn't seem to have that same competitive drive, although we sure could learn it.

While we wrestled with Kitty's question, many big motorboats passed us, which contributed to my nasty attitude. They sped through the big waves while we continued at a turtle's pace. Paddling was hard, and we were not maintaining our three-miles-an-hour average. The wind was doubling the time and energy we spent paddling.

The sky grew darker. For a break we pulled into a tiny bay, where floating logs created a barrier between us and shore. As I reached to put my water bottle away, Kitty shouted, "Snake!" I didn't understand her at first, but I saw the alarm on her face. She repeated, "Snake!" A snake was gliding across the top of the water straight toward me. I remembered Bob from the Leisure Harbor Inn saying that the ones with bright colors were poisonous. I scanned the snake as she came toward me. She was primarily brown, but some colors on her back could have been considered bright. My mind raced as I tried to figure out how bright it had to be to be poisonous. I anxiously tried to deflect the snake away from me with my paddle, but each time, she curled her body around the blade and continued to come directly at me. Soon she was too close for me to use my paddle, and I thought she would come right into the cockpit with me. Adrenaline surged through me as the snake lifted her head out of the water right next to the cockpit opening. I took a deep breath and envisioned how I would get the snake out of the cockpit. The snake raised her head higher. My body stiffened, but suddenly the snake dove under my kayak. Adrenaline surged again, and I paddled away quickly. I didn't want to see her come up on the other side.

The clouds continued to grow darker, and I felt a cool mist on my face. We paddled past a large industrial dock. Tied to the far end of the dock was a tugboat. Like other tugboats, it had the captain's name painted on the side in big, bold letters. This one said bruce t. I had a brother named Bruce who had a huge heart and a great sense of humor that kept everyone laughing. He faced issues straight on and reached out to anyone in need if there was a chance he could help them. Seeing his

name on the tugboat lifted my spirits and eased my discouragement.

A lone heron was perched on the highest point of a barge's load of coal. It looked regal yet out of place on the coal. We had seen many herons along the way around the barges and along shore. Each one was a pleasant reminder that a power greater than us was watching over us.

Fatigue set in for Kitty. The farther we paddled the quieter we became. I asked Kitty how committed she was to making it the entire distance we had scheduled for the day. Without hesitation, she said it was fine to call it a day, especially because the dark clouds building ahead of us concerned her.

Deciding to get off the water was the easy part, but actually getting off proved to be challenging. The shoreline was all either private property or too full of lotus plants to reach the shore. We paddled into the mouth of a creek, passing red-winged blackbirds perched on branches among discarded tires. Lis-

tening to them lifted my spirits and brought back memories of the first trip, when the birds had been our constant companions. We passed a refrigerator dumped at the mouth of the creek. It seemed odd that the trash remained there, since it was clearly visible to the homes along the shore.

We followed the creek upstream and came to an old bridge that only cleared the water by a few feet. Kitty hesitated as she approached it. She turned around and said, "I bet there are spiders under there." She paddled under anxiously then turned around to report no spider sightings. The bottom of the creek was sandy and weedy, and small fish darted

away from us. We continued up the creek until we got to the highway, where I pulled my kayak on the shore. Then I began the task of dragging it up the steep embankment to the road and breaking a trail through the brush and grass. Kitty followed. Pulling the kayaks uphill required muscles we didn't use while paddling, and I tired easily. We laid our kayaks to rest on the shoulder of the road. We called Gwyn for our shuttle to camp, sat on our kayaks, and waited.

Many cars passed by. We used the time to ready our kayaks for transport. A loud frog croaked in the background, resembling a creaky rocking chair. We discovered that we could lie down on our kayaks and nap once we had the cockpit covers on. I wasn't sure how long I slept, but it felt heavenly.

I explored the area across the road, which had a pumpkin patch ready for harvest. The clouds continued to thicken and the cricket song grew louder. Gwyn eventually found us and said that Kathy E. had arrived just as she was leaving to get us, so Gwyn had stayed to help get her settled.

On the way to camp we told Gwyn about the nine bad pelican sculptures we had seen along the shoreline. Our palm-tree sightings had shrunk to nothing, so we began to count bad pelican sculptures. We defined a statue as bad if we thought that a pelican with any degree of self-respect would not claim it as a likeness. Generally, the bad statues were in a comedic pose or their beaks and feet were painted Halloween orange, which wasn't even close to the normal coloring of a pelican.

We passed through Keokuk, Iowa, and drove to a campground in Warsaw, Illinois. Warsaw was known for being the town where the local newspaper had printed false statements about the Mormons in Nauvoo, which led to Joseph Smith's death there. In response to the false statements, the Smith brothers smashed the Warsaw printing press and were arrested. While they were in custody, a mob overran the jail and killed them.

Gwyn said that Penny, our football mascot, had been busy that day shopping and putting up tents. We suspected mischief when Gwyn said that she had documented the events. We would have to wait until the film was developed to know for sure.

We arrived at camp, grateful to have shelter from the rain. We greeted Kathy E., who seemed uneasy. She would paddle with us for three days. I had met Kathy E. the summer before at the Qigong Women in the Wilderness Retreat in Ely. I looked at the charts and grew worried about Kathy E.'s first day of

Kathy E.

paddling. Eighteen miles could be too much for her to start with.

Kathy E. and Gwyn began making a tasty fajita dinner in the electric skillet. We sat down to dinner and Kitty asked Gwyn, "Do you work with open mining?"

"It's surface," answered Gwyn.

"You mean strip mining?" I asked.

"They really don't want you to say that," said Gwyn.

"But isn't that what they're doing?" I said.

"Yes, that's what they are doing," replied Gwyn.

"What kind of coal is it? Is it good coal?" Kitty asked.

"Yes, it's lower sulfur and higher heat," responded Gwyn. "It outsells a lot of the East-coast coal because it causes less pollution. It's a different kind of mining in Wyoming. Back East they blow off mountaintops and throw it into the creek drainages; I wouldn't work for those guys. Our Wyoming mines sound bad, but the mining companies reclaim the land. It's never going to go back to exactly how it was, no doubt about that, but they do use native vegetation to reclaim it. It's an extremely strict process, very heavily regulated. It takes five years to get a permit each time they want to expand their activities. You might say about coal mining 'It's terrible; it's a big, ugly old hole in the ground.' But the reality is that Western coal is mined very systematically and disturbance is limited to one part of the mine at a time. Part of it is open and the rest is being backfilled or isn't mined yet. Surface mining does have an impact, but it's not the same as the disturbance associated with the natural gas industry. When we do aerial surveys, it's sad to see how much gas development has changed the landscape; it's hard to find areas that haven't been scarred. So even though the gas burns cleaner than coal in the long run, the way gas development is being managed now actually results in much greater surface disturbance than open pit mining.

"The reality is that we all consume energy. I want my lights to turn on when I flip the switch. I need my computer to turn on when I need it to turn on. But we can extract resources in a more responsible way. The surface mines in our area have a long history of doing that. Every coal mine we work with in northeast Wyoming does more than they are required to do for wildlife and actually compete with each other to win awards for their special projects and reclamation work. It's been really rewarding to see some of the coal companies change their attitudes about wildlife over the last few years and see them realize that it's in their interest to do things right."

"I remember when I moved to Ely, I was against logging," replied Kitty. "For me, it was as simple as: They are cutting the forest down, and that is bad. I don't remember what job I had, but as part of my job, I ended up in a fifth- or sixth-grade classroom, telling them that if they used toilet paper they were supporting the logging industry. I had to reconsider my beliefs."

"Since we have gotten so crazy about fire suppression, logging is the only way to clear out some of the forest," added Gwyn.

"Forest fires are a natural occurrence," I added. "Complete fire suppression doesn't make sense to me."

"No, I wish we would stop putting out all fires, especially in wild areas," said Gwyn.

"I heard that Canada doesn't suppress fires unless they threaten buildings or people," I said.

"Good for them," replied Gwyn. "They are doing that more in Yellowstone now. Smokey Bear was very effective. Many of us grew up with him, and it's really hard to undo that training. That was probably the worst thing that could have happened to forest health, in hindsight.

"Surface mining definitely does have impacts. There was one area where we had a really healthy prairie-dog colony. I used to watch the golden eagles take the prairie dogs to their nests. The mine I was helping was going to bury it. I asked why they had to put the overburden pile on top of that colony instead of somewhere else, but it was a scoria area. That meant the coal in the area had already been burned. They wanted to put their overburden on top of the dirt so they weren't burying good coal. I said, 'It's too bad we can't move the prairie dogs.' They said, 'Okay, why don't we do that?' 'I don't know how to right now, but I will figure it out,' I said. So I did.

"The first year I talked to a prairie-dog expert in Wyoming, and he said just drill a bunch of starter holes and throw them out free. We trapped them and hauled them over to the new reclamation spot where we had dug the holes, but they all ran away. I skipped a year and learned a better way to do it. The next year, we got out there with our pickaxes and shovels and buried chambers with little tubes and little cages on top. Before we put them in the cages, we mowed the area so it looked similar to where they had been. Once we put them in there they had to stay until they acclimated. The juveniles had a great time in the cages. It was like a little circus. Those little prairie dogs got in their new homes and reproduced. They had litters the next year, and the coal mine won four awards for the project. One award was from the Office of Surface Mining, which is the most prestigious award a coal mine can win. After that, they asked 'So how are our prairie dogs doing?' 'My prairie dogs are doing very well, thank you very much.'" We laughed.

"I don't have a problem working for the miners. They're really good folks who are trying to do the right thing. And as I say, I want my electricity when I flip that switch. Until I live entirely off the grid, I don't have the right to say, 'I want my energy, but I don't want energy companies to disturb anything to get it.' I have been very fortunate to have earned the trust of both the regulation agencies and the energy industry, and I'm astonished that little old me has been able to help some companies change their practices and attitudes about wildlife."

"Why does it astonish you so much that you have that power?" I asked.

"It just does," replied Gwyn with a smile. "I am just a little runt. A Sherpa."

After discussing the length of our paddle the next day, we decided that Kathy E. would join us after lunch. Kathy E. was relieved. She received a call from her husband, Bob. He said he had to pull over on his way home because of bad weather. A tornado had gone through Palmyra, Missouri, where he was headed. Palmyra was forty miles south of us and had been hit hard. We had been laughing and joking about the strong wind, hoping to convince ourselves that it wasn't that bad—turns out it was.

Night fell, and the wind died down. A paddlewheel boat passed us, moving upriver. Its sparkling lights were a spectacular site in the dark. We watched until it was out of sight.

I snuggled into my tent for the night but was interrupted by Kathy E. at my door. Her tent had leaked, so she settled into my tent, and we drifted off to sleep.

October 3, Day Thirty

Crawling from the tent, I could not have been happier to see calm water and a clear sky. Perhaps it was my fatigue or my growing discouragement, but Kitty was getting on my nerves. We had spent too much time together. I could have used a break from being together, and I guessed that she could have used one from me as well. Her tone of voice whenever she tried to cheer me up rubbed me the wrong way. We had listened to each other talk for thirty days straight, and we were starting to sound exactly alike. I would start focusing on the tone of her voice when she spoke and let it drive me crazy. I knew my discouragement had to pass.

On the other hand, I found that I wanted to spend more time with Gwyn. Other than the one day she had paddled, our time together was always short and filled with logistical details. Watching her work was like watching myself. I didn't like the reflection. Gwyn was also a driven woman who worked too hard.

Two cormorants perched on top of a windmill near the shore watched us with their wings spread, drying. I slid my kayak into the water and climbed in. I was apprehensive about the day but was looking forward to being joined by Kathy E. My kayak glided smoothly through the water, and I began to feel renewed. Discouragement melted away. Everything was beautiful in the fresh morning sun. Each paddle stroke

was effortless, and we moved quickly across the water. Kitty and I decided to try to beat Gwyn and Kathy E. to Fenway Landing for lunch. We knew they had a better chance at getting there first. A pileated woodpecker called from the trees, and we saw eagles, herons, and songbirds. We were engulfed by tranquility.

Kitty talked about the importance of faith. We'd had a conversation earlier about how she had watched me throw myself into situations, trusting that things would work out. I did have a deep sense that everything would always work out the way it was supposed to, but sometimes family issues tended to get me stuck, and I wouldn't recognize when my feelings were hurt. When it came to the Gatherings, it was easier for me to trust my internal knowing that things would be resolved as they should. Kitty talked about how she needed to trust her knowing more, since it could provide opportunities for new ways of seeing things. Watching me live that philosophy had been a great lesson for her.

Paddling around the west side of Buzzard Island, we enjoyed the intimacy of the trees. Kitty fished a butterfly out of the water and put it on her kayak so its wings could dry. It rode there for a few miles before flying off. There was more debris in the water than usual, due to the strong wind the night before. Logs, branches, leaves, and lumber floated near us. One log had an unusual shape. It was a round knot from a large tree that was missing its center. The floating log looked like a doughnut. Each time we stopped, the log floated past us. It became a quiet game of tag.

We increased our speed and managed to beat Gwyn and Kathy E. to the meeting spot after all. An older man in a plaid shirt, sitting on a white plastic bucket, greeted us. He was fishing for carp to feed his family. He proudly announced that his family ate fish every Friday. He was using a simple hook loaded with corn. A partially empty can of corn sat on the ground next to him. As we talked, he reached into the can and took a small handful for himself. "About half of the can is for me, and the other half is for the fish," he said. The man ate another handful of corn, tossed the rest in the river to feed the fish, and drove off in his old pickup.

Kitty and I settled in at a picnic table after scouting the area. We had found a plant nearby with an unusual-looking seed pod. It was a trumpet creeper, a fairly common plant there.

We learned our victory against Gwyn and Kathy E. was a hollow one when they pulled up in the van. They'd had trouble finding the landing due to road construction. At lunch, I watched Kathy E., who was quietly taking in our chatter. I sensed she was nervous, but I could feel her courage. She had been diagnosed with breast cancer two years earlier. After a year of treatment and another year restoring her strength, she was paddling the Mississippi. I commented on her courage, and she responded, "I couldn't do this without you."

"Me? Why?" I asked.

"I met you and knew you could do it. I read your book, and I decided I had to try," Kathy E. answered.

I was struck silent. What she said went to the heart of the mission of the trip and my work. That I could have that kind of impact on other women put cracks in the limiting beliefs I still held about myself.

We were giddy as we prepared to get on the water with Kathy E. She had trouble getting in her kayak and nearly tipped over. We decided it would be our common goal to keep her dry, and we gave her tips that we hoped would help. As I got in my kayak my doughnut log floated by. I wanted to bring it home, but it was too big to strap onto the kayak.

We followed Missouri Chute passed Nelson, Brownsville, and White Islands. Young trees grew on the islands. Kitty's back was bothering her, so after paddling a few miles we took a break on a sandy beach. She stretched while Kathy E. and I enjoyed the view. On the other shore was a flock of pelicans. I had begun to miss seeing them as frequently. Lock and Dam No. 20 crossed the river in Meyer, Illinois. Across from the dam, black smoke billowed upward from a large fire burning at a grain elevator.

We paddled toward the lock and joined a houseboat that was already inside. Kathy E.'s eyes were wide as she took in the process of locking through. While we waited for the water level to drop, I paddled over to talk with the couple in the houseboat. They were excited to hear about our trip. I had often wondered about the man in the little red canoe we had seen on Lake Pepin. The couple had seen him in Dubuque and said that he was doing fine and had even stopped to buy river charts.

On the downriver side of the lock, we encountered the Canton Ferry as it crossed the river from Canton, Missouri, to Meyer, Illinois. Gwyn had used the ferry earlier to get to our destination, Bear Creek Recreation Area.

We headed down Canton Chute and came across some creative duck blinds. One looked like a large, hairy bug. Many shades of green reflected off the calm water as we lazily paddled on. We passed Bear Creek and reached our campground, where Gwyn had laid the tents out to dry. We put them up so we could escape the heat with a long nap. Afterward, we made dinner while Gwyn talked about Penny's latest adventures.

"Penny and I had time to read about the Canton ferry while we waited our turn to cross the river," said Gwyn. "The ferry used to run using two horses that were on a treadmill hooked up to a paddlewheel. That ferry has been running year-round since 1840."

Penny (center) with new friends

Gwyn said that Penny had become brave and made friends with the ferry's captain. We enjoyed seeing the playful side of Gwyn that Penny had brought out. I sensed she didn't let it out often.

It was dark when we finished dinner, so we all headed for bed, except Kathy E. She sat on the picnic table and played her Native American flute. A pack of coyotes sang along with her. After Kathy E. stopped playing, Gwyn stood near my tent, calling to the owls, and they answered. I was amazed at how much she sounded like them. Gwyn's confidence, which was sprinkled with gentleness and compassion, was inspiring. I had seen signs of her talons and knew she could use them skillfully to defend those in her care, whether it was women on the trip or her treasured prairie dogs.

While we were in our tent, Penny wrote in the paddlers' journal:

> *This will be a little messy because I just learned to write (plus I don't have hands!)*
>
> *I just wanted to thank you for rescuing me—literally and figuratively. As you know, I was caught in a current that I thought was leading me down the wrong channel. Now I realize that I was supposed to drift in that direction—otherwise I would not have met you!*
>
> *I have had a great time with you ladies and I'm looking forward to seeing my new home in Wyoming. Gwyn (she spells her name funny—don't tell her I said that!) said we'll be riding home in Xena Warrior Princess. I am not sure what to make of the whole thing, but she's been good to me so far, so I guess I can trust her. I'm getting tired so I'd better stop. Gwyn says she has to work (she looked sad) and couldn't keep telling me how to spell words like figuratively—that was a BIG one! She said she would help me some more later if she can.*

So thank you for everything! You are wonderful.
Love, Penny

After Penny's entry, Gwyn wrote:

Dinner is over now. The barred owls are calling, a pack of coyotes sang a brief greeting to one another, the crickets are chirping, and we can't hear any trains or barges. It is a peaceful evening, but sad because it is the next-to-last night to camp with you special ladies.

I will not be able to put into words how much I have enjoyed my time with you during your adventure. It has been a privilege and a pleasure to share this experience with you. I have been 'lost' for some time now, and began to find myself again in Ely last summer. This trip has strengthened that reconnection with myself, my real self, and I thank you.

One of the most enjoyable parts of this trip has been the easy laughter. It has been so much fun for me to be with others my age, who get the same jokes and understand the subtle and not-so-subtle humor we shared. Penny has been an unexpected little delight and has allowed me to let my 'playful' side out for a breath of fresh air. I hope you will enjoy her many adventures with me from the photos, and I look forward to seeing what next week holds in store for her.

My day on the water was wonderful, especially because of my 'solo' with Nancy—very special indeed. An unexpected but much appreciated gift. Thank you.

One thing that has been late to click for me has been the Gatherings. It wasn't until the last one that I think I figured out why. My whole life, until about 2004, I have had a deep internal peace, for lack of a better word, about who I am. I have always felt sort of old inside, not in energy or attitude, but in a 'knowing' way that only comes with age. I have also felt that a part of me always walks alone, which is hard to explain, but I believe you'll understand. Anyway, since 2004 I have been feeling unsettled and not like myself. Listening to the women at the Gatherings has helped me solidify what I had identified superficially as the cause of my unrest. I thought I was sort of guessing, but after listening to those women, I have no more doubt. I stopped being happy when I started living someone else's dream. Our office staff has nearly tripled in size since 2004 to accommodate my business partner's ambitions to make more money. That expansion was driven by greed, and I was a reluctant participant from the start.

The point is, I was always so absolutely confident in my dreams that it never occurred to me that they wouldn't come true. But when I listen to these women, the common theme I hear is this—they spent most of their lives living someone else's dream. That is what I have been doing since 2004. Being able to identify with certainty the root of my unrest will help me stay on course and maintain my resolve to make whatever decisions I need to make in the future to get back to myself. That has never failed me before, so I see no reason to doubt my intuition now. The message gets louder and louder for me, and I am grateful to have had this time—this chance to catch my breath—to get back to trusting myself. Thank you again.

I just put my gloves on, so my handwriting is likely to get messier. The barred owls continue to play their vocal game of tag around our camp—one came in quite close for a bit when Kathy E. played her flute for us, which touched my soul. I have already committed to returning to Ely next summer, by the way, and will make it work.

As I mentioned yesterday morning, Nancy, the day on the river with you has brought your book to life for me. The connection of seeing the water over the tip of the kayak, experiencing the wildlife—not to mention some wild water—the easy feel of the paddle in my hand, are all more tangible for me now. I feel your story on a new level. It is a wonderful connection.

I will have to stop…for now. My hand and arm are both fully asleep—giving me a hint that I should do the same, I suppose.
Gwyn

October 4, Day Thirty-One

During the night, I crawled out of the tent and discovered a half moon lighting the campground. Morning was breaking, but a few bright stars glistened above me. A barred owl called as she had through the night. Earlier, several deer snorts near my tent had woken me. I had peeked out of the tent's screen door but hadn't seen them.

I thought about the thirteen feathers White Buffalo Man had given me. Handing them out was an honor I did not take lightly. I had given three out so far, and I believed another one should go to Gwyn. I struggled with that decision, wondering if I was too personally involved. With the other women, a strong sense of knowing came when I first met them, so it felt like the decision was out of my hands. With Gwyn the feeling was similar, but different. She was an amazing woman, but what I thought didn't matter. Gwyn was a Grandmother who cared for our world. She saw wounded or confused people and adopted them, drawing them into the circle so they could blossom. She single-handedly took on energy companies and held them accountable for their behavior toward nature and reclamation of the land. Nature was one of her children, and she did what needed to be done to care for it. I lay in my tent, trying to come to a resolution, when my struggle came to a sudden halt. I clearly heard the words "just get out of the way" in my mind. It was one of the clearest intuitive messages I had ever received, and I wasn't about to argue. Gwyn would receive a feather.

My thoughts turned to what going home would mean. A familiar feeling of dread and defensiveness began to settle in. Then I remembered my conversation with Kitty about faith and realized that I wasn't trusting my knowing that things would work out. I was approaching it with a faulty, old perspective right off the bat instead of being hopeful and joyful. I began to focus on how I wanted the experience of going home to feel. I tried to let go of the daunting task of trying to figure everything out before I got there. I already felt lighter.

Birdsong captured my attention. The sun broke through the trees, hit my tent, and motivated me to go to the river. Gwyn sat on the shore at the boat launch. I sat next to her and talked to her about what an honor it was to carry the thirteen peace feathers. She nodded. I pulled the feather out of my jacket and told her she was one of the Peace Grandmothers who was to receive one. She looked at it and said no, she couldn't be a Grandmother since she wasn't old enough. I told her my admiration for her had me questioning the decision, but that an intuitive voice had chimed in to set me straight.

She took the feather, shaking her head in disbelief. She was speechless. I told her she may not fit the traditional description of a

Grandmother, but that her role defending nature and working to make the world a better place made her one. I told her I had watched her reach out to people and take them under her wing. She was a powerful healing force in a tiny package. We shared a few moments of silence while Gwyn stared at the feather in awe.

Gwyn said she had something to show me. We got in the van and drove down the road that led into the campground to see a tree. Gwyn said the tree had spoken to her on the way in. We climbed out of the van once she spotted it. I was fascinated by the large cottonwoods. Gwyn's tree was huge, and it felt restorative to be near the special energy it generated.

Back at camp, we joined Kitty and Kathy E. for breakfast. I told Gwyn I thought her hooting back and forth with the owls the night before was incredible and thanked her for standing right next to my tent. She looked at me, grinned, and said, "I didn't call the owls last night. I thought about it, but they were going so well on their own that I didn't want to disturb them." We burst into laughter. It hadn't occurred to me that a real owl would be in the tree right above my tent.

Up to that point, Gwyn had been burning the candle at both ends as she took care of us and worked late into the night on her laptop. Her exhaustion was beginning to show. Kitty, Kathy E., and I ordered Gwyn to let us take care of everything for the day. She was only to drive and spend her time getting caught up with work so she could relax and enjoy the rest of her time with us. She was scheduled to paddle with us again the next day, and we were determined that her work wouldn't get in the way. It was a tough order for Gwyn, but she agreed, got up, and started putting things away. We raised our eyebrows at her until she smiled and stepped away from the table. We laughed as Gwyn said, "This is not going to be easy."

We gathered the boats together so Kathy E. could hear the morning song. Kathy E. wore a hearing aid most of the time but had it out while on the water and could not hear us during the day. It was important to her that she could hear the song that morning. While I sang, fish played in the water in front of us.

Paddling Canton Chute, we enjoyed the peace and calm that surrounded us. Kathy E. paddled well, though we continued to give her tips on entering and exiting the kayak. She was grasping the concept but still occasionally got wet. Though she paddled quietly, she was a full participant. She said she wasn't as nervous as she had been the day before.

Kitty talked about how she was going to try to do things differently when she returned home. I mentioned how trying could get in her way, since trying was not actually doing. I suggested that she drop the word try. She realized that saying "try" made her feel good about attempting to change but also kept her from actually taking the necessary steps to do so. She said, "I'm going to change it from 'I'll try,' to 'I'll allow myself.'" I wondered how often I was trying and not doing.

The weather continued to treat us well. We paddled on and stopped for lunch at the Canton Chute Recreation Area. Thick mud from the previous flood lined either side of the boat launch and stuck to everything.

In the distance I spotted a tree with beaver chews on it and went to investigate. Several fully grown trees had been gnawed by beavers. In the yard next to the boat launch the bottoms of the trees were covered with wire to prevent the beavers from doing any more damage.

There was a lot of mud stuck to my paddle from our lunch stop. Usually I wiped off any mud on my paddle, but I decided to see how many paddle strokes it took to remove the Mississippi sludge. I quietly counted as I paddled. At 425 strokes, I told Kitty and Kathy E. what I was doing. At 600 strokes, they could not believe that I was still counting. At 1,000 strokes, the amount of mud had diminished a great deal, but some still clung tightly to my paddle blade. I'd had enough of counting, so I wiped the rest of it off with my hand and watched the muddy swirl quickly blend in with the rest of the river.

The van was waiting for us at the Bob Bangert Park boat landing in Quincy Bay. Two artists worked quietly on the dock and barely noticed us. We loaded our boats and drove across the road to the Valley View Campground in Quincy, Illinois. Gwyn was proud that she had refrained from setting up the tents. After a short conversation, she headed back to work on her computer. While we made dinner, we told Kathy E. how impressed we were with how well she had paddled the thirteen miles. She had kept our pace and managed to stay mostly dry at every entrance and exit.

We took advantage of the warm showers at the campground. I enjoyed the electricity and internet access at our campsite and updated our website and uploaded pictures from my camera. Gwyn disappeared again to work, determined to get her tasks done so she could paddle in the morning. We asked her where she was headed since the campground club room she had used during the day was closed for the evening. She

Photo by Kitty Kennedy

said, "I have it all figured out," and walked away. Going into the shower room to brush our teeth, we found Gwyn settled in near the sinks. She was quite pleased with the makeshift office she had created.

Kathy E. played her flute under a starry sky. We all went to bed, except for Gwyn.

Kathy E. wrote a poem about her experience in the paddlers' journal.

A year of darkness
My soul in need of renewal
My body in search of healing
An inner struggle to find the light
A flute
A retreat in the wilderness
Encouragement
What do you do for fun
A friend with a camera
A friend with a kayak
A picture, a kayak and me
A book
A remarkable woman
An incredible journey
A longing deep in my soul
Questions with no answers
A hopeful plan
A gift of bloodstone for courage
The warmth of Friends and Family
The flash of a paddle
At last earth, wind and water connect me to what is here and now
My soul soars and the flute sings

October 5, Day Thirty-Two

Gwyn hadn't finished her work and wasn't sure she would be able to paddle that day. She made the responsible choice to take care of work duties, but she was clearly disappointed. Kitty, Kathy E., and I weren't ready to give up. We made an agreement that Gwyn would concentrate on work in the morning and switch places with Kitty at lunch. That put a smile on Gwyn's face, and she focused on getting us on the water so she could get to work.

We unloaded the kayaks at the landing and met a woman named Deb K., who had walked past our campsite the previous night. She was excited to meet other women who loved to paddle the river as much as she did. She lived on Quincy Bay, where she was refurbishing an old resort. We told her about our trip and invited her to the Gathering in Hannibal.

An egret fished near us in the shallow water, undisturbed by our activity. Its bright white feathers stood out against the deep greens of the water and trees. We left the channel and neared a train bridge with Kathy

E. leading the way. Two flocks of pelicans took flight right over Kathy E.'s head, which delighted her.

Gwyn called to us from where she was waiting at Kesler Park along the shore. We gave her a hard time about not working as we passed her and headed back into the channel.

Quincy, Illinois, was built along a limestone bluff. The town had originally been called The Bluff but was later named after John Quincy Adams. Arriving at Lock and Dam No. 21, Kathy E. pulled the signal cord. The Lockmaster didn't respond, so she pulled it again. The lock attendant came speeding toward us in his cart along the top of the lock wall and yelled, "I was wondering when you were going to get here. What took you so long?" He chuckled and said he had seen an article about us in the paper. A dredge was locking through first, so it would be a half-hour wait.

When the gates opened, we paddled away from the lock entrance to stay out of the way of the dredge. We had to paddle continuously while we waited for the dredge to clear the lock because the current moved us quickly toward the dam. The auxiliary lock gate was piled high with logs and other debris from the storm. Over the top of the downriver gate we saw the second half of the dredge waiting its turn. Loud bangs and clunks from the other side of the gate echoed in the lock chamber. It was unnerving, and made me feel tiny in the enormous lock chamber. I felt particularly responsible for Kathy E., who was about to face a situation that required more experience than she had.

The gate opened and revealed that the dredge was parked a few feet from the gate. It was enormous and had an intimidating drill-like blade with menacing teeth on the front. I looked closely to see how much room we had to get around it. From our vantage point, the clearance looked almost nonexistent. The path we would have to take led into the strong current coming off the dam on the other side of the lock wall. The all-clear whistle blew and startled me. Under my breath I said, "Oh boy, here we go." I paddled away as confidently as I could, hoping that I would encourage Kathy E. and Kitty. I approached the dredge and

Dredge barge—our exit point is the narrow space to the right of the barge.

headed for the opening. There was a gap of twenty feet between the wall and the dredge, wider than it had seemed from the lock chamber. I paddled around the end of the dredge, past the end of the wall, and entered the current. The current was demanding but was not as difficult as it had looked. I slowed down. The others grinned when they caught up with me, and Kitty said, "Wow, that was close."

We continued paddling the wavey current that ran the length of the dredge and turned toward a boat landing for a quick break. Kathy E. had done an amazing job getting around the barge. When we pulled into the boat landing, she tipped over and got soaked getting out of her kayak. She came out of the water embarrassed but smiling.

An older man sitting in a car and wearing a McDonald's uniform spoke to us. He said he had spotted us when we passed Kesler Park in Quincy. He drove to the lock to watch us and then came to the boat landing hoping to meet us. He was retired but worked at McDonald's part-time and was on his way to work. He was a pleasant man with a gentle, curious nature. He said he would have talked longer if he hadn't needed to get to work.

A tall, slender man with two black dogs walked up. He spoke with a long drawl and immediately imparted his knowledge of the river. He warned us to be careful when we passed the ammonia plant downriver. "Don't look up at that smokestack, even though you'll want to because it's a big one." He said cinders came out of the chimney and landed in the river. He had gotten his eyes burned that way before. He wanted to review our route, so I told him we planned to cross over the channel and follow the Fabius River for three miles. He approved.

Another barge approached the lock, so we stayed on shore until it passed. Kathy E. was the first one back in her kayak and paddled confidently after her lock experience. Kitty and I had to paddle quickly to catch up with her. The narrow Fabius River had duck blinds at the entrance. Grape vines hung from every tree and shrub. Logs obscured by the murky, green water clunked along the bottom of our kayaks, unnerving us. At the head of Fabius Island, trees were piled high from floods. The new additions to the log jam joined others that had aged.

We pulled into the Fabius River landing for lunch and called Gwyn. She was still not done with work and told us to paddle on without her. Instead, we created a new plan to meet her at the south end of Whitney Island that afternoon, which brightened her spirits.

We paddled out of Fabius River and hugged Goose Island, which allowed us to avoid the industrial plants on the Missouri side of the river. We passed a soybean plant that smelled like bad fried bacon.

The narrows on the Missouri side of Whitney Island were serene. We drifted, listening to the birds and enjoying our surroundings. Nearing

the south end of Whitney Island, we couldn't find where the road connected to the water. Houses crowded the shoreline. We paddled slowly along shore looking for a place to stop. On a piece of land between houses, we climbed out at a rocky slope and met up with Gwyn on foot. Downed trees from a tornado were scattered around the yards of the homes and had kept her from getting the van close to the water.

I couldn't tell if Gwyn or Kathy E. was more excited for Gwyn's switch with Kitty. We paddled lazily near the shore, crossing several wing dams. We paddled by a riverside home made from an old train caboose. Gwyn pointed out an eagle's nest high in a tree that I would have otherwise missed. We saw Hannibal in the distance, and

turned into the narrows on the west side of Ziegler Island to make our paddle last a little longer. We passed Kitty, who waved to us from high on an embankment. It felt odd to see her on shore.

The Hannibal Small Boat Harbor marked the end of our day and the end of Kathy E. and Gwyn's paddles. Kitty welcomed us with big hugs. Early on in the trip, Gwyn had taken to calling us her "little ducklings" and had purchased rubber ducks that rode in the van with her. Before we loaded the van, she insisted on a photo with all her little ducklings.

A marching band in the distance caught our attention. A parade came in our direction down Main Street, which ran directly out of the boat harbor. It was part of Hannibal High School's homecoming celebration, but we joked that it was for us.

People who'd been watching the parade wandered down to the river, and we became their new entertainment as we loaded gear into the van. Getting the third kayak on top of the van was a challenge. I climbed on top, and we managed to muscle it up. With Kathy E.'s kayak safely on top, we squeezed in among the gear in the van.

We drove to the gas station in New London, Missouri, where we were to meet Mary H. She was ninety-two and lived on a 200-acre ranch with her beloved dog, Joe. Kitty and I knew her sons, Bert and Phil, who lived in Ely and had connected us with Mary H. Her lime sherbet-colored Volkswagen Beetle was easy to spot. She climbed out of her car to greet us and immediately focused on feeding us. On the way to her home, we stopped at Mildred's, a friend of hers who was waiting to meet us. We would rejoin Mildred at Mama Mia's restaurant for dinner.

Mary H. showed us around her home. As we got settled in our bedrooms, I sensed that there were many wonderful stories about the beautiful antiques in the rooms. The paneled walls were adorned with family photos. The floor made me smile; I had not seen that particular shade of orange shag carpeting in years.

Gwyn, Kathy E., Kitty, Mildred, Mary H., and Nancy

We cleaned up and went to meet Mildred at the restaurant. Everyone in the place greeted us when we arrived. Mildred was talkative and very observant of her surroundings. Kitty ordered the catfish she had long awaited. Gwyn and I chose the local favorite, pork tenderloin.

Mildred generously invited us to her house, but we followed Mary H. home. We left the restaurant with an audience. I backed the van away while Mildred stood in the parking lot, throwing kisses and yelling good-bye. By the time I got out on the highway, Mary H. was already well on her way down the road, and I had to hurry to catch her. She had said that she didn't like driving in the dark, and she meant it.

Mary H. sat in the living room with Joe near her. She said she had lived in the house for thirty years, and it had been handed down through three generations of her husband's family.

"Bert is a friend of ours," I said. "When he heard we were going to paddle through Hannibal he said, 'You have to stop and see my mom.'"

"They're coming down on Thanksgiving," Mary H. responded. "Do you know my granddaughter Kahsha?"

"Yes, but not well. She's very sweet," I said.

"She calls me all the time," Mary H. said.

"She is the only girl on the Ely football team," I added.

"Why would she do that?" asked Mary H.

"I would not have got on a football field with a bunch of boys at that age," I said.

While we talked, Kitty looked at the photos on the walls, pointed to one and asked, "Who is in this picture of a woman in a riding habit with horses?"

"That's me. I used to do a lot of riding and showed horses," said Mary H., smiling.

"You mean when you were a kid?" I asked.

"Yes, and jumping," Mary H. said enthusiastically. "But that was a lifetime ago."

"Did you keep doing it after you were married?" asked Kitty.

"No," replied Mary H. "I rode often though."

"How many years were you married?" I asked.

"Oh, sixty-seven I think," answered Mary H. "Well, we were only married fifty-four years before my husband died."

"How old were you when you got married?" I asked

"I was twenty-seven," answered Mary H. "I suppose that seems kind of late, but it wasn't then. A couple of years go by in a heartbeat."

"What else did you do before you got married?" I asked.

"I worked at the construction company—where I met my husband," answered Mary H.

"Your land out here is beautiful," said Kitty.

"I like the quiet," said Mary H. "My kids think I'm crazy to live out here by myself, but I don't."

"What do you do in the winter?" asked Kitty.

"I go out everyday," Mary H. replied. "The handyman took part of the fence down so I can park right by the door. And when it snows, he calls me up to be sure I can get out. I have never been stuck in the house. I have a little John Deere Gator, one of those six-wheelers. I use it to get around the property. It's handy. It's gone today because my handyman is repairing it."

"With six wheels I bet it will go over just about anything," I commented.

"Yes it will—rocks and logs," Mary H. added.

Turning to Gwyn, Kitty asked, "What time do you need to be in town in the morning?"

"Becky is meeting us at the hotel parking lot at seven-thirty," answered Gwyn. "Nancy has to do her thing at the river, and then hopefully we will have breakfast before we head out."

"You have been a gift to us for all that you have done and how you have helped," said Kitty.

"Thanks. You caught me on my good days," said Gwyn with a big grin.

"You've had a lot of them," added Kitty.

"Yeah, in a row," said Gwyn. "I hope I didn't use them all up." We laughed.

"Uh oh, maybe we should call your husband to warn him," teased Kitty.

"He's probably not in danger: it's probably my staff," Gwyn said, still laughing.

It was clear that Mary H. was tired, and so were we. Mary H. headed to bed with Joe right behind her. Kitty and I joined Gwyn to sleep on the living room floor. The bedrooms felt too confining after being outside.

Kitty and I drifted off to sleep while Gwyn wrote in the paddlers' journal:

> *My last day and night with you. I had another chance to paddle today. Thanks for your patience as I addressed my 'real job' responsibilities.*
>
> *My husband and I have a new rule, forged over failed attempts to merge free and work time during the last several months, and fired into permanent gear on this trip—either play or work. Doing both does injustice to everyone and every activity. Imagine what fun it would be to share time with you without the 'evil one' lurking in the shadows—damn those computers anyway. Despite that, I so enjoyed myself and my Sherpa role of assisting you and looking after my ducklings. What a joy and a special treat it has been.*
>
> *That should cover it. I had a marvelous time, and I so appreciated this time with you. It has great meaning for me in many ways that*

I can't express in words very well.
Thank you–Safe Travels–Be Happy
Know that you are special!   Gwyn
P.S. I got to end this journey by joining Nancy by the river and
hearing her beautiful voice this morning–no better way. I think it is
interesting that Penny was able to say in so few words what it took
me pages to express. Hmmmm.
One more thing–I'm keeping both of my sticks to remind me that
I have the ability to let go of the unpleasant things. All I have to
do is open my hand.

October 6, Day Thirty-Three

Mary H. came out from her room in the morning and saw us on the living room floor and said "Oh my! Why are you out here?"

"We've been sleeping on the ground for so long that the floor felt better," I responded. She asked if we had slept on the floor all night, and when we answered yes, she simply replied, "Oh mercy."

With Gwyn's things in the van she and I headed to Hannibal to meet my friend Becky, who would drive Gwyn back to Burlington to get her truck for her drive home to Wyoming. Arriving in Hannibal, we headed straight to the river and sat on a concrete wall. I sang and made an offering of kinnikinnick as fish made bubbles along the surface of the water. A spectacular sunrise caught our attention. Layers of clouds created shadows on each other. Soft blue and bright orange fingers reached toward the heavens.

Becky waited in her truck at the Mark Twain Dinette with her loyal companion, her beagle Rusty. Breakfast conversation was lively, as it always was with Becky. She was an enthusiastic woman from St. Louis who had a gift for bringing humor to most situations. In the parking lot after breakfast I took advantage of Gwyn's computer to update the website. While online, I played the flower fairy for a change and ordered flowers for Gwyn that would be waiting when she arrived home.

Gwyn, Becky, and Rusty headed down the road to Burlington, and I  returned to Mary H.'s. Everyone was making breakfast when I arrived. We loaded the van and settled in to relax while Mary H. ran errands in town.

Kathy E. wrote in the paddlers' journal:

A book, a remarkable woman,
an incredible journey, a longing
deep in my soul, questions with

no answers, a hopeful plan, the gift of a bloodstone for courage, at last earth, wind, and water connect me to what is here and now, my soul sings.

The opportunity to travel with three extraordinary women is one I almost missed. Questions, questions, and more questions. Was I strong enough, would I slow them down, could I take care of myself and not be a burden, what gear should I bring? Breathe, everything will work out. Slowly things worked out and my longing became reality. The trip was everything I had hoped for and more. Nancy, Kitty, and Gwyn accepted me into their family without question.

There was time for lots of laugher, wilderness, solitude, and shared stories. Paddling along the Mississippi and its backwaters was peaceful and restorative most of the time. At times the water was like a glass mirror reflecting the life and land around it. Other times the wind churned it to a muddy brown and made the paddle a little more challenging for me. I learned about locks and dams, waffle waves, and wing dams. I learned I have enough strength, but not as much as I would like. I will take many memories home with me. The stillness of the water, playing my flute in an amphitheater of stars, the camaraderie of cooking and sharing a meal with dear friends, pelicans, mosquitoes that were far too friendly, and the good, the bad, and the ugly of duck blinds.

As my journey continues on a different path, my soul sings to the music of shared laughter, Nancy's lovely morning prayer, and the warmth of a helping hand. I wish you safe travels until our paths cross again.

Love, Kathy

I wrote in my journal while Kitty read. It was pleasant to be still. Mary H. returned from town and said, "Everybody was talking about us. They are so glad that you went to the restaurant last night."

A truck drove up the driveway pulling a trailer with Mary H.'s John Deere Gator on it. We greeted the handyman and his wife while he unloaded the Gator. Mary H. climbed into the driver's seat. "She only runs it in full throttle," the handyman said, which brought a smile to Mary H.'s face.

We said good-bye and drove to Hannibal to explore Mark Twain's birthplace. We checked into our rooms at the Hotel Clemens and headed to the historic section of Hannibal. The people of Hannibal were proud of Mark Twain, and had named many things after him. We wandered the grounds of his boyhood home, a two-story white building that had been converted into a museum in his honor. Becky Thatcher's house was across the street. Hannibal had been a sawmill town before Mark Twain brought it its notoriety. The sawmills had processed logs that were floated down the Mississippi from the northern states.

The heat drove us back to the hotel for a nap. Afterward, Kathy E. and I went to the bus stop to wait for Nancy H., who would be taking over as our car-support person. The bus pulled in right on schedule, and Nancy H. had no trouble spotting us. Our van was hard to miss with our three kayaks stacked on top.

Nancy H. told us about her bus adventure. She had been traveling for two days. She left her truck in Minneapolis at her brother's and caught the bus to Hannibal by way of Chicago. She'd had the opportunity to meet a rich diversity of people.

We picked up Kitty and went to the next Gathering location, which was in a shelter near the historic area of town. It was difficult to find, and we

Nancy H.

hoped that would not deter anyone from joining us. Becky rolled in and helped set up. Then Kathy E.'s husband, Bob, her friend Catherine, and daughter, Adrienne, arrived. They focused on getting Kathy E.'s kayak off the van and onto their car for the drive home after the Gathering.

I was surprised when Betsy K. and her friend Virginia, arrived. I had met Betsy K. several years before while facilitating a workshop in Milwaukee. A woman on a motorcycle pulled in and joined our group. I realized it was Kay Marie, a friend from Lakeville, Minnesota, who had driven down that day to be at the Gathering. She said it was the only Gathering that fit into her schedule and that it was a great excuse to ride her bike.

Elizabeth, from New Castle, Indiana, walked in and introduced herself. She had read my first book and had been determined to get to one of the Gatherings. Jan K., Ann P., and Ann P.'s daughter represented the Hannibal women. Then Deb K., who we had met in Quincy, arrived.

HANNIBAL GATHERING

When the Gathering began, Bob E. made himself scarce. It was a group of fifteen women ranging in age from ten to seventy-five. I turned to Virginia, the elder of the evening, and asked her to speak first. Her face lit up, and she was delighted to receive the mug as a gift. She began.

"One of the lines in the poem Kitty read especially meant a lot to me this evening. It spoke about the value of friends. Betsy and I have been friends and schoolmates since fifth grade, a long time ago. We went to a small enough school that we knew each other well, but we were probably fond acquaintances rather than good friends. We each had other things on our minds then. As I grow older, and particularly at this time in my life, I appreciate the value of my friends at age seventy-five. I appreciate Betsy much more than I did when she was younger. In the last six years of my life, I have lost five very close friends: four to cancer and one who did not survive a heart operation."

"That certainly goes both ways," responded Betsy K. "I think we have gotten to know each other better as the years went on, and we have an awful lot in common. I cherish my friendship with Virginia and am delighted to be here with her tonight. I am a farm girl, like Virginia, raised mostly in a small town and lived a while in suburban Washington, D.C. I remember when I was three years old and thinking that the adults didn't understand things the way I did. I used to walk out in the yard in the trees with my grandfather. It was the middle of the Depression, and we were temporarily living with my maternal grandparents. I walked through the trees with my grandfather, who was setting traps for moles. The moles ruined the mowing. We used a push mower in those days. There were a lot of trees. I could go with him to set traps if I would be very, very quiet and walk exactly where he did. I did this quite often.

"One day, after being out there quietly following him and thinking, I came home with a piece of wisdom. I said, 'I have discovered that there are three kinds of moles. There are ground moles, there are knee moles, and there are Eskemoles.' [Laughter.] Well, they all laughed at me. You laughed with me, but they laughed at me and talked about it, so I figured out right then that I understood things the way they didn't understand things. Even after my mother explained that was not the way Eskimo was spelled, it didn't satisfy me. I thought that since I understood things and had some sort of wisdom that they didn't have I was never going to share with them again, and I never did.

"I think I always had that inner voice speaking to me. You can call it intuition, the Holy Spirit or a hunch or whatever. The voice has always been there for me. I haven't always been there for it. I have often ignored it, almost always undervalued it, until I crossed paths with Nancy and took a class from her. The difficult growing-up time gave me insight that I never shared.

"It took me a long time and many adventures to find myself and like the me I found. Today, as my physical and mental capacities diminish, I am grateful that I have learned to follow my intuition. I am grateful that I have been rooted in God's presence. I am thankful for the Episcopal Church, especially during my childhood. I am grateful for the many adventures that I have had. The negative ones made me struggle to know myself and the positive ones helped me grow.

"In conclusion, I say don't ever put the blame out there, even though it might belong there. Use what seems to be missing and the tough times in your life as fertilizer for personal growth. Do your inner work. Find out who you are. If you get stuck on the journey, get help and don't wait as long as I did to find and like yourself."

Kathy E. spoke next. "I started on a journey two years ago when I found out I had cancer." Her eyes filled with tears. "I was forty-eight with a family and a future that didn't include cancer, but then it did. And I knew I needed to make a change. I knew that I couldn't keep doing things the way I had been doing them. Getting to where I am today was a team effort. In addition to great doctors, conventional and alternative, my parents put their lives on hold for almost a year to help. They stayed with us and kept my house and family going so I could focus on getting well. My daughter learned to be much more independent so she wouldn't add to my stress. My husband and son were very supportive, as well as friends and colleagues from work. Part of my healing is a place called the Wellness Community. It's for cancer patients, survivors, and their families. I met a lady named Cis who teaches Tai Chi in St. Louis. She told me about a retreat in Ely, Minnesota, where they teach Tai Chi and Qigong and healing for women. Ely is a long way away from St. Louis, Missouri, but I went home and talked with my husband and said, 'I think I need to be there.' He said, 'You're right.' I did something I don't do very often. I'm a computer-security analyst by trade, and I am a very analytical person. I usually weigh things out very carefully before I make a decision. The next day I went to work and I picked up the phone and I called Rebecca Kali in Ely, Minnesota, and made the commitment to go to the retreat.

"It was a wonderful healing experience. As a result, I read a wonderful book. I met a wonderful lady and began an incredible journey that ended with paddling three days on the Mississippi River. It took a lot of friendship, a lot of help, a lot of prayer, but it was a very worthwhile experience, and it's pretty remarkable. [Tears.] When I think that two years ago I thought my life was ending, and yesterday I paddled twenty miles of the Mississippi River, it's incredible. Thank you, Nancy."

"It was my pleasure and honor," I responded.

"I would like to speak to something that happened tonight as we were getting ready for the Gathering," added Kitty. "I knew as soon as I heard it come out of my mouth that it was something I know I don't believe. I was standing over there and Nancy asked me something and I said, 'I don't know anything.' As soon as it came out of my mouth I knew, uh oh, back up here. It really struck me how easy and quick it is to negate myself. I read a book called *The Four Agreements*, and one of the four agreements is to speak with integrity. It is not only speaking with integrity to others; it is speaking with integrity about myself. I find it much easier to do with others than to do with myself. It is something I need to work on, because I do know a lot. To hear myself say that so quickly and so matter of fact caught me off guard. Where did that come from? Thank you, I just needed to spit that out and forgive myself so that I can move on."

Nancy H. began to speak as a train rolled past. The sound of the wheels on the track a few yards away was louder than the whistle. Nancy H. spoke loudly over the train. "I feel that courage is the ability to speak your mind and say what needs to be said. I kind of coined a phrase, 'conditional ethics,' which I think kind of ties into that. Like Kitty, we are our own worst critics. I fall into that a lot. Have the courage to speak your ethics no matter what they are. Of course you don't want to be offensive to anybody, but have the ability to stand up for what you believe in, even though it might not be popular with everybody." Another train added to the noise. Nancy H. turned toward the train and yelled, "Shut up!" The passing train blasted its whistle as if in response to Nancy H., and we laughed.

"I am my own worst critic," she continued. "I wonder how honest I am really being with people at times. I can be rather quick-witted and can blow stuff off and make it fly by on a humorous surface note. I don't get to the heart of what I am really feeling or what I really need to say. Those are some things I discovered recently, and hopefully I am becoming more in tune with that."

"I rode down on a motorcycle from Minneapolis to join this group," began Kay Marie. "Like Kathy, I met Nancy in Ely at a retreat for Tai Chi and Qigong. The first two years, Nancy shared her story of the first part of the journey, and I somehow wanted to get to a Gathering this time.

"Life is but one journey after another. Some are very difficult. This one I am on right now, this phase of my life is wonderful. Five years ago if you told me I would be saying that I would not have believed you. There always seem to be dark parts of your life or shadows of your life. At the time they are happening, you can't hear or understand that it will get better. I loved what Betsy K. said about valuing the process. I know after my accident five years ago, I said, 'Wow, God, whatever the lesson is here I want to learn it the first time, because I sure as heck don't want to do this again.' There is value and information in every upset. I pray that I learn it and take it with me so I don't have to repeat the lesson again."

"I am probably considered a local because I just live up the road a little ways," said Jan K. "I saw your write-up in the newspaper, and that's what lured me to come tonight. Retirement is really coming close and we are anxious to get on the river and canoe when that happens. My husband and I are teachers and we love the river very much.

"I remember an instance when I was younger, twenty-eight, and I was at another meeting with ladies. I was the second-youngest person there, and the youngest person said she was most anxious for her growing family. I remember my remark was that I was most anxious to gain the wisdom of getting older. And everybody thought 'Now Jan, don't get old too quick.' At my school, we have foster grandparents, and I always tell the children that they are the smartest people in our building and that you won't be as smart as Grandma until you are as old as Grandma. That is the same with me. I have a lot to learn, and I learned most of what I know from the grandmothers at school."

Elizabeth, who had been sitting with a smile on her face most of the evening, jumped in with great enthusiasm. "It is such an honor to be here this evening and to see all these beautiful faces around this beautiful peace fire. I shared with Kitty earlier that Elizabeth is the beginning of a new journey for me. My given name is Elizabeth Louise,  but I have been Betty Lou all my life. Betty Lou is a fine name and she is a fine person, but Betty Lou is the person that everybody else wanted me to be. I feel it is time for Elizabeth to move forward and to develop the potential that I feel in myself and that I know is in every person. My advice to those of a younger generation is to lose the labels. Get rid of the labels that society and circumstance place on you, but in retrospect, I think some of those labels are a very important part of your life. We are all

Elizabeth

obviously daughters; many of us are mothers; some of us are grandmothers or aunts. You generally have some sort of label placed on you due to profession or a hobby, but a lot of times those labels become who you are instead of you becoming who you truly are. It is important to honor the labels and honor those tasks that come with the labels, but move beyond the labels as well and become the person you need to become."

"It's kind of an accident that I'm here, because I had no idea about any of this until yesterday," said Deb K. "I really didn't know what I was getting into tonight. I met these ladies in Quincy when I was walking. I came by and saw their van with the kayaks and I thought 'Oh, that is great.' There were three women, and they were there without any men around. It was neat to see women doing things like that together, but I didn't stop. I kept walking, and I made my route. When I came back around, there they were again, only in a different place. I thought that must be a sign, so I stopped. Nancy gave me the information about this meeting. I still had no understanding about what it was. I talked to my neighbor who had read something in the paper. She didn't give me much information either, so I didn't know I would have to speak. [Laughter.]

"If I was going to give advice just off the cuff, my advice would be to learn to overcome your own fear. We set our own boundaries and set the mark way too low. We have no idea what we are capable of until we challenge ourselves. It is amazing when you look back over your life some of the things that you have faced. You thought you couldn't do it, but you did. I do believe that a lot of it comes from my belief in God; a belief that there is a destiny and a purpose for my life. I am not sure most of the time what that purpose is, but I keep searching. I haven't come to any great revelation, but I have had lots of little revelations. I have enjoyed my life most of the time, even in the bad times."

"To me, spirituality is a very personal thing," continued Virginia. "I was brought up in the church, and I went to Sunday school faithfully, because my mother insisted that I do it, not particularly because I wanted to. I probably didn't get a whole lot out of the experience. When I became older, married, had children, then church started to mean more to me because I wanted to influence my sons. I had to make them go to church like I had to go to church. [Laughter.] Not really. I wanted them to believe in God and have a faith basis in their lives also. How has it influenced me? It has certainly given my life a purpose. It helped me considerably when I lost an infant son, when my sister and brother-in-law were murdered. If I hadn't had my faith then, I don't think I would have kept my sanity, either time. I did have my faith, and I did survive. Both of my sons, while one is a regular churchgoer and one is not, they are both very spiritual young men. I feel I have influenced them and helped them understand how important a belief in God is."

"One of the reasons that I came for the Gathering has to do with someone who lives in Pittsfield, Illinois," added Betsy K. "Griggsville, in Pike County, Illinois, was my hometown. In a retirement home in Pittsfield lives a woman who was always my 'other' mother. Did you ever have someone who was a little younger than your mother who lived close by who you could always run over and talk to? Annabelle is my other mother, and she is 101 years old. When I saw that you were stopping in Hannibal, I said to Jack, 'I want to go. I want to go to that, and I want to see Annabelle. I don't want to wait until I get a call to come to a funeral. I want to go and see her now.' I visited her already, and she looks healthier than I am, so it might go the other way.

"This whole journey of becoming aware has been so very important to me. It makes a lot of difference. I have learned a lot of things from a variety of sources. I have been keeping a journal for a long time—very off and on. Months might go by, but I still need to write, and I write. That is just a piece of the journey, I guess. It goes on. Right now I am very aware of my reduced faculties. I have a short-term memory problem in my brain and obviously I can't move as fast as I used to. So all this becomes more important as time goes on. Jack and I have been married for fifty-two years. We have three grown children and four grandchildren. We are very grateful for that. It is good."

The fan was passed again to Kathy E., and she said, "Spirituality has been different things to me at different times in my life. At one time, I thought it was all about going to church. Not that that isn't part of it, but for me, it is not the whole thing. In the last two years, I have learned how to meditate, and I experience a peace and openness inside that I don't find any other place.

"My Dad was in the Air Force, and we moved around a lot. About the time I had made a good friend we moved again. By the time I was in high school, I learned not to make friends because they go away. It took a long time for me to realize I could have and keep friends. One of those friends is here with me tonight. Catherine and my husband went to school together, but I met her for the first time when we went to Oklahoma and my husband became the godfather of their daughter. We have been close friends ever since. She was there to help me get through the cancer, and she is here with me now. That is a kind of spirituality, having that connectedness to friends and family and knowing you can pick up the phone or send an e-mail and there is someone at the other end who cares. Except for family, I don't have very many folks in my life like that.

"Another spiritual thing for me has been connecting with nature. I had the opportunity to do that this week. Being on the water with Nancy and Kitty, watching the birds, and listening to the splash of our paddles was almost as opening to me as the meditation I practice. In the backwaters, it is so peaceful and the water is like glass. It's just incredible. You can hear the wings of the birds, it's so quiet. I realized I need that part too. It reaches a part of my soul that nothing else does. And then there is the flute. Music has always been in and out of my life. In middle school and high school I played clarinet. It was kind of hard to keep up with it moving around, so I quit. Then several years ago, I tried the piano, but my teacher decided to quit teaching. Somehow I needed to fill the need for music that didn't involve having to have a teacher or somebody to show me the way. I went to a Renaissance festival and was walking by a flute-maker's tent. He was a Cherokee Indian who made Native American flutes. He said, 'I have music here, or you can play from your heart.' I think the minute he said that I knew this is what I had been looking for. I bought a cane flute and I tried it out, but it didn't have quite the right feel. I went back to the Renaissance festival, and I traded up for a wooden flute. The feeling I get when I play the flute is like no other. Time just seems to stop. Playing out among the stars this week was really a treat. Almost like playing by the lake in Ely. For me, those are the things that make up spirituality. It's not any one thing. It's a whole lot of things together."

Just as Kay Marie began to speak, another train blasted past. "So I get to compete with the train this time. I keep thinking that life has many chapters. In Minnesota, if you are Lutheran, your parents are mortified if you don't get confirmed. That reminds me of a joke. May I? [Everyone nodded.]

"There was a rabbi, a Lutheran minister, and a Presbyterian minister. They gathered once a week for coffee because they lived in the same town. They were all upset because there were so many squirrels. The rabbi said, 'I am going to get rid of mine. I am going to trap them and bring them down to the river.' He did that, and a week later they came back. The Presbyterian minister said, 'I am going to poison them.' Two weeks later he had twice as many. The Lutheran minister said, 'Well, mine are all gone. They just disappeared.' They asked, 'Well what on earth did you do?' 'I invited them all in; I lined them up; I confirmed them, and I haven't seen them since.' [Laughter.]

"That is kind of how my life was. I got confirmed and disappeared from church until I was going to get married. Then we came back. I did another twenty-year stint with the church, and then I got divorced and ran away again. Then I started another journey, looking for other churches and other ways of worshiping. You are so right, Kathy, for me it is nature. Nature is God's gift and his portrait and his presence among us. Leaving Dubuque this morning on my motorcycle, I was crying; it was so beautiful. Life is so wonderful for me right now. I am just so grateful that I could make this trip. The people in my life support me taking off on my own. Nobody is panicked or threatened or anything else. It is just a beautiful place to be. By the way, my favorite commercial on TV is one that says people who ride motorcycles are the only ones who understand why dogs hang their heads out the window." [Laughter.]

"I guess I finally found kindred spirits, because the spirituality thing with nature is what matters to me," added Jan K. "I was raised Methodist. My children were raised Methodist. I was a Methodist Sunday school teacher for a million years. Lately, I have not been as involved in my church because I get so much more out of being out in the woods or being out on the lake. We use canoes, not kayaks. I want to try a kayak, but my husband says no, so I guess I will listen to my husband for the time being. I just get so much peace out of being in the woods. I went for a hike this morning, and it is just so neat to watch the woods change and the birds and squirrels. It's where I feel peaceful and appreciate the beauty and thank God every day. I love sunsets and moonrises. If you have never seen the moon rise over the Mississippi, it's the most amazing thing. You can't even say how incredible the moon is over the Mississippi.

"I am also a migration freak. I like to be on the river during the migration to watch all the birds. To the ones that are up real high I say, 'Hey, what are you? You should have little name tags hanging from you so I know what kind of bird you are.' I am not real good at identifying birds. They have a habit of moving too quickly for me. 'Oh, what was that bird? Oh, it's gone.' I'm a nature girl. My husband and I keep a hiking journal. He is my best friend in the whole wide world. We hike all the time, and we go to Minnesota and the Boundary Waters every chance we get. Our son worked up in Minnesota in the Boundary Waters one year. We just like the nature and its peace and quiet and beauty."

"A comment was made earlier that someone believed that men were a taboo subject at these Gatherings," I said. "That is not true. Men are definitely not taboo. They are a part of our lives and will be a part of our stories and experiences. I prefer no man-bashing because that does not serve them or us, but that doesn't mean we can't criticize them." [Laughter.]

"Do men have groups that sit around like this, like we are doing this evening?" asked Elizabeth. "I don't know of any. I am privileged to have a group of women friends in Indiana, and we meet every third Monday of every month. We do something very similar. I think that it is so important to make the connection with the other women and to find out that we are all on the same spiritual journey in a lot of ways. A lot of us have grown up in traditional religions and now find our peace and our connection with the Creator through nature and through other means. We have sort of lost our religious labels or lost what people say is the 'right way' or the way that they feel that you should believe. I think it's a shame that organized religion has gotten so narrow-minded. Spirituality is a very important part of our lives and can be very broad-based, not necessarily connected to a specific church or teachings. I believe life is missing a large piece without some time for spirituality. If people do not make the time, spirituality is lost to them. In my busy world, it is often very difficult for me to find a time to go walk in the woods or a time to just sit and enjoy a sunset. I finally got enough wisdom to block out two weeks of my life each September and go to Ely, Minnesota, to get recharged.

"I have started a daily personal log in getting connected with nature. Actually sitting and meditating and being with nature rather than having to do something has become increasingly important. I tend to be a very analytical person, so I could relate to what Kathy was saying as far as being analytical. I have to schedule time for spirituality. That is the wisdom I would pass on to others and to the younger generation. Make time for your spiritual self, because it is a very important part of who we are, who we become, and how we interact with others.

"I think planning your spirituality is important," responded Deb K. "You said maybe it's a bad thing that you have to plan your spirituality. I don't think it's a bad thing. I think it's a good thing that you take that time to do it. Sometimes you have to plan things in order to include them in your life.

"I bought a place on the bay in Quincy a couple of years ago. It's really a trash hole to tell you the truth. It's nothing really special, but it's special to me. One of the reasons it's special is because I get to see the sunset almost every day. It's my special time."

"As we went around, every one of you talked about whether you went to church or not," said Betsy K. "What came to my mind was something that one of Virginia's sons said about church attendance. He said, 'It's about whether you are talking about religion or whether you are talking about spirituality.' Spirituality is important to me. It has been important to me since I was very young.

"Someone else said something about purpose in life. I have known since I was ten years old that I have a purpose in my life as a result of being very ill. I was left alone while they all decided what to do about me, tried to find another doctor or what have you. I had this great experience—it was like the inner voice talking to me saying, 'Don't worry about it. If you die, you will be with me, and if you live, there is a purpose for your life; there is a reason for your living.' I clearly remember answering back: 'That's fine with me, but if I die, my mother won't see it that way.'" [Laughter.]

Turning to her daughter, Adrienne, Kathy E. looked in her eyes and said, "Take care of yourself. If you don't take care of yourself, nothing else can happen. Keep it simple and allow yourself to be strong, because you are." There wasn't a dry eye after we witnessed the exchange between them.

"Kathy," I said, "you just told Adrienne to allow herself to be strong. Well, I watched you demonstrate that over and over in the past three days. I kept giving you opportunities to gracefully bow out if it was too much, and you kept taking a deep breath and saying, 'I want to try, I am going to try.' You accomplished it every time. You allowed yourself to do exactly what you are asking your daughter to do, and it was awesome to witness."

"Thank you," said Kathy E.

As I began to close the Gathering for the evening, Elizabeth said she had one last thing to say. "I would like to thank Nancy for doing her journey so that I could learn about her journey and be here tonight with you all. I just can't tell you how much reading your book and learning about what you have done has enriched my life. You have touched a lot of people who are touching other people. Thank you."

Cleaning up went quickly. I made a point to speak with Adrienne. "I was very impressed with you during the Gathering. I watched you soak up every word the women said."

"Well, yes," she responded. "I am formulating who I am right now, and this is good information."

I smiled at her. She was precious.

We went back to the Mark Twain Dinette for a bite to eat and then fell into bed, exhausted.

OCTOBER 7TH THROUGH 10TH

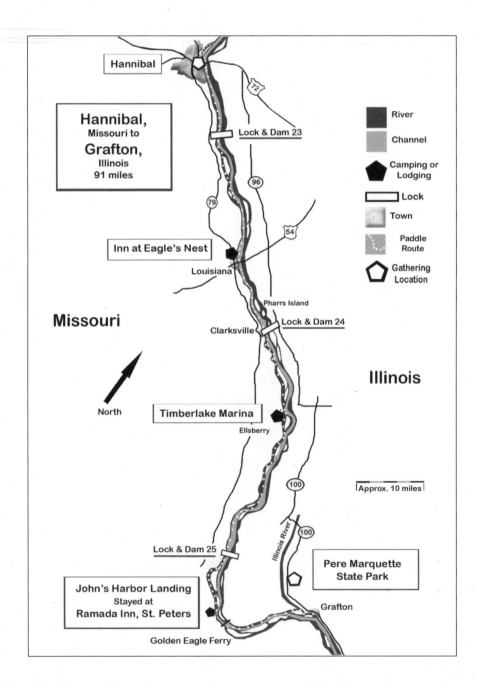

Hannibal to Grafton

October 7, Day Thirty-Four

With twenty-six miles to paddle and more hot weather predicted, we skipped breakfast so we could get an early start. Kay Marie joined Nancy H. at the boat launch to send us off. We paddled the Missouri shoreline and passed Lover's Leap, a rock outcropping at the top of the bluff. Legend held that two young Native Americans, a princess from one tribe and a warrior from another, fell in love, even though their tribes were at

Kitty, Nancy H., and Nancy

war. One night they ran off together and were cornered on the rock outcropping. Rather than be killed, they chose to jump to their deaths in each others' arms.

Driftwood continued to float along on the calm water. The bluffs were close to the river on both sides, creating a lush, green border. Two egrets seemed to play tag between the duck blinds on the opposite side of the river.

The river was quiet during the eight-mile stretch to Lock and Dam No. 22. We floated next to the Sir Richard tugboat parked in the auxiliary lock while we waited for a barge to lock through. We clung to the side of the tug, stayed cool in the shade, and listened to people on the barge and the Lockmasters communicate with horn toots. We couldn't see anything, but heard loud clunks and clanging. It took thirty minutes for the barge to pass through. The clinks from the large chains and tools they used continued as they cinched the cables and locked the barges together.

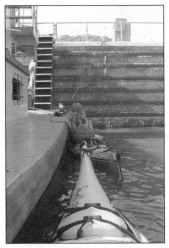

A hundred yards out from the lock, the tugboat continued to displace water. It churned between the walls of the auxiliary lock and the main lock. A horn blast indicated that it was our turn to lock through, so I paddled out. The tugboat's current spun me halfway around immediately. I dug in with my paddle to maintain control. Kitty followed and was caught in the same whirlpool. We paddled hard to reach the lock.

I looked at the downriver gate, where another barge waited on the other side. We floated in the lock and put our spray skirts on. The gate opened and revealed that there was barely any clearance between the end of the lock wall and an enormous, yellow, concrete pylon south of the lock wall. The barge was adjacent to the pylon, and there was no room for us to pass between them. I looked at the lock attendant, who was perched on the wall watching us, and said, "Are you kidding?" He shrugged his shoulders and said, "You have plenty of room." His words indicated that he was clueless that the tight space and strong current churning around the wall and pylon were dangerous for small boats like ours.

I looked at the raging water that swirled around the end of the lock wall. It whirled toward the concrete pylon before it divided: half churned around the pylon out towards the river, while the other half dove under

the barge. My heart raced as I mustered courage. The barge workers took seats on the front of the barge to watch. Seeing them provided the boost I needed. I refused to go down in front of them.

I paddled out, cutting close to the wall. I thought staying near the wall would give me time to deal with the current churning around the pylon. I was wrong. At the end of the wall, the current picked me up like a twig and spun me towards the barge. I screamed and heard the barge workers howl with laughter. The current forcefully propelled me toward the pylon. The yellow concrete grew more daunting the closer it got. The end of my kayak was heading toward the current running under the barge, and I knew I would be in trouble if I hit it. I dug in hard and fast, adrenaline surging through me. At one point, all I could see to my right was yellow. On the last stroke I felt my paddle hit the pylon, but I had propelled myself far enough to clear the current going under the barge.

Relieved, I paddled choppy waffle waves that bounced off the side of the barge. I was worried about Kitty, but turning around was precarious, and I was out of energy. I guessed that if Kitty were in trouble I would hear the men on the barge shouting. Hearing only the sound of the wind and waves hitting the barge, I was reassured. In calmer water I turned around and saw Kitty not far behind me. We paddled past the lock and pulled onto a sandy beach.

I was shaking and weak. Not eating breakfast that morning had been a bad idea. We sat on the sandy beach, ate almonds and cashews for protein, and drank our electrolyte replacement. I asked Kitty how she did. She had watched my exit, chose a different approach, and didn't get as close to the pylon as I had. She said it was the most dangerous situation we had encountered yet. We decided not to take rookies through the locks with us anymore. We could not afford to put anyone without experience in situations like that.

The current was fast, and we appreciated the easy paddling. Cicada song filled the air during lunch at DuPont Reservation Conservation Area. A couple who saw us paddling from the highway came to the boat launch to meet us. They warned us that the next day was Columbus Day and that the boat traffic would be heavy. We appreciated the information, since we had mostly lost track of dates, holidays, and days of the week.

We lay in the shade on a floating dock, exhausted from the heat. We listened to the water, wind, and creaking dock as we rocked gently. We searched the passing clouds and found some that looked like animals and faces. I could have lingered there all afternoon.

Paddling on, I heard Kitty humming over the light breeze. We passed a large piece of driftwood, partially buried in the mud on shore. It looked like a warthog wearing a bonnet of white asters. Fishermen sat alone on the shore. I wondered if fishing was a form of meditation for them. Catfish were the most popular fish to catch there. My connection to catfish went back to my youth, when my siblings and I fished for bullheads in a creek behind my grandparents' cabin.

We were exhausted, and the last two miles were windy and wavy. We landed at the Old Louisiana Ramp and met Nancy H. We headed into the Inn at Eagles Nest bed-and-breakfast located in the historic riverfront area of Louisiana, Missouri. Our room was charming. The town of Louisiana was started by tobacco farmers and used to have many cigar factories. It is the birthplace of Red Delicious apples.

A couple from California named Frank and Debby sat near us at dinner in town. Frank asked about the kayaks on our car, and we explained what we were doing. He responded, "There are only a couple thousand questions I have about what you're doing." He kept coming up with more questions about how many miles a day we paddled, the weather, and more. He told us that he and Debby had just completed a long-held goal of hers to visit every National Park. Debby said, "It's the best hobby a person could ever have."

When they left, Nancy H. asked, "So, how does it feel to be famous?"

"We've had this conversation with other people before," replied Kitty.

"This has been happening all the way down," I added.

"I always looked at people who did things like this differently, too," said Kitty. "Now I realize they are just ordinary people."

"But people don't want you to be ordinary," said Nancy H. "They need you to be idols."

"That is the weird part," said Kitty.

"I am still trying to work through it," I said. "No matter how it shakes out, the person across from me is hard to truly connect with, because they don't see me for who I am. I was thinking about the Gathering last night, and realized that we're still drawing mostly white women."

"That is true," replied Kitty.

"Did you have more Native American women on the first trip?" asked Nancy H.

"Yes," I replied. "The first Gathering on the first trip was on Leech Lake Reservation. I thought I did a lot to publicize this trip, as well as sending information to African American, Native American, and Asian communities. I just haven't found a good way to connect with them. I really want diversity. I would like to see more women of color at the Gatherings. They have a different perspective. We could learn so much from each other."

We headed back to the bed-and-breakfast. I had ordered a replacement kayak seat, which Lou had brought to the last Gathering for me. However, we didn't have the correct tools to install it. We made three attempts to connect with a kayak vendor in Louisiana for installation. Unable to reach him, I resigned myself to the fact that the new seat would keep riding in the van while I made the best of the broken one.

Photo by Nancy Hernesmaa

October 8, Day Thirty-Five

Our twenty-five-mile day started with calm, hot weather. My body was ready to be done, go home, and sleep in my own bed. Fatigue, heat, and hormones were not a promising combination for long days of paddling, but there were only five days left. Swallows darted around us, and watching their graceful dance cheered me up.

Six miles south of Louisiana was Pharrs Island. I thought of my son, Wade, whose last name was Pharr. I enjoyed a momentary connection to him while we paddled past the island.

The morning haze cast everything in a grey-blue tint. Distance became an illusion. Things in the distance came into view lazily, or we'd think our destination was several miles away, but within a few paddle strokes we were there. Such was the case with Lock and Dam No. 24. We took a break in a small bay before entering the lock. Several logs floated in the shallow, muddy water. Large fish splashed and swirled away from our paddle strokes, startling us. We paddled hesitantly. Each time we disturbed another giant creature, we squealed as it broke the surface and splashed away from us.

The Lockmaster instructed us to wait in the auxiliary lock until a barge passed through. The situation sounded familiar, and I got nervous. I asked if there were downstream barges waiting to lock through. I wasn't ready for a repeat of the last lock. The Lockmaster said he didn't expect another one for a couple of hours and then warned us to stay away from the channels on the dam-side wall, since their currents could sweep us through to the dam. We paddled into the auxiliary lock and waited far from the channels. My anxiety rose when the barge passed through and headed upriver. The lock attendant blew the all-clear whistle. We didn't move. The barge was several yards upriver, but the water in front of us was still churning from it. My heart pounded when the whistle blew again. The water was not calming down. Kitty said, "We're waiting until we feel it is safe."

Channels leading from the auxiliary lock out to the dam.

The water calmed a bit, and after another whistle, Kitty went first. The churning water spun her around, but she paddled hard and disappeared safely around the wall into the lock. I took a deep breath and began repeating "relax and paddle, relax and paddle," knowing that tense muscles wouldn't help the situation. The current grabbed me momentarily, but I paddled hard through the turbulent water and safely into the lock. Seeing Nancy H. on the observation platform also helped me relax. I anxiously waited to see what was on the other side of the downriver gate. I heard a familiar clanging and began to worry. However, the gates opened to calm water with no boats in sight. I was thrilled.

We pulled into the boat launch at Clarksville, Missouri. Clarksville was a small river town nestled into the side of a 200-foot bluff with Native American burial mounds on top. We stowed our boats on the shore and jumped in the van to have lunch with Nancy H. at Clarksville Station. After lunch, we walked out of the air-conditioning back into the hot air and melted. A gentle breeze urged us back to the river to paddle. We stuck close to the shore and claimed what shade we could, ducking behind Eagle and Amaranth islands and into Slim Chute.

The water in the chute was calm, and herons lined the shore. Sandy beaches connected the islands. We heard a large animal crashing through the woods and assumed it was a deer. Turtles plopped into the water from their sunning spots. It was so quiet that I could hear water rushing past a buoy a quarter mile out in the channel. Our paddle strokes resonated loudly across the water. Spider webs stretched across the chute, brushing our faces, and redwing blackbirds sang from the trees.

We paddled silently, lost in our thoughts and immersed in the beauty around us. In the silence, I processed the events and stories of the past weeks. Normally I liked to process my thoughts out loud so I could hear what I was thinking and sometimes seek some- one's opinion or approval. I considered it

a sign of personal growth that I wasn't looking for approval outside of myself that day. I knew that the truth I sought would only be found internally.

I thought about Elizabeth, who mustered the courage to change her name and claim her identity after many years. I agreed with her that labels affected us. Labels were not empty words; they molded our view of the world and altered our choices. I had not enjoyed the rare treasure of a long-standing friendship like Betsy K. and Virginia's in my lifetime. They had been witnesses to each other for the better part of their lives. I envied their connection and the rich, supportive history they shared.

A snake swam across the river in front of us. She had the same markings as the one that had approached my kayak earlier. I wanted to know if she was poisonous.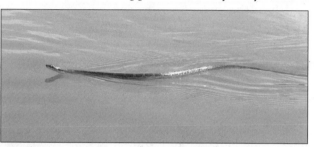

I chased her down with the camera while Kitty kept her distance. I eventually identified her as a nonpoisonous broad-banded water snake.

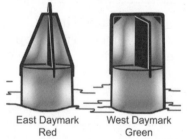

East Daymark
Red

West Daymark
Green

I looked downriver and understood why buoys came in a variety of shapes. When the light was behind them their color was indiscernible, but I could tell them apart by their shapes. Buoys rose four feet out of the water, which was very tall from our vantage point. I passed a red buoy bobbing in the current, and for some reason, it reminded me of a sauntering cartoon character. I half expected it to say, "Hey Baby."

We rounded a bend into Thomas Chute, which was heavily wooded and dotted with duck blinds. One resembled the head of a strange animal. We passed two men relaxing in lawn chairs who yelled, "You two from Minnesota?" They were delighted when we said yes. "We saw you in the paper, and we wanted to catch a glimpse of ya!" Down the shore from them, a yard was dotted with colorful plastic figures. Excitedly, I
said, "Penguins!" Kitty said, "You mean pelicans." Throughout the past few days I had accidentally called the few pelicans we had seen penguins. "No, I mean penguins," I replied. Kitty looked at the yard and burst into

laughter. Seven plastic penguins stood in the yard, with pink flamingos and other plastic birds scattered among them. We noticed two palm trees on the deck and laughed harder.

To get to our campsite, we had to go through yellow caution tape that marked an area covered in shotgun shells. Apparently there had been a turkey shoot a few days earlier. Nancy H. had Kitty's tent up, but mine befuddled her. Hers was set up under the shelter without the fly on it. She suggested that we join her under the shelter because it would be much cooler without the flies on our tents. She had not finished speaking before a gust of wind sent her tent rolling down the embankment and into the river. I ran to the end of the dock and saw Kitty, chest-deep in the river, dragging the tent and laughing. Nancy H. and I ran for our cameras, and Kitty crawled unaided out of the water with the tent securely in hand. With our cameras pointed at her, she laughed and said, "I don't feel the love right now."

Photo by Nancy Hernesmaa

The campground was a disappointment. The women's toilets didn't work, and we weren't brave enough to look into the shower stalls. We used the men's room, which wasn't in much better shape. There was no fresh drinking water, so Kitty and Nancy H. went into town to get some. The tables under the shelter were covered in bird guano. Behind us stood a large garage, where men were welding and fixing large equipment. We headed for bed with lights shining around us and a party going on at the neighbors' site. We could hear the partygoers talking about us as we fell asleep. We had been spoiled by the quiet of the more rustic campsites.

October 9, Day Thirty-Six

The calm water and warm sun on my skin indicated that it would be another hot day. Swallows lined up on a power line near our campsite. They alternated between perching motionlessly and swirling around us in the air. While the swallows danced over my head, I again attempted to fix my kayak seat with an extra piece of padding, duct tape, safety pins, and athletic tape. It wasn't pretty, but it felt a little more comfortable.

Westport Chute was peaceful. I realized that the mud particles suspended in the water created shapes that mirrored both the cracked, dried mud on the shore and the patterns in the clouds overhead. I was amazed at how nature's patterns repeated themselves in unexpected places.

We pulled into Norton Wood access area for a break. The adjustments I had made on my seat only made it worse. While I tried again to repair it, Kitty watched airplanes overhead. The closer we got to St. Louis the more planes we saw. She said it was a clear indication that we were headed back to civilization.

I paddled away from the shore. An enormous fish leaped out of the water, and I screamed. Kitty thought I had splashed myself. The fish sailed three feet in the air before splashing back into the water near my kayak. I suspected it was an Asian carp, but until I knew with certainty, I decided to keep my apprehension to myself. The video I'd seen showed them flying more than five in the air. The carp had invaded the Mississippi River when they escaped from a fish hatchery during a flood. The fish hatchery had used the carp to keep their ponds clean because they would eat anything.

We paddled slowly, searching for a good spot for lunch. Our shoreline choices were either thick mud or rocks along the levee. We chose rocks. With one foot out of the kayak, I saw a flock of coots sitting on the rocks ahead of us. Their little black heads popped up in succession and peered at us. First one, then two, then the entire flock scooted across the water

and took flight, landing in the channel a hundred yards away.

Settled in on the rocks as best we could, we noticed that pelicans had claimed a dry, sandy beach across the river. Butterflies flitted around us. They varied widely in size, shape, and color and kept us company for a few miles when we resumed paddling.

I approached Lock No. 25 with trepidation. We had no phone service and couldn't ask the Lockmaster if there were barges downstream waiting to lock through. I anxiously waited for the upriver gate to open. I was relieved when I saw that there was nobody else inside the lock and that the downriver gate also looked clear. However, while the water lowered in the chamber I heard familiar clangs and a deep, loud bang. Fear rose in me as another bang echoed outside the downriver gate. I was convinced there was a barge we couldn't see. The gate moaned as it opened, as if announcing doom. It seemed to take forever. My heart raced until it was all the way open, and I saw nothing but water and a lot of debris floating in the water downriver from the lock. The river was still being cleaned up after a tornado. A hefty wind out of the west created waves that pushed us sideways across the water.

Our previous two lock experiences had unnerved us. The next two, which were also the last two of the trip, were considerably larger than the others we had encountered. We would have new people paddling with us, and we had no idea what their skill levels were or the types of boats they would be in. The risk was not worth it. We would not paddle through the last two locks.

We chose to head down Cuivre Slough, even though we were tired and it would lengthen what was already our longest day at twenty-eight miles. It would be our last opportunity to paddle in narrow backwaters, and we wanted to relish it. We drifted on the current through the slough, which was fed by the Cuivre River. We passed a few homes, but for the most part, the shoreline was wilderness. We passed areas where the vines had taken over trees and created unusual shapes. One looked like a cross between an aardvark and a rabbit.

We met a couple in a boat coming back from spending time at their "club house." Kitty asked what club house meant, and the man said it was a weekend cabin on the water. He questioned us about our trip. He shared stories about men who had paddled the river and the challenges they had conquered. He made it clear he didn't think women should be paddling the river.

The rest of the day's paddle was in the main channel, where the heat was relentless. We focused on the showers and beds that awaited us at the motel. In our minds, the motel had transformed into a luxurious spa by the end of the day.

We got off the water at a private marina because it was the only place Nancy H. could connect with us. While waiting for us she had tried to make contact with the people who ran the marina, but the building was closed. When we were completely out of the water and had all the gear loaded except one kayak, a man emerged and angrily asked us what we were doing. We explained our situation, but he kept insisting that it was a private area. I tried a new tactic and asked what we owed the owners for using their dock. He said he would not charge us, but it was private and we were not welcome. We had broken the rules and were not to come back in the morning to put back into the water. He said there was a boat launch six miles downriver we should go to instead. He moved a short distance away and watched us closely.

Photo by Nancy Hernesmaa

While trying to put my cockpit cover on, my efforts were thwarted by a chow that appeared out of nowhere and decided to sit on it. I made the mistake of petting her, and she moved closer. I had to shoo her off the cockpit cover several times before I could secure it enough for transport.

As Nancy H. drove toward our motel, Kitty and I thought she was speeding. She was actually driving the speed limit, but the trees flashed by much faster than the pace we were used to. We arrived at the Ramada Inn in St. Peters, Missouri, and quickly showered and headed for dinner at a fast-food place across the parking lot.

At dinner, we talked about what the next few days would bring. I talked about how I still hadn't resolved my issue about being the center of attention. I said that I wasn't making the trip and writing women's stories for personal fame. In fact, it hadn't occurred to me that the project would bring me any attention at all. I hadn't considered how the project would change my life. During the first trip there wasn't much media attention, and public interest in the trip was moderate at best. I paddled the river in Minnesota—my own backyard. The only notoriety I received was at home, where around town I began to be known as "the woman paddling the Mississippi." I could easily dismiss that, because there are many people in Ely doing unusual things; for example, it is home to Arctic explorer Will Steger. In comparison to what others were doing, I believed my trip was small. After the book about the first trip was published, things changed. I received attention from a broader audience. Women from other states began to follow the project and told me how the book had helped and inspired them. Women I had never met thanked me, some for changing their lives. I began to see a star-struck look in their eyes that surprised me. I felt a great sense of responsibility that I wasn't sure I wanted and knew I hadn't asked for. Women saw me as the reason things changed for them, even though all I did was create a space for things to happen. I didn't make them happen.

As planning for the second trip began, more volunteers came forward to help. I found myself in a position of leadership and made decisions for many women that affected them. Kitty became a partner in decision making. As things progressed, I watched her confusion when people changed how they viewed her too. I found myself in a tricky place, stuck between wanting to be acknowledged for the work required to make a project like this happen and wanting to stay in the background so the project stood on its own merits. I was a confident leader at the Gatherings because my role was clear. On the water or in camp, my role was not as clear, and I resisted using my strengths as a leader. I didn't like that leadership meant not being equal to the other participants or that it put me in the position of telling other people what to do. I wanted to keep everyone happy but needed to accept that it would be impossible to do that.

After the trip was over, I spoke on the phone with Lynne from the Prairie du Chien Gathering. She said, "Things have opened up since you came. You opened a portal or something with what you are doing. I felt so alone before you were here, and now I know that I'm not. There are others in the vicinity who are like-minded." I was delighted by Lynne's experience. I felt acknowledged and that we were making a positive impact. While listening to her, something shifted within me and fell into place. My struggle to find balance and being the center of attention had eased.

I crawled into bed as Nancy H. wrote in the paddlers' journal:

> It is an honor and a privilege to assist you both on your journey. It is so easy to become caught up in our own little worlds, and forget about helping others, which can spin one out of balance.
>
> It is truly inspiring to reconnect to life's real purpose, one of giving.

October 10, Day Thirty-Seven

I woke up wondering why I hadn't considered what this work would mean to my life. I guess I thought I would still be in the background and the women who shared their stories would be in the foreground. I realized that there is always a face out in front of any project, and that face was mine. It was certainly a different way of being in the world than I was used to.

The sun was rising, and I wouldn't be able to get to the river before it rose fully. I wanted to be near water, so I headed to a small pond near the parking lot. I sang in the cool morning air with traffic noises in the background. I was joined by the honking of a pair of Canada geese floating on the pond.

When I returned, Kitty was doing an interview with WELY, the Ely radio station, and sounded relieved when it was over. Doug heard her while driving to work and called to say that she had sounded great. I told him about my trepidation over the next few days. He simply replied, "Enjoy it. You've worked hard to get there. Enjoy it." His words reverberated in my ears throughout the day.

Photo by Kitty Kennedy

We grabbed bagels, juice, and gorp and headed to the river. We unloaded our kayaks and watched Nancy H. drive onto a ferry to cross the river. The cold breeze motivated us to get moving before Nancy H. landed on the other side. I got in my kayak and drifted while I waited for Kitty. Drifting turned out to be a bad idea. I broadsided a log and got hung up. I nearly flipped while trying to dislodge my kayak. Two large fish jumped high into the air and startled us. I told Kitty about the Asian carp. "Wow," she responded. "I think I'm both scared and excited by them."

We let a barge go by before I made an offering of kinnikinnick. Kitty paddled quickly downriver. I caught up with her and asked if she was in a hurry. She smiled and said, "I'm in the rhythm and ready for twenty miles!" I said we only had twelve miles to go and that I would prefer to take it easy and paddle a bit more slowly. "Only twelve miles–I think I will slow down and savor it too," she agreed.

Continuing our conversation from the night before, I told Kitty that I just wanted to be a regular gal but that it was getting in the way of being a leader. Kitty reminded me of what Nancy H. had said about how people didn't want to hear that from me. I realized that paddling the Mississippi was something few had done, but I believed that most people could do it if they put their mind to it. It had become routine and simple: get up, paddle, camp, and repeat the process the next day. I realized it wasn't really that simple, but many people faced more demanding challenges in their daily lives.

I had changed because of the trip. I felt it but was unable to put it into words. The change had begun after the first trip. I had not seen myself as someone that would go on such a big adventure. On this trip, the change was more pronounced. There had been more women involved and more conversations that challenged my beliefs about the world and myself than on the first trip. I had seen the evolution of the river as it moved south. I was evolving and growing along with the river.

A quiet sadness surrounded me, which I assumed was the grief that often accompanies change. It would pass with time. I sensed my own fear, which was connected to my perceived expectations and "what ifs." What if I made a mistake and let everyone down? What if they expected more of me in the future and I couldn't or didn't want to do it? The "what ifs" created anxiety that contrasted with my faith that everything would work out. Then the "why me?" question surfaced. Why was I chosen to do this work? Who did I think I was? The questions were echoes of a young girl who lacked self-esteem and believed that she was innately broken. It wasn't up me to decide why me. I needed to lean into my faith and show up each day to do what was in front of me. After all, the true adventure in life is showing up to see where each day will go. I stopped analyzing myself and let Doug's simple wisdom to enjoy echo through my mind. He was right, and his words soothed me.

We floated next to a small stone bluff with a variety of colors, shapes, and outcroppings. Blooming asters speckled the shoreline among the cedars. A sharp-shinned hawk flew out of a tree above my head and traveled down the shoreline. I saw a heron trying to hide from us down a narrow offshoot. I realized we hadn't seen any purple loosestrife in the last few pools, and I was glad that it hadn't invaded those waters yet.

There were definitely Asian carp in the shallows. A firm, sudden paddle stroke brought them leaping three feet out of the water near us. We learned to paddle gently so we would not alarm them. They no longer scared us, but they continued to startle us each time they jumped.

A barge headed upstream. It was a tanker, so it most likely carried propane. The tugboat captain was a woman, Captain Cheryl Stegbauer. It was the second female captain we had seen, and she was moving hazardous cargo.

Our destination was around the next island, but we weren't ready for the day's paddle to be over. We stopped at the Pohlman Slough Access Area and rested, staring out at the water. A frog leaped out of the water and immediately blended in with the rock she landed on. The frog was gray, like Mississippi mud. My presence did not disturb her, and she let me get close.

I saw a Mylar balloon that read "You're Special" caught in branches near shore and retrieved it. Kitty and I thought it would be a perfect river prize for Nancy H., who hadn't received one yet.

We landed in Grafton, a commercial fishing village. Before leaving the boat ramp, we presented Nancy H. with her special prize. She graciously accepted and asked, "What would be the appropriate length of time that I need to keep this? I don't want to seem ungrateful by tossing it too soon."

"Oh, about an hour would do," Kitty responded, smiling.

We headed to Pere Marquette State Park, four miles north of Grafton. Nancy H. joked with the park host before we went to our campsite, which was on a ridge lush with trees. A poison ivy vine grew up tree at camp. I was astonished at how differently the plant grew in Illinois compared to Minnesota, where the shrub rarely grows more than a foot tall.

For dinner, we warmed up chili that Nancy H. had received from Susan, a woman from Grafton. Susan would be at the Gathering and would paddle with us the next day. Hot homemade chili was perfect after our cold day.

GRAFTON GATHERING

We were not at the Gathering site long before the women began arriving. We began the Gathering with eight women ranging in age from forty-four to seventy-five. "As the honored elder, Bonnie D., you get the fan first," I said, handing her the fan.

"I am a grandmother," began Bonnie D. "Well, spirituality has had a tremendous influence in my life. Four years ago, my daughter had a brain aneurism. She is my only child, and she was in the hospital for thirteen weeks. Shortly after that, my husband had a lung removed, and he was in the hospital nine weeks. Without a lot of good spirits and good thoughts we would have never made it through. My daughter is now running her own business, and my husband had four good years after that."

Bonnie D.

"Spirituality has influenced my life in so many areas," said Carol G. "You know, actually, I couldn't even say which area is the most important. One of the most important is that I don't see myself as invisible, like society does. Age is kind of irrelevant for me. I don't think getting older means that you are not valued, even if we live in a society that looks at it like that. I don't look at it like that. My daughter, granddaughter, and I don't look at it like that either. We are all very close, and we all value where each of us are in our lives. Actually, the more I studied spirituality, the more I understood why organized religion just wasn't making sense for me. I did try organized religion and tried the beliefs that you were supposed to believe. It never worked for me. It just never did. At some point I began studying spirituality and philosophy, and it has taken me on a journey where there is so much wisdom for me. Of course people think I'm a rebel, but I really don't care, you know. Spirituality has just brought out my individuality."

Nancy H. thought for a moment before speaking. "I want to address the value of good friendships. To just appreciate people while they're with you in your life and letting them know that. So often we get so busy and forget about what really matters. For me, what matters is connections with other people—good, pure connections. I like to take the time to appreciate people while they are with me on the journey of life. I know that nothing lasts forever, so I let them know that I love them."

Bonnie H. took the fan. "I didn't really come here today to talk about anything specific. I wanted to just be a part of this. Looking at these questions, I think I did set myself on this path. I'm trying to give as much as possible, trying to be everything that I chose. What I wanted to be, despite what other people would think of me. Doing it right, not in any negative way. I just feel as though I have done the very best in raising a child. Now I have an empty nest. [She choked up.] Oh my God, I'm going to cry. As of a month ago, I have an empty nest and I turned fifty, all in a two-week period. So it's kind of neat, because I'm at a point in my life now where I'm at a crossroads. I'm looking at what's next. The hard part is done, I think, which is good. I am very proud of my daughter. My husband is retired, and I am looking at retirement as soon as possible. We would love to travel.

"I work with children. Even though I believe most everyone here has already raised their children or are in the process of doing that, one of the things I wanted to mention tonight is about children. I work as a counselor in a school and I want to impart that giving everything we can to raise them with morals and character is probably the most important thing we can give to anyone. It doesn't cost a penny to do that. I see so many people in our world today that are not raising their kids with morals and character. The kids are getting lost. It's just very sad. If there were younger women here who haven't started a family I would be asking them to please raise your children with morals and character. Those are my words of wisdom to begin with tonight."

"Bonnie H., welcome to the new journey in your life," responded Kitty. "I have the empty nest syndrome now too, and it brought me 600-plus miles down the river, so you never know where the new journey will take you. In reflecting on the trip, today feels almost like the beginning of the end of the journey to me. We have been on the river for a while now and the journey took on a life of its own. We're in the rhythm of nature, usually getting up at daylight and going to bed at eight o'clock at night, thinking that nine o'clock seems too late. Time has not really been a factor on the river. I think of time and entering my life again when I go back to work, and I do not wish to do that. I want to be able to keep following the rhythm that I have been following. It seems better.

"Something that I am trying to do is simplify my life. It can get so complicated sometimes. It isn't that life is so complicated. It's that I make it complicated. Just keep it simple and stay open. I just need to allow life to happen."

"There is something to be said about being in tune with what is going on around you," responded Bonnie H. "Just moving slow and really paying attention. I'm trying to think of the right words for it, paying attention to the pace of life. Set the pace yourself and don't let what's around you set that pace, because it's just like a whirlpool going around and around if you can't slow down somewhat. You need to appreciate what is happening. It's hard in our fast-paced society to really rein that in. There are times in my life when I do that very well and other times when it's just a whirlwind all the time. The whirlwind is mostly professional as opposed to personal.

"There is always a struggle with that balance and helping others to find that balance in life. Particularly in relationships—very clearly in relationships. There are many people I know that have never been able to come to grips with good relationships with people over an extended period of time. I feel very fortunate that I have that in my life and try to impart that to others.

"I just wish life would slow down a little bit for all of us. I think it's particularly hard on women because of the multiple roles we play as mother, as spouse, as full-time employee, and oftentimes as a single parent. It's a very, very fast-paced world in the era of 2007 and growing up in the past fifty years. If there is anyone who has some wisdom on slowing it all down, I would appreciate hearing that."

"I have an empty nest for the first time in my life," added Bonnie D. "My husband died April the second. We'd been together for seven years. This was my second marriage. The one thing that I have found is that you can't live in the past. You can have good memories; you can have wonderful memories; you can have bad memories or horrible memories, but you can't change the past. You have the choice to remember the ones you want. You can't live in the future, because you really don't know what the future is, so we have to live in the now. I think old age has just been a blast. I liked sixty-five, because when you are grumpy—well, it's my age. When you are seventy-five, you can pull anything and they say, 'Well, she's getting senile.' [Laughter.] And that's fine. I have an animal sanctuary and I'm in the process of breaking twin fillies that are three years old. I just finished cleaning my basement after five years. I started right after Bob died. It took two months to do that. My daughter said, 'You can't break those horses.' I said, 'You just keep still. If I can clean that stinking basement and do all that work without a single bit of help, then I can and I will break my horses.' I have a younger friend who says, 'I'm getting so forgetful at forty, and my mom said it's going to get worse.' I said, 'It is going to get worse, but the good is that you forget you forgot, so you don't care.'" [Laughter.]

"I'd like to say something about getting older too," said Carol G. "I can remember the only birthday I got bummed out about. If you can believe this, it was when I turned thirty. That's when I felt I wasn't young anymore. And you know, there was just something that clicked in my mind at that time, and I decided I am never going to get in that mindset again. I am not going to think like that. I am not going to act like that. I'm just not going to. I've never had a birthday since that I felt like that.

"I had the empty nest with my daughter, oh, I don't know how many years ago. Now my granddaughter is grown and in college. Every phase of life brings new adventures. My husband passed away a couple of years ago, which was not unexpected. He had lots of health problems. You just look for the adventure in whatever occurs in life. The only constant in life is change.

"Last summer I got two new little Yorkies. I love animals. I dearly love animals. I was telling my daughter what some friends of mine were saying when I got the two Yorkies: 'You know, Yorkies can live about fifteen years.' I was sixty-four then, and my daughter laughed. She said, 'Well, just tell them when they die you'll just get two more.' I am not going to get into the mindset that I am too old for animals or too old for anything. I am just not going to do it."

"I want to speak to the age thing for a moment as well," I said. "The year I turned forty, a friend of mine threw me the biggest party. It meant something very different to me than it did anyone else I knew. I was thrilled to be forty. I didn't understand for many years what that was about. Later, I read a book called **Motherless Daughters**, and it all fell into place. My mother died when I was eleven and she was thirty-nine years old. What I learned from that book is that when a parent dies, a child can believe that they will die at the same age. So, unconsciously I was sure I was going to die at thirty-nine, but I hit forty. Wow! All that changed how I view age. Nine times out of ten I can't remember how old I am. I have to do the math. I can't tell you my age tonight—I'm fifty-something. It doesn't matter to me. How old other people are doesn't matter to me either. I decided I am going for one hundred and five. I don't know why, but that's where I'm headed. I find it fascinating to watch how age affects people. For some people it's thirty; for some it's forty; for my dad it was seventy. He said he didn't feel old until he had to say he was seventy. I find every decade gets better than the one before. I am really looking forward to what's next. I sure as heck would never have dreamed that I would be doing this at this age."

"I am fifty-one," said Nancy H. "So I'm on the young side of grandmotherhood. I have never had children and married later in life, which I'm kind of glad I did. I waited a long time, and it wasn't that I couldn't continue on by myself. I was extremely independent. I just felt like the time was right to have a partner, so I did. I changed my name because it seemed like something fun to do. I think being fifty-one has given me a new vision. I no longer worry as much about what people think. I am rather proud of my age, and who I am, what I represent. It feels good. A reality check came a couple of summers ago while I was working. I work in the Boundary Waters Canoe Area Wilderness and paddle a canoe as part of my work. Because we have a lot of lakes to paddle to, we recruit volunteers to paddle with us. Many volunteers are from our community college, and they are usually about eighteen or twenty years old. I have been doing this eighteen years now, and my volunteers never seem to get any older—they're always eighteen or twenty years old. I was paddling along, and I just had to stop paddling and say, 'You know I'm now not only old enough to be your mother, I could be your grandmother.' It was kind of a reality check, but the age feels good. I can foresee it only getting better. It's a fun path to be on."

"As far as age, I have never admitted it to people before, but I hear a voice once in a while," said Bonnie D. "I am third degree Reiki; I think it was a year ago in May that I took third degree. It's a Japanese form of alternative healing. I took my first degree Reiki July thirtieth of '06. So I took first, then second, and I thought, 'Well, I'm awful old. I don't know if I want to go ahead and take the third one.' I think about things at night when I can't sleep, and the voice said, 'You can live to one hundred and twenty.' Didn't say I was going to, but you talk about one hundred and five, that's just a baby. I don't expect to live to one hundred and twenty and don't want to, but I did take third degree Reiki and I'm glad I did. It's just a matter of how you think about things. My husband was ten years younger than I am, and I kept teasing him, saying, 'I got to trade you in for a younger model. You're too slow.' Life, age, has nothing to do with it. It just doesn't have a thing to do with it.

"Life definitely has not followed the path that I expected," added Carol G. "One of the things I learned in life, things that have been the best teachers for me, well, don't anybody faint now, but relationships have been a disaster for me. I always seem to choose the ones that cannot be fixed. After I'm out of the relationships, I look back and think, 'Why didn't I see this? Why didn't I see that? Why? Why? Why?' Actually, as soon as I think that, as soon as I start going over the relationship, thoughts come to me about what I learned and what I gained. The

Carol G.

people I chose were not stable or responsible, which required me to be very stable and very responsible. I always had to take up the slack for whatever wasn't there. Actually, I'm so independent, responsible, and stable that it's very contrary to my relationships.

"I like who I am, and I like the fact that I don't need other people's approval. I like the fact that I don't need to be taken care of. I have ended up with a great ability to take care of myself and make decisions and organize my life, because I have always had to do it. Maybe it wasn't a mistake, the relationships that I chose and the ones I got into. I benefited a great deal from them, even though many times I thought, 'Couldn't you have learned an easier way?' You know, maybe for me I couldn't. Maybe it really took some hard situations to experience the benefit."

"This is my second marriage," I added. "I tried to stick it out in the first marriage because I was a good Catholic girl, but there are times when you just need to get out. I did and got married again, to another alcoholic, to my Dad's confusion. Only this one had been sober for five years, and now he's been sober for over thirty years. About a year and a half ago, Doug and I were going through probably the worst time in our marriage. One of the things I figured out is that when you're in a committed relationship and things get hard, don't bail. That's assuming you have two people committed to each other with the same goals. I figured that if I left him I would most likely find another man just like him, and I would have to do it again, so why don't I just hang with this one. I know what the problems are, where the warts and bumps are, and we have very meaningful history together. During that hard time, I had a thirty-six-year-old friend who said, 'You should leave. Why don't you leave?' And I said, 'Because I have almost twenty-five years invested in this, and I don't want to do it again. We'll figure this out.' And we did. And as she watched, she realized, 'I get it now. I get why you stuck it out. If my husband and I were in the same place I think I would stick it out too.' We have relationships so we can learn from them. We learn from leaving, we learn from staying."

"This might sound like a soap opera," added Carol G. "but I have been through some really scary situations and circumstances in life. As a result, courage just means you must be careful; you will recognize when it's a disaster, and you just keep moving forward.

"In '93, when we had the flood, my husband and I lived down by the Lock Haven Country Club and it was flooded. We had rental property too. We lost our house, seven rental properties, and of course everything in them. There was a long period of time, which seemed like forever, that we dealt with FEMA and the Small Business Administration trying to find out if there was going to be a buyout of our property. That was another whole long story. I never ran around and found another place to live so fast in my life. My husband was one of those that couldn't deal with stress. His way of dealing with the flood, and most of life, was that he just never drew a sober breath until the water went down. Of course, at first I was frantic that he wasn't there to help when I desperately needed help. I quickly realized, 'Don't sober up until I get it all figured out. I can do it better if no one is in my way.' Strangely enough, that did work out the best. I got a new house, got more rental property, got a FEMA loan, and he sobered up. I said, 'Here is where we live now.' Looking back on that I thought, 'My God, all the things that we lost in our house.' But you know, at some point it just settled in my thoughts that it was just really stuff. Nobody lost their life, and we didn't lose anything that couldn't be replaced. A lot of that stuff needed to be lost. It was an amazing thing to go through and realize that life can be tragic and unimaginable and then it can be good again. You can work through the tragedy and recover. I didn't know I had that much courage."

"Because we are a small group this evening, I would like to know if the younger women, Susan and Frances, who have been listening so earnestly, would like to share anything?" I asked.

Hesitantly and after a moment's thought, Frances said, "I want to thank everyone for being here. Nancy and Kitty, thank you for taking on this adventure and inviting everyone to partake. I think it is very good of you. You all had many great words of wisdom, and I have just been soaking it in. I work in a hospital, and I realize with age that there is so much to be learned from everyone older, and I am grateful for you all. Thank you."

Susan jumped right in. "Just listening to all of your stories, I'm struck by the courage to be yourself. I loved your comment, Frances, about it all soaking in. The courage to not be what everybody wants you to be. To really sink into what you are yourself. Bonnie D., you said you hear voices. I think we all have voices that tell us things. I think that somehow that's how we make a difference. It's not being what people expect us to be, but being the people who we truly need to be.

"I have a story I just heard yesterday. This woman I work with has a husband who inspects and appraises houses in the area. He's very methodical and always sticks to the book. One time he was appraising this house. There was this statue of a frog in this elderly woman's yard, and on a whim, it just struck him to take it home with him, so he took it. They were about to go on a trip to Europe. He took the frog with and then took pictures of the frog everywhere, like at the Eiffel Tower. He sent the pictures to the woman like postcards. He never identified himself. It was just this little secret thing that her frog was going on vacation. Then he returned the frog in the yard one night and left a little box of touristy gifts for the woman. Later he read in the paper: Whoever took my frog and took him on vacation, please contact me, because you saved my life. They went ahead and contacted the woman, and she told them that her husband had just died, she was selling the house, and she was at a low point. She was actually suicidal. Then when she started getting these postcards, it cracked her up so much to see her little statue traveling all over the place. This story struck me as so bizarre. He was not the type to have the nerve to do things either. I think that sometimes spirits or God work in funny ways, so if you just listen to them, it really does make a difference in other people's lives."

"Wow," was the resounding response.

"As we were driving down to the river this morning, I had an overwhelming feeling of gratitude for everything, for the day, for the friendships that I have, for the ability and willingness to take part in an adventure as this has been," said Kitty. "Gratitude has really been important in my life. I need to remember what I am thankful for because it helps get me through times when I am not feeling good about where life is taking me. If I can remember what I have that is good in my life, it can change my attitude so fast. Thank you for being here tonight and sharing."

The conversation continued after we completed the aspiration-stick ritual to close the Gathering.

"Maybe it's an age thing," said Bonnie D., "but we all burned our sticks, and all the young ones piled them up over there to go in the river." We all laughed.

"That was an interesting observation," I replied.

After the Gathering, Susan and Frances joined us at camp for hot chocolate and to talk about the paddling planned for the next day.

Susan asked Nancy H. about her background. Nancy H. replied, "I work for the Forest Service. I go out on eight-day canoe trips for my job, talk to campers, check permits, do law enforcement, clean campsites, trail maintenance, rehab projects, shoreline restoration, and a variety of things. I have also conducted some archaeology surveys. We call the archaeology people the 'stones and bones resource people.' It's a really fun job. I don't have people over my head. I'm out there doing my thing."

"I have a real practical question about tomorrow," Susan said shyly. "Where do we go to the bathroom?"

We laughed, and I said, "That's a fair question. We usually try to find a sandy beach with woods, but that is not always what we get."

"It's getting late," I said. "We were serious earlier about wanting chili for breakfast. Do you two want to join us?"

"Yes, and we will heat the chili," said Susan.

I slept outside that night and loved snuggling into my sleeping bag against the cold.

October 11th through 13th

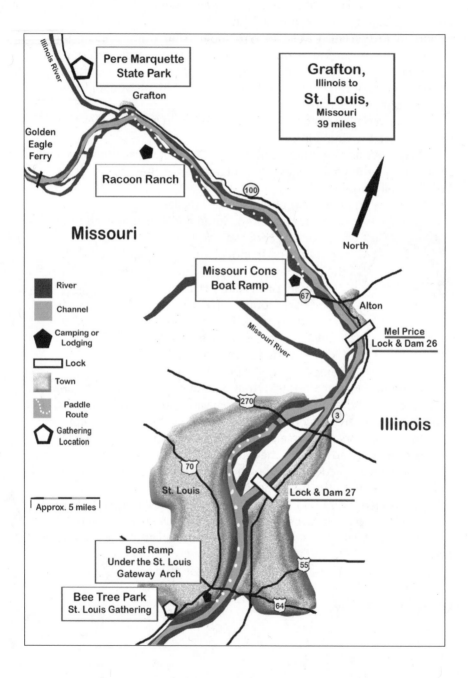

Pere Marquette State Park

Grafton

Golden Eagle Ferry

Racoon Ranch

Missouri

Grafton, Illinois to St. Louis, Missouri 39 miles

North

Missouri Cons Boat Ramp

Missouri River

Alton

Mel Price Lock & Dam 26

River

Channel

Camping or Lodging

Lock

Town

Paddle Route

Gathering Location

Illinois

Approx. 5 miles

Lock & Dam 27

St. Louis

Boat Ramp Under the St. Louis Gateway Arch

Bee Tree Park St. Louis Gathering

Illinois River

Grafton to St. Louis

Back: Nancy, Christine, Jill G., Susan
Front: Cathy G., Karen P., Kitty, Frances

October 11, Day Thirty-Eight

We woke to a serenade of hooting owls surrounding us. It would be our final campsite of the trip. Closure was an odd experience. I loved being in nature most of the day and knew I would miss it, but I also knew that I would quickly settle back into being in buildings. I got disconnected from Spirit and the energy that nature gave me when I was inside too long. My motivation declined, and I could become complacent. I didn't want that.

I had recognized two of the Peace Grandmothers late. We needed to stop in Fort Madison on the way home to deliver a heron feather to Esther, and I also needed to deliver one to Bonnie D. I hoped that at the St. Louis Gathering I would be less preoccupied with details and more in the moment so I would be aware if anyone there was meant to receive one. My intuition often faded into the background when I was focusing on tasks.

While taking down our tents, I saw a large, lime-green object fall from a tree. It hit the ground with a loud thud and rolled away. I found the odd fruit, which was six inches across, under a shrub. I brought it to the table, grateful that it hadn't landed on anyone's head. It was a hedge apple, also known  as an Osage orange. They aren't edible, but people place them around the house to keep spiders away. We gave it to Kitty.

Susan and Frances joined us for a breakfast of chili, yogurt, fresh bagels, and other leftovers. At the river, our paddling team included Susan, Frances, Karen P., who had paddled with us before, Cathy G., Christine, Jill G., Kitty, and myself.

It was heartwarming to see so many women on the water. We hadn't had a group that big since we left Red Wing. Everyone was gabbing as we paddled away from the shore and waved good-bye to Nancy H. We enjoyed a cool breeze and slightly choppy water.

We followed the wooded Missouri shoreline. On the Illinois side, the shore was only a few yards from the highway, which ran along the base of a 150-foot bluff. A high limestone rubble wall sloped from the highway down to the river. The entire town of Elsah was tucked into the

bluff's ravines. On the top of the bluff stood large homes with majestic views. Some of the women told us that the bluffs on the Illinois side were limestone, while the bluffs on the Missouri side were granite. Remnants of old quarries were still visible on the Illinois side.

We passed Portage des Sioux, the site of a historic portage that French fur traders had used. They had portaged to the Missouri River to save

themselves thirty miles of upriver travel. On shore
stood an enormous statue of the Madonna, Our
Lady of the Rivers. Our paddling partners told us
that every spring, hundreds of boats gathered in
front of her to receive a blessing for safe travel.

Our paddle was leisurely, and we enjoyed lots of
laughter. For lunch, Karen P. directed us into the St.
Louis Sailing Club marina. She had been a member
of the club and felt right at home. With everyone
safely off the water, Karen P. proceeded to lay out a
spread of fruits, cheeses, crackers, and more. She even had a tablecloth
for the picnic table. Cathy G. said she could always count on Karen P. to
bring wonderful food.

The women asked Kitty and me if we had seen the Asian carp. I said
yes, and told them that we had screamed every time one jumped near us
because it was so startling. Cathy G. was adamant that she was not a
screamer and insisted that she wouldn't scream. Others in the group
were nervous about the fish, but we reassured them.

We got back on the water. When the first two women paddled away,
a few small fish jumped behind their boats. As more of us got on the
water the fish became more active and larger ones jumped, making some
of the women scream.

The industrial docks and
equipment along the shore were
larger than those along the
northern part of the river. Our
flotilla of boats was insignificant in contrast. A bucket on
one of the cranes attached to a
dock could have easily held all
of us.

Our laughter and conversation continued. I paddled
between the boats, trying to talk
with everyone. Christine and Jill were in a tandem kayak and were a
wealth of knowledge about the area. Approaching Alton, Illinois, they
pointed to the Piasa Bluff and the giant
pictograph of a mythical bird, called the
Piasa, painted on the white limestone
wall across from it. The Piasa was named by
the Illini Native Americans and meant "a
bird that devours men." Downriver from the
Piasa was a floating casino parked at the Alton
docks. The bright purple paint made it stand

out against the backdrop of downtown Alton.

Nancy H., Frances's husband, and Cis waited at a Missouri Department of Conservation boat ramp north of Lock No. 26, also called the Mel Price Locks and Dam. The fifteen-mile paddle had gone by too quickly. The flying carp became active closer to the shore. Cis told us that the fish had been stirred up intentionally by a speed boat in the bay. A large carp sailed close to Cathy G., and she screamed loudly. Laughing, she yelled, "Oh, I screamed!" We all laughed.

Cis was on the phone with Kitty's mother, Mary K., who was from Arkansas, and Kitty's sister, Ann S., from Colorado. They had wanted to be at the boat launch to greet Kitty as she paddled in, but they had gotten lost. We said good-bye to everyone and headed out. Kitty was very excited when Mary K. and Ann S. caught up with us at a gas station. They were disappointed about missing our landing and promised that they would not miss it the next day.

The four of us drove across the Highway 67 bridge toward the Mel Price Locks and Dam and its river museum. I was stunned by the size of the two locks as we crossed the bridge. They looked twice as big as the other locks we had passed through. I watched the intense current around the dam with awe. Kitty, who had been riding in the car with her mother and sister, jumped out of their car, and in unison we asked, "Did you see that water? Oh my God!" The water churned up into big waves as it moved quickly past the lock walls. We wandered onto the observation deck and tried to imagine our tiny boats approaching and entering one of the locks. Kitty said, "Wouldn't it be exciting!" Her mother raised her eyebrows at her.

The museum had a tugboat simulation room. Cis tried driving the tugboat and kept crashing into a bridge. I tried and nearly took out the bridge as well. The process of driving the simulator helped me understand the visibility and steering challenges the tugboat captains had. Steering was not as simple as turning a wheel like in a car; there were multiple steering functions to coordinate at the same time. My respect for tugboat captains grew.

We left the museum and drove to Raccoon Ranch, Cis's family's hunting lodge. Even though I had seen the ranch before, I was impressed by its beauty and size. The stair-way was lined with giant pumpkins. Hunting photos and taxidermied birds and animals were everywhere, including a bear, a deer, a moose, raccoons, and a stunning display of several ducks. Cis showed us rooms to choose from, and we settled

in and then headed to the main room for dinner with Cis, Mary K., and Ann S.

At dinner, Kitty's mother asked her about the man in her life. The rest of us giggled. Then Mary K. began matchmaking and mentioned a nice man she knew. Kitty's sister joined her mother asking questions, indicating that they felt it would be best if Kitty were in a stable relationship, which we all knew meant married. Kitty listened for a while and then, with a smile and soft tone to her voice, ended the conversation.

I asked Cis, who was knowledgeable about the outdoors, about the trees in the area. I told her I found it odd that there weren't other species besides maple and cottonwood. She said maple, and particularly cottonwood, could "hold their breath" for sixty days during the floods. Her simple explanation put the effects of flooding into a context I could appreciate.

October 12, Day Thirty-Nine

Out my window, the peaceful sky transformed from the darkness of night to a brilliant pink kaleidoscope of color as the sun rose on our final day of paddling. For safety and river-access reasons, we would travel only nine of the twenty-two miles we had originally planned. I was sad I would not paddle past the confluence of the Missouri and Mississippi rivers, since I wanted to experience the impact the Missouri had on the Mississippi.

We drove into St. Louis, considered the gateway to the West. St. Louis was a boomtown in the mid-1800s, when its population had doubled every twenty years. We put our boats in at the Missouri Department of Conservation boat launch south of the Highway 270 bridge. Cis, Nancy H., Mary K., and Ann S. helped unload our gear onto a shoreline thick with mud and strewn with trash. The city's impact on the river was obvious. The overcast sky made everything gray and threatened rain, but team spirits were still high. Kitty's mother was noticeably nervous and watched closely as we put things in place and made sure our rain gear was close at hand. We planned to meet two hours later under the Gateway Arch.

The Arch stood in the distance like a ghost in the gray sky, beckoning us forward. The water ran faster than we had experienced before.  Even when we stopped paddling to sing, the current kept us moving quickly. A heron took off from Mosenthan Island. To have Kee bless our last day was a powerful feeling.

Other than the heron and a few sea gulls, there were no other signs of wildlife, not even Asian carp. The sounds that engulfed us were a dramatic change from the rest of the trip: sirens, buzzers, tweets from motors, drones, dings, bangs, voices, and screeching trains. The St. Louis side of the river was industrial. Beyond the barges parked along the shore, we saw the flood wall, which was painted with murals depicting St. Louis's colorful personality and history.

The water was fast and churned in the main channel. Waves came at us that weren't created by the wind or any object we could see, instead emanating from something below the surface. Maneuvering in the waves and current required focused attention.

A disabled bridge crossed the river and stood tall against the gray industrial backdrop. Drab fabric draped over it swayed in the breeze and hung below the bottom of the bridge. A crane held two men high above the bridge who were doing repair work. Paddling underneath the bridge, workers hidden behind the gray curtain waved and yelled to us.

Photo by Kitty Kennedy

South of the bridge, a dark building stood against the shore, making us feel like we had been transported to Batman's Gotham City.

We approached the graceful stainless-steel arch, which rose six hundred and

thirty feet above the river. It gleamed against the gray sky, its polished surface magnifying what little light there was. We passed a statue of Lewis and Clark, and as we paddled the last few yards, we scanned the landing for our greeting party. Due to the fast current, we arrived a half hour earlier than anticipated. We saw our van and other cars we recognized but no familiar faces. We quietly paddled to the shore with no fanfare or hurrah.

We pulled our kayaks onto the historic cobblestone paddleboat landing, where boats had landed since St.

Louis was founded. We stood under the towering arch and laughed about how Kitty's mother had missed our landing again. Our attempts to reach them by phone were unsuccessful. We got our kayaks ready for transport home but paused and looked at each other when we realized that it would be the last time we would tear down our gear.

Kitty took out her journal while I called Doug. He was ecstatic. The pride, excitement, and relief in his voice touched my heart. I could see his face in my mind. He laughed when I told him that we were sitting at the landing alone waiting for everyone. I hung up when we saw the group coming down the stairs toward the landing. One by one, their smiles turned to momentary disappointment as they realized they had missed our landing. They had been exploring the arch museum.

After photos and hugs, Kitty and I went to a trash container and ceremoniously disposed of her water shoes. She couldn't stand the stench wafting off of them any longer. Then we went to see the statue of Louis and Clark. Karen P. took us upriver to see a segment of the flood wall where an artist had installed clay tiles on the wall. The tiles had been created by schoolchildren and depicted the evolution of life. It was a fabulous display of color that ran several yards down the Riverfront Trail.  Our entourage had lunch at Soulard's where Bodhi, another friend, joined us to help celebrate the end of our journey. I ate crab cakes and enjoyed the wonderful celebratory atmosphere.

Back at Raccoon Ranch, I had a sweet surprise of flowers from Doug waiting for me. Nancy K. arrived with her massage table to provide the pampering our bodies craved. Exhausted and relieved, I took a nap before the dinner party Cis was throwing that evening.

Cis had decorated the dining room with a New Orleans theme. Rubber ducks and tiny umbrellas lined the table, even though she had not known that Gwyn referred to us as her "little ducklings." A backdrop of palm trees stretched across the room, and inflatable pink flamingos hung all over. One umbrella playfully hung from the black bear's mouth. A large group of women arrived, and lots of conversation and laughter ensued.

Cis put Kitty and me in the front of the room and began roasting us. She explained to the group the significance of the items she had decorated with, like the palm trees we had counted along the way. Then she turned her focus to what the rest of my journey down the river would be like.

"I have often wondered about Nancy as she makes her way down the Mississloppy River," Cis said, using the river's nickname. "The mud gets thicker as she goes, and she will need to be careful of the jumping carp."

She produced a big orange stuffed fish and handed it to me. "When you go farther south, you are going to have bigger things to look out for than jumping carp. You'll have to really be careful of the alligators." She produced a large lime-green stuffed alligator and handed it to me while everyone laughed. "It's one thing to blend in here, but when you get farther south to New Orleans, you really have to blend in." She placed a jester's hat on my head and tossed bright purple and green beaded necklaces to everyone. Above the raucous laughter she said, "I don't know, but we might just have to put beads around everyone's neck, because you know during Mardi Gras we all want to get beads."

Cis became serious. "As you travel further south, let the river take you down. Let it take you and immerse yourself in the water. I never really understood on a visceral level what it meant to walk in someone else's shoes—such a cliché!—but I had an opportunity to paddle, usually behind Nancy."

"Until you put your headphones on," I interjected.

"Yes," Cis laughed, "Until I put my headphones on. Four days, compared to forty-some days, of paddling is just a little taste of what it was like to get in the water, get out of the water, and get stranded in the sand and the mud. We didn't have many bugs, but I know they had bugs. It was a unique opportunity to be a part of this journey. I am so glad all you women are here to be a part of this thing that is bigger than two kayaks going down the river."

"Thank you," I responded, with joy and gratitude in my heart. "I have to admit I have heard from many women on the trip how my journey has impacted their lives, and I have a really hard time taking that in. When I started this journey, I had no idea that it would become what it is now, or I might not have signed up for the job. [Laughter.] I had no idea it could have such an impact on other women. I am so grateful for and totally amazed by this reaction, because the act of traveling the river for this long has become so routine to us. Kitty and I were explaining to someone earlier how this gets to be ordinary."

"Next time you think you or your life is ordinary, just send me an e-mail, and I will explain to you again how extraordinary you really are and how paddling with you changed my life," Kathy E. chimed in.

"Kathy," I responded, "when I heard you speak in Hannibal, it was the first time I really understood how deep the impact is for other women. You were powerful that night at the Gathering. I got it and am letting it in. I believe anyone can do what we did if they just put their mind to it. We all have the same potential. If I can do big things, anyone can. Doing this doesn't make me any different." Every woman in the place raised her eyebrows. "Okay, stop looking at me like that," I said, to another round of laughter.

"When is the next trip?" asked Carole.

"Two or three years," I answered. "One of the things that stands out for me about the trip was our car support. They did a stellar job and went beyond all expectations. Kitty and I thought we might lose some weight paddling 600 miles. [Laughter.] We may have put some on. We had an unending supply of good food and desserts."

"When I joined, they said, 'Don't buy anything!'" Nancy H. added. [Laughter.] "They got in the car after a day of paddling and said, 'Did you buy that gorp?' 'No, I found it in the food box.'" [Laughter.]

"We are going home with as much food as we started with," I added. "Our car support kept going to the store, which was great because we had salads and fresh food almost every night."

"If anyone is interested in my job on the next leg," said Nancy H., "I would highly encourage anyone to join them. It was just a joy, it really was."

"Have you seen your husband since you left?" asked Carol S.

"No," I answered. "He's on his own adventure. He took on our coffee shop all by himself for the first time. Because of that and cell phones, a whole new dimension was added to the trip. I'd be paddling and my phone would ring. Of course I usually couldn't get to it in time because it was in a waterproof container. I'd call Doug back and he'd say, 'I can't figure out payroll on the computer.' [Laughter.] Then I'd walk him through it step by step, pulling up a visual in my head of the different computer screens required for payroll. It was just weird to be floating on the river, enjoying the beauty and quiet around me, while handling payroll and taxes hundreds of miles away."

We answered the women's questions and shared river stories and photos while enjoying more laughter. The party wound down late in the evening, and the women headed home. Kitty and I looked at each other and smiled. We hugged and told each other that we had done a good job. Heading to bed, our hearts and souls felt joyfully full.

October 13, Day Forty

At sunrise, Cis drove me to the river to sing. The water was calm and beckoned to me, but there would be no paddling. I soaked in its strength and beauty for a few moments and then went back to Raccoon Ranch, where Nancy K. gave me a massage. As she worked the tension out of my muscles, I thought about how acceptance of who I was and acknowledgment of the impact I had on others were key to moving forward for me. One of my dark sides was not letting people in, a behavior I intended to change. The heavenly massage came to an end too soon.

Breakfast went by quickly, like the rest of the day would. We rode the Grafton Ferry across the river to Bonnie D.'s exotic-game refuge to deliver a heron feather to her and to meet Drayas the baboon. We easily recognized the refuge from the lion statues that stood watch on pillars on both sides of her driveway. Two dogs greeted us and an albino peacock ran behind the house. Bonnie D. popped out of the house with her friend Linda. I spoke with Bonnie D. privately and gave her the feather. She was overwhelmed by the story of the thirteen Grandmothers and humbled to receive a feather.

"I have a blue heron that has lived on this farm for five years. Oh, it's a beautiful feather," she said and immediately put it in a safe place.

The others joined us in the house to meet Drayas. The baboon sat, looking around, while some of us joined her on the floor.

"She is a hamadryas baboon, and I think she's a little deformed," said Bonnie D. "Her father looked like a basketball too, but our other baboons didn't." We laughed when Drayas roughly petted a stuffed horse. Bonnie D. said, "She eats watermelon, chicken, and pretty well everything. She will be eight January second. My husband Bob just died April second, and Drayas was so crazy about him. He was Drayas's favorite person." Drayas walked between Carol S. and me and let us pet her, which Bonnie D. said was unusual.

Bonnie D. went into another room and came back with a ferret. As soon as Drayas saw it she grunted. Bonnie D. said, "I don't want any of you petting her ferret." She handed the ferret to Drayas, who hugged it tightly. "She just loves her ferret, but she doesn't like the other ferrets. If one of the other ones comes up to her she scoots it away. Okay Drayas, it's time to go in your cage. Do you want me to take your ferret?"

Drayas went into the cage carrying the ferret.

"She is the funniest little girl you

ever saw," said Bonnie D. "Every time we tell her to go back in, she always goes back in. I'll let her keep her ferret for a while—she's never hurt him."

Bonnie D. and Linda took us to meet the other animals in their care. "As part of my license I have to have entertainment for them, so there are toys and other things I keep in with them," said Bonnie D. "This is our sloth. Look at her claws; she's a member of the bear family."

"This is the spider monkey," said Linda. "His tail is something else; it's like a hand. The first time I was out here, I got close to the cage and he put the tail around my neck, and I was stuck there."

Bonnie D. spoke of her husband's death while introducing us to the coatimundi, which is an African raccoon that lived in a cage in the same room as Drayas.

"What Linda and I went through during Bob's death was one of the most interesting experiences," said Bonnie D. "I was up at a friend's taking care of their horse's twins."

"I was here with Bob," said Linda, "and he said, 'I am lifting up.' I thought maybe he had a little too much morphine. But he said, 'I want to talk to Bonnie.' I found the number and called her."

"Within fifteen minutes I came home," said Bonnie D. "He was upset. I calmed him down. That was on a Thursday. On Friday morning, he slept later than usual, and I kept looking in to see if he was okay. I looked in once and he said, 'I got to ask you a question. Am I dead?' I said no. 'Are you sure I'm not dead?' he asked again. I assured him he was not dead. 'I thought I died last night,' he said, 'but when I opened my eyes and saw you I knew I wasn't in Heaven.'" We all laughed.

"I thought that was so funny. Sunday he slept all day, and when I was putting him to bed he said, 'Now Bonnie, you are going to wake up and find me dead, but you are going to be okay. There is something that you have got to do, I don't know what it is, but taking care of me has helped prepare you for it.' That was something." Bonnie D. said. She was still not sure what he meant, but was convinced it would come to pass.

We went into a small room in the basement to see a black labrador puppy that was found and brought to Bonnie D. for care. "Look, the bullet went in here," said Bonnie D., pointing at a spot on the puppy while she tenderly stroked it. The puppy tried to stand, but its back was paralyzed. "I give him Reiki treatments three to four times a day. At first we thought he had been hit by a car. I don't generally take dogs or cats in the sanctuary, but that's all right."

She gave the puppy water, and we walked through the barn past dwarf horses and a llama to see the mountain lion. Bonnie D. petted the huge cat, which rubbed against the cage door. "About four years ago, I could put a harness on her and take her to the nursing home and let people pet her."

"That gives a whole new meaning to pet therapy," said Kitty. We laughed.

"If you heard her crack chicken bones it would curl your hair," said Bonnie D.

On the way back to the house, the llama greeted us. "I didn't know what to name him," said Bonnie D. "I am real particular. You can see what a royal look llamas have. And as I told you earlier, I hear voices at night. So I saw him in a dream and he said, 'I am all you want, I am all you need. I am all. So his name is Amall, which is llama spelled backwards.'"

Bonnie D.'s entire life revolved around the animals in her care. She told us that her animals came mostly from zoos that could no longer care for them. Some came from individuals who had cared for them until the animals became too big or law enforcement had intervened.

It was hard to leave because Bonnie D. had so many fascinating stories to share. As we left, Bonnie D. gave me a bundle of peacock feathers.

Cis and I went to a book signing for my first book at REI, an outfitting store. Carole joined us there, and her great smile and people skills brought many people to the table. After the book signing we enjoyed a quick lunch with Pat G. and left to prepare for the final Gathering.

We arrived at the Bee Tree County Park shelter. My emotions were running high. The weather wasn't cooperating. The gentle rain had me wondering how many women would come. I took a deep breath and leaned into my knowing that everyone who was meant to be there would come.

Women began to join our group. I took a break from the crowd to collect my thoughts and walked to an overlook to gaze at the river below. I spoke quietly to the river, thanking her for our safe travels and the countless gifts she had given us. I watched the current flow southward and wondered what the next leg of my journey downriver would bring.

St. Louis Gathering

Women began to join our group. I took a break from the crowd to collect my thoughts and walked to an overlook to gaze at the river below. I spoke quietly to the river, thanking her for our safe travels and the countless gifts she had given us. I watched the current flow southward and wondered what the next leg of my journey downriver would bring.

The energy level was high at the shelter. There were twenty-nine women, ranging in age from forty to seventy-five.

Mary K. was proud to be the honored elder at the Gathering and didn't hesitate to speak. "So many thoughts go through your mind at something like this. I'm Kitty's mother. I came here from Arkansas to greet Kitty at the river. When they came paddling down the river, we were going to be there waiting. Well, we missed them the first time. And we missed them the second time. [Laughter.] We never

Mary K.

saw them land. They were already here when we got here. Kitty will probably be traumatized for the rest of her life. [More laughter.]

"I really admire Kitty. First I was apprehensive when she told me what she was going to do. And then I thought, when I was growing up and about Kitty's age I probably would not have had the courage to do what she has. Growing up in the age I did, in the 'thirties and 'forties, a lot of women were not apt to get very far out into the world. It seemed as though they kind of married into the community, started having families, and just kind of settled where they were, which was very true of me. I grew up in the community, and we lived there for fifty-five years before we finally moved. We never moved from our safe little area. I really think women are finding their way much more and more easily than they did when I was growing up. Maybe it's the community that you live in where people have certain expectations, certain customs.

"I was married very young. When I look back, I probably would not recommend that to most girls now. I think you need to have a little maturity to be able to be married and have a family. I don't think I had that right at the beginning. I could probably have done a little bit better when I was first raising my children. I don't regret the things that I did. They all turned out fine, and I'm thankful for that.

"The other thought that came into my mind while we were sitting here is that women need to support other women more. I find that it's happening, but I don't believe it's happening enough. I think women are just not as supportive as they could be with one another. Whether we agree with them or not, I think we should still try to find their side of whatever is going on and to be supportive."

"I have been to one other Gathering before, because I paddled with the girls for a few days, and that was wonderful," began Karen P. "I got an e-mail the other day that I thought was pretty neat. It's from the Dove company, which is making a big push to help improve the self-image of women. They have a little video on their web site, which I watched; it's really good. They offer a space where you can make comments about body image. Even though they are a company that's in it for profit, they're taking a tack that could potentially be very helpful for women in general. I think that is a good sign."

"I have a story to share about a friend that I deal with during work that relates to self-image," responded Kate. "I talk to this woman on the telephone for work. I talked to her on Friday, and she opened up and created even more of a powerful way for us to examine our lives and our lives in relation to one another. She whispered into the telephone that she had recently lost all of her hair, and they don't know why. She doesn't have a thyroid problem, her blood tests are just fine, and she hasn't had any kind of chemotherapy. She whispered into the telephone, 'Katie, I don't know who I am.' My hair is getting very long, and I had decided just to let it grow into long gray braids. When she said that, I looked into myself and put myself in her place. Who am I if I'm not what I look like? What do people expect to see when they look at me? I think that is a powerful lesson for all of us to keep in mind."

"Like Nancy said, I was in the support team from Savanna, Illinois, to Burlington, Iowa," said Pat G. "It was just so fabulous to be included in the group and not have to worry about anything. Everyone there was included, no matter who was around. Any of the women that came in were just part of the group. It was a group of just fabulous people. I must say that it was one of the most enjoyable and enlightening and rewarding experiences. It was definitely one of the most rewarding. I am not going to say it was the most, because there are many other rewarding things in my life. I thank you both for allowing me to participate. I really enjoyed it."

The fan was passed to Jane K., who looked at it nervously and said, "I thought I had a little more time. It's not easy for me to speak in places like this. I had my own business for many years and it's very easy for me to get up and speak about business with people. I am not quite sure why. I guess it's a bit more impersonal.

"I was thinking about something Carol C. and I were talking about it earlier. I asked her if she had ever been in a hot air balloon. As we talked about that, I was thinking about the sensation I had being in a hot air balloon. The peacefulness I felt was unexplainable, but more than that it was because I was riding above everything.

"I am an observer of life, and because I have my own business, I work out of my home. I talk to people on the phone. I am always a little bit hidden, and I like that. But I'm finding now that it's time to not be so hidden. There is something in me that is pushing another way. I'm not sure how to broach that. Today was one of the first efforts I made when Carol C. invited me to come here. I believe we have so much to share with other people, and you never really know when someone is going to be impacted by something you say in a positive way. I hope that I can be braver and be more outgoing."

"I now realize that most of my life I was very external and unconscious," said Carol C. "In the past twenty years, after being hit over the head with what felt like several two-by-fours, I realize that I have been on a fascinating spiritual journey, and I'm aware of the slow changes in my beliefs, emotions, and behaviors that have taken place. I'm aware of how spirituality has influenced my life with more ease of living and contentment. Now, I feel an internal awareness and awakening of my self, my soul. My personality history is diminishing. My soul history is guiding my life. As a result, I find that the hardships of my life experiences have led me to this awareness. I have an appreciation of myself at a deeper level of self-knowledge and self-honesty. I practice deep soul work by studying the mystics and their practices to reach enlightenment."

Cis took the fan and said, "I, too, had the honor of paddling a few days with Nancy. It was an extraordinary experience. I resonate a lot with what you say, Jane K., with what you say, Carol C., with what all of you women are saying. It really took about forty-five years to get me to speak. Sometimes you can't shut me up now. Today I don't think I can get going. I am still processing internally all that I experienced."

"For the past six years, I have been caretaking for my mother, who is ill," began Mimi. "I'm not doing that anymore. I have traveled. I think I have reinvented myself so many times. But, it's funny, I'm back now in the same area where I was born. So my radius has spread, and now it's coming back to center.

"I just did some work that I would like to share, because it had a lot of impact on me. I have a big family conflict. I just learned this practice where you internally confront whatever it is that you are having problems with. I bring someone, like my brother, into my heart-space, and then I dialogue with that person. This is actually a practice that was passed on to me through the Integral Approach, which is Ken Wilbur's work. I dialogue with whomever in whatever fashion works. Then I let myself become the enemy or the problem. I did this with my brother, who I had a big conflict with, and I started crying for my brother. It took this whole turn where I understood, because all these aspects that are parts of myself are split off. For me to be able to come around to have such deep compassion and not just 'Oh God, please just let me forgive,' was so real. It was a big heart-opening. I wanted to share that practice, because it moved a lot for me. I find, obviously, that shadow work really is enlightening for me. And I'm really so happy to be in a place where being over fifty is so honored! I could strip down naked." [Laughter.]

"That was beautiful, Mimi," responded Christy. "I came tonight because I found out from Mimi that a group of women were meeting to welcome two women who kayaked the Mississippi. She said kayak and I said, 'I'm there.' Oh my God, I couldn't believe it. That is just fantastic news. Congratulations to both women. Congratulations and best of luck on your future ventures. It sounds like a fabulous thing to do."

As Christy finished speaking, four deer lazily passed by a short distance away. For a few moments, we took in their beauty, and I recalled the deer that had greeted me at the beginning of the journey.

"For me, Mimi came up with a perfect example of courage," said Dancing Coyote. "When I was doing shadow work, my Jungian therapist said, 'Courage is a word that has a much broader meaning than just doing something really spectacular like saving a buddy in wartime, which is the usual way you look at courage. Courage is when you can do your shadow work and face your demons. Look at the things that hold you back, the issues that you have that are impediments to where you want to go, where your visions would take you if you could deal with them.' You can do exactly what Mimi did. It's looking into yourself and seeing how much responsibility you have for where you are, and then taking the responsibility for getting yourself out of that place. The best way to grow is to have the courage to take a look at your shadow and make your shadow your friend."

"I am one of several Nancys here tonight," said Nancy R. "I am well over fifty, but it is the best time of my life. It's not at all where I thought I would be at this stage of my life, and yet it's better. I love the fire. It takes me back to when I was growing up and I was a Girl Scout. I was a Girl Scout well into high school because my mother wanted to be the Girl Scout leader. [Laughter.] I still camp and have campfires and things that I didn't appreciate at the time. This fire really takes me back. I just lost my mother this last year, although I have been losing her for many years to Alzheimer's, so it was a long good-bye. Things like this bring her right back to me."

"Nancy R.'s comments just brought to mind my mother," Dancing Coyote continued. "When my mother was my age, I was twenty-six years younger. I had no idea what her life looked like. Now that I am where she was, I know what her life was like. I can imagine what her life was like when she was my age. I wish that there was some way that she could have stood still and I could have grown twenty-six years, so I could have had the kind of conversations about gratitude that I would love to have with her right now. I would like an understanding of why she did certain things that she did that I didn't understand at the time. I'd have liked a conversation about the skills she passed on to me and the wisdom. I don't know how you do something like that. It leaves a kind of echo inside of me that I can't do that. I felt that way about my father, also. I would have loved to have a conversation with my father as a contemporary."

Ellen

"The question that interested me is about life. Did it turn out as you expected or follow the path you expected?" began Ellen. "Oh, heck no! It's had so many twists and turns, but obviously I am supposed to be where I am now, which gives me great comfort. I have two beautiful daughters, and I have to say, it was just such a joy raising my daughters. I remember when I was pregnant with my first one. That was when they had all the hostages in Iran. I remember thinking, 'Please don't let this be a boy.' If it's a girl she can play piano and play baseball and nobody will tease her. If it's a boy he is going to have a hard time playing the piano and playing baseball, so I was blessed with two daughters who are totally different, as Becky can attest. They were quite a challenge. I wouldn't have traded any of the hardship. I buried my mother when she was forty-eight years old. My father remarried; I buried my step-mother thirteen years later. For the last couple of years, I have lost a friend every six months. I wouldn't have traded any of it.

"I have a personal message for Nancy from Jesse. He is very excited to be here and he is back in the light and very happy. He has a message for everybody. Jesse is a nephew of ours that was killed in a car crash just a couple of months ago. When I met Nancy, Jesse had just died a week before. He came to the group that we were in and wouldn't leave. Nancy asked him to quiet down and he said, 'I'm staying. I want to see what you all have to say.' I think it's when he hears 'sisterhood,' and when I hear 'sisterhood,' that I realize there are so many men out there that need us. Men want to be able to speak emotionally, but also want to be able to know the right things to say but were never given the chance because they were supposed to be masculine. Be men! Men were expected to do the job, take care of the family, and they get very lost. Jesse's spirit is also hoping that you will keep all the men in your prayers. Know that some of them are striving almost to be as good as us, but not quite." [Laughter.]

Bodhi quietly took the fan from Ellen and paused a few moments to gather her thoughts. "I'm going through a lot lately," she began. "I've been crying a lot the last few weeks, and I haven't done much of that in years. Part of it is that I have been talking to a very dear friend whose son was my son's best friend growing up. This boy just went into Iraq this week. I've also heard so many stories from friends over the last year of their illnesses, their loss of people who they've been close to during the difficult times they've been going through. In fact my life has been really devoted to exploring spiritual paths. Shamanism, Tibetan Buddhism, Zen Buddhism, Hinduism, as well as traditional religions. I find myself sitting the last few weeks feeling like I haven't gone deeply enough into those things. That I've been dabbling too much, and I've been doing some relooking at my life.

"On the subject of courage, I'm just hoping that I will have the courage to really hear my friends' stories and be supportive. I need to be with them through the things that they're going through in their lives, have the courage to be there, listen, and be present. I must find a peace within myself."

"I am really excited to be here tonight," said Anna enthusiastically. "When Bodhi e-mailed me about this I really wanted to come and meet the two women who had done the upper Mississippi. Rivers have always been at the heart of my spirituality. I was raised down in the Ozarks and on the Current River with my cousins running up and down the river in johnboats. When I was eleven, my Dad bought a boat on the Mississippi. He and I spent almost every weekend out there. When I was about eight or nine, I found a boat that was sunk. It was a metal rowboat. I dug it out of the mud and fixed it up. I whittled little pegs to put in the little holes that were in the bottom where the rivets had come out. I actually took it out on the Mississippi. My father found out about it later, and he was not real excited about that." [Laughter.]

"At that time, I remember I used to talk to the river a lot and tell the river that someday I was going to do the whole thing right from the top all the way down. About thirty years ago, my husband said, 'What about living on a sailboat?' We had three kids at the time, but we went ahead and bought a boat and built it in our backyard. We did the lower river in that boat. We took it from here down to New Orleans and down into the Caribbean for three years. We lived in the Caribbean with the kids, so I did do the lower river. When we came back, people asked me, 'What was the best part of the trip?' We went all the way down as far as St. Martin and in the area of Martinique, but my favorite part has always been the Mississippi. Last year I had a chance to do the upper Mississippi in a motorboat. My husband and I did that. The further north we got the prettier the river seemed to get. We'd go through a lock and it opened up into what seemed like a whole other river each time. It's real exciting to me to meet two women that are adventuring and out there. It's neat what you've done with it, gathering women together in these groups to share feelings and emotions and their lives."

"I am Carol from Chicago," began Carol S. "There are many Carols, so I thought I would identify myself that way. When my mother gave birth to me in 1950, she went to the hospital, and they put her to sleep, and she woke up a while later, and there I was. When I gave birth to my daughter, there was every effort by my doctor for me to use medication. My husband was one of the first fathers to actually be present in the hospital room with me when I gave birth to my daughter. He was horribly hospital averse and blood averse, but he did it anyway. When my daughter gave birth to her children, she invited me to come and be with her. It was a beautiful thing. About two weeks ago, my god-daughter was ready to give birth to her child, and I was invited. That was the last circle I sat in. I was invited to a Blessing Way, which was a small, intimate event. I, as her god-mother, and her mother were there. We sat in the space where she planned to give birth in her home and blessed her journey toward her labor. That night she said to me, and I live almost 200 miles away from her, 'Carol, if I give birth to this baby tomorrow, would you come and be present? I would love it.' And I said, 'Sure.' Well, she didn't give birth that day, but about three weeks later, I was back. I was there for the birth of her baby. She gave birth in a tub of water in her home in a very natural way. It was really beautiful. I am still just kind of savoring the moment of watching that baby come into the world.

"I believe that all of us, as well as all of those generations, have enormous courage. I think it takes a lot of courage to be a woman in our society, because of the long, oppressive patriarchal push in which we have had to exist in the whole context of our lives. I wanted to discuss the birthing moments because I think giving birth is a time that takes enormous courage. I think it takes a lot of courage to be who we are. I have struggled my whole life with that. I have taken some courageous steps to take charge of my life and make decisions in my life, which led to me being me. Knowing that I want to be authentic, even though there has just been so much pressure to live in life, go on day after day, and just fit in."

Kitty's sister, Ann S., spoke next. "My life has been good, so I don't really have anything too serious to share with you. I would like to say that I work with lots of guys, and I am with guys all of the time. We all sound way more intelligent than all the guys I deal with all of the time. We should keep it up.

"When Kitty told me she was going to go on this adventure, I just thought 'Wow, this is terrific!' It was like the 'You go girl' thing. It was just terrific. I couldn't believe that she was going to do something like that. I thought this was a great adventure. I hadn't planned on coming here for this, but I am really happy that I did. I can't remember when I have ever been in a room with this many women. Ever! It's overwhelming. But it's really nice, and I think we should all remember that we are special. We should be thoughtful and caring and let each other know how we feel.

"I just wanted to say that we all think our mothers are great, but Mary K. is my mom, and I think she is really the best too. I am happy to be here with my sister, Kitty, and with my mom, and thanks for everybody being here and having me. Thank you for this little bit of sunshine."

"I just met everybody this afternoon at REI," said Barbara S. "I really had no idea what I was coming to. I haven't even read more than the front page of your book. [Laughter.] It sounded interesting, so I grabbed my friend Debbie, who had no idea what she was coming to either, and here we are.

"I know that my life has changed a lot in the last ten years, because I got separated and moved out on my own. It was the first time I had moved out on my own, which was a humongous step. I went from sharing a room with my sister to going to college and sharing a room with roommates to getting married. I got married at twenty-four, and I think that's too young, but that was what everybody else was doing, so I got married. I got to my fifties and life was not where I wanted it. It took me months to finally take the step and actually move out. I finally said, 'Things aren't working here. Counseling is not working, so I'm moving out.' It was one of the best things that I did for myself.

"When I turned fifty I wanted to do something really different. I was working with these guys in England, and one of the guys had this big dream. He said, 'I want to hike to the top of Mount Kilimanjaro.' I thought that sounded really neat to do, and I said, 'Sure I'll do it.' Then I started reading about the adventure and thought, 'Oh my gosh. What have I signed up to do?' We had a group of six or seven who were going. Everybody else started reading and they fell out. There were only three of us that did it: the guy that initiated the trip, another guy from the UK, and me. We got all prepared to do this thing and we did it. We actually made it to the top. It was the most incredible and the most challenging thing I have ever done. The thing it taught me was if you really want to do something, you may have to exert an extra amount of energy to do it, but it is possible to do. I never would have thought, five years before that, that I would be able to go to the top of Mount Kilimanjaro, and enjoy it too. I would tell younger women to strive for what they think might be impossible, because it may be possible."

"As we were going around the circle," added Jo, "I've heard so many wonderful stories. Now I look at the fan and hope that it will help me to be wise or say wise things.

"I wish I had taken my three children down the Mississippi and lived in the Caribbean for three years. I have always wanted to do something really wild like that. My brain is over here thinking, 'Where did they go to school? How did she do that?' Carol S. talked about how the childbirth experience was completely different for our mothers. Things are so much more open for young women today. Most people don't really know how it changed. The changes in attitude about labor and delivery came about not because of doctors but because of women themselves. Many of us said, 'We want something different.' There was a lot of reading and classes that happened. The environment of the time was such that the baby boom was over, so doctors were competing for patients. We took back giving birth as the natural event that it is. Childbirth is not an illness. Women's bodies are designed for it. The best medical treatment is the least treatment possible. It was a stretch for me to be outspoken then, but it was also very rewarding. It was a privilege to be part of that movement."

Sarajane took the fan. "I had the great opportunity of meeting Nancy in Ely in July. I have a really hard time talking about myself, even one-on-one. One of the things that I can say, and then I want to pass the fan on, is I brought a poem that I would like to read. It has to do with the kind of healing that I am going through right now, at this moment, as I speak. I think it is the best way for me to speak my truth and give something to the circle. It's a poem that a very dear friend of mine gave me about six months ago to read, and it evoked a deep response from me. It keeps coming up. In the past week, it has come up many times, and I would like to share it with you. It's a poem by Mary Oliver entitled "The Journey." [Sarajane read the poem.]

"I heard that this evening come out in different ways from all of you. Thank you."

Kitty stood a long time with the fan in hand. "Tonight I felt sad and teary-eyed over this being the end of this journey. It gets replaced with gratitude very fast. I am very much in a place of gratitude today. This has been—and I am going to use the word that Nancy has heard many, many times on this trip—this has been amazing."

After the closing ceremony the women remained for a few moments and talked.

"It was great to meet you," Jane said to me.

"It was good to meet you," I said. "Thank you for being so brave and speaking tonight."

"I don't know you any other way than being brave and speaking," said Carol C. to Jane. "So I don't know who you are talking about."

"I know what she's talking about," I said. "We're kindred spirits. I've done public speaking and I am great as long as I don't have to go here," I pointed to my heart. "That's when I choke up, so I know exactly what you mean."

"Thanks, me too," responded Jane. "I want to be genuine with it, so I start thinking about it too much and then don't speak."

"I understand. That's why I said thank you for your courage," I added.

Our conversation was interrupted by a police officer who told us we had to wrap up. We had stayed past the park's closing time. Darkness and hunger drove us to a local pub for food.

The energy from the Gathering bubbled over to our dinner table. With fourteen of us seated at the table, the conversation was raucous. We laughed, talked, and had a wonderful time together. By the time we headed back to the ranch, I was ready for a good night's sleep.

HEADED HOME

October 14, Day Forty-One

I took my time getting out of bed, but still ended up downstairs before everyone else. I attacked the list of tasks I needed to complete before we could leave, only taking a break to join the others for breakfast.

While we ate, Mary K. told us how she had driven a beet truck in North Dakota early on in her marriage. It had been beet harvest time, and she agreed to drive the truck when a friend asked her to. She had never driven a truck before and was intimidated by the beet truck's eighteen gears. She took out the telephone wires on her first trip to the railroad station to deliver the beets. Luckily, she wasn't fired. Mary K. said the adventurousness of driving the truck felt similar to what Kitty was doing paddling the river.

We fell silent as Mary K. spoke of a time that changed many lives. She remembered her father listening to the radio during the Pearl Harbor attack, and the worried look on his face had never left her memory. She was nine years old, and the adults around her talked about their fear that the Japanese would start bombing our shores. As she relayed her story, I felt the fear she described and remembered how it had affected my own father's life in a similar way.

After breakfast, we went to the river. I stood silently with the others around me. I was unable to describe my feelings; words seemed too hollow for the occasion. It felt sad and sacred. Something stirred within me as if awakened

Photo by Kitty Kennedy

from a deep sleep. I had felt protected by the river while on the trip. I felt my vulnerability begin to rise now that it was over, yet I was excited, knowing that I would return to the river. I sang a farewell to my dearest friend, the Mississippi, knowing that I would steal glimpses of her every chance I got on the way home.

Kitty, Nancy H., and I packed our gear, said good-bye to everyone, and finally headed toward home. We intended to drive to Red Wing and spend the evening with Sherry. I sat in the backseat of the car, reading, journaling, and processing the past six weeks. I was grateful for everything that had happened and the amazing women we had the joy of connecting with. While Nancy H. and Kitty chatted, I read more of Grandmothers Counsel the World and felt that the women's words spoke directly to me and about me. The Grandmothers wrote about how indigenous people function as one with their environment and how having close contact with nature facilitated an inner journey. I realized that was why I intuitively knew that the Gatherings must be held outside.

One of the Grandmothers in the book said that we forget who we are and that was the cause of our illnesses. She was right. If I strove too hard, my spirit became dull, and I couldn't hear the voice from within. A gift from the river was a chance to slow down and hear that precious inner voice more clearly.

We drove on into the darkness, singing along with the oldies on the radio and trying to stay awake. When we reached La Crosse, we were too tired to drive any farther, so we abandoned our quest to stay with Sherry. We checked into a motel. Nancy H. and Kitty fell asleep with the lights still on, and I was right behind them.

October 15, Day Forty-Two

The next morning we stopped and saw Sherry on our way through Red Wing. Kitty gave Sherry party favors from Cis's, which included ten feet of the palm-tree backdrop.

We arrived in the Twin Cities and dropped Nancy H. off at her brother's house, where she'd stored her truck. Nancy H. continued on to Ely, but Kitty and I went to my daughter Naomi's house for the evening.

We showed Naomi and her fiancé, Nick, a few of our photos. We realized that they weren't interested, so we stopped. Kitty went out for the evening with friends while I hung out with Naomi and Nick. I wanted to share my experiences and talk about what I had accomplished on the trip, but I fell silent. They talked with each other about their dog and how to handle someone who had broken the townhouse organization's rules as they worked on their computers, planning their wedding. The wedding was all they could focus on. I remained silent and went to bed feeling hurt.

October 16, Day Forty-Three

Kitty and I read the paddlers' journal aloud on the drive home to Ely. We laughed, cried, and felt blessed. I felt like I was living in my body differently because I was living with my spirit differently. I could not live in nature, sing a sacred song each morning, and set my personal desires aside for the greater good for forty-three days without being forever changed.

I lay in my own bed that night thinking about my behavior the night before at Naomi's. Why hadn't I spoken up and told them what I wanted to say? Why had I fallen silent? I realized I was one of the silent ones the journey was designed to reach out to. I was sensitive to the subtle cues of disinterest. Because of those cues, I chose to believe that Naomi and Nick didn't value what I had experienced or had to say. I also wondered if I had been using my role as leader to hide so that I would not need to speak at the Gatherings.

When I was growing up, I felt like I had no voice and wondered if I was invisible. After graduating from high school, I eagerly anticipated college. I talked to my father about it, knowing he had been putting my mother's social security benefits away to pay for our educations, but he told me that money was for the boys. I was devastated. He saw how hurt and determined I was and said I could try community college, as long as my focus was on something practical like teaching or nursing. I desperately wanted to go to art school, but that was not a "practical" choice, so I was afraid to bring it up. I began studying elementary education, knowing it was not what I wanted. In a moment of bravery I talked to my father about trying one semester of art school. When he said yes, I felt overjoyed, alive, challenged, and terrified.

I loved art school, but I compared myself to others in the class, and my insecurities rose to the surface. The pressure to do what a "good girl" should do never stopped echoing in the back of my mind. My feelings of incompetence won out. Silenced by cultural pressures and my fear of failure, I left school, got married, and had children.

Those cultural pressures still influenced me. I still looked for clues from other people before I spoke. Were they interested in what I had to say? If I thought they weren't, I often wouldn't say anything. I was saddened that my self-limiting beliefs were still present but elated that I had begun to break free from them. My struggle with those beliefs was connected to the difficulty I had experienced on the trip. On the trip, I had been visible and able to stand in my power. Returning home, I could feel the shackles of my insecurities attempting to limit me again. The trip had altered those feelings in a significant way and had the potential to change the remainder of my life for the better.

Our culture has made some women believe that we are useless and insignificant, particularly as we age. In actuality, we are the hope. We hold within us a knowing, born out of time and experience, that is the key to truly healing the world.

May you harvest the knowledge and blessings of your life.

MORE WOMEN'S STORIES

FROM THE GATHERINGS

BETSY F.'S STORY

"I grew up in California, moved to Minneapolis to go to school, and lived in Edina, where I said I would never live. I have retired in Ely, Minnesota, and I am very happy there. I don't have a lot of answers, but I have little pieces of answers in my life. Things that seem to work.

"I am not a church person. I was raised a church person. I used to write editorials for the school newspaper about being saved. In those days you could do that. I was Baptist, and we read the Bible. The one class I got an A in at college my freshman year was Old Testaments. But then I started reading too much, and I started asking questions. I think the one thing that has stayed with me, as kind of a fallen-away church person, is I really like the story of the Good Samaritan and some of those Bible stories I was told as a child. I liked the story of Ruth that was written for children and taken from the scripture. In my older years, I think there are lots of ways to live. I don't know that I have really found one. I feel like the story of the Good Samaritan influenced my life a lot. I also like the concept, although I am not a Quaker, that there is a bit of God in everybody. Like many of you, I find a spiritual experience in the outdoors. Though, I don't know if I always think of it as spiritual. I love being in my garden, even if I don't always get everything planted.

"One thing I like to do, but we haven't done in the last couple of years, is canoe. When I've gone canoeing, I like the fact that I can out-portage a lot of people. A piece of advice I have is to have a sense of patience, a sense of humor, and good friends. Look for the neat things about other people. One of the neat things about Ely is that there are lots of people my age who are really busy contributing to the community. Maybe that is just part of a small town, but I just see this contribution to the community as something to look forward to."

Jan F.'s Story

"I saw the article in the paper and I thought that it's so cool to go down the river like that. That's something that I would love to do, but I've got two little dogs, and at this point in my life, I cannot leave my girls.

"I am fifty-eight. I had my daughter when I was eighteen. At that time, I was really a dumb, little, naïve, innocent girl who the first guy I dated, I swear, knocked me up so he could stay out of Vietnam. I left a father, who was very verbally and emotionally abusive, [and] a mother, who was very submissive and took it. She just took it! Mainly I guess I escaped from the house by getting pregnant, which I wouldn't recommend to anybody.

"That was a ten-year marriage that was very mentally and verbally abusive. And Mom is all the time saying, 'You can't leave him. You can't get along by yourself.' I finally said, 'I deserve better than this. I'm not taking it anymore.' So I left him with a job for $4.75 an hour. I got $25 a week child support. I worked a full-time job and added on a part-time job. I worked nine years part-time in addition to full-time. I raised my daughter, Wendy, who really put me through hell. She really was a pistol. We are very very close now. I told Wendy tonight I was going down to the riverfront to get some wisdom. And she said, 'Mom you have a lot of wisdom to give those ladies.' I said, 'If you say so, Honey.' She's forty years old. She just recently married. She has a step-daughter who is putting her through it. I keep telling her, 'It's payback time, Honey.'

"After my divorce I sampled a lot of fruits to be offered. There were a lot of fruits out there, seems like I found a lot of not very good men. I finally realized I could take care of myself. I deserve to be treated with dignity and respect. That is a Dr. Phil line. I did attract and marry a very wonderful man.

"Like Oprah says, you need to find your passion in life. My passion in my life, what I can hardly wait to get back to when I am away, is my home. I truly love my home. I volunteer with the Discovery Center, down at the Humane Society; my second home is the Y. I love to go there. I have been a member at the Y since I was twenty-one, and I am fifty-eight years old. It's a great place to go; you meet a lot of ladies. You can make a lot of friends. I keep busy. I garden. I'm so busy I don't know how I got things done before when I worked outside my home.

"Life is good. I started wearing 'Life is Good' T-shirts a few years back when I developed heart problems. Anything illness-wise or physically wrong you could get, I think my parents passed on to me. Out of all of the kids in the family, I am the one that got their stuff. I have eleven stints in my heart. I've had two back surgeries. I've had both knees worked on. I've gone through a lot of pain, but you just keep trucking. Whatever gets thrown at you, you just keep trucking. I do the best I can and sometimes I get down, but I get over it.

"My little dogs are my friends, my companions. Life is very full. I have good friends. My daughter calls me every day. I exercise with a gal that is eleven years younger. She keeps me going. When the girls complain about their husbands I tell them, 'Honey, they can't help it, they're men.' My philosophy is that men are from Mars, and they are just a totally different breed as far as I am concerned! They are here to share this world with us.

"A party is what you make it. I try to be happy and just keep chugging on, and whatever comes my way, I will handle it. I handled it before, and I will do it again."

Constance's Story

"I love that I'm sharing this experience with my mother, Katie. I am a teacher. My area of work is developmental guidance. I work with young children and with an Employee Assistance program.

"Spirituality is something that I didn't think I would ever understand in life. I remember a book I had on my shelf written by Billy Graham. He wrote about the Holy Spirit. I tried to read it, and it didn't make sense. It didn't click until a few years ago when I was asked to give a talk at the federal prison. I work with a program called Charis, which nurtures inmates in terms of their spiritual life. Of all the talks possible, I was asked to give it on spirituality. I found that choice to be very interesting, because I felt very inadequate about that topic. I was preparing for the talk while I was out hiking as the sun was beginning to set. The sun was in the trees and they were aglow. It was as if they were lit from inside, they were so intense—the golds, reds, oranges, and the bronzes. I caught a glimpse of the trees where the sun was not shining and then again of the sun on the trees. It was an 'aha moment.' All of a sudden, I realized that spirituality—however you want to define it, by the Christian term of being the Holy Spirit or by some other religious influence—is that power, that incredible power from within that we can access through becoming attuned to ourselves and our environment. It was incredible to really understand what that was about. It is tapping into a power that we ourselves are not capable of. I think we are capable of a great deal, and I think women especially keep needing to hear that we are so capable of so very much. But there is a power beyond us and within us that I think contributes to us becoming more than what we could be without it. That is something I have really tried to remain true to or tuned into and come to peace with.

"When I find that I need to decompress and level off, I come to the water. I just started back to public-education teaching yesterday. As much as I love what I do, it is challenging to leave the out-of-doors environment. Yesterday and today I came to Lake City. I live here part-time and part-time in Rochester. I drove here with the intention to bike, kayak, or sail to get my inner being as calmed as it had felt during summer break.

"My life hasn't been what I expected. I experienced a divorce ten years ago that I didn't choose. And yet, in the last ten years I have had incredible experiences and met people I never, ever would have experienced. My life has been rich, full and very wonderful.

"I have a son, age twenty-six, who is brilliant. His sophomore year of college he experienced a schizophrenic break and struggles with severe mental illness. He is a young adult wanting to be independent, a young adult struggling to accept his condition, but can't accept it and all of the challenges that go along with that. It's frustrating for me, being in the mental-health profession, to come to an inner peace with the choices he's making while continuing to be positive and encouraging for both of us. I need to truly draw upon a spiritual strength for that and, in doing so, become enlivened.

"The wisdom that I think I've gained over time is to be hopeful about life. In spite of adversity, to look at what a given situation can do to strengthen me and not to become bitter or despondent about life. I need to always believe that there is something meaningful within all of life. My son's illness has helped me to become even more of an advocate for mental-health issues. There is a patience and calm that has evolved and strengthened me as a person, a mother, a professional, and a friend. Remember my analogy of the tree. I feel like the tree that is aglow when I seek peace and spirituality within me and the beauty of land and water around me."

Leslie's Story

"I just take what life brings to me, no matter what it is. Sometimes it means just sitting with it for a while and not going off the deep end about what is happening. Just sit with it for a little while and see what you can take away from it. There is always something. It's not always apparent right away. Sometimes things are not the way you would choose for things to go, but I do believe things happen for a reason, and there is something to be learned from them. Be hopeful and don't let it change who you are for the worst.

"Life hasn't at all followed the path I expected. When I was young I had expectations. When I was sixteen, I was going to change the world. I was going to go out and make everything the way I thought it should be. My Dad reeled me in and said, 'I don't think you can do that. I think that is kind of asking a lot of yourself.' I didn't like hearing that, but I slowly learned that he was right. It is a big job, and I can't do it alone. What's more important is being the person I want to be, being more than the pebble in the water. If I change who I am, maybe that will affect someone else in a positive way and they will affect other people. That is actually much more powerful, much more effective, and not as much work. [Laughter.] So I thank my dad for reeling me in when I was sixteen and planning to stop the Vietnam War. [Laughter.] I was sure I could find a way. What I have learned now is that I no longer have expectations. When you talk about what you expect for your life, I really don't have expectations. I just take it a day at a time and look for the good in it. I am never disappointed. I find if I have really high expectations, or my expectations are over here and life takes me over there, then it makes it seem like life isn't as good as what I had planned for myself. I have learned I am a lot calmer and a lot happier if I'm always looking for 'Now what?' I have that sense of 'Where is the next good thing I can go do?' and 'Who is the next nice person I can meet?' If it's not a nice person, there's still something nice there. It's just so much easier when I don't go in with an expectation. I don't have high expectations and I don't have low expectations. I don't want to think, 'Oh, this is really bad,' because then I can be pleasantly surprised when it's not. I just want to accept life for what it is. That has been a huge weight off of me."

Bonne O.'s Story

"I want to share my extended family situations, which I think made my life very, very rich. I have two younger sisters and a younger brother. Four siblings, mom, and dad all in the house. At times, we had two extra people, cousins, living with us and sometimes two other cousins. We did have four bedrooms, thank goodness, but only one bathroom. We had a grandmother with us one time and a grandfather at another time. My dad was the only breadwinner. It amazes me that my mother and dad just used the money that they had so effectively. We finally added a half bath upstairs so we could get along. I look back on that time and I remember the house was never quiet. You went outside to find quiet or you went in the bathroom and locked the door. The bathroom was the only place you could be alone, but how rich all that made my family and my life.

"My grandfather came to the United States from Germany when he was sixteen. I can't imagine a child leaving their home country and coming over to the United States at age sixteen. I don't know if he knew anybody in this area, but he did settle in Minnesota. My family is from Minnesota and Wisconsin. He didn't speak English when he came. My father was raised speaking German and didn't speak English until he went to school. He never had an accent, but my grandfather did. My father died when I was fourteen, so my memory is more of a child with my grandfather. Instead of Northern Pacific Railroad he would say 'Northern Pasafick'. Now I greatly understand the immigration issue better than I did at age fourteen. Living with multi-generations and various people in our home, as some of you have done, added so much to my life. I feel l like I had a rich life."

Mary Loraine's Story

"I grew up in this area. My husband and I have been here all of our lives. We sold our house a while back, and we are full-time RVers, so we now follow the radiator cap. We are back in La Crosse for a month or so. We are here to help move his mother into assisted living. When we get her settled we're going south for the winter.

"I have become very good friends with someone that is part Heron Native American. Lynne is very involved in following the Red Road as her life path. I have learned so much from her, so much about life and the things that really matter. I have had a chance to read many of the books that she has recommended about the Native American life and teachings.

"Life kind of threw me a curve in my early fifties. It helped explain many of the painful things I have experienced and this taught me a lot. Without going into a lot of detail, I learned on my mother's deathbed that the mother I had known was not my biological mother. It was a life-changing revelation for me, and it shook my very foundation.

"At her funeral service, the priest that did the service used the analogy of being a child and shared that he liked to do puzzles. He said he liked to do the frame and that he never finished the puzzles. He only does the frame. And he said, 'When we look at someone's life, that's all we know is the frame. We don't know the whole story.'

"I have learned so much about not being judgmental. Because no matter what anybody is doing or what choices they have made, we don't know what went into it. I was very angry with my mother for not telling me sooner. My father had passed away years before that so I couldn't ask him anything. He was my biological father, so it wasn't a perfect marriage since he did stray. How hard it must have been for mother to raise somebody else's child. They never had any children, so after twenty years of marriage, my father convinced my mother to allow him to keep me. What they basically did was tell everybody that I was adopted. I would hear that rumor and I would ask her if that was true and she would say, 'No, no, you're not.' Well, I was. I found out that my biological mother was a nursing student. The nun who was in charge of the school of nursing got the doctors to forge the birth certificate. It's not a legal thing that I can trace back or do any research into it. It happened; it's over with. I have finally come to terms with it, but it did change who I was and how I saw things.

"The puzzle analogy has stayed with me ever since. It just made so much sense. We look at somebody and say, 'Why would they live like that?' or 'Why would they make those choices?' We don't know the whole story. And I think that is something I would encourage you to remember. Let's not be quick to judge people. It's an easy thing to do, and sometimes I still do it. I speak too quickly and then I think back, 'Why did I do it?'

"Traveling has given us a chance to meet so many people from so many walks of life and from so many cultures. Hopefully we will get to do a little more traveling. It's been an interesting way of living, not like paddling the river. We are following the engine, but it's an adventure, and so far it has been an interesting journey."

Barbara C. H.'s Story

"I come from Native American background on my mother's side. My father had none in him, he was a complete chiimookimin. In Ojibwa that means 'white man.' When he turned seventy-two, he decided to learn the Ojibwa language. It was the biggest embarrassment my mother ever had. He learned it well; he spoke it fluently. He also learned the Red Path, and he passed that on to me, being his only kid. Now here I am, having lost all of my family. [Tears.] Just myself and my daughter are left in the line. And yet, whenever I would have a hard time with these things, betrayals or deaths or pain, he would say, 'You know what? This is your opportunity. This is your chance because this is the thing that's going to build your character. This is the thing that's going to make you who you are. If you can overcome this thing, if you can see beyond it, you are going to grow inside. So the next time something happens, you can face it. You can get through it, you can learn from it.'

"My dad was also a writer, an artist, a musician, a humorist, and a really good father. I am so lucky to have had the parents that I have had. They were the ones who said, 'You can do anything you put your mind to. You just have to go for it. Just make your goal and go.' So I am lucky, real lucky and real honored to be here with these grandmothers and these young women starting out in the world."

Sue H.'s Story

"Years ago, my boyfriend Dale and I were country-western dancers. His best friend and wife, we were like a foursome. We were all close. The husband came over to meet us to go dancing, but Dale hadn't come over yet, and this guy said that my back was out. He told me to lay down, and he was going to straighten my back out. I trusted him. I shouldn't have. What he did no man should do to their best friend's girlfriend, at all. I was so angry. I could not tell Dale about it. It took me weeks to tell him. After all that, we broke up.

"A year later, I'm working in the woods, and I'm still angry, mind you. I'm carrying this chainsaw, and I got my chaps on and my hard hat, and I am grumbling through the woods. There is another friend of mine, also named Dale, who is an Echencar. That's religion of the light. This guy, strange little creature, everybody teased him to death because he would eat grubs and do all this weird stuff. Those loggers would give this guy a heck of a time, so I could not understand how he smiled all of the time. Nothing ever got to him, and here I was, carrying around this anger with me all the time. So I asked him, 'How do you do it?' He said, 'Well, do you have a God?' I said, 'Kinda.' He said, 'Pray.' I said, 'That's it?' He said, 'Yeah.' 'Okay.'

"So I was sleeping in the back of my truck and I was praying. Next morning, I got up just as angry as when I went to bed, and I couldn't understand it. Here I was going through the woods again, carrying the chainsaw and the chaps, and all of a sudden, and I swear to you this is true—I am going to have to get up, [She stood] because I am like this. [She demonstrated walking with her head down and stomping forward angrily.] Suddenly, something stopped me. It felt like a swoop. She swooped down and kinda caught my shoulder and said, 'My dear, why are you so angry?' I couldn't see her, but she was here. I couldn't see her, but I felt her. [Tears.] I call her the Lady of the Woods because she was a female. I tried to answer her question, but I didn't use my mouth, I was using my mind. She caught my answers before I was able to finish! I started to explain to her about Dale and Bob and my anger. I was telling her all this when she stopped me and she said, 'Way too many people accept this type of people in their lives versus being alone.' I realized these perverted characters are accepted in a lot of ways that they shouldn't be. Then she said, 'You have not been a warrior. This is your first life to be such a warrior, to be so angry over this issue.' I asked about my daughter, Bonnie, and she said, 'Bonnie. It is the same situation as your last husband. It will take her thirteen years to get out of it, just like you.' I asked about Dale, and she said, 'Dale was fine. He had a good heart. He is a young soul, a young spirit.' We both said simultaneously. 'Lessons repeated until they are learned.' Then she said, 'What lesson have you learned?'

"I gasped, because I was taken aback, and I said, 'Me?' And suddenly my life flashed in front of me. My whole life I had been presented with perverts and liars. My grandfather was a child molester, my father was a child molester, my mother was molested, and I was, my daughter was. Throughout forever, and that is why molestation is such a hard thing with me. All these perverts had been part of my whole life. I have always taken them in and tried to make them better. She made me realize that my life is for me, and allowing these negative entities to keep me from growing is something I have to work on. I have to identify a personality as that type of personality, and I have to back off from them. I have to allow myself to grow spiritually and not let them hold me back. My whole life was that way. After she got done talking to me, that anger I had been carrying for a year was gone. I have not been angry since. People think I'm nuts when I talk about the Lady of the Woods, but she was real. Physically, I felt her. I heard her. I couldn't see her, but she was there. It was a fascinatingly spiritual experience for me."

Karen P.'s Story

"I want to tell a story of something that happened to me this summer, which I find kind of curious. I don't generally like to camp around a whole lot of people. If I'm going camping I think, 'I should be out there by myself to really get near nature, be alone so I can get calm and have a cool experience with the stars.' But I had to camp one night in a very crowded campground. I had paid the campground host my fee and he sent me on around. When I got to my campsite, it was taken up with a big RV. A man and his two young boys were there, and they were just getting back from getting some take-out dinner. They had a trailer parked there for their boat as well. It was funny because I thought, 'I guess I can go back, but the campground was pretty full.' But then the man said, 'You can park your truck here, and you can camp in the back of your truck. You can just park right here, and I'll move the trailer out of the way. We won't be in your way.' I said, 'Well, you aren't really in my way. Am I going to be in your way?' 'Oh no, no. Sit down and have some dinner with us if you want.' I had already had dinner, but we sat down and chatted a little bit and then I went on a walk around the campground. I found a bench that overlooks the lake, and I just sat there. Then it struck me, I was working on a Bible study about Abraham: where he goes up to the mountain to find the Ten Commandments. When he comes back down he is going to tell all his people that they are doing things wrong and they now have the Ten Commandments and that they are going to follow them.

"As I sat there, I noticed there was a lot of noise: barking dogs, children playing, and a couple arguing over there. It was this community of people, wrapping all the way around me. It was comforting, and it didn't bother me. I thought, 'This really is a community, this whole little microcosm of community.' And then I was thinking, 'Maybe Abraham went up to get away from the noise for a while. Maybe he needed a little peace and quiet.' I reveled in being kind of a voyeur in this little community and not part of anyone in this community. I was enjoying being in the ambience of it. I slept really good that night."

Amanda's Story

"I would say that the women in my life have influenced me greatly, especially the women in my past. A great-grandmother I never knew, because she came from the old country. She had a ten-dollar name that I have written down somewhere. They were tenement farmers back in Finland. My grandmother was eighteen when she came to this country. My parents have a phobia about just coming out of the house and walking down the street, but when my grandmother was eighteen she came across the ocean on her own.

"My families were tenement farmers in Finland. They saved money for a long time so that my great-grandmother's husband could come to the United States, make his fortune, and send for the rest of the family to bring the rest of the family over. It's a time-old story; everybody comes here for a better life. He wrote quite often, sent some money, and then he quit writing. Then my great-grandmother, one more time, with six kids, started saving money to send their oldest son to the United States. When he got to America, he looked up his dad and found him homesteading in Minnesota with a new wife, a new family, and a major amount of land. He turned around and left.

"The oldest son settled in Ohio, and he helped earn money to send for each of his brothers and sisters. My grandmother, Elphinia, came here next; she was the second-to-youngest. She spent one week in Ohio with her brother, and she also had to see her dad. She went to Minnesota to where he had his farm. She stepped on the doorstep and knocked. When he answered the door, she said, 'I'm your daughter.' Then she turned around and she left.

"Everyone came over here except for my great-grandmother. She said she was too old to pull up roots. But my grandmother went to northern Wisconsin where the mines were. They had a Finnish community there. Women in those days had nothing! They owned nothing! Everything they had belonged to their husband. The fellow that she married ended up taking just about everything. These women were strong. My great-grandmother was strong. My grandmother was strong. My grandmother figured out that her husband played poker all the time. He gambled. She coerced her husband into getting a boardinghouse so they could have boarders. All the money from the boardinghouse was his. She did all the work, but he got the money from the boardinghouse, and he had money from the mine. Then what she did, instead of letting him go someplace else to gamble, she would say, 'Ask them over to my house to gamble,' and she would stand and watch. When they were short somebody to play, she would play. What money she earned she kept. When they moved to central part of Wisconsin, she had enough money to buy a farm. She bought a farm!

"Grandfather would go north during the good months and mine, and she would stay at the farm. Now, not only did she stay at the farm, but she was the horse. She was the horse that pulled the plow. She was the horse that pulled the stumps! These were strong women. Strong women. My mom, Adel, is the youngest of nine children. They really don't want to talk about it. Those were bad times. They were hard times. There was nothing good to say about these years. They assumed Grandmother had tuberculosis at one time, so she fenced off the middle of the yard and the house. No one was allowed to come into her portion of the yard. Even though it was fenced, she ran the whole place from that fenced-in area, thinking she had tuberculosis while she had children to care for. She outlived two husbands. She was amazing.

"Yet, these women turned around and taught the women in their family that the man is top dog. You live like that just so long and you think, 'Not my family.' My sisters say, 'Not my family. I am going to have equal rights to be top dog myself.' This is the era, the turn around, where the women also get to say, rather than obey. It's good. I think it's good. So if you've got a tough lineage, I think that is something to be proud of.

"My son was almost an Elphinia. We couldn't agree on a girl's name after my daughter was born, and my second child was due to be born on my grandmother's birthday. I told my husband, 'You come up with a name I like, or I will name her Elphinia after my grandmother.' He said, 'Over my dead body.' My son was born on my grandmother's birthday."

Joyce's Story

"As someone who was certainly not raised with a spiritual life forced on them, but certainly put in the position of accepting a spiritual life, I have not always appreciated the physical. I have not appreciated the joys that are within the physical, but kayaking probably fills that for me now. There is nothing I can think of that is as totally soothing and lifting as when that kayak slides into the water or that first moment of just feeling buoyant on top of the water. So I find no words of wisdom right now, but I am just appreciating the physical at this mature stage of my life. I think I kind of got it backwards, but at least I am kind of catching up with it."

Kitty's Story

"When I admitted I was an alcoholic, I felt like a failure in life. I felt I could not manage my own life, and I had to ask for help. That was very difficult for me because, up until that point, I thought I could do it all myself. I had done it all myself, but I had done a very bad job of it. I was not moving myself forward in a way that I wanted to move forward.

"To be powerful, for me, has been the ability to ask for help when I need help. There aren't six billion people on this planet so that we can all figure everything out separately and not use the knowledge from others around us. That is part of what I get from some of these Gatherings. The more I open myself up and am willing to talk about what is going on in my life and share, I feel more power over my life.

"Recovery has been a journey, and I didn't do it by myself. That is where part of acknowledging my power is being grateful for all those who have taught me and I have listened to. I didn't come to be where I am today by myself, and I don't want to move forward by myself. I need others. This is what I tell my twelve-step group, 'I need you to tell me when I am a little bit off or I am acting a little bit weird, because I live by myself, and I need the perspective of others to help me remain open and honest.' Others in my life make life so much easier. I think part of the motivation to finally admit I was an alcoholic was because I was tired of trying to figure everything out by myself. I don't have to do that anymore. That is really something to rejoice in."

Joyce's Story

"I live on a farm that is a century farm, over one-hundred years the same family. My family has lived there about 110 years. I have had people who have rented it before I came back to live there, and they had stories of spiritual happenings with figures that they acknowledged or thought were family members. I had a step-mother who lived there for a period of time, and she had similar experiences. She had to leave. It bothered her that much. My children have had similar experiences. I don't see anything nor do I really feel any presence. I feel energy. I feel very comfortable. I'm not trying to draw any conclusions from any of that; I just ponder a question in my mind since other people have had these experiences over a period of time. Who knows? That's just a question I sometimes ponder because I feel so secure there."

Nancy L.'s Story

"I am fifty and I am a grandmother. I have one grandson, and he is the apple of my eye. There is another one on the way. My one daughter lives close. She has a wonderful husband. She went through a few losers first. She found a good one and latched on to him. So I'm happy about all of that.

"I had a job that I got let go from in January. I had worked there for twenty-eight years. I thought I would retire there. There were changes in the administration. I didn't get along with them, and I wanted to leave just as much as they wanted me to go. That changed a lot of things in my life. I'm dealing with it. I found another job in the same industry. There are good points and bad points to that. I don't want to leave the area because of my family. I don't have a husband. I tried that once and have not tried it again. I have a lot of wonderful friends, both male and female. I grew up with just brothers. I tend to work with men, and so I get along with them fine. I just don't want to take one home with me. [Laughter.]

"A comment that struck a nerve was the one about the dog. Last year, I lost a dog that I had for fourteen years. He was a very good companion. I live up along the river here, and we used to walk along the river every day. I still miss him every day. That's probably my longest relationship.

"There are a lot of good things in life. The whole job thing threw me for a while, and on certain days it's hard. I don't think I'll leave the area until I retire, because those grandbabies are too good."

Jean's Story

"Carolyn and I are really good friends, and we both have a lot of enjoyable times talking about our spiritual life and our relationship with Jesus Christ, that he did come, he did die on the cross for my sins as well as everybody else's. Through all the problems that I'm hearing here, he is the only answer. He really is the only answer to anybody's problems in anybody's life. My wisdom to my kids and my grandkids is to accept him as their personal savior and, whatever comes along in your life, talk to him in prayer. He has promised to guide you and lead you. I have that definite comfort that he is always with me and will always guide me. He has given me courage when I don't have it.

"God has blessed me with a Christian husband and two Christian kids. Now we're trying to relate to our grandkids about this personal relationship, because we all know about God, but we all need to know about the very personal relationship of Jesus Christ. Thank you."

Judy's Story

"I married an incredible man. We are different. I'm more outgoing. He's an accountant and everything is straight, in a row. Drawers are all lined up perfectly. He can be very boring, but I love him. I fully intend that if and when he retires I will go back to work. He's going to drive me nuts. He's a good man, and he provided me with opportunities like early retirement. I worked for seventeen years at a terrible place to work. I am grateful I could leave there and he allowed me to stay home."

Connie H.'s Story

"I turned sixty-five this year. All my life, I planned to retire from a job and do nothing, but in the year 2000, our company here in Muscatine decided they were going to close their doors. So when you add it all up, I was at the end of my fifties trying to locate a job. I thought it was the worst thing.

"In October, at the end of the year, I was just going to go ahead and take a couple of months off and not work just to see what it was going to be like because I would have severance pay. It was great. I got all my cupboards cleaned. I couldn't really volunteer for anything because I was going to have to work. In the back of my mind I believed I had to have a job. Well, I love mysteries, that is just my thing. I was very fortunate that I got a job that kind of relates to that. I turned sixty-five in July and they said, 'Do you think you could stay a little longer?' It made me feel really good. I had to do that. So now I'm set until the first of May, then we will see what happens.

"My children both moved up to Minneapolis. So I am pretty much on my own here. I have a group of friends, but this is a real shocker for me to come down here on my own without calling somebody and saying, 'Hey I'm doing this. Do you want to come?' It really made me feel kind of good. I'm going to be able to stand on my own two feet. I think this ten months that I'm working with here is going to open up some doors and make me see what I really want to do. My car broke a couple months ago. All on my own I went out and bought a car. I didn't believe I could do that! If you see an atomic-orange little car running around, that's mine. I always lost the other one, which was red, but now at Wal-Mart, I can go right out and find my car. [Laughter.] I don't think you're really supposed to be buying a car because of the color, but that's what I did, to be honest with you.

"I've had a pretty good time trying to get my life organized and see what I'm going to have to do. I found out right away that I am not going to be able to sit home. I'm going to have to volunteer, find a part-time job, go up and bug the kids in Minneapolis. I have five grandchildren. I try to be a role model for them. I try to make them understand that life isn't so bad when you're on your own. You just need to try to be the best that you can."

Jan F.'s Story

"I guess I feel that life is really good and that you can keep going. You just need to tackle all the things that come at you, use all the resources that are available to you. Friends are wonderful. I'm a talker. When I have a problem, I need to talk about it. I need to get it out. As wonderful as he is, my husband doesn't always understand that.

"You just have to accept life as it gets thrown at you. A lot of things don't turn out the way you think they should when you expect something from somebody. Lots of times you're disappointed. I just think you have to take that person for the way they are. See their face value and take from them what you need and what you want. If a friend disappoints you in one area, there are a lot of good things about that person you can usually find and say 'Yeah, you're still my friend and I value you.' So life is good."

Linda L.'s Story

"At age thirty-nine, I was an alcoholic, and I knew life had to change. I went to treatment and discovered an entire new life. So for the next several years, it was a journey to find out who I was. I had divorced my spouse of twenty-two years and set about this journey. Today, I know that was exactly as I had to do it. I have been an active member of AA for twenty-two years this fall. It made me realize that nature has always worked for me as a spiritual place. As a child, I lived on one-hundred acres of land that my folks cleared to create a farm. The surrounding woods and creeks were my refuge when my dad was ill. He died at thirty-five after an eighteen-month illness.

"My adoptive mother was very religious. As a child, we did what she wanted, but as an adult, I had no use for organized religion. I got lost, but thankfully the Great Spirit guided me to a safe harbor. Via AA, my escape to northern Wisconsin, and a sponsor who I love dearly, I discovered the raw beauty of Lake Superior and the north woods. It was my refuge once again. Today, it still is and will always be. Today, the Mississippi River and surrounding area where there is still a small piece of nature is my refuge. I'm so grateful for this, my father and my adoptive mother who loved nature. They showed me a peace I didn't realize till I aged.

"Life has not really followed the path I expected. I had always thought I would become a scientist or naturalist. I guess in some ways I have, but not officially. I love color and ended up being a fiber artist most of my life, but due to health and arthritis, I've had to give up many of my loves. Today I know my Great Spirit will lead me to the next thing I am to do in this lifetime on earth.

"I, as most of the women I have sponsored over the years, do not change without some outside force. Then it seems we struggle. So, today I try not to, as I know the past struggles have shaped me into the being my Creator wants me to become.

"After nearly two years, my spouse and I remarried, and today are quite happy and enjoying retirement near our sons and our grandchildren, who are the joy of our lives!"

Lorrain's Story

"My son met the President last Tuesday–that was the big news. I was e-mailing everyone because his picture was in USA Today. He was right next to the President and the Vice President. He sat eight feet from Condoleezza Rice. The vetsforfreedom.org and his officer asked him to enroll and paid for his trip to go to up on Capitol Hill. There were about 185 veterans there and about 700 family members who have lost loved ones over in Iraq there.

"I was disappointed that one of our congressmen, who was against the bill and wants to pull out of Iraq, wouldn't even say hello to soldiers and marines who had come that far. He could have said, 'I am the delegation from here in support of our military, and while I disagree with you, I'm so glad to meet you. Thank you for serving.' Though he wouldn't even see him, my son did meet a lot of wonderful people."

Sue D.'s Story

"I am a grandmother, and my life growing up was a lot different than a lot of people's lives were when I grew up. I was born in 1950. I came from a very small family; I only have one sister. Many of my peers came from very large families with a whole lot of different experiences. We went out to eat once a week, and I hated it. We had to go to a restaurant and dress up, stuff that some of my peers would have thought was a really wonderful thing to get to do.

"I grew up with a lot of confidence. At that point in time, my parents were a little non-traditional. I went through college, and I did a lot of things that were important to me and really worried my parents. I backpacked in Europe for six weeks. I did things that were pretty adventurous for someone who came from a family with one sister and was more or less protected and told what to do, when to do it, and how to do it.

"People in that time married very early age, eighteen, nineteen, twenty. I didn't get married until I was twenty-five, which was again an exception to the rule. Then, lo and behold, my husband and I ended up with seven children. Kind of a flip-flop. I almost felt like I was cheated growing up because I had one sibling. We got along okay, but it wasn't great. I just enjoy my kids so much, especially the youngest, who is almost twenty. They always have each other, and they all still get along together. So far, I only have two grandchildren. I am hoping for more, but I haven't asked for any. It's just a joy to see two different ways of life and how they both can work to make people good people who do their own thing.

"I think it's interesting that with our kids we don't have any carbon copies. They are all pretty unique individuals, and yet our oldest two were twins. You would think they would be the same, and yet they couldn't be more different. I just find life very interesting and very satisfying at this point in time."

Cindy's Story

"My dad doesn't think he likes feminists, but I told him he taught me to be a feminist. We had cattle and he gave me a calf when I was nine or ten. You had to raise it by yourself and take it to 4-H fairs. You groomed it, and it became your best friend. I was never really very big; the calf was obviously much bigger than me. I would be holding on to the rope and drug across the gravel on my belly—teaching the calf to lead, right? [Laughter.] I think it worked like that. Eventually the calf did learn to lead. After Dad gave me a calf to raise, I don't think there was any telling me that a girl couldn't do something.

"I found myself in a lot of places I never imagined I'd be. That makes me think about fear. The most scared I ever was in my life was on top of Devil's Tower. I don't know if anybody is familiar with that rock. It was in the movie Close Encounters of the Third Kind. My husband had a climbing accident the year before. He would have died if it hadn't been for a fifty-dollar helmet. We got on that rock and were talking to this lady whose husband was climbing. We found out later that her husband, that very day, rappelled off the end of the rock and died. The next day it was our turn to climb. It was really cold, and it was windy. The straw on my Camelback broke and peed a liter of water on my pants. That made the windchill somewhere around freezing for me. I was so cold. I was so scared. I have pictures of me, and I had my helmet on backwards. I wear my climbing helmet all the time, and I had it on backwards! It was like, 'Get me down off this rock! I don't ever want to climb again!' But the next day we got a guide, went up, and it was just so fantastic. We were on top of the world. You can get to a lot of places that you didn't ever think you would."

Carol T.'s Story

"I'm a little older than Sue D., so I was one of those who got married real young. I was raised by overprotective parents. I hardly did anything growing up. I thought that if I got married, I would be out on my own and get away from my parents. 'I'll get married, and I'll have my own life.' Well, it doesn't work that way. I was married for thirty years, but it wasn't much of a marriage. Actually, my life didn't follow the path I expected. I thought my married life would be great. I do have six great kids from that marriage, but finally I decided I had to divorce him to keep my own sanity. Two years later, I married a wonderful man and was married thirteen years before he died suddenly.

"As a result of my parents being so overprotective and my marriage not being what I thought it would be, I became kind of a rebel. I became my own person. I have done quite a few things. I think that my early life really made me become the person I am now.

"I ended up with three more kids from the second marriage, so I have six kids, three step-sons, and seventeen grandchildren, with another one on the way. I do a lot of traveling because none of them live very close. While I can continue to travel, I am traveling, and when I can't anymore, they will have to travel to visit me."

Nancy H.'s Story

"I would like to touch on spirituality, because I am still searching. It just seems like it has been so ongoing for all my life, and I haven't found anything that resonates. Being out in nature, like Kathy E. says, is extremely important to me. I guess if I had to put a label on it, that would be where my spirituality is.

"I was raised Jewish, and I found a lot of prejudice growing up, so I tended to stifle traditional religion because of that. It was very painful. My family wasn't very traditional in their following of Judaism. They said, 'We don't really believe in God, but we are supposed to go to a synagogue because that's what everybody does.' I didn't quite have a foundation of anything that really came from the heart. Being nontraditional was compounded with teasing, and I just went tilt, big time.

"When I did get out on my own and started following my own path, I did a lot of reading. I don't want to put a label on spirituality. I just want it to be kind of free-flowing, whether it's playing a musical instrument, which I agree can be very spiritual, or paddling down a lake, or standing on a frozen lake in the middle of winter and not hearing anything but silence. Those experiences give me that little hair-raising experience on the back of the neck that makes me feel like, yeah, this is what it is."

Cindy's Story

"The first time I ever hunted I was fifteen. I had gone hunting with my dad a lot, but never carried a gun, and I had never really shot at anything. When I was fifteen, I went out with a gun, and I shot this rabbit. It was the first thing I had ever aimed at. The rabbit cried, no, actually it screamed. I didn't know rabbits screamed. I grew up on a farm and that was enough of the killing thing. I didn't try to hunt anything again. I had some friends that liked to bow hunt fish. That was pretty challenging. Somehow fish were a little bit more like sparrows than they were like Bambi. So fish were fun to shoot with the arrows, and I got rather proficient with it.

"At the time, I was writing articles for the local outdoors magazine. My son had told me they hunted wild boar with dogs in Florida. I thought it sounded exciting to go and watch those dogs run out through the cane fields and chase down the hogs. I told my Dad I would like to go, and, sure enough, he knew somebody that would take me out so I could take some pictures and write a story. About that time, I had written an article about bow-fishing, and Dad took that story to his friend. The guy said, 'Well, yeah, I'll take her bow-hunting.' I'm thinking that wasn't really what I said, I just wanted to watch, but the gauntlet was laid at that point.

"I had about six weeks to learn to shoot a compound bow instead of a recurve bow. It's a whole different game with sights and guessing distances. There was a lot to learning to shoot that bow. It was really a challenge because I had to learn an awful lot about technique with the bow, and I had to practice a lot. I've had a different experience than Connie K., in that I found men to be very helpful. They were very good about showing me how to shoot and telling me what I needed to learn to shoot this hog. They were very encouraging.

"I ended up in Florida and there was a hog being chased by these dogs. I aimed at it and flat out missed the first time. The guide was really nice about it and said that happened to a lot of people. I took another shot at it and killed it with a perfect shot. Before I shot the hog, the men literally grabbed that hog by its back legs and threw it out in the open where you could shoot it. I couldn't imagine that they did it that way, but they did.

"It was really interesting to hear those guides tell about their sport. The one thing I found particularly interesting was that the biggest weapon they carried was a jackknife. It wasn't really used for a weapon. It was used to dress the hogs. So that was bow hunting hogs in Lake Okeechobee, Florida."

Bonnie D.'s Story

"One more voices story. I had a llama; it was a year ago last December. There is a thing llamas get where they can't walk. He went down on December the thirteenth. My husband was pretty bad at this time. I kept working with this llama at night. I didn't have time during the day. This voice came and it said, 'Carrots and apples.' It did say that! The next day I went to Krogers Center. They give me food for the animals that they can't use. They gave me four forty-pound bags of cleaned carrots, three fifteen-pound bags of little baby carrots, and about eighty boxes of lettuce. I had to buy my own apples. I worked with this llama. I got up every night in the night. Finally, I don't know why and I don't need to know why, but I just knew he wasn't going to make it. Four months he lived. Full of carrots, I got him to last until May. I wanted him to die so bad if he wasn't going to walk. I was the one that had to call the vet and put him down. I held him in my arms, and I put him down. That was another voice I heard, and I just think it is fascinating because I don't think *I* was supposed to eat the apples and carrots. [Laughter.]

Carol S.'s Story

"I have been more intentional since I turned fifty. For my fiftieth birthday I did several things. I got a belly ring, I went hiking, and I had a croning, which is a celebration that acknowledges active wise women and celebrates the third stage of life. I went hiking in the Andes. I have been trying since then, and I am very intentional about it, trying to set out some things that enlarge my world. The reason I am here is that I think Nancy is on a mission to enlarge her world, both in terms of inner spirituality and in an awareness of what is out there. We can do that by watching a river flow by or flowing along with it, or we can travel. We can do any number of things.

"I have a granddaughter. She just turned six and she started first grade. I was visiting her a few weeks ago. We went over to her neighbor's house and she said, 'Oma,'—she calls me Oma—'this is my friend Morgan.' Morgan looked up at me and said, 'You're Julia's grandma who goes all over the world, aren't you?' She was five years old. Julia has told her stories of her Oma who travels around the world and brings her things and tries to teach her about the world. It's my own journey, but I know it's being passed along.

"I know and hope that Julia will see my courage in doing things when others are saying, 'Why are you going there? What in the world are you doing?' They don't know my inner journey. My inner journey is just as much connected to just getting out there in the world. I hope for all of you to experience that kind of courage, especially my grand-daughter, Julia, and to know what it means to have courage in this very difficult world. Life is good."

Carole's Story

"Lately I have been thinking a lot about the circle of life. I have been sitting here thinking about us in this circle. I was born in 1940. When I was forty, I lived in Columbus, Indiana, and went through a divorce, and I found myself single. I am an artist, and I had a studio there. Cummins Engine had hired all of these wonderful new, young folks from Harvard, Yale, and Stanford. My studio became the eighteenth-century salon every Friday night, because they would all come to my studio.

"I knew a woman named Gertrude, who was ninety. When Jane K. mentioned the hot air balloons, I remembered what Gertrude told me:

'Oh honey, you have given me years.' I was thinking, 'I'm forty and she's ninety.' Then she said, 'I've decided to hot-air balloon across France as my last hurrah.' [Laughter.] And then she said, 'My family is very mad at you that you have given me these young ideas.' Well, she hot-air ballooned, and she came back and everyone just loved her. I mean they just loved her. Then she said, 'I'm going to China.' Again the family was really upset then. She could barely walk, but she found this young male that would put her on the back of his bicycle and take Gertrude all around China riding on the bicycle.

"We would all go to this little place and have dinner on Friday nights and listen to Walter and Liz play their bluegrass music. We loved their music, only I didn't really know their last name. I just knew I loved Walter and Liz's music. I moved to St. Louis, and I work at Barnes & Noble. I worked with this wonderful young male, about twenty-two, named Andrew. We were such good friends. He had a really cute girlfriend. And he kept saying, 'My aunt and uncle know you from Columbus.' I didn't know who they were. In 2005, Andrew and Kelly were married. When I got to the wedding, Walter and Liz were playing the music and I said, 'Oh my heavens!' Walter and I just spent the most wonderful time talking about everything that evening.

"A week ago Walter died. Andrew was not even born when I knew Walter and Liz. Andrew and his wife called me Friday, after the funeral, and they said, 'Your art is so present here. There are all these musicians that have come from everywhere to celebrate Walter and Liz, and we're going to play some songs for you.' I thought, 'Here is another circle.' Here was Andrew, playing music at Walter's funeral. I thought how wonderful the question 'Has your life taken the path you thought?' I just thought about all of the people we've met.

"I had forgotten about Gertrude flying in the hot-air balloon, but I thought, 'Goodness, she is ninety!' and I'm thinking how incredible that is. Just sitting in this circle and sharing these stories, you think about the strength that people have given you in your life and how important people are to you. It's just a real gift to be here today."

Ielah's Story
Ielah's House Building - The Ripped Tent

"While we were building our house, we had one tent that had a screened-in area, which we used as a kitchen. Its back canvas section was our private area for cleaning up, et cetera. Our tent for sleeping had been a gift to us from a friend who would have liked to have shared this adventure but opted to live vicariously through her gift of canvas. It had space for our four cots—my partner in this had two daughters, ages ten and sixteen—and a trunk containing our 'go to town' clothes. Our main living area was a table under a tree between the two tents. We were comfortable. Then one day our errands in town took longer than expected. At least longer than our dog expected. She was tied safely behind the sleeping tent. She either got bored or afraid we weren't coming back. Whatever it was, she stretched her chain to the corner of the tent and ripped out enough canvas to pull my cot through. Considering the size and population of mosquitoes in the woods of northern Minnesota, there was no way could we sleep in that tent now. It was already late afternoon when we discovered the damage. We had to rebuild before dark.

"After a frenzied trip to town for materials, we framed in a cabin and covered it with pressed insulation board. I cut the screen window and flaps out of the tent and used them to cover a window on each side of the cabin. It was a rustic, eight-foot by sixteen-foot space, which was bigger than the tent. It allowed us to bring the table inside. No more sitting on our cots to eat when it rained. We hung a lantern over the table, and that place truly became home. That was where we organized and planned the building projects for the day at breakfast, re-energized at lunch, and became a family that summer over our nightly card games. I think I'm starting to sound like John Boy Walton, but it was all an interesting lesson in psychology that carried through to moving into the house.

"We had moved out of a four-bedroom, two-bath, family room, et cetera type house. The house we built was one-bath, three-bedroom. The living room and kitchen were one big room. The first winter we hauled our hot water from the wood stove in the basement to the bathtub upstairs, but after living in the tent/cabin, it felt like we were in a mansion. We had also learned to live quite happily without all that stuff we had packed, hauled, and stored from our previous house. Simpler is so much easier!"

Ielah's House Building - The Invitation

"It has been my experience in the past that when a person is new to a neighborhood, one of the neighbors will usually come forward with an invitation to coffee. Well, we must have looked pretty scary after the first couple of weeks of tent life and ground-breaking, because our invitation was quite unique. Our nearest neighbor sent her two teenage sons over to invite us to use their shower any time. We took this invitation in the spirit in which we were sure it was given—no offense taken— and cleaned ourselves up and paid a social call on the neighbor. We did, by the way, get coffee and friends."

Ielah's House Building - Just One Goat

"Just one goat. Yeah, right! Let me explain about this goat deal. See, if you want to have a goat for a pet, you can have just one goat. Having a goat for milk is another story, since things that give milk only do so after they give birth. Right away, you know you are going to have to have more than one goat. Also, goats are herd animals, so they really aren't happy being the only goat. Anyway, that's how it was explained to me when Annie, my partner in this little adventure, brought home Ruth and Naomi, our first two goats. Besides of the aforementioned reasons, these girls had been together for several years. They were friends. We couldn't split them up. I'm sure Annie got some kind of a deal on them. She always gets a deal. I don't remember where we got the next two does. Annie may have gotten one good deal from the previous owner for all of the goats or got two good deals. Whatever, we now had four goats. Two is company. Four is a herd. Things like this happened a lot with Annie. It made life interesting and gave me memories to talk about.

"Then, when the time came, we had to take the does to visit a buck. It's the buck that gives goats their reputation for smelling so bad. We decided we were not going to have a buck on the property. They only work ten minutes out of the year. The rest of the time, they eat and get into mischief, so no buck! Okay? I came home one day to find the biggest damned goat I've ever seen standing behind the barn. We were told he weighed 300 pounds, and I'm sure he weighed at least 200 pounds. It was every ounce muscle. His horns were at least three inches wide at the base and at least a foot long. His eyes always had the same glazed look. I often felt that he was some sinister being in a goat suit. His name was Tony. He was awesome, . . . and he was all ours. I think Annie traded a stained-glass lamp shade she'd made for Tony. Somebody got a good deal that day.

"I had really hoped to only have one goat to milk at a time. I thought they could take turns having babies. That was my idea of birth control on the farm. Now it was spring, and we had four pregnant goats. Annie got a book about goats, and we read up on kidding. I'm sure the book was for me. Annie had foals, puppies, kittens, and two daughters. I had no experience with the birthing process. I had lots of confidence in Annie though. I figured I would just be her assistant. I don't know if all goats prefer to give birth later in the day or if that was just the arrangement our goats had. Annie worked nights. She went to work around three p.m. They knew it and waited until she left, every time. Fortunately, the first three does didn't need my help. However, Naomi, who was the oldest, biggest, and most cantankerous doe—we lovingly nicknamed her Pig Bitch—had problems.

"It was feeding time, so I was in the barn when Naomi became restless and started breathing heavily. She turned her backside to me, lifted her tail, and this little face suddenly appeared. It was sticking out just enough to open its eyes and look right at me. 'Well hello, Sweetie,' I said. 'Blaaaaa!!' wailed the little face, as it disappeared back inside Naomi. 'On no, Baby,' I said. 'Come this way.' The little face poked out again, and I heard 'Blaaaaa!' as it disappeared again. Now Naomi is looking back over her shoulder at me like 'You want to do something here?' I knew what needed to be done but was afraid my inexperience would make matters worse. I ran to the house and called our neighbor, who was a dairy farmer. He was in our barn in less than ten minutes. It wasn't long after when there were two adorable chocolate-colored kids with white stripes on their noses, standing next to Naomi. The male was the one that had played hide-and-seek with me. Naomi would have nothing to do with him. I took him to the house and kept him in a stall in the basement for a few days. They all had to be bottle-fed anyway, if the does were to be milked.

"When all was said and done, three of our does had twins, and the fourth was a single birth. Counting Tony, that made twelve goats. Did I mention that I don't drink milk?"

Jo's Story

"Several women spoke about doing inner work. It takes courage to identify the problems we create for ourselves and to work to change ourselves. It's equally hard to really see the world from another person's point of view. I've been working on challenges similar to those already mentioned. I am working to heal physically, mentally, and spiritually. Not necessarily in that order. One of my hardest issues is to honor myself and to have confidence in my own being. I'm learning to find the things I need to thrive and then do them. Like so many women, I've been a caregiver for so long that I haven't taken very good care of myself. There is a fine line between caring for others and being able to care for yourself. It's hard to know sometimes which things are legitimate needs for myself. I am getting better at it. My advice to younger women would be to take time out to find out what you need to have in your own life."

Debbie's Story

"I had no idea what I was coming to tonight. My friend Barb called me this afternoon and said, 'Hey, there is this lady going down the river in a kayak, and she's going to have this gathering of women near your house. Do you want to go?' I really didn't know what to expect here. I was surprised, but I think it is really very cool what you are doing.

"Myself, I get involved in things mostly through my work. They have programs where we get to mentor younger women in colleges and in grade schools. I always do that when I can because I grew up when it wasn't the thing for women to be in science and things like that. I am in computers, so at the time, I was one of very few women going to school in that kind of field. I still see an awful lot of areas where women still aren't as advanced as the men. I think a lot of it is something you mentioned earlier. A lot of women just feel like they can't speak up or do what they want to do.

"Working with these younger girls, the ones in grade school and also some in junior high, they come from the lower-class part of town and schools in those areas. It is amazing how they just think that their place in life is to get married, have kids, and do women types of work. I really like to encourage them to do other things. The older girls in college are always trying to figure out, 'What is my first job going to be? Should I get married right away? Is it bad to have a career first?' They are always worried about planning all these things out. One of the things I try to tell them is that you can't plan what is going to happen in your life.

"I certainly didn't end up anywhere near where I thought. When I actually started college, I thought I was going to go for a year or two, find somebody, and get married. When I got there, I just kept going, ended up finishing and getting into the workplace. I did get married right after that. You know, I never planned to have the job I have, which is a nice job. I always thought that my husband would be the strong person in my family, but as it turned out, he wasn't–I was. Unfortunately, we have since been divorced, but I always ended up taking care of him. You just can't plan how life is going to be. I tell these girls, 'Don't worry about what your first job is or try to plan anything out. This is your stepping stone to wherever you are going next. Don't worry that once you take this job it's going to be forever or the boyfriend you have now is forever. You just can't plan for things like that.'

"One thing I will say about courage is that because you don't know where your life is going to take you, it could be that something very good happens to you; it could be that something very bad happens to you or the people around you. I think courage is when whatever happens you find something good in it. Don't be scared to face what life presents. Everybody counts on everybody else. If you help each other through the rough spots, there is always something good that comes out of it."

Roberta's Story

"My nephew is in Iraq. I guess just seeing his vulnerabilities and my son's vulnerability and photos of him." She choked up. "He was so excited about going. He's a West Point graduate, an Army Ranger, and had three months of incredibly rigorous training. He was excited to go in and led forty troops. I got a picture of him in the Kuwait Desert with his machine guns and grenades. Recently I got another email from his mother saying, 'He has been there two days and already he is really disturbed. It's just not what he thought he was getting into, what he thought he had prepared for. The vehicles are full of bullet holes and are broken down that he is supposed to be using.' It's hard to witness his disillusionment. I feel so helpless."

Nancy H.'s Story

"This is Nancy the van driver, forever known as The Van Driver. [Laughter.] I would like to spin off one of the questions that talked about 'Did your life go where you wanted it to go?' My thoughts on that are: it really doesn't matter. It is probably a good idea to not have a lot of preconceived ideas and just be kind of fluid and open and let things happen. I had some ideas of where I might be headed, but it didn't really turn out that way. I am very comfortable with that, which makes it kind of like it did turn out that way I wanted it to. That brings a lot of inner peace with me for where I am at the moment. To acknowledge the beauty of what is going on at the present and looking forward to the future without a lot of preconceived ideas and structure in it. I like keeping things open."

Barb V.'s Story

"My youngest son, Andrew, has been an addict and alcoholic since the age of at least fourteen. My husband, our older son, and I have been

through a number of events over the years with Andrew, including legal entanglements that were a result of his drug and alcohol use. We have always told Andrew we love him, but there have always been consequences—natural or logical, whichever seemed to fit the situation. In other words, we never bailed him out! He had to face the music but not alone. We made it clear we believed he was an addict from early on, that we did not support that behavior, but we loved him.

"A number of years ago, Andrew ended up in jail in Wisconsin over Memorial Day weekend. At that time, we told him any further event would result in him having to move out of our house. That next event occurred in June of 2007, which was a very stressful time for our family. My father-in-law had been placed into hospice the week before and died about two days after Andrew's event. As a result of his behavior, Andrew lost his car, and his job was at risk because he needed a car for work. In addition to dealing with the police and insurance company, he had to find a place to live. He moved out within three days of his grandfather's funeral. Andrew was unable to find a consistent living situation. His new car was unreliable, and life was hard for him. The hopeless nature of his circumstances is hard even now to handle. His contact with us was very sporadic during this time.

"On July nineteenth, I received a call from our oldest son, telling me that Andrew had left him a voice-mail message he was in the ER at Regions Hospital in St. Paul. I called Regions and confirmed Andrew was there. Immediately our oldest son called again to tell me he had spoken with Andrew and that he needed his dad or me to come so he would be physically okay. I was with friends in downtown Minneapolis. They drove me to Regions, and it took forever to get there that evening–the traffic was awful. Andrew's face was pretty banged up on the right side. Both arms were wrapped up in bandages. I laid over him and cried in relief, anger, and sadness. I spoke to the doctors and heard the story of his jump and the results of the many CT scans and X-rays that had been done since he arrived by ambulance several hours earlier.

"He had jumped off a bridge after being in court and having his license revoked—the last straw of a very disheartening series of events over the previous month. He jumped forty feet onto a hard surface, not into water. After the jump, he stood up and planned to jump again. A pair of city workers stopped him and called 911. His injuries were minimal for the type of jump he had taken. It was a miracle there were no structural damage to his skull, neck, spine, or legs. He did have a pelvic fracture of uncertain significance; both wrists were broken and required surgery, and his face required stitches. Those were the first of miracles that just kept coming. Regions Hospital was a Level 1 trauma center and that team was treating Andrew. His broken wrists were operated on by Dr. Fletcher, who had the reputation of being one of the best plastic surgeons in the city. He was a small, gentle man with glasses, who was kind and reassuring.

"I spent most of the next week at the hospital with Andrew. Over that time, we discovered the extent of his injuries and the recovery required. Thankfully, the pelvic fracture would not require surgery, but he would have the pins in his wrists for twelve weeks. He also needed to use a walker for that same time frame due to the hip fracture. He was given a specialized walker that did not require he bear weight on his wrists. It was quite a contraption. Andrew had no insurance, and now, no job.

"After a week on the trauma ward, Andrew was transferred to the psych ward. He experienced a fair amount of pain and was medicated around the clock. He was sometimes a difficult patient. He continued to heal physically, and his face had almost no sign of any injury in less than a week after he jumped. He continued to use the walker while the social worker continued to work on plans for where he would go next. This was a very frustrating process. It involved working with the Hennepin County system. We worked with multiple social workers, making multiple calls, and often they gave different messages. After about two and a half weeks in the psych ward, arrangements were made to transfer

Andrew to the chemical-dependency treatment program at St. Joseph's Hospital in St. Paul. I left work early on a Monday to transport him to St. Joe's. He was relieved to be moving on to the next stage of his healing. I was relieved, and everything seemed to be continuing in a positive direction.

"Shortly after that, he started calling me to tell me about the extent of his pain and that he'd been taken off his pain medications and put on methadone. It was a very frustrating and confusing experience. Andrew told me he was yelling at the staff, demanding they call the doctor to come and provide pain medication. Wednesday afternoon, I received a call from the counselor on the chemical-dependency unit, telling me Andrew was not being cooperative with treatment, and because his stay was funded by the county, they had to release him. I was frantic! Release him where? I told the counselor he could not come home and that he had not been living with us when this whole thing happened. It was a bizarre series of phone calls and messages over a half-hour period of time. I quickly decided to go to the hospital and called my husband, Chris, to meet me there. When I arrived, they were packing Andrew's things to send him to the Dorothy Day Center next door. The Dorothy Day Center is a homeless shelter. It's a two-block walk from the hospital, but it was a long walk for Andrew, who was still using the walker. Chris arrived as we walked to the Dorothy Day Center. All we could do now was move forward.

"We arrived at the Dorothy Day Center at about four p.m. The social worker told Andrew he could stay for dinner, and then walk over to Mary Hall, another two-block walk within the complex that housed the hospital and the center. We left Andrew with the things he would need, told him we loved him, and walked out of the center, leaving my twenty-three-year-old son there. The drive home and the rest of that evening were awful. I alternately called an Al-Anon friend and one of my sisters every half hour. Andrew called us later that evening at around nine p.m. to tell us he was settled at Mary Hall. It was less than ideal, but he was indoors, safe, and fed.

"The next day, my other son and I went to see Andrew. We brought him some things and spent about fifteen minutes with him. He was sitting in the lobby, had an appointment with a social worker to get medical care and determine next steps for him. He was tired, angry, and physically in pain but seemed to know he needed to figure things out for himself.

"I continue to struggle with my role. Should I be making phone calls for him? What is the healthy thing for all of us? I went to an Al-Anon and spoke with supportive friends and family.

"The following weekend, my husband visited Andrew and had a serious discussion with him regarding his need to recover. The next day, I picked Andrew up from the shelter, took him to a nearby hotel for a shower—he still needed help with daily activities—and took him to dinner. My husband and I both showed Andrew that we loved and supported him in the ways that suited each of us. I believe that was when Andrew decided to live and be sober.

"He remained homeless for another month after he left the treatment center. He found his way through the social-service networks. He stayed sober and attended AA meetings, while family and friends supported him with visits and meals. He was admitted to a second treatment program that used a treatment model called Health Realization, which Andrew found more helpful for him. He said it supplemented the twelve-step program. From there, he went to a halfway house, started a new job at a coffee shop, continued his recovery, gradually gained some maturity, and became more and more enjoyable to spend time with. He moved into a sober house where four young people support each others' sobriety. Over the last ten months, Andrew made amends to all of his immediate family and continues to work a strong twelve-step program. From my current vantage point today, over a year after all of these events, I know we did all the right things for Andrew. I am so proud of him and so happy to have my son back. His level of maturity grew substantially during his recovery. I am so grateful."

MORE WOMEN'S WISDOM

FROM CONVERSATIONS ALONG THE WAY

Children

"My children have young children, and I look at them and I see myself. 'Oh dear,' I think, 'I did the same thing.' Unfortunately, I didn't have a mom to lean on at the time, so I try to guide my children in a nice way. I suggest, 'Maybe you should approach this in a little different way.'"   Linda B.

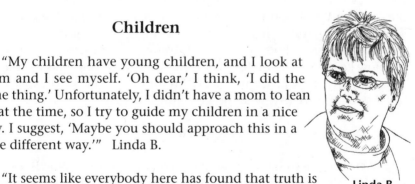

Linda B.

"It seems like everybody here has found that truth is the most important thing that you can have in life. God is truth and light. It is very simple, and a lot of people overlook that. With my grandchildren—well, you know how kids are: they'll lie to you in a heartbeat—I stop and remind them that 'Remember God and the truth and light. Who are you serving if you choose to lie?' Kind of puts them at a standstill and makes them think a little bit. Truth is something that we are taught to avoid a lot in life. It's not easy to be truthful with yourself, and it's not easy to be truthful with your boss or your friends and coworkers and people like that, but once you are known to be a truthful person, that is something nobody can ever take away from you. So to me, God in everybody is people finding their truth in themselves and in their life. I find it amazing to watch people. I wrote a poem for my grand-kids when they were quite little: 'If it is nestled in a lie, fear lives forever.' The one thing all kids should learn is to live without fear and enjoy the freedom of truth." Sue H.

"I heard a story, I don't even know where, that babies see auras. If your aura is a color that isn't for the higher good, a baby will not respond well to you. If your aura is of a color that is for the higher good or of love, the baby is going to respond positively to you. I'm talking little babies, the newborns. There is always going to be the six-month-old who doesn't want anyone but Momma, so don't think you have this horrible aura because some baby doesn't want to come near you. I was watching my granddaughter and thinking about that. I was watching her look over to her mom and then over to me and over to her mom and over to me. It was like she was looking above our heads, and it was just so cool. I wondered if she was looking at our auras. She was happy both times, so that was good." Lynne

"My daughter is in college right now. Three years ago, I was in Bemidji, taking a walk with her on Easter Sunday before I headed back home to Ely. We were walking in the state park there. Through our dis-cussion, I realized she was going to be okay. It was going to be okay for me to go and move on with my life. I giggled all the way back to Ely. It was just wonderful. 'This is so cool. This is so cool. She's going to be okay!' The reason I knew that is that, through our discussion, I realized she now knew how to ask for help from somebody other than her mom. Twenty years—so what comes next? I didn't know what to expect, so I just stood there, 'Okay, what do I do now?'" Kitty

Courage

"What I have to say is about what courage means. There is a young man I hadn't met until recently. He is forty-five; he has boys age eleven and eight. Five years ago, his wife left him, and he is raising these boys himself. Two percent of households have a single father as the head of the household. He worked as a plumber, sometimes in ditches. He had been in three cave-ins, so he quit his job in July. His brothers told him he was nuts. His girlfriend told him he was nuts.

"As soon as I met him I said, 'I wanted to tell you how much courage it had to take for you to quit that job. You either have guidance or you are awful smart. Those boys are healthy and happy at this point. If you wait until they are teenagers, you'll have a mess trying to get on with your career.' My sister knows him well, and she says that has absolutely just changed his life. He has applications for two very good jobs in. We don't know if he has them yet. I think it took all the courage in the world, and he just says, 'I want to be home with my boys for a while.' That is courage." Bonnie D.

"As far as being courageous, I probably am not courageous; nevertheless, that is okay." Lou

"Being courageous means having fear but doing it anyway, knowing that one's Great Creator is there with them every step of the way. Faith can move mountains, fear doesn't." Linda L.

"I think some of us think we are not courageous because we are just common people who don't do big things in life. But courage to me is when you are scared—you are shy, maybe you are scared of talking like this—but you do it anyway. You are scared of opening yourself up and talking like this and afraid you will forget what you're going to say. You don't have to be the president of the United States to speak publicly. To just be in a group and speak when you are afraid takes a lot of courage. Going to a party with strangers takes courage! Bravery is taking small actions and growing as people when we confront our very small demons." Lydia

"At times, we think courage is about these great big accomplishments and tackling great problems, but sometimes, it's the simplest little things. It is the courage to be myself. Sometimes that is what most of us are so terrified of: allowing anyone to see who we really are. What are they going to think of me? How am I going to present myself? This should be the simplest thing for us. If we could do anything right it should be to be ourselves. That is what it means to be courageous. When I come across someone who is truly genuine and not afraid of looking silly or laughing at themselves, I love it. I don't care what anybody says. I am true to myself. I don't do this to the point of hurting other people but just fully being who I am and embracing it. You either like me or you don't. I don't take offense, and I won't get a big head. This is the way I am, and I am happy to be that way." Leslie

Honoring Elders

"It is really nice to honor older women. In America, we are not spoken for that much, nor are older men actually. We don't respect people who are aging, but hopefully the baby-boomers, which some of you are, will change that. There will be so many of you out there. We are already seeing changes in the commercials on TV. Commercials are now more pertinent to older people." Lydia

Know yourself

"I am from south Minneapolis, and I have taken a path in my life different from most people. I decided it was important for me to get to know myself really well, so I am doing that through therapy. It has been fascinating. It has really changed my life a lot by helping me to understand myself and what is going on around me. I come from a family that truly values therapy. My daughter is going to be a therapist."

Penny K.

Laughter

"I think the most important thing in my life has been laughter. If I can spend time laughing with my family and friends, that just really makes my day." Penny K.

Life Philosophy

"I like sayings so much, and one of my favorites is 'No now is for- ever,' and that is so true. If things are going bad, it is not forever; hang in and it will get better. One thing I have really learned is that if it is good now, stop what you are doing and savor, savor, savor every minute of that good now. Sometimes they even get better. It might get worse, but it won't last forever. When it is good, boy it is great, so really take time and enjoy it. Look at the sky and watch the birds. There is so much to do. You can do it anywhere you are or any time you are down. Nature has magic." Bonnie D.

"I am looking forward to simplifying. I am looking forward to a much simpler lifestyle. I am not sure how I am going to get there, but I think it might come from opening doors and looking through. I have always been one to take advantage of every opportunity that comes my way. I will find my path. I love to have fun, and my motto has always been 'If I'm having fun, then we are going to just keep on going.' I do enjoy the outdoors. I do enjoy adventure travel and being outside."

Bonnie H.

"The other day I was sitting along the river when I had a little free time being the support driver. It was a beautiful day, and I was watching a leaf float down the river and made an analogy between the leaf and the path we choose in our lives. The leaf floated with the current, the leaf hit turbulence, the leaf went into rough waters, and the leaf stagnated during calm times. I wondered if it takes current or agitation to create change in our lives. When things are too easy, we tend to not make any moves and get a little lax, a little lazy. Then all of a sudden there is a gust of wind and things are shaken up and we have to react."   Nancy H.

"'Things happen as they happen, and whatever happens happens.' That is what I said during the planning when things would get kind of crazy. Then I would wonder 'Am I just taking all this too lightly? Am I not looking at how serious this can be in the whole scheme of things?' I still come back to things happen as they are supposed to happen. When I can believe that, I do okay; I won't get all shook up. Everything has worked out and moved along the way it should beautifully.

"That is kind of how I hold my life, too. No matter what I have gone through, here I sit. I am fifty-two years old, and I just keep coming through everything. No matter what takes place in my life, I am going to come through it in some manner, and it may be life-changing for me or it may not. If I keep putting that foot forward, it is going to be okay. I don't always know how. I must let go of some of the fear by learning to embrace whatever the emotion is. It is hard sometimes, depending on what the emotion is, to go through it, to embrace it and hold it for what it is worth, but I always do, and that is the good part."   Kitty

"I think everyone has to rethink what success is. Success has such a wide possibility of definitions. My idea of success is when you are healthy and if you are happy. If you're not healthy, you're probably not going to be happy. Maybe you don't know it, but many rich people are not happy. So what is success? I think pretty much it is if you are healthy and if you are happy."   Bonnie D.

Marriage, Relationships and Friends

"A piece of wisdom I'd like to share is that I got married at age forty-five, and I encourage everyone to wait until they are at least forty-five, unless having kids is important to them."   Deah

"My marriage was my life; the church was my life, and then our divorce came along. This was a big blow that just shook me up. For a while, you sort of pull in, at least I did. I pulled back. It's sort of like a death of these things I used to believe in. What do I believe anymore? Who am I? I had to go into myself and find strength within, because I could no longer rely on those people I knew and for understanding myself. Since then it has just been great."   Sherry

"I've had a lot of best friends. One of them is right here. What is it we usually say? 'If you don't get in trouble, I will lead you there.' 'Cohorts in crime,' that was it. Amanda has been a great friend, and she always has a different twist on things, which is so neat. I love her for it. I say, 'We got to do it this way.' She replies, 'Well, maybe if we did this or that.' That's what's really neat about friends, learning different perspectives."   Linda B.

Be Remembered

Kandy

"I want to be remembered as Nana the Crazy Cat Lady. I say this because, although I don't have any of my own children, I am surrounded by children in my town who refer to me as Nana. They have over-nighters with me. Because I'm hanging with these young kids and I am not their parent, I can be the crazy person. We spontaneously go miniature golfing, roller skating, swimming or hiking. It's just the best.

"About the cat lady part, I am down to six cats from nine. My husband is trying to get me down to two. I am a kind and gentle person that takes in strays. You just love them, and they love, and I think it's this caring part that makes me who I am. I'm called Nana, which reminds me of the child in me and the children that I love. The crazy part has to do with the fact that I will get up and do anything, at any time, to be with the children. And then the really crazy part of always having cats in my life."   Kandy

"I don't really care if family and friends remember me or not. I will be quite truthful with you. I have two granddaughters, both in college, and a grandson. I am sure they will remember me one way or another."

Lou

"I would like to be remembered by family and friends as a woman of peace and love, giving and sharing what I could of myself and that I have made a difference by being on this earth. I truly believe that is what life is about."   Linda L.

"I would like to be remembered as myself. To be remembered as someone who did what she liked to do when she liked to do it. Remembered as a go-getter who enjoyed her family and her friends. I would try anything once, as long as it was something I should try. That's also something that I would have to say to the young people: Don't wait. I have kicked myself many a time and said, 'Why didn't I do that?' When the time presents itself, take advantage of it, do it today because tomorrow you might not get that chance."   Karen S.

"I was in a women's group about ten years ago, and the question posed there was, 'What would you want on your tombstone?' I thought for a while as they went around the circle and people said things like 'She was sensitive' and 'She was kind.' I said, 'She was frugal.' [Laughter.] I want to be known as frugal." Kay W.

"I have a friend who enjoys working with people to plan their own funerals, which in the one sense, might sound a little maudlin and odd, but on the other hand, it's not. I was recently at a celebration of a small, country church's 200th anniversary. They were singing some old-time hymns to bluegrass music. They were singing 'I'll Fly Away.' I very much have birds in my life, professionally, spiritually, and in just about every other aspect. I thought, 'I really want them to sing that at my funeral.' Then I remembered that I don't think about the future. I try very hard to just be present. And yet when you're gone, you have no idea what they are going to say about you. I wouldn't have any idea what anyone would say about me. I have never really taken myself all that seriously. Every now and then I hear something, and I think, 'That would be good to have at my funeral.' All because I have a friend who wants to plan her funeral." Cis

"I don't care what they say at my funeral. I don't want to know." Marsha

"I would like to be remembered by family and friends as the crazy lady!—which fits with my desire to not follow any tradition. I have tried a little bit of everything. I have driven a semi-truck across the U.S. by myself. I try anything once, almost, except sky-diving and bungee-jumping. I am not there. I fell off a cliff when I was a little girl. That's why I have a natural fear of falling, so those two I know I can't do." Sue H.

"I have thought about the word legacy a lot. I think it is important for all of us, to leave at least something, not a monument, but leave something behind to help somebody or make a difference. That goes back to the parable of the Good Samaritan." Betsy F.

Respect

"We asked a lot of questions as we got a bit older. Before I left home, I learned some of the Finnish language. My grandmother didn't speak English, but when some of the kids started school, she insisted that they take English so she could learn English. Grandmother had the foresight to know that when the kids were around people, they didn't speak their own language. They spoke English so that people wouldn't assume that they were talking about them." Amanda

Spirituality

"The one thing that I keep thinking about is what Black Elk said: 'Everything our Creator made is round.' Now everywhere I look outside, I see it's true. The circle of life!" Esther

"Has life followed the path that you expected? The first thing that came to my mind was a refrigerator magnet that I used to have that said blessed are those that expect nothing for they shall not be disappointed. [Laughter.] I never thought about expecting anything from life, except just to try to be happy. The spiritual path, the Native American spiritual path has helped me to do that. Connecting with the oneness and nature has a great deal to do with my happiness. As far as wisdom, I would say, 'Don't quit having adventures.' That is the best thing I can think of, and that gets wrapped up with being courageous. All it requires is the gumption and conviction to follow your own dreams. That is life-changing in itself." Ielah

"I want to describe how spirituality has influenced my life. I was brought up in a Christian family that was very involved in church. My mom said that since the time I was a babe, I attended Sunday school and church. I tell you I couldn't have gone through many of the deep valleys and climbed the high mountains that I have faced without having spirituality as a very, very important part of my life." Katie

"To me, spirituality is being outside, like we are doing tonight, and being with friends. Being outside is really important to me. On a daily basis, I have to be outside, whether it's cold or hot. It's just important, even though I live in a condo in the midst of the city, and I'm really an urban girl at heart.

"I quit praying the way I used to about six years ago. You know, the begging prayers. You know how you do that, and you never get your prayers answered? That is because God does whatever he or she wants to do. Now I am thankful in my prayers. I start listing what I have to be grateful for on a daily basis, which makes me more positive. When I am feeling down or depressed, it's really a big helpmate in my life to be able to realize what I have to be grateful for. When things are really bad—not just like regular depression or sadness, but when stuff is really problematic—reaching for something positive in your life helps." Lydia

"Spirituality has really changed me, and it's growing. There are no limits to possibilities for any of us. As we live our lives, we experience our lives mainly within the parameters of what our senses and our environment have taught us. We feel that we have limits. We can't envision our experiences much beyond what we think we know. 'Oh no, I can't do that,' we claim. But, like Kathy said, it's all there. I feel my responsibility is to be a steward of my life and the earth. This chance to live is an opportunity to search and push as far as I can go with my life and help other people that I come in contact with." Sherry

"Spirituality has helped me on my path. It has given me the courage to move forward and look at different parameters in life and different belief systems. I have learned how to open my life to different perspectives, which has been just a tremendous gift. Right now I want to move forward in how. I call it the 'big how' versus the 'little how.' The 'big how' is about me being honest, open and willing, rather than the 'little how,' which has always got me stuck my whole life. The 'little how,' which to me means 'How can that possibly happen?' I missed so much in my life because I just didn't know how to move forward with it. If I am open, honest, and willing, then anything is going to be possible in my life. When I put it out to the universe, it opens up many possibilities that can take me places that can help me in how I am going to move forward, whether it be the 'big how' or the 'little how.' My brain is too little to think that I can move forward on my own. There are so many facets to learn from mindful meditation and yoga or going to the intuition workshop that Nancy put on. Now I have a life coach in my life." Kitty

"The word 'spirit' is in the word 'spirituality.' To me it is spirit. The things I think about are what hold my spirit down from being able to take off and fly and live as fully as I could. Those things that limit me are the things I have to watch out for. For me, the church was that way. There were too many parameters, too many rules and theology." Sherry

"Since 2000, spirituality has been a big part of my life. It has been through my whole life, but it feels like I have been on a new awakening, and thanks to my younger grandmothers-in-training, as you call them, I share a lot of revelations. The revelation I discovered recently that's important for me is that spirituality is not one thing. It's not being a Catholic or being Protestant or being Muslim or being Jewish. It is all of it. The light is in every single one of those. It has recently become very clear to me that this is so important, because if you take all of everything, including all of your sisters of all ages and all of their experiences, you are then becoming a more whole woman. You take all of the information and the light out of each one of those spiritualities and you become a whole spiritual person. Don't get stuck in one little spot. I don't get stuck in being sixty-two. I don't get stuck in being a Catholic. It is just a matter of being a whole person by reaching out towards the universe."
Lynne

"Some Jehovah's Witnesses came to my door one time. There were two men and a little boy, and they wanted to come in and talk with me. I said, 'No.' They did the 'But, but . . .' thing, and I said, 'Now listen. I don't want to talk to you because to me there are two powers in this world. They both want your money. They both want your obedience. One keeps you out of jail, and the other keeps you out of hell. So for me, it's just two organizations.' The next week, two women came by with a little girl. They started again; they thought maybe switching sexes would work. Not with this old lady. I said the same thing. You know, they never bothered me again after that. Talk about ornery. But that to me is organized religion. It's a powerful group, and they expect obedience of their laws and rules. One will keep me out of hell with fear and the other of course would be jail. I've got to classify those concepts and put them that way. I kind of separate politics and religion, which is probably helpful. I've always been mean like that."   Sue H.

"I've come to the conclusion that no matter what I am doing, whether it's a rendezvous or a gathering, whatever circle or meeting, if I'm sitting there, there is a reason. There is an absolute reason why I am there, and there is something for me to learn. I need to pay attention to that. Whether I figure it out at the meeting or gathering or not doesn't matter, it will happen. Maybe I will figure it out later, but I know there is a reason for each and every one of us to be here. I am grateful that everyone is here, because I know I am going to learn something from every one of you."   Lynne

"I joined this group of people I work with, and they were all very organized religious people. It was very strange. I could sit and talk to them about religion and stuff, but I am not a Christian. Not that I don't believe in Christ, it's just that I'm not an organized follower of their religion. I'm not like them. I believe differently than they do, and that is okay with me. Sue H.

"I have also been on a spiritual search. It kind of waxes and wanes with a lot of effort going into it. Sometimes it just sits there and waits for the next little piece. I found I do not fit in a traditional Christian church anymore. I found a church called St. Sophia's Liberal Catholic Church. St. Sophia is the saint of women's wisdom. At St. Sophia's church, the priest is married and doesn't follow the line of the pope. Wally, the priest, has a medieval mass every other week, and on the alternating weeks we have discussion group. It gets into quantum theory, spiral dynamics, Ken Wilbur, some really wild stuff that you don't find in most churches. It's taken me on a really great trip of discovery."   Sherry

Wisdom for Youth

Barbara S.

"What I would share with a younger woman is that sometimes you need to step outside your comfort zone. If you are used to something, sometimes you just have to go one step farther and take a chance on doing something else." Barbara S.

"My advice to younger women would be: Cherish your sisters and know that we are all sisters; be there for one another. I am blessed to have three biological sisters but also many other sisters of the heart. I appreciate my women friends more the older I get. I hope I am learning how to be a better friend. I am very pleased to be with all of you tonight to share this circle of sisterhood. I thank Nancy and Kitty for what they are doing. It is really an inspiration to me. I would not have the courage to do what you are doing, so I really admire and appreciate what you are doing for all of us." Nancy R.

"I say don't judge, enjoy. I had to walk around in shorts at the age of twenty-one with these big, thick stockings on my legs because I had blood clots. As far as trying to think I was sexy, that threw that idea right out the door. Just enjoy and accept people for who and what they are. As soon as you think that someone doesn't have anything to offer, that will be the person who offers you the most. Whether it be man, woman, or child, that is true. I have a granddaughter who is only two and can't talk, but her eyes speak volumes. Enjoy life and be at peace with wherever you are at in your life. Tomorrow is another day, and it will bring another challenge and another blessing." Ellen

"The wisdom I would like to share with younger women as they travel the river of life is: Keep paddling. That's it, basically. Happiness is a journey, not a destination. So that would be basically how I would describe, you know, just the river of life." Lou

"One of the things that I would love to say to younger women starting out is to love and honor yourself first, because all of the rest of your life will be so much better if you can do that. When you spend so much of your life feeling like you are not valued and loved, it's just awful. So many of the turns I have taken in my life, things that have happened to me, would have been different if I could have learned that at a much younger age. I would have had better experiences. I was talking to my friend Liz one time, and I said, 'You know, it finally occurred to me that it wasn't during the times when everything was going so well and everything was just falling into place that I was really learning and growing; it was during or right after those bad times.' So remember when things are really going bad or you are going through a lot of pain or whatever that you will look back and say, 'Wow, I have really come a long way from that.'"   Connie K.

"I have a niece. She is sixteen, and she cannot imagine herself without a boyfriend. She breaks up and quickly gets into another relationship. And now she's getting married. These are the types of young ladies that I wish could be rescued some day, because they are missing so much of life. They have already fallen into this trap. Marriage is like a little prison. They are only allowed to be a woman 'this way.' They will not be adventurous, but afraid to travel the world or jump in a canoe or whatever. This freedom is something young women still haven't found. I'm shocked at how many of them are still in the cuffs and ankles stuff. Hopefully women will spread the news and say, 'Hey, guess what. There is a life out here above and beyond.'"   Sue H.

"What I would tell somebody younger is: Forgive yourself and see some humor in your faults. I also deal with OCD, Obsessive Compulsive Disorder. I look at courage in my life as having to deal with that and the struggle it caused between my husband and myself for a number of years, and still does sometimes. And yet I go on, I get involved, and I like being the age I am. It never occurred to me to do anything that would be a lot of work, like dye my hair. [Laughter.] I have daughters that can do that. I like being active. I don't find that I have to be fit, but I would like to be. I do things like take the dog for a walk."   Betsy F.

"I would tell younger people: Don't be so hard on yourself. Don't be afraid to have fun and laugh at yourself. Don't take yourself so seriously. Just live your life fully and be true to yourself. Be who you are and think it will all work out okay."   Leslie

"There are a couple of things to share with the youth. I used to be a size twelve, and I thought I was really fat. I always wanted to lose weight. And then I was a size fourteen, and I felt I had to keep losing weight. Now I am bigger, so I tell my friends who are size twelve who want to lose weight, 'Just be happy with your body and make the most of it.' That is a wisdom I wish someone would have told me when I was a size twelve. 'Hey, be happy. You will never have anything like that happen again.'"   Deah

Greet each day as a marvelous Adventure!
Believe your heart's desires are possible,
and will arrive when you are ready to receive.
Dream and Manifest into reality.
Like a loving parent who supports, encourages
and cheers us on to reach our goal,
the Universe is benevolent, generous and
waiting to hear your requests.
The potential Magic of Life
lies within your heart and mind.
You create your reality.
Do it with ease, opulence and grandeur.
May you have Mystical, Magical
Surprises on your Journey.

                                        -Anka

EPILOGUE

Life is truly a journey and journeys, like rivers, have twists and turns. This trip has evolved from having a personal focus to answering a larger calling. The Mississippi reflects this change metaphorically and the books reflect it literally.

The first book focused on my personal journey. I interacted with the River and was inspired by the Gatherings. The beginning of the River is small and intimate. She periodically opens up to explore larger spaces then contracts again—much the way I did while paddling her.

This second book offers more women's voices and more messages from the River, along with my personal journey. Between Red Wing, Minnesota, and St. Louis, Missouri, the River grows wider yet offers quiet backwaters with opportunities for personal reflection and intimate moments with nature.

As planning for the final leg proceeds, it is clear that the primary focus of the third book will be the women's voices. The River and my experiences will be more of a backdrop. The southern part of the Mississippi is expansive and open to many possibilities.

My life's journey between river trips has offered joyful and challenging events that have given more meaning to the words of the women I met paddling and at the Gatherings. The birth of my first grandchild reminded me of my own time as a struggling young mother and helped me appreciate the awesome adults my children have become. The personal sacrifices I felt compelled to make for the success of my husband's business moved me through layers of understanding what is truly important to me. The value in serving others became more significant for me. A hysterectomy taught me that I don't need to suffer. I learned how to slow down and let others care for me. Through these and other events I have learned to listen more carefully to my inner voice, to the messages the River offered, and to others who have come into my life as a result of this river journey. I have learned to look forward with less of an agenda and more of an attitude of showing up to watch and experience how things unfold.

I made a planning trip to the banks of the Mississippi River in the spring of 2010. The River spoke to me. I experienced her as angry and dangerous; not as the gentle, yet powerful, friend I had known. The water was turbulent. Huge waves traveled upriver at breathtaking speed. I heard her say I was not to give my life for this mission and that it was time to revisit my approach to this journey. With reflection, I realized there were two messages: one for me and one about the River.

The personal message for me was to stop allowing this mission to drive my life. This had increased to a point that had become unhealthy. It was time to step back, assess things, and approach with a new vision that will bring more joy to the mission. The message also meant that I needed to become more collaborative, to stop trying to do it alone.

I postponed the paddling trip that had been planned for fall 2010. A team of women began working with me to bring new vision to Ripples Of Wisdom. Our intention is to be on the water in the fall of 2011 and to create opportunities to meet many women from diverse backgrounds.

The message about the River was that she needs everyone who cares for her to send her positive thoughts and prayers, and to do what they can to heal her. I assumed she needed this help because of the usual pollution and disrespect she endures. But on my last night on the River, the media was full of news of the oil spill in the Gulf of Mexico and the likelihood that it would impact the delta. The Mississippi River serves us all in a myriad of ways large and small. The health and well being of her water impacts all the water of the Earth. At the time of this writing the complete damage of the oil spill is yet to be determined.

It is with great anticipation that I move toward the final leg of the journey down the River. What experiences will unfold and who we will encounter is a divine mystery. The planning team moves forward leaning into the faith that the River will carry us to the messages we all need to hear, carry us toward ripples of wisdom with great healing potential.

Book Club Questions

1. Which woman's story touched you the most and why? How can find
   ing commonality with other women enrich your life?
2. A theme of leaning into your faith runs throughout this book. How do
   you lean into your faith and let life flow?
3. In this journey the term Grandmother is a term borrowed from the
   Native American culture and is a title of great respect that recognizes
   wisdom born out of time and experience. It embraces women age 50
   and older, whether or not they have had children or grandchildren.
   Do you consider yourself a grandmother? Who are the Grandmothers
   in your life that have been significant? How does this definition change
   how you perceive yourself now or in the future?
4. The Mississippi River is essential to this story because it was important
   to Nancy. Is there a body of water that is essential to you? How do you
   feel when you are there and what is the significance of it for you?
5. Many of the women started out by saying they didn't have wisdom to
   share and then went on to say profound things. What are the messages
   you tell yourself about your wisdom? How does that affect the
   way you share it with others?
6. What is a story from your own life that you regard as unimportant, but
   if you heard someone else tell the same story you would find it
   significant?
7. It was a leap of faith for Nancy to begin this journey. What is some
   thing that you would love to do if you could find the support and the
   faith in yourself and your dream?
8. Life on the river is a much slower pace than life on land. This allows
   the paddlers to be present in the moment and appreciate life's gifts.
   How can you slow down the pace of your life so you can absorb more
   of life's simple pleasures?

The Gathering Questions

1. Describe how spirituality has influenced your life.
2. Has life followed the path you expected? How have life's circumstances
   shaped who you are?
3. What wisdom would you like to share with younger women as they
   travel their own river of life?
4. What does being courageous mean to you?
5. How would you like to be remembered by family and friends?

Imagine A Woman

Imagine a woman who believes it is right and good
she is a woman.
A woman who honors her experience and tells her stories.
Who refuses to carry the sins of others within her body and life.

Imagine a woman who trusts and respects herself.
A woman who listens to her needs and desires.
Who meets them with tenderness and grace.

Imagine a woman who acknowledges
the past's influence on the present.
A woman who has walked through her past.
Who has healed into the present.

Imagine a woman who authors her own life.
A woman who exerts, initiates, and moves on her own behalf.
Who refuses to surrender except to her truest self and wisest voice.

Imagine a woman who names her own gods.
A woman who imagine the divine in her image and likeness.
Who designs a personal spirituality to inform her daily life.

Imagine a woman in love with her own body.
A woman who believes her body is enough, just as it is.
Who celebrates her body's rhythms and cycles
as an exquisite resource.

Imagine a woman who honors the body of the Goddess
In her changing body. A woman who celebrate the accumulation
Of her years and her wisdom. Who refuses to use her life-energy
Disguising the changes in her body and life.

Imagine a woman who values the women in her life.
A woman who sits in circles of women.
Who is reminded or the truth about herself when she forgets.

Imagine yourself as this woman.

Patricia Lynn Reilly
www.imagineAwoman.com

To purchase a copy of this book or of
Water Women Wisdom, Voices from the Upper Mississippi
go to the Ripples Of Wisdom web site:

www.ripplesofwisdom.com

At the Ripples Of Wisdom website you can:

• Learn the details about the final leg of the journey

• Follow the planning and execution of the 2011 journey

• See photos from the first two legs of the journey

• Discover ways you can get involved and support the journey

• Purchase other Ripples Of Wisdom products

• Find out more about the Ripples of Wisdom team

• Learn about opportunities to paddle Ripples Of Wisdom in
  the Boundary Waters Canoe Area Wilderness

Water * Women * Wisdom